AT WAR WITH W(

AT WAR WITH WOMEN

Military Humanitarianism and Imperial Feminism in an Era of Permanent War

Jennifer Greenburg

CORNELL UNIVERSITY PRESS   **ITHACA AND LONDON**

First published 2023 by Cornell University Press

Library of Congress Cataloging-in-Publication Data

Names: Greenburg, Jennifer, 1983– author.
Title: At war with women : military humanitarianism and imperial feminism in
    an era of permanent war / Jennifer Greenburg.
Description: Ithaca [New York] : Cornell University Press, 2023. |
    Includes bibliographical references and index.
Identifiers: LCCN 2022012866 (print) | LCCN 2022012867 (ebook) |
    ISBN 9781501767739 (hardcover) | ISBN 9781501767746 (paperback) |
    ISBN 9781501767753 (pdf) | ISBN 9781501767760 (epub)
Subjects: LCSH: Women soldiers—Government policy—United States. |
    Afghan War, 2001–2021—Participation, Female. | Iraq War, 2003–2011—
    Participation, Female. | Counterinsurgency—Iraq—History—21st century. |
    Counterinsurgency—Afghanistan—History—21st century. | Sex role—United
    States—History—21st century. | Imperialism—Social aspects. | United States—
    Armed Forces—Women—History—21st century. | United States—
    Military policy—Social aspects. | United States—Military policy—
    21st century.
Classification: LCC UB418.W65 G74 2023 (print) | LCC UB418.W65 (ebook) |
    DDC 355.00820973—dc23/eng/20220831
LC record available at https://lccn.loc.gov/2022012866
LC ebook record available at https://lccn.loc.gov/2022012867

Dedicated to Anne Greenburg

Contents

Acknowledgments

Single authorship disguises what is actually a collective endeavor. This book is the product of so much generosity it is impossible to properly acknowledge all of those who shepherded it along. But I will try. The seeds of this project were planted at the University of California, Berkeley, where I was extraordinarily lucky to have Gillian Hart as my mentor. I have yet to meet another person whose sheer intellectual force is matched by their commitment to students. Donald Moore's kindness, bibliographic recall, and ability to connect scholars to one another led me down personal, political, and intellectual pathways woven together here. Michael Watts and Jake Kosek sponsored a reading group in critical empire studies during the post-9/11 wars that introduced me to Rosa Luxemburg and many of the theories of imperialism I constantly returned to during this research. I would not understand social practice in the same way without Jean Lave.

The Watson Institute for International and Public Affairs at Brown University provided the most generative space I can imagine to write a book. Heartfelt thanks to Catherine Lutz, whose pathbreaking work in critical military studies and ethnographies of US empire inspired me for so long before her guidance and insight supported this book. I benefited tremendously from a Watson author workshop and will always be grateful for the feedback Deborah Cowen, Catherine Lutz, and David Vine gave to make this a better book. I could not have been more fortunate to discover the brilliance and friendship of Jordan T. Camp and Christina Heatherton while writing this book. Their intellectual generosity and optimism of the will have enriched my work and my life. I thank Cécile Accilien, Jordan T. Camp, Jessica Katzenstein, and Shaina Potts for reading and commenting on various parts of this book before publication and Jacqueline Larson for her superb editorial hand.

Intersecting at Brown with the Costs of War project was a constant reminder of the stakes of researching the post-9/11 wars. I am especially grateful for the interaction I got to have with Catherine Besteman, Neta Crawford, Allegra Harpootlian, Heidi Peltier, Stephanie Savell, and the whole Costs of War team. Thanks also at Brown University to Peter Andreas, Robert Blair, Steven Bloomfield, Beshara Doumani, Claudia Elliot, James Green, Michael Kennedy, Elena Shih, Edward Steinfeld, Debbie Weinstein, and Nicholas Ziegler. For making our work in progress series the generative space it was, I thank Rawan Arar, Narges Bajoghli, Nicholas Barnes, Michelle Jurkovich, Ali Kadivar, Almita Miranda, Duff Morton,

Yusuf Neggers, Anthony Pratcher, Aarti Sethi, Lucas Stanczyk, Aileen Teague, Adaner Usmani, Darío Valles, Elizabeth Williams, and Alex Winder. Staff members Stephanie Abbott-Pandey, Kathryn Dunkelman, Deb Healey, Alex Laferrière, Megan Murphy, Anita Nester, Hayden Reiss, and Ellen White made all of this possible.

I benefited from so many panels, opportunities to present work in progress, and other conversations, short and long, while writing this book, including with Javier Arbona, Jenny Baca, Teo Ballvé, Sarah Besky, Lisa Bhungalia, Keith Brown, Joe Bryan, Jen Casolo, Kate Chandler, Erin Collins, Jennifer Devine, Lieba Faier, Jennifer Fluri, Emily Gilbert, Roberto González, Hugh Gusterson, Caren Kaplan, Laleh Khalili, Julie Klinger, Sarah Knuth, Shiloh Krupar, Jenna Lloyd, Kenneth MacLeish, Greta Marchesi, Brittany Meché, Andrea Miller, Adam Moore, Diana Negrín, Trevor Paglen, Nomi Stone, and David Szanton. The Haitian Studies Association has been a long-standing source of support and insight, especially the guidance and inspiration of Mark Schuller and Claudine Michel. Thank you to Laurent Dubois, Greg Beckett, Jessica Hsu, Jonathan Katz, Chelsey Kivland, Pierre Minn, Claire Payton, Mamyrah Prosper, and Lynn Selby. Thanks to friends in Haiti and the diaspora whose insights and generosity have informed so much of my thinking along the way. It is painful that many violent factors shaped through US domestic and foreign policies make me fearful to name you here. I am especially grateful to Laura Wagner for her prose and humor and, of course, her creation of the Radio Haiti Archive and to Lindsey Dillon and Beth and Casey Lew-Williams for blending professional guidance and friendship over the years.

At Stanford University, I appreciate being included in conversations at the Center for International Security and Cooperation. For the stability and kindness they facilitated during COVID, thank you to Dayo Mitchell and Parna Sengupta. I am indebted to my seminar students at Stanford University, whose commitment to a better world energized me. Thank you to the Department of Politics and International Relations at the University of Sheffield for creating a home for critical, feminist, and decolonial approaches to international relations and, now, a home for me.

This book would have been impossible without the willingness of those involved in its social processes to speak openly with me. They necessarily appear under pseudonyms here, but it would be difficult to overstate how much I learned from speaking with the hundreds of military service members, veterans, trainers, contractors, cadets, development workers, governmental officials, interpreters, and advocates who allowed me to spend time with them and taught me to disaggregate "the military" into a much more complex social process. I am indebted to archival and library staff at the US Marine Corps Historical Resources Branch, the National Museum of the Marine Corps, the US Army Women's Museum, the US National Archives and Records Administration, the Saint-Louis de Gonzague and

National Libraries in Port-au-Prince, the Special Collections Center at New York University, and interlibrary loan at Brown and Stanford Universities. Research and writing for *At War with Women* were made possible through generous financial support from the Association of American Geographers, the National Science Foundation, the Social Science Research Council, Stanford University, the Watson Institute for International and Public Affairs at Brown University, and the Department of Geography and the Graduate Division at the University of California, Berkeley. The University of Sheffield Institutional Open Access Fund made an open access ebook edition freely available. This book is derived in part from an article, "'Going Back to History': Haiti and US Military Humanitarian Knowledge Production," published in *Critical Military Studies*, 2017, copyright Taylor & Francis, http://www.tandfonline.com/10.1080/23337486 .2017.1313380.

Jim Lance at Cornell University Press provided extraordinary editorial support throughout the process of writing this book. Jim's enthusiasm for writing, metaphor, and music—and most of all his humanity—was a lifeline during a pandemic publication pipeline. Thanks also at Cornell to Emily Andrew, Clare Jones, and two anonymous reviewers. Thank you to Kristen Bettcher and Mary Kate Murphy and all of their colleagues in production, composition, and marketing.

I do not know how to convey my gratitude to my friends and family who put up with me during a drawn-out and pandemic-interrupted writing and revision process. The warmth of Brown Play School and all the women who watched my kids during these years was a comfort blanket insulating me from how hard academic writing can be. Thanks especially in Rhode Island to Claudine Taylor and family and to Jackie Courtemanche, Melissa Loiselle, and the Freda-Krebs, Rufino, and Sorrenti families. Thank you to Sabine Henry and the Bustos, Brogan-Powell, Erbe-Talbot, Safranek, Skemp-Cupp, Stotts, Terence, Weber, and Zimmer-Kelsey families. I would have never pursued writing without the support of my parents, Deborah Newstat and Steven Greenburg, and my brother, Matthew Greenburg. There is nobody I admire more in this world than my grandmother, Anne Greenburg, to whom this book is dedicated. Thank you, Lisa Greenburg, for adopting my kids; Lisa and Aaron Clyman, for so much laughter; David McCollum, for letting me transform your guest room into an ever-expanding pile of books; the Binnings, for expanding my family; and the gaggle of Newstat sisters, for ensuring that I have cousins wherever I go.

It is definitely more fun to write a book than to watch someone else attempt to put words on paper. Thank you, Peter Binnings, for being a true partner through this process. My deepest debt of gratitude is to you and to our children, Leo and Rose.

Abbreviations

ASCOPE   areas, structures, capabilities, organizations, people, and events
CORDS   Civil Operations and Revolutionary Development Support
CST   cultural support team
DOD   US Department of Defense
DSF   District Stability Framework
EMSIs   *équipe medico-sociales itinérantes* (mobile medical-social teams)
FET   female engagement team
NGO   nongovernmental organization
PMESII   political, military, economic, social, information, and infrastructure
PNAC   Project for a New American Century
PRT   Provincial Reconstruction Team
PTSD   post-traumatic stress disorder
QDDR   Quadrennial Diplomacy and Development Review
S/CRS   Office of the Coordinator for Reconstruction and Stabilization, US Department of State
SOI   source of instability
SWAT   special weapons and tactics
TSCTP   Trans-Sahara Counterterrorism Partnership
UN   United Nations
USAID   US Agency for International Development
VA   Veterans Affairs
VSO   village stability operation

AT WAR WITH WOMEN

INTRODUCTION

In a large cement building on a remote part of Camp Atterbury army base in south-central Indiana, a group of US soldiers prepares to visit a mock Afghan village. The village, part of a simulation, is populated by privately contracted role players acting as Afghan farmers, merchants, religious figures, elders, and other villagers. As part of their predeployment training, the soldiers will survey village needs to identify projects that could bolster local support for the provincial government—a key tenet of the counterinsurgency doctrine their team is implementing. The survey was designed by the US Agency for International Development (USAID), which hired and sent contractors to provide the military with instruction in international development "best practices." Another contractor—an Afghan American woman working as a translator—wraps a pink headscarf around a female soldier and secures it under her chin. A second female soldier wearing a blue headscarf looks on, eager to learn how to wear the scarf under her helmet and draped over her military-issued camouflage blouse and body armor (figure 1).

The two female soldiers are members of what the military calls a "female engagement team" (FET). The simulation includes a "women's tent" populated by Afghan women actors crocheting, preparing food, and talking. In this context, "FET" denotes the two women on the deploying team who, based on their gender, are presumed to have access to any female villagers the team may confront during the simulation. It is 2011, the height of the US military's FET program in Afghanistan. The headscarves identify the soldiers as female to villagers and send what the military calls a "powerful and positive message" that its "intentions are

1

good and that the United States is there to protect them."[1] The female soldiers plan to "engage" women they encounter, viewing this as an opportunity to make a positive impression as well as to gather any information about the village that might be strategically useful. This striking combination of actors came about when the US military integrated development into counterinsurgency training, a process that relied on military understandings of the colonial past and new forms of labor for private contractors and female soldiers.[2]

At War with Women examines the forces that brought this simulation into play. These forces drive the modern assembly of imperialism, a concept I will explore more fully and redefine through what political economist Giovanni Arrighi conceptualized as a post–World War II "struggle for world-hegemony."[3] Fought through new forms of US financial and military power, the post-9/11 wars in Afghanistan and Iraq revived counterinsurgency doctrine through explicit reference to the colonial past.[4] Counterinsurgency returned through military uses of development and humanitarianism as weapons of war—for instance, the military's pronounced interest in the mid-2000s in building schools in Afghanistan to gain civilian support for the occupation. The US military looked to women in its ranks, still technically banned from direct assignment to ground combat units, to do the so-called work of "winning hearts and minds," and to access Iraqi and Afghan women and their households. Servicewomen were assembled into FETs that searched and questioned women at security checkpoints and took part in outreach projects distributing humanitarian supplies.

From 2010 to 2017, I observed counterinsurgency trainings and interviewed women who had served on FETs. Drawing on this material, I investigate how the post-9/11 turn to counterinsurgency did not convince soldiers to reimagine themselves as "armed social workers," but it did give rise to what I call here a "new imperial feminism" under which servicewomen came to understand themselves as global ambassadors for women's rights. This new imperial feminism framed members of female counterinsurgency teams as feminist trailblazers for women's equal right to serve alongside men in combat units. Over time, all-female counterinsurgency teams were increasingly attached to special operations missions, in which female soldiers were expected to calm women and children during violent night raids of Afghan homes. The military came to explicitly value women's labor through gender essentialisms, such as claims that female soldiers were "naturally" more emotionally equipped to "soothe and calm" war's victims. Such forms of emotional labor make up what I call a "new military femininity," one component of a broader imperial feminism. Gender operates here and across imperial encounters in relation to constructions of racial difference. In interviews and journal entries, servicewomen contrasted their position as icons of modern women's liberation with that of Afghan women, whom military trainings framed as universally oppressed by "backward" cultural practices that could be modernized through foreign occupation. Soldiers viewed the subjects of occupation through such cultural and imperial racisms that were enabled by official military rhetoric of "color blindness."

At the height of the FET program between 2010 and 2012, all-female counterinsurgency teams were attached to Army Ranger and Green Beret units and, in violation of military combat exclusion policy that still banned women, participated in combat-intensive special operations missions.[5] Thus, female counterinsurgency teams have been popularly understood as a prehistory to the military overturning its ban on women in combat in 2013 and, since 2016, opening all military jobs to women.[6] Soon after combat exclusion ended, media images proliferated of women such as Kristen Griest (one of the first to graduate from Army Ranger School) performing a firefighter's carry of a fellow soldier. One *New York Times* article describes Griest "joining a branch of the Army that has long been considered the last bastion of traditionally male combat roles, and with the move, the Army has crossed another barrier in its promise to consider women for all roles without exception."[7] The article typifies a popular way of understanding post-9/11 shifts in military gender policies as reflecting a gradual progression toward gender equality in the US military.[8] At the same time as women's integration into US military combat units was popularly interpreted as the achievement of equal rights, a liberal feminist tradition has supported justifications of the US invasion of Afghanistan as a defense of Afghan women's rights. The post-9/11 wars were framed through "the twin figures of the Islamic fundamentalist and his female victim," who appeared everywhere from the *New York Times* to the Feminist Majority to popularize the view that the wars were "for Afghanistan's own good."[9] Counterinsurgency's claims to protect civilians and to operate through development and humanitarianism were central to this liberal feminist narrative. We see these forces at work in Samantha Power's endorsement of the *Counterinsurgency Field Manual* in a *New York Times* book review shortly after the manual's 2006 public release. Power—President Joe Biden's USAID administrator and former ambassador to the United Nations (UN)—criticizes President George W. Bush's policies in Iraq while urging readers not to give up what is otherwise a worthy counterterrorism effort. "The challenge now is to accept that just because George W. Bush hyped the threat does not mean the threat should be played down." In her efforts to redeem what she calls "our war on terror," Power lingers on the manual's introduction, penned by her close colleague at Harvard, Sarah Sewall. Power claims that Sewall "can say what the generals who devised the manual cannot," referring to her argument for the greater effectiveness of military strategies that reduce civilian harm in retort to those who see the manual as a mere "marketing campaign."[10]

There is even more that Sewall—and, I add, Power—can say that the generals who wrote the manual cannot. Through figures such as Power and Sewall, we see how liberal feminism and development joined hands to forge a path to permanent war. Power embodies a liberal feminism that was key to securing consent for the post-9/11 wars. Emphasizing workplace equality and sexual violence, she self-identifies as a feminist through a singular focus on gender as the basis for equal rights. A liberal feminist tradition—prominent in the United States and often uncritical of imperialism—informs Power's self-identification when she explains to a reporter that "being the only woman in the UN made me a feminist." Her feminist awakening occurred when she looked up from her seat on the UN Security Council at school tours and was struck by the symbolic harm of being the only woman.[11] On the other hand, she frames her efforts to balance work and home—emphasizing how her young children were "everywhere"—as a positive professional model. "When you are the only woman on the Security Council and you hear men talk about sexual violence in war with great authority and dogmatism, about how certain events couldn't have happened because the men who were accused of rape would have had their wives to go home to, so why would they? Certainly now I'm focused on that set of issues."[12]

Power's understanding of gender and women's rights reveals what Chandra Mohanty calls a "white, Western, middle-class liberal feminism," singularly focused on "gender as a basis for sexual rights." This singular focus stands in contrast to feminist politics forged from an understanding of "gender in relation to race and/or class as part of a broader liberation struggle."[13] As Power's emphasis on workplace equality demonstrates, liberal feminism focuses on legal and economic equality between men and women within a capitalist system.[14] An autonomous, self-determining individual is the subject of liberal feminist scholarship and politics.[15] This subject has produced a "Third World woman" as the "Other" of Western liberal feminism, often homogenizing and victimizing women who are the subject of its gaze.[16]

This liberal feminist tradition underpins interpretations of both the Afghanistan War as being in the name of women's rights and of combat integration as a milestone on a progressive march toward universal women's equality. In contrast to these dominant narratives of war, I offer an alternate framework of a new imperial feminism that has been central to the broader operation of US hegemony and its redefinition of post–World War II imperialism.[17] Counterinsurgency offers a particularly salient lens for examining how imperial feminism is assembled through military doctrine, living colonial and Cold War histories, and practices of US military soldiers and contractors. If Power's endorsement of the *Counterinsurgency Field Manual* is a key articulation of liberal feminist narratives of war, it also indicates the significance of development and humanitarianism in reformulating the occupations of Iraq and Afghanistan from the mid-2000s onward. To understand how the new imperial feminism has taken shape through these interconnected forces, I focus on three key features: the US military's adoption of development and humanitarianism as counterinsurgency weapons, military instructors' reliance on colonial and Cold War histories to produce modern counterinsurgent soldiers, and women's incorporation into those ranks through new forms of gendered labor.[18] This nexus of development, colonial historiography, and gender is crucial to understanding how military labor and militarism as a social way of life were redefined over the course of the wars in Iraq and Afghanistan in the early twenty-first century.

A key marker of militarized development's role in counterinsurgency was the military's so-called cultural turn, a response to the realization, soon after President Bush announced the end of major combat operations in Iraq in May 2003, that the war was not going well.[19] The *Counterinsurgency Field Manual* indicated militarized forms of development and humanitarianism as central to its "population-centric" approach, which emphasized winning the population's support over annihilating the enemy.[20] In an effort to follow counterinsurgency guidelines for engaging local populations and winning their support, military trainings in subsequent years began to include development "best practices" that had been repurposed for military objectives.

Part of what distinguishes counterinsurgency's revival in the mid-2000s from its historical precedents involves private contractors' role in translating development into a counterinsurgency weapon. In 2005, USAID established the new Office of Military Affairs to liaise with the Department of Defense. One of the primary tasks of the Office of Military Affairs was to contract civilian experts to teach a development framework that USAID had written for military instruction. Military personnel learned how to conduct a village needs assessment and then design, evaluate, and monitor irrigation, education, commerce, and other types of projects intended to fulfill a need and draw support away from the Taliban.

The contractors' introduction to bases was framed by gendered counterinsurgency, which Laleh Khalili describes as offering new forms of masculinity "in which 'manliness' is softened, and the sensitive masculinity of the humanitarian soldier-scholar (white, literate, articulate, and doctorate-festooned) overshadows the hyper-masculinity of warrior kings (or indeed of the racialised imperial grunts)."[21] In my research on military bases, I found that both the contractors themselves and USAID's instructional framework embodied this softened masculinity apparent in counterinsurgency doctrine. But in predeployment trainings, contractors' lessons often conflicted with other dimensions of soldiering, such as a security force's prior training in aggressive searching and patrolling tactics. Soldiers made sense of the conflict they experienced in terms of competing definitions of masculinity: longer-standing associations of masculinity with combat came into direct conflict with softened counterinsurgent masculinity. Some of the soldiers resisted being transformed into what they mockingly called "an NGO with guns." In its most extreme form in the US Marine Corps, trainees challenged the developmental counterinsurgency material outright, claiming they would rather be, in the words of one marine, "kicking in doors, blowin' up something." This resistance was often related to previous specialization in infantry and artillery, including home raids and detonating explosives, and involuntary assignment to more civilian-oriented and developmental military jobs.

In reaction to soldiers and marines who argued that this new material was not part of their job, military instructors provided historical explanations of how, for instance, the Marine Corps built roads and schools, trained local militaries, and managed the civil service of Haiti, Nicaragua, and the Dominican Republic during the early twentieth century.[22] Marine instructors frequently used Haiti as a case study to exemplify a number of unconventional deployments the students might find themselves on. Such examples included the invasion and occupation of Haiti from 1915 to 1934, when US marines turned to developmental projects in education and public health following a massive peasant uprising; peacekeeping operations in the 1990s and 2000s in Haiti; and the humanitarian response that followed the 2010 Haiti earthquake.[23] Lessons the marines learned in Haiti were incorporated into the *Small Wars Manual* (1940), which became the basis of the *US Army and Marine Corps Counterinsurgency Field Manual* (2006).[24]

The history of US imperialism directly informs the present, incorporated into modern military doctrine and in military trainings as evidence that developmental approaches are part of skeptical students' identity. At the same time, military doctrine erases historical geographies of imperialism, particularly their brutality and associated antisystemic movements, in favor of abstract tactics that are removed from time and place.[25] Placing the new imperial feminism within a longer history challenges military historiographies, which are generally told from the colonial officer's perspective, by surfacing the body counts as well as the cultural practices of colonial rule. Keeping the present in tension with the past clarifies where colonial ideologies of race, gender, and sexuality have resurfaced in the present and where they have changed.

New Military Femininity in All-Female Counterinsurgency Teams

Counterinsurgency in its post-9/11 incarnation targeted the household as a key site of military conquest.[26] Military literature from the mid to late 2000s understands the household as the link to the central counterinsurgency category of "the population," whose loyalties determine military success. According to the influential counterinsurgency theorist David Kilcullen, "Win the women, and you own the family unit. Own the family, and you take a big step forward in mobilizing the population."[27] By 2009, anxieties in the military that it was "only reaching half the population" (the male half) became palpable in official statements as well as more informal actions of those deployed, including the assembly of all-female teams to reach Afghan and Iraqi women. Female soldiers increasingly served as a conduit to this coveted domain of the household.

Despite military rhetoric, all-female counterinsurgency teams served an important intelligence dimension of providing opportunities to question women and children residing in a militarily surveilled home and allowing secret missions to remain under the cover of silence by calming the subjects of a home raid. Women's sexuality took on new meaning in these contexts. Whereas historically ✘ the military treated women as a sexual distraction that could undermine "unit cohesion," in the context of female counterinsurgency teams, servicewomen spoke of their "allure" as a benefit to collecting intelligence from young Afghan men. Such allure was conceptualized in terms of heteronormative sexuality as well as a racialized emphasis on physical traits such as blond hair and blue eyes—something so exotic that it captivated foreign populations, enchanting them into answering questions that were useful to their military team's intelligence goals. Participants also described their mission as global ambassadorship for women's rights, serving as a beacon of "Western" liberal feminism in a land they understood as backward in history.[28] Servicewomen's understandings of themselves as models of moder- ✘ nity and female empowerment articulate a new imperial feminism that, on the one hand, further entrenches gender stereotypes within the military and, on the other, imagines helpless Afghan people, especially women, requiring benevolent occupation. These linked processes in domestic and foreign spaces challenge popular framings of the post-9/11 wars liberating women abroad at the same time as combat integration brings the US military closer to gender equality.[29]

In the context of women's historical exclusion from combat, scholarship has largely theorized femininity in relation to military support roles, ranging from women's indirect familial or domestic support for male soldiers to long-standing direct employment by the military as secretaries, nurses, and, more recently, combat support roles in logistics, communications, and engineering.[30] Debo- ✘ rah Cowen explores the relationship between sexual violence in military culture and how "military models of masculinity have historically been built around the suppression of femininity and the objectification of women."[31] Scholars have developed a more robust understanding of masculinity's centrality to the construction of war, as well as masculinity's role and associations in structuring military institutions.[32] Women's integration into previously male and masculinist military domains, along with military praise for their unique contributions, calls for a concept of military femininity akin to more robust theorizations of military masculinity. This requires a move beyond what scholars such as Aaron Belkin have called for in considering military masculinity in its relation to, rather than simply disavowal of, femininity and queerness.[33] Instead, we need a concept of military femininity that captures how the repression framework in foundational work on gender and militarism has not disappeared but has undergone significant change.

New forms of gender inclusion, such as women's integration into previously male-only combat positions, have been accompanied by new exclusions, such as the denial of Veterans Affairs services to women who were "temporarily attached" rather than formally assigned to ground combat units and thus lacked formal documentation of their combat. Leading up to the integration of women into all combat units, the image of a certain military woman—white, heterosexual, capable of soothing and calming civilians—became emblematic of military claims to women's value in the post-9/11 counterinsurgency era. This racially and sexually circumscribed military womanhood is itself a form of exclusion and repression that has accompanied combat integration. By analyzing the female counterinsurgency teams leading up to women's formal inclusion in combat, I found that the forms of inclusion in policy changes have reinforced gender essentialisms such as women's capacity to soothe and calm war's victims.

Although FETs were initially used to search Iraqi and Afghan women, military proponents described them as a way to win the hearts and minds of Iraqi and especially Afghan civilian populations. This distinguishes counterinsurgency from so-called conventional theories of war, which focus on how to defeat another military force. If USAID trainings were one arm of the military's effort to create a force capable of winning such civilian support, gendered counterinsurgency is a second arm of this same military effort to remake itself in a counterinsurgent image. Military and popular media represented female counterinsurgency teams as performing humanitarian work to win the favor of both Afghan civilians and US domestic populations critical of the wars.[34] However, this humanitarian representation conceals a more strategic military interest, particularly in later iterations of the teams, related to intelligence collection and the seizure of high-value targets.

The initial wave of academic literature examining female counterinsurgency as a form of military humanitarianism was accurate in its attention to the affective and emotional dimensions of this military work.[35] But the prevailing military, media, and academic framing of it as an attempt to use humanitarianism to cover up forms of military violence does not adequately explain the combat uses of gendered counterinsurgency. Female counterinsurgents' own experiences, articulated through interviews and program material, speak to how this new military femininity was constructed through combat. Female counterinsurgency team members spoke of public affairs officers photographing them conducting a medical clinic and distributing supplies to an orphanage, even though most of their day-to-day experience entailed collecting information, which, although technical military language referred to it as "atmospherics," was related to intelligence. Through attention to the gender essentialisms at work when female counterinsurgents are, for example, praised for their emotional capacity to extract valuable intelligence, I develop a concept of military femininity that is formed through the interrelationship between humanitarianism and combat. This emphasis on combat contrasts with the focus on humanitarian rhetoric within scholarship on female counterinsurgency teams, which echoes military and popular media's own representation of the teams as a more humanitarian dimension to war.[36] Taking military and media narratives of humanitarian gendered counterinsurgency at face value, we miss the teams' strong association with combat and what this association might mean for an adequate understanding of military femininity. Women's own narratives of their time on female counterinsurgency teams call for a theorization of "combat femininity" that is akin to Jennifer Fluri's concept of "combat masculinity," which combines violence and heroism with gendered bodily performances.[37]

We must take into account how women's emotional labor—the work they do to manage their own emotions in order to produce a desired state in others according to job requirements—is directly tied to military combat. Writing specifically about flight attendants, although with regard to many gendered forms of labor, Arlie Hochschild defines "emotional labor" as requiring "one to induce or suppress feeling in order to sustain the outward countenance that produces the proper state of mind in others—in this case, the sense of being cared for in a convivial and safe place."[38] Female counterinsurgents recalled various strategic uses of emotional labor in interviews. Women described placing their hands on the bodies of Afghan women and children, adjusting their voice tone, and removing their body armor to elicit feelings of security and comfort in civilians so that they might allow the military operation to continue smoothly or provide useful information. Particularly among early Lioness teams (from 2003 onward), who received no additional training or preparation for combat operations, women performed emotional labor to suppress their own fear or misgivings about the missions they were on to "get the job done."

Hochschild argues that emotional labor "behaves like a commodity," carrying with it all the vulnerabilities and alienation of the worker established in classic political economy.[39] Because the soldier's labor is a different sort of commodity, female counterinsurgents' emotional labor creates an interesting puzzle. Cowen has noted the soldier's absence from labor studies and political economy, even though the soldier has been central to modern welfare and citizenship regimes. Military work has also structured civilian work; modern workplace discipline and principles of industrial production and workplace organization originated within the military.[40] Taking from this insight that war work has structured civilian labor, in particular through social welfare, I present soldiering as a form of labor and, in the context of FETs, of emotional labor.

Military women's emotional labor is central to a new military femininity that upholds gender essentialisms such as women's emotional capacity at the same time as it promotes their role in combat. Lioness teams, FETs, and cultural support teams (CSTs, a later special operations program) all operated in violation of military policy that banned women from combat. Women were often in combat roles without the same training as their male counterparts and without the forms of documentation required to access certain Veterans Affairs health care and benefits. By examining where the push within the military to do these illicit forms of labor came from, how these teams were discussed in official military discourse, and how women serving on them understood their work, we see the emergence of a new military femininity that contains a more complex interplay between repression and inclusion than academic frameworks currently provide. I track the emergence of this new military femininity within the military's own labor force, in contrast to the stories the military tells about itself to the public at large. The years leading up to combat integration show how gendered counterinsurgency has taken on a new face of alleged inclusion whereby inclusion reinforces conservative gender roles and in fact exposes some women to heightened risk of injury.[41]

Imperial Histories of the Present

In US military trainings, instructors commonly used colonial history to convince trainees of the value of population-centric techniques such as military development projects. Different historiographical narratives create different historical lenses through which soldiers understand themselves. When instructors teach imperial history, for example, soldiers are asked to imagine themselves in the place of the British colonial soldier on the African continent or the US Army scout "pacifying" Indigenous resistance in the West. Such imperial historiographies operate at multiple levels of military knowledge production, including the *Counterinsurgency Field Manual*'s authors drawing directly on historical writings on colonial counterinsurgencies in Algeria, Malaya, Indonesia, and Vietnam.[42] David Kilcullen, one of the most important counterinsurgent voices during the post-9/11 period

and a member of the manual's writing team, considered the Phoenix Program—
which tortured, imprisoned, and killed tens of thousands of people during the
Vietnam War—a success that had been "unfairly maligned." He thought it was in
fact "highly effective" and should be treated as a model for counterinsurgency
in Iraq and Afghanistan.[43] If such military historiographies that treat Vietnam
War–era counterinsurgency strategies as successful and call for their revival are so
central to the making of the modern soldier, an alternate critical historiography of
imperialism raises a series of questions about the forms and scale of military violence enacted upon those who inhabit sites of US military occupation. Critical
histories of imperialism flip the script, which in a military historiography focuses
on the role of the occupying force, and instead ask about continuity and change of
colonial ideologies of race, gender, and other forms of social difference. Finally,
alternate historiographies of imperialism enable us to ask what alternate futures
may be possible that diverge from military doctrine.

"Small wars" theory originated within the US military in the context of the
nineteenth-century Indian Wars of US westward expansion. Tactics the army had
derived from the Indian Wars became the "necessary, if unwritten, manual for
subsequent overseas asymmetric warfare, in the Philippines, the Caribbean, and
Latin America."[44] The use of reservations, Native and settler scouts, and language
of "civilization" as instrumental to pacification circulated through the military
governors who traveled between sites of expanding US imperial power in the early
twentieth century. The Treaty of Paris in 1898 saw the ascendency of the United
States as a major imperial power, taking on sovereignty over not only the formerly
Spanish-held Philippines but also Puerto Rico and Guam as well as Cuba in the
form of a protectorate. The United States was embedded in intra- and interimpe-
rial circuits of government in this period, with Native rule and Native racial categories employed in the Philippines.[45] Inseparable in this period were "these two
histories—of the racial remaking of empire and the imperial remaking of race."[46]
Gail Bederman demonstrates US promotion of racism in this period through the
notion of the "strenuous life," exemplified in Theodore Roosevelt's "embodiment
of manly virtue, masculine violence, and white American racial supremacy."[47]

This high point of US imperial expansion at the end of the nineteenth century
was not so much an aberration—the only time the United States became a "proper
imperial power"—but instead, as Amy Kaplan argues, indicated the "multiple historical trajectories of the anarchy of empire," including violent continental expansion in the 1840s and colonization of Hawaii before its annexation as well as
imperial ventures that came after.[48] Following this dense imperial node of 1898,
the United States undertook military interventions during the first third of the
twentieth century in Cuba, Panama, Honduras, Nicaragua, Mexico, Haiti, and the
Dominican Republic. Collectively known as the Banana Wars, the period between

the end of the Spanish-American War and the beginning of President Franklin Delano Roosevelt's Good Neighbor policy marked another crucial turning point in twentieth-century US imperialism.[49] The almost twenty-year US Marine Corps occupation of Haiti (1915–1934) was administered through what historian Mary Renda calls a racialized paternalism. Following the occupation of Haiti, the United States renegotiated race, gender, sexuality, and national identity in direct relation to its imperial orbit.[50]

In the period before US entry into World War II, national debate framed by limitations on defense shifted to Roosevelt's much more expansive concept of national security.[51] The vast network that today encircles the globe in up to eight hundred US military bases has its roots in the World War II era. David Vine pinpoints the birth of what would become "base nation" to September 2, 1940, when Roosevelt exercised presidential power in the destroyers-for-bases deal that promised Britain a fleet of aging naval destroyers in exchange for ninety-nine–year leases on a group of air and naval bases in its colonies.[52] In tandem with this massive military expansion was the establishment of a political and economic order that by 1945 secured US hegemony. In the bipolar world unfolding after World War II, the United States pursued a "positive American world order" that built a network of regional alliances across the capitalist world.[53] Not just security alliances, these were the basis of social, political, and economic transformations cementing American control. As journalist I. F. Stone baldly stated, "Pax Americana is the 'internationalism' of Standard Oil, Chase Manhattan, and the Pentagon."[54] In the postwar era, the 1944 Bretton Woods agreement led to the formation of a global finance system as well as the International Monetary Fund and the World Bank, central banking institutions that were part of an emerging economic infrastructure dominated by US interests.[55] US military, political, and economic power was fortified in the context of a Cold War whose nuclear character threatened to annihilate humanity, eroding distinctions between soldiers and citizens.[56]

Counterinsurgency returned as the United States became increasingly embroiled in Vietnam. The US wars there were at the center of an early Cold War geography in the late 1940s and early 1950s that was "reorganizing the post–World War II world according to the principles of liberal capitalism."[57] By the time the United States had adopted its fully fledged policy of containment and rollback of Soviet power through the violent suppression of communist and anticolonial movements all over the world, the US war in Vietnam had also become a mirror reflecting bald-faced racism within the United States.[58] At the same time as draft resistance actively intersected with antiracist struggles and Dr. Martin Luther King Jr. delivered his "Beyond Vietnam" speech that drew connections between domestic racism and imperial wars, the "prose of counterinsurgency" provided the logic of racialized criminality that mainstream media outlets used to describe the Detroit and Watts uprisings. Counterinsurgency directly influenced urban policing in this period. For example, following the Detroit rebellion, President Lyndon Johnson's national security adviser, Walt Rostow, argued, "At home your appeal is for law and order as the framework for economic and social progress. Abroad we fight in Vietnam to make aggression unprofitable . . . [to] build a future of economic and social progress."[59]

The Cold War's "center of gravity" shifted to a series of proxy wars connecting southern Africa, Central America, and central Asia in the period following US defeat in Vietnam in the mid-1970s.[60] Within this broader geography of terrorism, a US-Saudi-Pakistani alliance formed in the late 1980s through which "the CIA [Central Intelligence Agency] created the Mujaheddin and bin Laden as alternatives to secular nationalism."[61] Cooperation between the CIA and Pakistan's Inter Services Intelligence recruited the most radical versions of political Islam to the region and imported large numbers of weapons to fuel the CIA paramilitary anti-Soviet operation. US intervention in Afghanistan and the surrounding region during the Cold War precipitated 9/11 by organizing, arming, and training previously diffuse right-wing Islamists. US proxies recruited Osama bin Laden to promote this newly consolidated notion of global jihad.[62] He circulated between Saudi Arabia, Afghanistan, and Pakistan with financial support, construction equipment, and civil engineers who built training camps and other infrastructure for the mujaheddin.[63]

With this in mind, we should understand the September 11, 2001 attacks as what Mahmood Mamdani calls "the result of an alliance gone sour, . . . first and foremost as the unfinished business of the Cold War."[64] Although a geography of interconnection produced the events of 9/11, which were themselves global in nature, the moments following the attacks saw an enormous amount of discursive and explicitly spatial work that produced those events as a US "*national* tragedy."[65] One example of this hardening of geographical boundaries is captured in war college professor Thomas Barnett's division of the world into a "functioning core" of countries, "where globalization is thick with network connectivity, financial transactions, liberal media flows, and collective security" and a "non-integrating gap" distinguished mainly by its "bloody boundaries" as well as poverty, disease, and "most important—the chronic conflicts that incubate the next generation of terrorists." Barnett argues that 9/11 did the security establishment a "huge favor" by showing where the boundaries between the "core" and the "gap" lie and revealing the dangers posed by the "gap." Imaginative geographies such as Barnett's underpinned the ensuing wars in Iraq and Afghanistan.[66]

The "Terminal Crisis" of US Hegemony

Fueled in part by the binary spatial logic of the "Pentagon's new map," the Bush administration quickly set in place the conditions of possibility for a military response to the 9/11 attacks, swiftly signing into law a joint resolution authorizing the use of force against those deemed responsible for the attacks.[67] Weeks later on October 7, 2001, the US military opened the Afghanistan War with a British-supported air assault against Afghanistan followed by a ground invasion. Although none of the nineteen hijackers hailed from Afghanistan, this was allegedly a war against terrorism and specifically the terrorist attacks of 9/11. At its height in 2011, about one hundred thousand US forces were deployed to Afghanistan.[68] As we move into the war on terror's third decade, the turning point from "boots on the ground" to covert and air wars whose battlefield spans the globe is a crucial opportunity to understand how the first twenty years of war were fought and to reckon with the consequences.

The 9/11 attacks also served as the catalyst for a group of neoconservative activists to implement a long-standing plan for regime change in Iraq.[69] In 1997, neoconservative activists founded the Project for a New American Century (PNAC), a foreign policy pressure group advocating military intervention to maintain US interests amid a shifting geopolitical landscape in the post–Cold War era. More than half of the PNAC's founding members, including Donald Rumsfeld, Paul Wolfowitz, and Elliot Abrams, went on to assume high-level positions in the Bush administration.[70] In 1998, the PNAC authored a letter to President Bill Clinton advocating for regime change in Iraq as the pillar of the US-centric foreign policy they promoted. Regime change in Iraq became "an obsession" for Wolfowitz, which he continued to advocate for right up until 9/11.[71] Reporter George Packer describes how "within minutes of fleeing his office at the devastated Pentagon" after the 9/11 attacks, "Wolfowitz told aides that he suspected Iraqi involvement in the attacks." Surrounded by longtime PNAC proponents, Bush requested the very next day, even after being told that al-Qaeda was responsible for the attacks, that his counterterrorism team investigate "any shred" of Iraqi connection to the attacks.[72] Based on false premises of weapons of mass destruction, he declared war in Iraq preemptively.[73] The Coalition Provisional Authority, which governed the country in the occupation following invasion, was staffed through the sole criteria of loyalty to the Bush administration.

All of this came at the hefty price of US$8 trillion.[74] Economist Linda Bilmes calls Iraq and Afghanistan "credit card wars" for their historic financing through deficit spending.[75] The human cost of the wars is no less staggering. In Iraq and Afghanistan alone, over 250,000 civilians died violent deaths as a direct result of the wars. When Syria, Pakistan, and Yemen are included, this number grows to about 387,000 civilians or 929,000 people total (including civilians, military, contractors, opposition fighters, journalists, humanitarian workers, etc.).[76] At least 38 million people have been displaced as a result of the wars the US military has fought globally since 2001.[77] During just the first dozen years of the global war on terror, 6,656 members of the US military were killed in Iraq and Afghanistan, with this number rising to 6,956 by the war's twentieth year.[78] More than 40 percent of US service members who returned from Iraq, Afghanistan, and related locations, or 1.8 million people, have a service-connected disability from their deployment and qualify for lifetime disability benefits. The cost of caring for Iraq and Afghanistan veterans into the future will be as high as US$2.5 trillion.[79] These are just some of the human and economic costs of the post-9/11 wars.

Among the many post-9/11 analyses of resurgent US imperialism, Arrighi provides an especially compelling framework of the post-9/11 wars as the "terminal crisis" of US hegemony, following the "signal crisis" of the late 1960s and 1970s marked by defeat in Vietnam. Arrighi argues that "the Iraqi adventure definitively confirmed the earlier verdict of the Vietnam War—that is, that the Western superiority of force has reached its limits and shows strong tendencies towards implosion."[80] In analyzing the distinctive financial, military, and spatial dimensions of the US position in the world after World War II, Arrighi moves from a concept of "imperialism" to a theory of "world-hegemony."[81] This move breaks from extensions of classical theories of imperialism into the present, instead charting a new course that acknowledges how post–World War II US hegemony was formed through very different political, economic, and military conditions than the competition over territory among capitalist states that distinguished the late nineteenth and early twentieth centuries.[82]

Arrighi's concept of a "struggle for world-hegemony" globalizes Antonio Gramsci's concept of hegemony as "the *additional* power that accrues to a dominant group by virtue of its capacity to lead society in a direction that not only serves the dominant group's interest but is also perceived by subordinate groups as serving a more general interest."[83] It is precisely Arrighi's Gramscian understanding of the political, economic, and military forces through which a *struggle* takes place that distinguishes his theory of US hegemony from more pervasive references to US imperialism. Understanding the social processes at work within this struggle requires concrete attention to military doctrine and practices. I see imperialism as redefined through the specificity of US power that Arrighi calls "world-hegemony." Yet I retain the term "imperialism" to signify new, violent, and expansionary dimensions of US financial and military power and continuities of colonial ideologies of race imported into the present through military trainings.[84] These imperial processes are intertwined with and transformed by struggles for consent signified by the term "hegemony."

Extending Gramsci's understanding of how economic crises alone cannot lead to historical events—"they can simply create a terrain more favourable to the dissemination of certain modes of thought"—Arrighi analyzes how the PNAC could not be implemented from above, but necessitated stoking domestic fear.[85] He draws a series of parallels between the Bush administration's response to 9/11 through adoption of the PNAC and President Harry Truman's embrace of Arthur Vandenberg's advice to "'scare hell out of the American people' by inflating the notion of global communist menace" in the early Cold War period.[86] In the post-9/11 period, scaring the hell out of the American people included making a racialized enemy centered on a Muslim "fundamentalist" threat.[87]

The military lessons I examine here contain a counterpart to domestic anti-Muslim racism in their representation of an imagined Afghan Other. But in contrast to the imagined Afghan Other, the new imperial feminism mobilizes particular valuations of racial identity. All-female teams are represented through civilizational rhetoric that attributes value to whiteness but employs the military's actual multiracial composition to do so. A prevalent military rhetoric of color blindness simultaneously denies this valuation of whiteness within the military as it couches imperial racism in the language of "culture" and "civilization." Such civilizational rhetoric is apparent in military claims that Afghan people are incapable of self-government. In contrast to the rugged masculinity reflected in notions of the "strenuous life" at the end of the nineteenth century, a white femininity now associated with counterinsurgency promotes the value of a delicate touch, sensitivity, and tropes of an imagined common humanity. These coupled understandings of race and gender give meaning to female counterinsurgents' work, allowing them, for example, to imagine a common solidarity of womanhood between themselves and the Afghan women they interact with on missions. In contrast to the military historiographies underpinning military doctrine, the alternate critical history discussed here frames the post-9/11 return of counterinsurgency as continuous with a longer imperial enterprise, asking what is distinctive about the modern assembly of imperialism.

Feminist Critics of Imperialism

Rather than accepting combat integration as a milestone on a progressive march toward universal women's equality, and the Afghanistan War as a defense of women's rights, we must ask how liberal feminist narratives of war enable and normalize US imperialism. For example, Judith Butler reflects on the "frames" of war—"the ways of selectively carving up experience as essential to the conduct of war."[88] She considers how sexual and feminist politics have provided a certain frame for the war effort, including defining modernity in terms of sexual free-dom.[89] If feminist politics have been framed in a way that fosters consent to war, the defining features of liberal feminism have been central to this framing. In contrast to the dominant frame of war that liberal feminism offers, feminist crit-ics of imperialism provide an alternative to framing the Afghanistan War as lib-erating women, or combat integration as indicative of gender equality.

Marxist feminists such as Rosa Luxemburg and Raya Dunayevskaya under-stood imperialism as a manifestation of capitalism's geographical need to expand. Luxemburg theorized imperialism as a form of ongoing "primitive accumula-tion," or capitalism's impulse to pillage noncapitalist or "outside" systems in or-der to reinvest surplus value and continue expanding.[90] Luxemburg develops a concept of militarism as a "province of accumulation," driving imperialist ex-pansion by taxing workers' wages to support an army acting in the bourgeoisie's interests. At the same time, armament manufacture becomes a new opportunity for accumulation.[91] Although Luxemburg wrote little on gender explicitly, she lived out a feminist critique of imperialism. Under her influence, the Second Women's Congress in 1910 called for a day of action against imperialist war, dem-onstrating the progressive force that women played within early twentieth-century socialist movements.[92]

Marxist understandings of imperialism as rooted in the logic of capital influ-enced Hannah Arendt's argument in *The Origins of Totalitarianism*. Although Arendt critiqued and ultimately departed from Karl Marx, she drew heavily on Luxemburg in her writings on imperialism.[93] Arendt came to understand impe-rialist expansion as a solution to nineteenth-century capitalism's contradiction of "superfluous money and superfluous men." As she saw it, "these two superfluous forces, superfluous capital and superfluous working power, joined hands and left the country together."[94] Such foundational thought linking imperialism to capi-talism also informed women's anti-imperial and antifascist organizing through the Cold War period.[95] Historiographies of such organizing describe how liberal feminist framings have silenced this history in favor of a dominant narrative of the women's movement that focuses on equal rights.[96]

Following the post-9/11 wars in Iraq and Afghanistan, contemporary feminist theorists have furthered such critiques of capitalism to dissect how gendered, ra-cialized, and sexualized practices consolidate capitalism through imperialist wars.[97] They examine how the trope of "saving and/or protecting women" has been used in Afghanistan to further military violence, which in turn harms women.[98] Such impulses grow out of a much deeper colonial legacy of what Gay-atri Spivak famously called "white men saving brown women from brown men."[99] Spivak was writing about Britain's justification of its imperial presence in India based on its abolition of widow sacrifice. Military rhetoric of liberating Afghan women justified counterinsurgency in Afghanistan, reflected in the photographs of unveiled women handed out to US soldiers as evidence of their "triumph."[100]

Many servicewomen I interviewed described their interactions with Afghan women as an opportunity to demonstrate what a liberated, rights-bearing woman looks like. The female soldier became emblematic of a new imperial feminism that ties Afghan women's liberation to US military occupation. The linkage of this imperial violence to liberation resembles Spivak's critique but with some important differences. Here a multiracial group of US military women does the "rescuing." Many female soldiers also struggled with the dissonance between their imagined Afghan subject—a timid, oppressed, and "traditional" woman hidden under a burka—with some of the women they actually met who were vibrant and modern and resisted patriarchy however they could.

As female soldiers became symbols of feminist liberation, in contrast to their imagined Afghan counterparts, they took on a larger cultural valence within the United States as an equal rights issue. The American Civil Liberties Union advocated for women's rights to serve in all capacities alongside male service members and in 2012 sued the Department of Defense. Feminist critics such as Angela Y. Davis and Zillah Eisenstein have, in the face of ongoing wars, rejected the "fight for the equal right of women to participate in the military, for the equal right of women to torture, or for their equal right to be killed in combat."[101] This equal right to be killed is linked to the framing of US military women as "saving brown women from brown men." Female counterinsurgency teams' allegedly humanitarian activities such as medical clinics were often directly linked to intelligence gathering and combat. The teams were then used by advocates of combat integration as proof that military policy should reflect reality by allowing women to serve in ground combat units. The link between allegedly humanitarian activities and violent forms of combat and intelligence suggests that a more expansive definition of violence is necessary to include the "humanitarian" activities I examine here. This more expansive definition of violence is at work when USAID deploys private development contractors to military bases and when female counterinsurgents offer medical clinics.

Counterinsurgency as a Contingent Social Process

Counterinsurgency's uses of development, how it relies on past histories, and the gendered ramifications of those uses involve multiple interdisciplinary conversations. A conjunctural understanding of development shows how its relation to security must be produced through the intricate, messy social relations between soldiers, marines, military trainers, contractors, and development pro-fessionals whose experiences shape the following analysis. Conjunctural analysis is a Gramscian method for understanding historical moments of crisis, the long duration of which reveals "incurable structural contradictions" and "the politi-cal forces which are struggling to conserve and defend the existing structure. . . . These incessant and persistent efforts (since no social formation will ever admit that it has been superseded) form the terrain of the 'conjunctural,' and it is upon this terrain that the forces of opposition organize."[102] A conjunctural analysis of counterinsurgency demands attention to how the relationship between de-velopment and security is produced through the political, economic, and mili-tary "relations of force" that shape the conjunctural terrain.[103]

Emphasizing the *production* of the relationship between development and se-curity makes military trainings especially relevant sources of evidence. Within these settings, instructors encourage military personnel to internalize a securi-tized language of development. Such trainings also provoke contention over development personnel's role within military missions, or whether military personnel should be fulfilling a development objective. Trainings and other sites of military knowledge production reveal militarized development to be contin-gent, or coming into formation through multiple determinations that operate without guarantees.[104]

This contingent understanding of development is markedly different from Mark Duffield's "security-development nexus," which frames underdevelopment itself as dangerous and development as merged with security.[105] By categorizing develop-ment as a type of biopolitics within a "liberal problematic of security," Duffield predetermines development as always already conceptually and discursively tied to security.[106] In contrast to this pregiven relationship between development and secu-rity, which emphasizes the analytic identification of development's biopolitical traits, my contingent understanding of development emphasizes the practices, meanings, and processes through which development comes into formation.[107]

Examining the practices at work within military trainings allows for perspec-tive into how war making can challenge, reinforce, or change the understandings soldiers carry within themselves. By analyzing military instruction in develop-ment, adaptations of colonial histories, and assembly of female counterinsurgency teams, this book advances scholarship on development as a contingent social pro-cess by elaborating how development's militarization has also taken shape through efforts to resolve the contradictory impulses of empire making. For instance, FETs were a direct response to soldiers' contradictory role in counterinsurgency of win-ning hearts and minds with one breath and enacting lethal force in the next.

Considering what happens within military trainings, history lessons, and fe-male counterinsurgency teams also diverges conceptually and methodologically from much of the existing scholarship on what is often referred to as "military humanitarianism." Derek Gregory has written of the US military's "cultural turn," which was defined by counterinsurgency's emphasis on the "human terrain" as opposed to the physical terrain, and a shift in military optics from territory to population.[108] Gregory's definition of the "cultural turn" as a second phase of the Revolution in Military Affairs is an important intervention into scholarship that sees military emphasis on population and culture as opposed to the use of drones and high-tech lethal instruments. He frames the cultural turn as part of the "re-enchantment" of war in which developmental forms of war are merely a "dress uniform" to distract the public from actual violence.[109] The analytical burden then becomes to strip away the dress uniform to reveal the more significant aspects of war making. Developmental and humanitarian projects pursued as part of counterinsurgency operations become less legitimate objects of study than the "kinetic" (violent) operations they are attempting to "dress up."

Gregory's intervention filled an important political need when counterinsurgency was presented to the public as a "kinder," "gentler," "humanitarian style of military intervention."[110] At the same time, emphasis on revealing humanitarian and development projects within counterinsurgency for their actual military objective has directed attention away from the internal workings of such projects. It has unintentionally replicated the military's own language of humanitarianism, at times neglecting how such projects not only acted as window dressing to obscure military violence but were also themselves part of the operation of such violence.

By delving into the inner workings of developmental and humanitarian forms of militarism, this book shows how their unintended consequences alone merit attention. What may begin as an attempt to dress up militarism in the garb of humanitarianism can also produce new institutions that change the financial and bureaucratic relationship of security to development within the US government. More than an attempt to conceal the truly violent nature of militarism, such projects are themselves integral to military violence. For example, the paradigmatic cups of tea female counterinsurgents describe drinking, often in the language of "winning hearts and minds," actually support intelligence gathering. By asking more about what happens when those cups of tea are consumed, the institutional and financial structures leading up to the "key leader engagement," and the type of soldiering entailed, this book reconceptualizes violence by holding development and humanitarian activities in relation to their military objective.

Such a reconceptualization demands that we move beyond binary military language of "kinetic" (violent) and "nonkinetic" (nonviolent) activities. Counterinsurgency's critics have focused on unmasking the nonkinetic dimensions of counterinsurgency as a "therapeutic discourse" that simply deflects attention from kinetic operations such as the air strikes that intensified in the very years the counterinsurgency manual was released (2006 and 2007).[111] In doing away with the binary of violent/nonviolent (itself the military's own making), we need to ask how those activities the military describes as nonkinetic are entirely implicated in violence. Pushing on the violent/nonviolent boundary even more, I also treat the dry delivery of a PowerPoint presentation and the seemingly sanguine exchange between Afghan role players and marines in a simulated village meeting as violent processes.[112] It would be a misreading to view such activities as nonviolent military acts. Nor are they simply papering over the more violent aspects of war. Rather, the subtle, even boring aspects of war making such as PowerPoint constitute violence. They make possible the air strike, the civilian casualties, and the thirty-eight million or more displaced: the female soldier's emotional labor facilitates the night raid in which civilians die.

I do not describe in great detail the violence enacted upon Afghan civilians. Studies exist that rightly draw our attention and horror to this violence. We know that about 929,000 people have been killed directly as a result of the post-9/11 wars.[113] But we know very little about how the military's revived penchant for development and humanitarian activities is part of this broader spectrum of violence. Although they have been central to the wars that continue today, we lack an understanding of how developmental military technologies are produced.[114]

The product of military trainings is not the canals the military promises to build but rather the transformation of gendered and racialized meanings of military labor. These struggles are a far more significant outcome of changes in military discourse than the promised wells, schools, and clinics. In contrast to the stated aim of such trainings to convince soldiers of the value of doing "armed social work" in all its feminized light, soldiers' rejection of these lessons ends up reinforcing traditional associations of combat with masculinity. Trainings produce racist, paternalistic understandings of Afghan civilians as incapable of managing their own lives. Within female counterinsurgency teams, gender essentialisms such as women's emotional expertise have taken hold through allegedly humanitarian projects that might otherwise be disregarded as public relations distractions from actual military violence. Female soldiers describe the gendered uses of emotion as a weapon to collect intelligence and raid homes. These activities are integral to, not an adjacent distraction from, the actual violence of war. An eye to the production side of military labor blurs the boundary between what the military claims is and is not violent and reveals the stakes of this boundary: for instance, female counterinsurgents' invisibility in combat limiting their ability to claim service-connected disabilities.

In contrast to existing analyses of counterinsurgency, *At War with Women* offers a contingent understanding of how the relationship between development and security has taken shape in the post-9/11 era. Focusing on practices inside the programs that other scholarship has dismissed as part of a dress uniform covering up the real stuff of empire reveals the unintended consequences of new bureaucracies and funding sources that have changed the development landscape. This focus also situates the history of colonial and Cold War counterinsurgency in the present, in military classrooms where instructors need this history to make claims for a military identity rooted in "armed social work." All of these components of war making feed into the construction of gender, race, and social difference in the modern imperial United States.

Methodological and Conceptual Approach

I first encountered development contractors working on military bases during fieldwork I began at USAID's Washington, D.C., headquarters in 2010. I had arranged a series of interviews with the agency's Office of Military Affairs because I was interested in a new federal financial mechanism that allowed a small portion of discretionary defense spending to be transferred via the State Department to development projects led by nongovernmental organizations. Some employees there and especially their counterparts in other USAID offices were concerned about the military's encroachment into what they understood as USAID's territory. The new funding stream was one among many institutional linkages in this period that created new relationships between military and development bureaucracies. The Office of Military Affairs was itself a major conduit of these new development-defense linkages; it contracted development experts to provide the military with predeployment training that repackaged development "best practices" for military use. After I interviewed several USAID employees about this military training, my numerous questions resulted in the invitation to observe the training for myself (and perhaps stop asking so many questions!). I spent the following year shadowing contractors hired by USAID as they traveled to different military bases across the United States, observing how they taught the material and interacted with their military audiences. This initial entry into military trainings through development contractors opened into much more extensive opportunities to learn about military training, military knowledge production, and military life more generally. Over time I was able to observe the pieces of predeployment training that came before and after the contractors' materials. Eventually, I was invited to entire trainings that were related to the transformations associated with counterinsurgency but did not include the contractors directly.

This book reflects changing definitions of ethnography.[115] My research questions could not have been answered by a more traditional ethnographic approach

of spending a sustained period of time in one field site. Access to military trainers depended on my ability to circulate with them between different sites as they
traveled to interlinked military bases all around the United States. Rather than
a year- or years-long engagement in a particular place, my observations on military bases were concentrated into periods ranging from several days to eight
weeks. I conducted these concentrated observations on six military bases within
the United States, returning to some more than once, mainly between 2010 and
2012. This did not include observations at war colleges (treated separately), which
were often located on different military bases. Since base access is often possible
only with permission for a specific purpose, my observations were structured
by the trainings I was able to observe.

This book uses an ethnographic lens to understand the question of how development became weaponized during the post-9/11 era of counterinsurgency. Applied to military trainings, this lens foregrounds how instructors confronted
resistance as they tried to transform soldiers into "armed social workers."[116] The
perspective from the training classroom, training material, and informal conversations with military personnel, contractors, and role players reveals the production of "armed social workers" to be quite contentious in practice. Analytically,
this provides a perspective of the US military—an object often popularly and aca-
demically seen as monolithic—as being full of contradiction and requiring constant work to maintain.

My methodological approach of following the historical examples and justifications that military instructors used into their archives grew out of my observations from these contentious classrooms. The combined action platoons of the
Vietnam War—which deployed a small US Marine Corps rifle squad with a South
Vietnamese military platoon to a targeted village to deprive the Viet Cong of village access and support—were a key reference point in the trainings I observed.[117]
Haiti also featured prominently in these classrooms because my research period
dovetailed with the large military response to the 2010 Haiti earthquake. The
earthquake was prefigured by the long-standing relationship between the United
States and Haiti, the first occupation of which was itself a strong source of military
"lessons learned" regarding training local militaries and the uses of development in counterinsurgency.[118] To clarify the historical texture of these military
lessons, I spent six months in Haiti mainly working with collections from the
early twentieth-century Marine Corps occupation. Reading this archive against
military uses of this same history to teach post-9/11 counterinsurgency revealed
how military historical instruction often erases political dynamics in favor of abstract tactics that instructors argue can travel between times and places.

As I saw these histories used in predeployment trainings on military bases, I
wanted to know more about their broader role in military knowledge production.

In my initial observations of military trainings, I sat in on instruction at some of the armed forces war colleges, which are the top leadership schools for each of the military's armed services. Initially, I observed several UN-taught courses on humanitarian emergencies as well as military curricula focused on counterinsurgency history, strategy, and policy. In 2016–2017, I conducted a more systematic set of observations at one of these war colleges to gain a greater understanding of how historical material was treated at the highest echelons of military academic instruction. Here, mainly college-educated officers and some civilian defense professionals received detailed lessons on Vietnam War–era counterinsurgency. Vietnam was treated as a case study in relation to the present day in many of the classrooms I observed, but, at this high academic level of military instruction, Malaya and Algeria were also key references that shaped doctrine during the Vietnam War. My methodology of following such historical material from war college classrooms into historiographies and archives is part of a conceptual argument that colonial and Cold War histories actively shape the production of the contemporary soldier. Critical theorists have noted the intensity of US counterinsurgency practitioners' awareness and invocation of historical cases, but we know much less about how these histories inform lower-level trainings and soldiers' everyday experiences.[119]

Through the fieldwork I began in 2010 on military bases, I started to encounter women who had served on all-female counterinsurgency teams. By 2011, the height of the FET and CST programs and my most intensive period of training observations, I also noticed various military trainings promoting the FET program. During a five-week Marine Corps training for civil affairs specialists—a military specialization in civilian interaction that encompasses everything from humanitarian response to processing condolence payments—I spent the final week of the training sleeping on a lumpy plastic cot in the women's barracks alongside the handful of female marines enrolled in the training.[120] Some of these women had been previously deployed on Lioness teams and FETs. Two female public affairs officers were especially interested in my research and invited me to run through the humid forested trails around the training exercise and to join them in early morning sessions completing the "Insanity" workout mix they had downloaded before a breakfast of foamy dehydrated eggs and clumpy oatmeal. I was captivated by their motivations for joining a masculinist institution that so often treated women's bodies as "foreign."[121] The enthusiastic conversations in some military circles about the FETs as the cutting edge of counterinsurgency tactics ran counter to established academic understandings as well as my own taken-for-granted notions of the military as masculinist.

I remained interested in the military women I had met during my first phase of intensive fieldwork on bases and in the female counterinsurgency teams that continued to play a central role in the post-9/11 wars in Iraq and Afghanistan. By 2016–2017, in part because the program had ended and many of its participants were by then able to speak about their experiences, I could again spend several concentrated periods of time on military bases interviewing former members of Lioness teams, FETs, and CSTs. I interviewed twenty-two women who had deployed on these teams and another ten who had trained, partnered with, or commanded such teams. Most of these interviews were on bases. For women who had separated from the military, we had coffee in the towns where they now resided or talked by phone or video call. I was also granted access to twenty-five video interviews conducted by the D.C.-based leadership and professional development organization Women in International Security and housed at the Army Women's Museum. These two sets of interviews, supplemented by media coverage, military documents, and training materials, provide the basis for my discussion of female counterinsurgency teams and their associated gender politics.[122]

Methodologically, this book draws together ethnographic observations of military trainings, archival exploration into the histories that military instructors used to create post-9/11 doctrine, and servicewomen's interviews, journal entries, and other primary military sources. Together, these sources provide insight into the practices within military institutions, how history shapes those practices, and how shifts in military doctrine took shape through changing notions of race and gender. Centering analysis on the practices within military institutions is a methodological preference but also a conceptual argument that these practices are central to understanding the shape of contemporary imperialism and thus warrant scholarly attention.

The Rise of a New Imperial Feminism

The following chapters trace the arc of the US military's integration of development into counterinsurgency training and the reliance of this weaponized development on particular understandings of history, through to its gendered effects in the deployment of all-female counterinsurgency teams. The foundations for this arc are rooted in changes that took place in US military doctrine and training during the occupations of Iraq and Afghanistan. Given the *Counterinsurgency Field Manual*'s significance in enlisting development, chapter 1 analyzes the development rhetoric located within the manual and related texts. Development has been historically considered a weapon of colonial and Cold War counterinsurgencies. Post-9/11 military discursive and policy shifts provoked institutional changes within the US government that linked the administration of development to defense in new ways. Military claims for soldiering to now resemble "armed social work" led to the imperative for military trainings commensurate with this newly conceived soldier.

The reemergence of counterinsurgency provoked new forms of military training. Chapter 2 follows a Provincial Reconstruction Team as it moved through the different dimensions of predeployment training for Afghanistan.[123] Drawing on ethnographic observations of development experts whom USAID contracted to train military personnel, I focus on contractors' instruction of a USAID-written framework of development "best practices." The framework most often came after the segment of training on counterinsurgency, offering development as a weapon in the broader counterinsurgency effort. As students moved through the classroom instruction and simulations involved in training, they established intensifying critiques of what it meant to be "an NGO with guns." In response to soldiers who rejected the material through taken-for-granted notions of combat masculinity, trainers invited famous generals to class to explicitly describe the "population-centric" form of war they were learning as "manly." Such visits did not succeed so much in changing soldiers' minds as they did in provoking debate among soldiers, contractors, and military trainers about what it meant to be a soldier today.

At Quantico, instructors used history as a retort to marines who rejected the civilian-centric and nonkinetic (nonviolent) aspects of the course. Instructors met students' critiques that they did not want to be "armed social workers" with stories of how famous marines such as Smedley Butler and Chesty Puller were shaped through their deployments to Haiti training local security forces in the early twentieth century. Chapter 3 follows the construction of military historiographies as they inform present-day doctrine drawing on interventions in Haiti and the Caribbean in the early twentieth century, Algeria in the 1950s and 1960s, and Vietnam and Malaya during the Cold War. These three times and places were central to the lessons I saw taught at Quantico Marine Corps Base, Fort Bragg Army Base, and the US Naval War College, respectively. Through a reading of Marine Corps archival documents, the chapter first examines how small wars doctrine was shaped through historical US marines' experiences in places such as Haiti, Nicaragua, Honduras, the Dominican Republic, and the Philippines. Beginning from a war college classroom, the chapter then traces the influence of Walt Rostow and the Strategic Hamlet Program through post-9/11 military learning about counterinsurgency and connects a Marine Corps instructor's lesson on gendered counterinsurgency to French colonial programs and writings during the Algerian War of Independence.

The legacy of women's military labor being used to shore up empire continues through the military's incorporation of development and humanitarianism. Chapter 4 focuses on how militarized development required new forms of servicewomen's labor through army and Marine Corps Lioness teams, army FETs, and special operative CSTs. After an overview of the temporal and conceptual development of the teams, I narrate each iteration through in-depth interviews with counterinsurgency team members. Interviews, journal entries, letters home, and training materials pose a paradox of female soldiers as central to militarized development at the same time as they were marginalized within military institutions. We meet women who served on the earliest Lioness teams—who combine memories of searching Afghan and Iraqi women at checkpoints and on home raids with being denied Veterans Affairs services once they returned because their combat was never documented. FET members recall their emotional labor "soothing" and "calming" Afghan women following their infantry division's home raids. Such stories illustrate pervasive military understandings of women as the emotional experts of war.

Humanitarian rhetoric deployed in support of the FETs morphed into promotion of women's utility in combat, often on the basis of their emotional expertise. The work performed by special operative CSTs forms the basis of chapter 5. CST narratives show how even combat-intensive special operative missions further

FIGURE 1.   Female engagement team training, US army base. Author photo.

entrenched the basis of women's inclusion in emotional labor. Women also focused on how their physical and biological difference—often framed in terms of sexuality—provided value to special operations missions. Servicewomen established understandings of themselves as global ambassadors for women's rights, a notion that took on gendered meaning through constructions of racial difference. Military representations of phenotypically white women performing counterinsurgent labor not only erased the labor performed by soldiers of color but also articulated a broader imperial feminism that framed female soldiers as a beacon of women's rights that could guide Afghan women into the modern world. Racialized language of culture and civilization is linked to military discourses of a "color-blind" approach to race, which structures racism within military ranks as it enables civilizational arguments for military intervention on the basis of cultural differences.

The United States has been reshaped by twenty years of war. The effects of imperialism and militarism on the country are profound. As the military expands its recognition and inclusion of transgender people, one of these effects is the military's increasing prevalence as a site at which gender and politics produce one another. Through study of the years leading up to the formal integration of women in combat, this book offers a window into how understandings of military labor were being constructed in conjunction with race, gender, and imperialism during the post-9/11 revival of counterinsurgency. This return to counterinsurgency relied on colonial and Cold War histories while military thinkers glossed over the body counts of the Phoenix Program. A new imperial feminism has promoted military women's inclusion at the same time that it has entrenched essentialist understandings of femininity defined through emotion, motherhood, heterosexual marriage, and domesticity. Grasping the construction and dimensions of this new imperial feminism is crucial to understanding how the United States' longest wars have been perpetuated and how their legacy will shape the social fabric of war for years to come.

DOCTRINAL TURNING POINTS
IN THE NEW IMPERIAL WARS

In a sprawling shantytown by the sea in Port-au-Prince, Haiti, the US government has funded an open-air marketplace, a park, and a community space. The US funding sources are unsurprising amid the alphabet soup of nongovernmental organizations (NGOs), United Nations (UN) agencies, and private companies, all clamoring for a piece of Haiti.[1] What does stand out, however, is a money trail from these projects in Haiti to the US Department of Defense (DOD). The projects were part of a pilot US government program that used a small part of the Defense Department's discretionary budget to support reconstruction, stabilization, and security projects around the world. By 2010, I had interviewed many of the actors involved in this new funding source and was invited to see how the funding had been used in Cité Soleil, a marginalized group of neighborhoods in a flood-prone area of Port-au-Prince and one of the largest shantytowns in North America. A major US government contractor led the tour with its local Haitian partners, showing off to State Department and other US and local representatives what they had accomplished. At the time of our visit, the marketplace, intended to increase opportunities for local commerce, sat empty. A Haitian contractor explained this was because of its undesirable location away from the *tap-tap* stop, an informal local transit system of converted pickup trucks and buses. As we walked from project to project, one guide pointed out a series of drains a contractor had been hired to build that were flooding nearby family homes instead of being properly directed to gutters.

The projects were part of the Haiti Stabilization Initiative, a program in Cité Soleil funded through a new blended source of development and defense funding.

In 2005 following the 2004 coup against Jean-Bertrand Aristide, the area was subjected to an extremely violent UN raid. Peacekeepers sprayed bullets from helicopters and drove armored personnel carriers through informal settlements. Using counterinsurgency language, peacekeepers talked about their mission as "clear-hold-build" to pacify this part of the city. The UN and the State Department imagined the new infrastructure and economic development programs as "holding" the area following the 2005 raids. The Haiti Stabilization Initiative exemplifies how counterinsurgency military theory has been imported into development projects across a much more expansive geography than the wars in Iraq and Afghanistan.

This more expansive geography was produced through a key turning point after the public release of the *Counterinsurgency Field Manual* in 2006, which rearticulated development as a weapon of war. This chapter examines three key dimensions of this turning point, beginning with the genesis and pervasion of "stabilization." Although explicit reference to counterinsurgency may have faded since its initial appearance in military doctrine, counterinsurgency has morphed into the language of "stabilization" and a "whole of government" approach. Such language has become entrenched in government institutions and funding streams even as military policy has shifted. The ill-fated projects in Cité Soleil came into formation through government, contractors, and NGOs imagining development through a counterinsurgency lens. The various actors touring the empty marketplace used the language of "stabilization" to convey the project's counterinsurgency purpose.

These changes in US military doctrine, government institutions, and finances are connected to a longer imperial history—our second dimension—reaching back to US westward expansion. That history telescopes into the present at each moment a defense intellectual directly uses colonial and Cold War histories to make counterinsurgency doctrine.[2] By tracing counterinsurgency's recent life cycle to its "forebearers," unearthing how military thinking about development specifically draws on historical referents, we see how modern soldiers are asked to identify with imperial figures such as T. E. Lawrence (of Arabia).[3] This imperial lens reimposes colonial hierarchies through a color-blind language that is commensurate with today's multicultural, multiracial military. Counterinsurgency's post-9/11 revival shares continuities with the longer history that Lawrence is a part of. One challenge of understanding this continuity is parsing the specific, distinctive characteristics at each juncture along a road of ongoing imperial intervention. The post-2006 turning point was distinguished through a series of new institutional formations—our third dimension—and entangled with the significant role of private contractors. The counterinsurgency language of "stabilization" came together with recycled colonial histories and new bureaucratic and financial entities to drive the imperialism of the mid-2000s, propping up the post-9/11 wars as it entrenched counterinsurgency logic within development around the world.

Counterinsurgency and the Conscription of Development

The *Counterinsurgency Field Manual* was an attempt to reform military policy that was clearly faltering amid growing insurgency in Iraq.[4] In addition to the invasion's scant public support, squandering of hundreds of billions of dollars, and incorrect information about weapons of mass destruction and Saddam Hussein's alleged role in the 9/11 attacks, the initial invasion's aftermath itself fostered an insurgency that was already picking up steam by the time of President George W. Bush's "Mission Accomplished" speech declaring the end of major combat operations in May 2003. The US invasion of Iraq did not contain plans for the country's reconstruction following the first battle of March 2003. By disbanding the Iraqi army, disenfranchising a large segment of the population, and lacking a coherent strategy, the US Army effectively created an insurgency that it then had no plan to fight.[5] The prisoner abuse scandal at Abu Ghraib, which became public by 2004, further fueled recruitment and support for the insurgency that by this time came to define the war in Iraq.

Derek Gregory has coined the military's response to this period of failure as a "cultural turn" that emphasized the human over the physical terrain.[6] The counterinsurgency manual was written in this moment of previous strategies' failure and of a turn toward the cultural and population-oriented dimensions of warfare. An interim army field manual was hastily assembled in 2004, which drew on a 1986 army counterguerrilla publication, heavily shaped in reaction to the Sandinista revolution in Nicaragua, as well as the 1980 US Marine Corps guide to counterinsurgency and its 1940 predecessor, *The Small Wars Manual.*[7] The 2006 manual was the product of a hybrid military-academic writing team that was at once celebrated in defense circles for its scholarly poise and critiqued by academics for its inaccuracy and absence of scholarly citation.[8]

Sarah Sewall wrote the introduction to the University of Chicago Press edition of the manual. At the time, she was the director of the Carr Center for Human Rights Policy at the Kennedy School of Government at Harvard University. Her background as a human rights scholar indicates how the counterinsurgency shift branded itself as more academic and thus a "smarter" way to wage war. The role of human rights figures such as Sewall is also dissonant with how counterinsurgency may have contained a cultural turn, but this turn was entirely consistent with targeted killings, drone warfare, and other means of violence that did not disappear when counterinsurgency reemerged. The manual's 2007 edition marked the first time in modern history that the US Army had worked with a private publisher to produce military doctrinal publications.[9] Its publication by the University of Chicago Press lent the manual the sort of legitimacy that comes from the rigor of an academic peer-review publication process. However, significant parts of the manual are plagiarized, "borrowing" without attributing numerous passages and phrases. Given the manual's documentation issues as well as its misreading and manipulation of prominent anthropological theory, critics argued that it enjoyed the status of a university press without being subjected to regular peer-review standards.[10] David Price stated that its "republication transformed the manual from an internal document of military doctrine into a public 'academic' document designed to convince a weary public that the war of occupation could be won: it is an attempt to legitimize war by 'academizing' it."[11]

Civilian figures such as Sewall's scholarship in the human rights field worked alongside military figures such as David Petraeus's and David Kilcullen's academic credentials to do this work of "academizing" the manual. Sewall's human rights credentials were equally important to her position as a scholar in this exercise. Her introduction to the University of Chicago Press edition highlights the importance of development to counterinsurgency: "Equally important, success in COIN [counterinsurgency] relies upon nonkinetic activities like providing electricity, jobs, and a functioning judicial system."[12] The word *nonkinetic* appears throughout the manual, in contrast to *kinetic* (meaning violent) military tools, such as an armed offensive. Although "nonkinetic" still denotes military activity, Sewall says that many of the "operational capacities" required by this mode of warfare are not readily available within the military. She identifies what she calls a paradox of the field manual, that "some of the best weapons do not shoot. A corollary follows: some of the most important actors in counterinsurgency warfare are not self-identified warriors. In COIN, civilians and nonkinetic actions become the Soldiers' exit strategies."[13] The sections that follow Sewall's introduction spend a significant amount of time explaining "nonmilitary counterinsurgency participants," such as civilian government agencies, NGOs, intergovernmental organizations, and private companies.[14] Development becomes redefined within this framework as a "nonkinetic" military tool essential in transferring the responsibility for economic development, security, and government to the host nation government.[15]

Elaborating on Sewall's point that civilians and nonkinetic actions become the soldiers' exit strategy, the manual states a preference that nonmilitary actors should take responsibility for the "welfare and support" of the people who are so vital to success.[16] Yet in the same breath, it also argues that "effective implementation of those programs is more important than who performs the tasks. If adequate civilian capacity is not available, military forces fill the gap."[17] This point is repeated throughout that when civilians best qualified to fulfill developmental tasks are not available, military forces must step in, often learning the necessary skills along the way.[18] Historical precedent serves as a touchstone. The manual's authors call upon T. E. Lawrence to argue that military forces must fill developmental roles in lieu of appropriate civilian professionals but also that they must, in Lawrence's words, do so "tolerably." Lawrence is chief among the historical figures the manual uses to illustrate its arguments.

Following a brief discussion of the division of activities between Vietnamese and American forces during the Vietnam War, the manual recalls T. E. Lawrence's account of leading the Arab Revolt against the Ottoman Empire in 1917: "Do not try to do too much with your own hands. Better the Arabs do it tolerably than that you do it perfectly. It's their war, and you are to help them, not to win it for them."[19] Vietnam is the other main historical reference in post-9/11 counterinsurgency discussions of development. Here the manual describes how

> during the Vietnam War, one of the most valuable and successful elements of COIN was the Civil Operations and Revolutionary—later Rural—Development Support (CORDS) program.... CORDS achieved considerable success in supporting and protecting the South Vietnamese population and in undermining the communist insurgents' influence and appeal.... Keen attention was given to the ultimate objective of serving the needs of the local populace. Success in meeting basic needs of the populace led, in turn, to improved intelligence that facilitated an assault on the Viet Cong political infrastructure.[20]

In its uses of both Lawrence and Vietnam, the manual reduces complex historical instances to sources of evidence for the effectiveness of military campaigns that have incorporated development into wars of pacification.

In contrast to a more dominant historiography of a murderous and strategically flawed US war in Vietnam, the manual treats the CORDS program as a success that just arrived too late and too underresourced in the war. It is also notable that Lawrence, who collected the lessons so enthusiastically cited by US military sources while fomenting rebellion against a foreign occupying force, is repurposed for the post-9/11 wars to explain how a new foreign occupying force might better fight an insurgency against its occupation. In both of these cases, military doctrine glosses over the finer grain of political and historical detail to create abstract lessons—"do not try to do too much with your own hands"—that can be applied to the most pressing military interventions at hand.

This process of what I am calling abstraction more broadly indicates how the military assembles imperial thought and practice in the ongoing wars. As I discuss at greater length in chapter 3, military instructors undertake a particular approach to selecting historical cases, such as Lawrence and Vietnam, with the explicit goal of identifying what they call "tactics, technologies, and procedures" that can be applied to interchangeable locations and time periods of military intervention. In constructing these abstract tactics, technologies, and procedures, instructors erase history from place and people from the places of war. The erasure of history is also an erasure of politics that creates an apolitical list of military tactics applicable to human war fighting on the grandest scale. In this particular military frame of mind, the political history of Vietnam is insignificant, since the specific tactic of, for instance, CORDS is framed as a *technical* piece of the broader tool kit of tactics, technologies, and procedures that forms the conceptual skeleton of what military trainees are to take away from such lessons. This exercise of abstraction has masculinist power that the (in this binary frame, feminized) selection of individual case studies does not.

Often, the colonial subject is entirely absent from the examples that military instructors invoke in classrooms. Instead, the colonial administrator's or military officer's experiences form the basis of the lesson. When the colonized are visible at all in such stories, they appear as savage subjects located "backward" in history—their inability to manage basic human functions such as hygiene, let alone their own territory, justifies military occupation. Military trainees are asked to identify with the white colonial officer such as T. E. Lawrence. This is another process of abstraction, given the multiracial character of the US military. Many of the soldiers asked to identify with, for example, Lawrence have been shaped by the legacies of racism and colonialism that Lawrence is a part of. The process of abstraction allows instructors to claim that the colonial hierarchy underpinning a lesson about Lawrence is not about racial war so much as a set of neutral tactics useful in any war campaign.

The US Army and the Marine Corps rereleased the *Counterinsurgency Field Manual* again in 2014 as an official joint publication. The manual's internal rerelease (without a corresponding press edition) speaks to the ways in which counterinsurgency has continued to inform military doctrine even as it has faded from the public eye. In many ways, the 2014 manual codifies many of the lessons featured in its previous iteration: the importance of a "whole of government approach," the centrality of "stability operations," and "nonkinetic" instruments of military power. It is organized somewhat differently than the University of Chicago Press edition and has a different title, *Insurgencies and Countering Insurgencies*, placing counterinsurgency in a particular discourse of insurgencies and how to counter them. In place of the multiple lengthy forewords and introductions by renowned soldier-scholars such as John Nagl and civilian human rights proponents such as Sewall, the 2014 edition gives just two paragraphs as framing remarks and then outlines the various chapters, which follow in a broad sense from the earlier version.

Whereas the 2006 manual is very tactical, written quickly while troops were actively engaged in a counterinsurgency, the 2014 manual is organized differently, spending more time defining an insurgency, discussing the context and range of military responses, and generally fleshing out the thinking behind many of the tactics in the earlier version. The 2006 manual defines an insurgency as "an organized movement aimed at the overthrow of a constituted government through the use of subversion and armed conflict," while in the 2014 edition insurgency is defined as "the organized use of subversion and violence to seize, nullify, or challenge political control of a region," removing reference to a government.[21] The manual doubles down on its claims for the power of "softer" developmental tools for reconstruction and a method of limiting the direct involvement of US forces. Accordingly, influential defense voices critiqued the 2014 manual for, like its predecessor, sounding as if it "belongs in a social science faculty lounge instead of a war room."[22] For example, Bing West, who was assistant secretary of defense for international security affairs under President Ronald Reagan and later embedded himself with patrols in Iraq and Afghanistan, wrote in the *Small Wars Journal* that "the 2014 FM hurtles down the wrong track. . . . If we cannot put our enemies six feet in the ground and infuse that same fierce, implacable, winning spirit into the host nation forces, friendly persuasion and development aid will be seen by our enemies as weakness and fecklessness."[23] Counterinsurgency continues to spark gender horror that its preferred mode of engagement is weak and unmasculine.

Since military manuals are updated and republished often, the 2014 edition is not necessarily exceptional but does call into question some scholars' claims that the counterinsurgency era has ended. Following President Donald Trump's 2017 use of the "mother of all bombs" in eastern Afghanistan and his announcement later that year to send four thousand more military personnel to Afghanistan, Oliver Belcher argued that "to be sure, counterinsurgency has recently returned to its status as a dead letter."[24] The 2014 manual imagines a different subject than the massive deployment of ground troops actively engaged in counterinsurgency warfare that was the impetus for the original document. But treating counterinsurgency as if it has disappeared from military thinking would be a mistake; instead, this version amplifies a "whole of government" approach and refers to "stabilization." A related joint military publication on counterinsurgency states in 2021 that "insurgencies will continue to challenge security and stability around the globe."[25] The concept of "stabilization" has become more entrenched in security discourse and institutions as the post-9/11 wars have morphed and their geography has expanded. To understand the extent and meaning of this pervasive language linked to counterinsurgency, it is worth examining a few of its key locations.

In 2005, the DOD issued a directive that elevated the status of "stability opera-tions" to the same level as combat. DOD Directive 3000.05, "Military Support for Stability, Security, Transition, and Reconstruction," defines "stability operations" as "military and civilian activities conducted across the spectrum from peace to conflict to establish or maintain order in States and regions."[26] The directive was so significant because it changed military policy to now consider stability opera-tions a "core US military mission" that the DOD needed to prioritize in a way that was comparable to combat operations. The directive ordered the DOD to inte-grate this emergent notion of "stability" into *all* of its activities, from doctrine and training to personnel and facilities. Following the directive's emphasis on "inte-grated civilian and military efforts" and military support for and coordination with civilian agencies, one effect of this shift in military policy was the extension of the military's already-long reach into civilian parts of the US government.[27] The new institutions that channeled parts of the defense budget to development projects in Haiti and brought development contractors onto military bases were all part of this broader shift in the mid-2000s that saw new administrative path-ways between development and defense bureaucracies.

The language of "stabilization" was also implemented through the less noted release in 2008 of *The US Army Stability Operations Field Manual (FM 3-07)* that, following the *Counterinsurgency Field Manual*, was the second military docu-ment to be republished by a university press (the University of Michigan Press) in 2009.[28] The *Stability Operations Field Manual* changed military doctrine's rela-tionship to development. In the foreword, Lt. Gen. William Caldwell argues that

> America's future abroad is unlikely to resemble Afghanistan or Iraq, where we grapple with the burden of nation-building under fire. Instead, we will work through and with the community of nations to defeat insurgency, assist fragile states, and provide vital humanitarian aid to the suffering. Achieving victory will assume new dimensions as we strengthen our ability to generate "soft" power to promote participation in government, spur economic development, and address the root causes of conflict among the disenfranchised populations of the world. At the heart of this effort is a comprehensive approach to stability operations that integrates the tools of statecraft with our military forces, interna-tional partners, humanitarian organizations, and the private sector.[29]

The manual defines stability as "establishing civil security" and rule of law, essen-tial services, and representative political institutions.[30] It emphasizes cooperation with NGOs, the UN, and other international organizations and includes in its definition of stability such tasks as the "alleviation of human suffering" as well as "support to economic and infrastructure development."[31] The manual also advocates for a "whole of government approach," another key phrase appearing in the reissued DOD Stability Directive in 2009 and the 2010 National Security Strategy that, like Directive 3000.05, elevates stability operations to the same priority as combat.[32]

The *Stability Operations Field Manual* returns repeatedly to a "comprehensive" approach, declaring that "throughout US history, the Army has learned that military forces alone cannot secure sustainable peace."[33] International organizations, NGOs, and humanitarian aid are listed as key elements of "securing sustainable peace." The manual addresses the military's role in supporting economic and infrastructure development, job creation, and public health. Much of this discussion is framed in terms of the eventual transfer of responsibility for these components back to civil authorities while still recognizing that they are an important and increasingly visible aspect of military campaigns, including but not limited to counterinsurgency operations.

If the earlier language of "winning hearts and minds" represented the initial post-9/11 counterinsurgency moment in the mid-2000s, it was considered inferior to the narrower technical language of "stabilization" that later military trainings favored. In a training I observed in 2011, US Agency for International Development (USAID) contractors used the language of "stabilization" to explain their work, which they also understood as more scientific, current, and precise than the outdated language of "hearts and minds."[34] One USAID trainer speaking to a military audience explained how he had become converted to "stability" over "winning hearts and minds" by using his own experience in Afghanistan:

> My team spent eight million dollars doing all kinds of stuff. We built a dozen schools; we built one hundred kilometers of road; we built a hospital and a day care center. The list went on and on. And it looked great on my AAR [after-action report]. But at the end of my tour, things had actually gotten worse in terms of stability. There were more TICs [troops in contact], more IEDs [improvised explosive devices], fewer NGOs that had freedom of movement in the area. And we honestly had to look back and say "Hey, my AAR, your AAR looks great, but we didn't really accomplish anything in terms of stability." We didn't have a framework like this to help us focus our attention. We just, like, sprinkled fairy dust all over Helmand province. We had no measurable effect, so that's why this process exists. The SOI [source of instability] matrix is a way of focusing our attention on what's driving instability. Then the TSM [tactical stability matrix] is the logical thought process to say "Okay, this is the problem I'm trying to solve. How do I identify the appropriate activities to solve that problem?" So, we do the systemic causes. What are the root causes?

What am I trying to achieve? The impact indicators will tell me how I will know if I achieved it—and on down the list. So that's sort of the high-level view for why this process exists and why they carved out three and a half days to give you some starting points.

The contractor likened building schools, hospitals, and roads to "sprinkling fairy dust all over Helmand province." His comments represent a broad rhetorical shift that occurred in this period. Whereas in 2006 military training material described counterinsurgency as "winning hearts and minds," by 2011 "systemic causes of instability" had become standard language when this contractor delivered a training. The matrices and concepts the contractor mentions—tactical stability, sources of instability, measurable effects, and impact indicators—come from the social scientific framework that USAID established to bring development tools overtly into military trainings. His language also indicated stabilization's close relationship to social science at this time.

If the language of "stabilization" pervades military documents from this period, it also appears in associated development discourses, again in the spirit of drawing development and defense institutions closer together. In 2009 early in her term as secretary of state, Hillary Clinton launched the Quadrennial Diplomacy and Development Review (QDDR). The process mirrored the long-standing, legislatively mandated Quadrennial Defense Review conducted by the DOD every four years to review defense strategy and priorities. The first QDDR, released in 2010, refracted Clinton's earlier reference to "smart power" and a "3Ds" approach—or mutually reinforcing and linked fields of development, diplomacy, and defense—through the language of "civilian power." An official fact sheet for the 2010 QDDR announced that "at its core the QDDR provides a blueprint for elevating American 'civilian power' to better advance our national interests and to be a better partner to the US military."[35] Civilian power was described as multiple civilian agencies working together to address conflict and poverty.

The 2015 QDDR further amplifies a vision of development as "conflict prevention," marking a certain continuity with Mark Duffield's discussion of underdevelopment as "dangerous."[36] Part of what is distinctive, though, about this particular iteration of militarized development is the institutional changes it has wrought. The State Department established a new office, which directly emerged from the QDDR, specifically tasked with institutionalizing the linkages between development, diplomacy, and defense captured in the "stabilization" and "whole of government" language that is emblematic of the post-2006 landscape. The language of counterinsurgency has not so much disappeared as it has morphed into the language of "stabilization" and "whole of government." Materially, this has meant that parts of the federal government have been reorganized to integrate defense, development, and diplomacy. Counterinsurgency's associated language and institutions continued to affect development and defense policy and practice even as military policy shifted. Extensive financial and institutional rearrangements associated with the language of "stability" and "whole of government" led to development contractors' entrance onto military bases. These institutional changes and post-9/11 counterinsurgency discourses had deep historical roots.

Counterinsurgency Histories in the Present

The *Counterinsurgency Field Manual*'s uses of development grow directly out of its authors' own knowledge of counterinsurgency as a tool to repress resistance to imperial occupation. Kilcullen and Nagl both served on the manual's writing team, hold PhDs alongside military officer credentials, and made many influential media appearances that were part of a more pervasive conversion of the press to support counterinsurgency.[37] Soldier-scholars such as Nagl, Kilcullen, and, most famously, Petraeus played a key role in promoting the manual as a "smart bomb" that would reverse the downhill trajectory of the war in Iraq.[38] Development's role in counterinsurgency is also rooted in the *Counterinsurgency Field Manual*'s focus on what the military calls a "population-centric" approach that emphasizes "protecting" the security of the local population and luring them away from supporting the insurgent movement in question. This is opposed to an "enemy-centric" approach that focuses on capturing and killing the enemy.

The dichotomous language is of course misleading, because in practice a "population-centric" approach still involves killing, a dynamic apparent in Kilcullen's and Nagl's own writings. Just one example of this doublespeak was at work when the US military's counterinsurgency campaign involved completely razing several villages in Helmand and Kandahar provinces in 2010. When one of these villages was rebuilt to exemplify counterinsurgency's more "humane" side, the building style inscribed new forms of violence in its deviation from local norms, including a lack of internal walls around homes in the village. This increased women's confinement to their homes, which became so hot in the summer that they were uninhabitable.[39]

Counterinsurgency's referents compose a layering of historical sources in which the argument for the Vietnam War's relevance to the post-9/11 wars relies on knowledge of colonial counterinsurgency in Algeria. Kilcullen's and Nagl's ideas were heavily influenced by David Galula, a French military officer turned counterinsurgency theorist who drew on his experience during the Algerian war of independence. Particularly in Kilcullen's writings and most elaborately in

Galula's, women's bodies are key sites of struggle over the meaning of military intervention.

A former Australian army officer, Kilcullen served as Petraeus's senior counterinsurgency adviser in Iraq before becoming Condoleezza Rice's special adviser for counterinsurgency, where he continued to work within the State Department as a chief strategist for the Counterterrorism Bureau. He then entered the private sector and founded several security-related companies, including a tech startup focusing on social and spatial data. Kilcullen was also, in 1996, a fellow of the Royal Geographical Society, an institution formed through the involvement of senior ex-military officers and commitments to imperial notions of "exploration" and "discovery." Kilcullen's biography reflects geography's problematic disciplinary history in its entanglement with military and imperial objectives, not to mention counterinsurgency's linkages to spatial analytics.[40] To complete his PhD in political anthropology from the University of New South Wales, Kilcullen did fieldwork using military leave and travel allowances the military afforded to officers within their "target country," which allowed him, as the commander of military advisory teams for the Indonesian army, to conduct research on Darul Islam.[41] Kilcullen describes the seamless overlap between his military career and academic research in the preface to his book, without mention of the ethical implications of conducting ethnographic research in foreign military uniform with foreign military funding. He does not disclose how his position as a foreign military adviser could have undermined his research participants' ability to grant informed consent, violating a key ethical requirement of anthropological research.

Kilcullen's doctoral research became the thesis of his highly influential book *The Accidental Guerrilla: Fighting Small Wars in the Midst of a Big One.* Considered "an intellectual foundation for the Surge of 2007," the book describes the "accidental guerrilla syndrome" whereby would-be neutral civilians end up fighting alongside "extremist forces" not because they are ideologically on board but instead because they object to outside interference in what Kilcullen describes as local affairs.[42] This is part of his larger argument that identifies a biomedical (and biopolitical) syndrome of *infection* (a terrorist organization moves into a remote, "ungoverned" area and takes hold through intimidation and co-optation), *contagion* (the extremist group's influence spreads), *intervention* (external authorities take action against the extremist presence, and local groups begin to close ranks against the external threat), and finally *rejection* (resembling an "immune response" of rejecting a foreign object whereby local people become "accidental guerrillas" fighting against outside interference although not necessarily in favor of the extremist group).[43]

Kilcullen's medical analogies naturalize the accidental guerrilla phenomenon. They also allow him to generalize this theory across geographical sites. Just as the human body generally reacts to a virus or an infection (i.e., a foreign body), so too do people react to extremist forces, or so the logic goes. The influence of such biomedical and biopolitical language is palpable in the *Counterinsurgency Field Manual*, which describes "three indistinct stages" of counterinsurgency. The first stage, "stop the bleeding," is likened to "emergency first aid for the patient," where the goal is to "protect the population, break the insurgents' initiative and momentum, and set the conditions for further engagement." The second stage, "inpatient care—recovery," describes "assisting the patient through long-term recovery or restoration of health—which in this case means achieving stability. . . . As civil security is assured, focus expands to include governance, provision of essential services, and stimulation of economic development." Third, "outpatient care—movement to self-sufficiency" refers to when stability operations can geographically expand, eventually transitioning responsibility for counterinsurgency to the host nation.[44] Kilcullen's and the counterinsurgency manual's medical analogies do powerful work to professionalize and sanitize counterinsurgency. Theorists of counterinsurgency have generally interpreted this as part of the military's attempt to anesthetize and distract the public from counterinsurgency's violence. Gregory has written of biopolitical language such as Kilcullen's as "intrinsically therapeutic" in that "the walling of Baghdad neighborhoods becomes the military's equivalent of 'tourniquets in surgery.'"[45] The language likens each of these steps to precise, surgical medical interventions, further contributing to the notion of counterinsurgency as a "smarter" form of war. It also naturalizes the occupation, imagining the world as the operating table for the US military, which in this metaphor has somehow become a professional surgeon with all the attained and self-evident status that makes it the unquestionable authority.

While scholarship has attended to the implications of Kilcullen's biopolitical language, there is also a spatial aspect to this argument that has garnered considerably less attention. An understanding of place as a bounded unit underpins Kilcullen's argument. Writing of debates over "locality studies" in geography in the 1990s as well as popular conceptions of place over the previous decade, geographer Doreen Massey critiqued views of place as bounded, fixed, and singular. This static view of space is an important part of the theoretical underpinning that allows Kilcullen to construct the accidental guerrilla syndrome. Particularly in the last medicalized phase, rejection, the argument depends on an understanding of local and global as opposed to one another. The key turning point in Kilcullen's argument is when "local populations"—framed in Massey's words as authentic, singular, fixed, and unproblematic in their identity—join an extremist movement, which they associate with "local society," for the sole reason that they oppose the intrusion of "outside interference" in their affairs.[46] Kilcullen imagines the local as enclosed and harboring a fixed identity.

Medical analogies do further work to naturalize the local response to the binary global. "If, however, the spatial is thought of in the context of space-time," as Massey writes, "and as formed out of social interrelations at all scales, then one view of a place is as a particular articulation of those relations, a particular moment in those networks of social relations and understandings."[47] Massey argues for an expansive sense of place in which the global is part of what constitutes the local, a view of place that challenges claims to "internal histories or timeless identities."[48] Applied to Kilcullen, a Masseyan sense of place negates the possibility that the localities he considers had no previously existing relations to the global. The multiplicity of identities contained within Massey's sense of locality complicates the automaticness with which Kilcullen imagines the local community will band together against uniform outside influence.

Also drawing on a bounded sense of place, Kilcullen sets up his accidental guerrilla thesis through a series of models of what he refers to as the "threat environment." One of these models is the "globalization backlash thesis," which adopts Thomas Friedman's understanding of globalization as a technologically driven process that has sped up the circulation of people, capital, and goods, carving the world into, in Friedman's words, the "flat" technologically connected world and the "unflat" world of those too sick, disempowered, and frustrated to participate in globalization.[49] Kilcullen also refers to regions of Africa, the Middle East, Latin America, and Asia as "gap countries," adopting the map that military theorist Thomas Barnett uses to explain terrorism as a by-product of "gap" countries' economic, technological, and "cultural" disconnectedness from the "core" of the developed world.[50] Friedman's understanding of globalization influences Kilcullen's "globalization backlash" model in which "traditional societies" are subjected to the "corrosive effects" of globalization on what are conceived as fundamental cultural and religious views, sparking violent backlash against symbols of "Western-led modernization."[51]

Development occupies a particular role in Kilcullen's thinking, given his spatial argument that insurgency is caused by certain populations being "left out" of globalization, exiled to Barnett's "gap" or Friedman's "unflat world." The corollary to Kilcullen's "globalization backlash" model is the "globalized insurgency" model in which he argues that given the globalization backlash, insurgency is also globalized: its target is the entire world. Here Kilcullen espouses the notion of a "population-centric" strategy, emphasizing programs addressing the conditions that terrorists exploit over killing and capturing terrorists, which he deems "strictly a secondary activity."[52] As captured in the language of "stabilization," such a population-centric approach to counterinsurgency underpins militarized forms of development that seek to accomplish what Kilcullen describes as the prevention of future terrorism. Kilcullen's is an implicit argument about development as potentially part of a population-centric military strategy to entice would-be accidental guerrillas away from supporting an insurgent movement. Development within this framework targets Barnett's "gap" or Friedman's "unflat world," operating with an explicitly spatial conception of development as a means of incorporating those "left out" of globalization. Many of the institutional shifts that took place in response to counterinsurgency's influence in this period were based on an understanding of development as part of this population-centric approach.

Kilcullen elaborates elsewhere an argument related to his notion of development influencing military doctrine—that counterinsurgency is "armed social work; an attempt to redress basic social and political problems while being shot at."[53] This highly cited piece of advice appears in Kilcullen's "Twenty-Eight Articles: Fundamentals of Company-Level Counterinsurgency," first published in *Military Review* in 2006 and then reprinted and circulated through multiple other defense publications. This was Kilcullen's first and most widely read piece on counterinsurgency, self-consciously modeled in its title and structure after T. E. Lawrence's writings during World War I. "Twenty-Eight Articles" draws on Kilcullen's doctoral work that became the basis of *The Accidental Guerrilla*.[54] The article is written as a series of enumerated, practical pieces of advice for a military unit about to deploy to Iraq or Afghanistan. In contrast to the historical orientation of Galula's writings or the doctrinal level of the *Counterinsurgency Field Manual*, Kilcullen's article is tactical—it distills the prevailing theoretical frameworks of counterinsurgency into a few takeaway points, followed by a numbered series of "commandments" including the advice to conduct "armed social work," which he also calls "armed civil affairs." Kilcullen points to the importance of civil affairs—a military specialization focused on civilian interaction—encompassing everything from the sort of humanitarian response seen in the 2010 Haiti earthquake to the population-centric counterinsurgency projects he discusses. Whereas civil affairs has historically been seen as a less-glorified specialization within the military than combat jobs such as infantry and artillery, particularly in the Marine Corps, the military has found it necessary to fill an increasing number of civil affairs positions, often to the dismay of personnel who are reassigned there from historically more valorized combat positions.[55]

Laleh Khalili situates Kilcullen within a genealogy of counterinsurgency thinkers that reaches back to the colonial era. She notes that the basis of Kilcullen's accidental guerrilla thesis—that the majority of the population in an area of insurgency will support whichever side can provide security and basic needs and "most closely aligns with their primary group identity"—recycles David

Galula's writings on counterinsurgency.[56] Galula claims that "in any situation, whatever the cause, there will be an active minority for the cause, a neutral majority, and an active minority against the cause. The technique of power consists in relying on the favorable minority in order to rally the neutral majority and to neutralize or eliminate the hostile minority."[57] Khalili notes the extent to which Kilcullen relies on Galula's "Machiavellian understanding of politics," alongside the influence of former army officer and coauthor of the *Counterinsurgency Field Manual,* John Nagl.[58] Kilcullen thanks Nagl in his book's acknowledgments before quoting Galula's *Counterinsurgency Warfare* in the prologue to *The Accidental Guerrilla.* These lines of gratitude also trace a clear lineage of colonial thought that underpins the 2006 manual.

T. E. Lawrence, whose *Twenty-Seven Articles* Kilcullen borrows from to title his own "Twenty-Eight Articles" is a touchstone in these multiple pathways between colonial and contemporary counterinsurgency thought. In *Seven Pillars of Wisdom,* Lawrence wrote that "to make war upon rebellion is messy and slow, like eating soup with a knife."[59] Writing almost a century later on the eve of the war on terror, Lt. Col. John Nagl used these very words as the title for his book *Learning to Eat Soup with a Knife: Counterinsurgency Lessons from Malaya and Vietnam.* The book, which is based on Nagl's doctoral dissertation in international relations at Oxford University, compares the organizational cultures of the British army during the Malayan Emergency (1948–1960) to the US Army during the Vietnam War. Nagl earned his doctorate after deploying to Iraq during the Gulf War (1990–1991), then returned to Iraq in 2003 as an operations officer in Al Anbar Province.[60] In 2004 the *New York Times Magazine* ran a cover story on Nagl's doctoral dissertation.[61] The article, which brought Nagl to Pentagon officials' attention, is a perfect example of how seductive Nagl's and Kilcullen's academic representations of war were to mainstream media outlets.

Nagl was a key figure on the writing team for the *Counterinsurgency Field Manual,* integrating many of the arguments from his book into the eventual doctrine. His book argues that the British army was a "learning institution," while the US Army was not. "The United States Army resisted any true attempt to learn how to fight an insurgency during the course of the Vietnam War, preferring to treat the war as a conventional conflict in the tradition of the Korean War and World War II. The British army, because of its traditional role as a colonial police force and the organizational culture that its history and the national culture created, was better able to learn quickly and apply the lessons of counterinsurgency during the course of the Malayan Emergency."[62]

The crux of Nagl's argument comes from his comparison of British army doctrine in 1957 versus 1951, allowing him to track how the British army developed tactics in response to its experience fighting the insurgency. Nagl attributes the

Malayan counterinsurgency's success to British "population control" measures that, in addition to a detention and deportation campaign, forcibly resettled hundreds of thousands of Malays into "New Villages." The villages were surrounded by barbed wire and guard towers, and food was rationed to ensure that none was passed on to the guerrillas.[63] One cannot possibly squint hard enough at this aspect of the Malayan campaign to see a benign institution, as Nagl does, in the business of "protecting" the population. Yet Nagl frames the British in Malaya as a "successful" example of militarily suppressing an insurgency and securing the interests of the (colonial) military power in question, a perspective echoed in multiple other military instructional contexts from enlisted trainings to war college classrooms.

Khalili shows the incoherence of Nagl's celebration of "population control" on its own terms, pointing to the direct descent of Malaya's New Villages from the concentration camps the British used during the Anglo-Boer War. "In the Boer war, the language of protection and refuge was used to herd thousands of civilians into barren compounds after their farms and houses were ordered torched by Lord Kitchener. In counterinsurgency doctrine, however, Boer war tactics are held up as enemy-centric (with an odor of disapproval wafting from the term), while the New Villages are considered a source of emulation for practitioners of humane, population-centric quashing of rebellion."[64] Historians highlight the inaccuracy of the phrase "hearts and minds," whose origins are attributed to British general Gerald Templer during his reign as high commissioner of Malaya, that "the answer [to the uprising] lies not in pouring more troops into the jungle, but in the hearts and minds of the people."[65] While the phrase was used in Malaya to denote the use of "less coercive tactics against insurgents," in contrast to the use of conventional warfare tactics that deploy overwhelming force and are willing to incur civilian casualties, critics have noted that in practice the "hearts and minds" campaign in Malaya involved free-fire zones, detention camps, and mass incarceration.[66]

Nagl also does not follow the New Villages into Vietnam, where the Malayan example was used as a template for forced villagization. Recycling Templer's language from Malaya, in 1965 President Lyndon Johnson proclaimed that "we must be ready to fight in Vietnam, but the ultimate victory will depend on the hearts and minds of the people."[67] In Vietnam, a "hearts and minds" strategy entailed forced displacement of villagers, poisoning crops, assassination campaigns, saturation bombing, and free-fire zones in which anyone alive was presumed to be hostile.[68] This violent history underpins the authorship of the 2006 field manual. Nagl recounted how the writing team for the *Counterinsurgency Field Manual* drew not only on historical case studies but also on the primary source writings of historical counterinsurgent figures such as David Galula. Nagl wrote the foreword when, in 2006, Praeger Security International reprinted Galula's treatise, *Counterinsurgency: Theory and Practice*.

In his essay on Nagl's use of Galula, anthropologist John D. Kelly describes "Nagl's Galula" as "the voice unheard, the lost genius."[69] The *Counterinsurgency Field Manual*'s authors adopted wholesale elements of Galula's eight-step tactical solution to "destroy or expel the insurgent guerrilla area by area (mobile forces) and also, area by area, control and get to know the local population (static forces)."[70] Galula's influence is also prominent in the manual's discussion of how civilians would often be the more appropriate implementers of developmental tasks required of a counterinsurgency, though military personnel must step in when civilians are often not readily available. As evidence to support this claim, the manual recalls that "David Galula wisely notes, 'To confine soldiers to purely military functions while urgent and vital tasks have to be done, and nobody else is available to undertake them, would be senseless. The soldier must then be prepared to become . . . a social worker, a civil engineer, a schoolteacher, a nurse, a boy scout. But only for as long as he cannot be replaced, for it is better to entrust civilian tasks to civilians.'"[71] In the manual's recycling of Galula's words, it specifically adopts the idea of the flexible soldier capable of becoming a social worker, among other educational or caregiving tasks (the boy scout metaphor is slightly more curious, given the relationship of scouting to imperial militarism).[72]

Galula's own thinking on counterinsurgency was shaped through the ties binding colonial to Cold War counterinsurgencies. His most famous book, *Pacification in Algeria, 1956–1958*, was produced in direct relation to the Vietnam War. In 1962, Galula had come to the United States as a fellow at Harvard's Center for International Affairs. He participated in a symposium during this time at the RAND Corporation, which brought together military officers and civilian officials to distill their experiences in Algeria, China, Greece, Kenya, Laos, Malaya, Oman, Vietnam, and the Philippines into lessons to apply to the US campaign in Vietnam.[73] So impressed was the organizer of the symposium with Galula's comments on counterinsurgency that he invited him to write a more detailed study for RAND. Galula wrote *Pacification in Algeria, 1956–1958*, published by RAND alongside *Counterinsurgency: A Symposium* in 1963. RAND reissued both documents in 2006, the same year the *Counterinsurgency Field Manual* was published, in the spirit of now applying to Iraq those lessons Galula had originally distilled from Algeria for the Vietnam War.

Galula begins *Pacification in Algeria* by describing his enthusiasm to test the theories he had developed about counterinsurgency during his post in China during the civil war, as a UN military observer in the Balkans, and then as a military attaché in Hong Kong, where he visited the Philippines and corresponded with officers serving in French Indochina and British Malaya at the height of their anticolonial insurgencies. He explains that "I left Hong Kong in February 1956 after a five-year assignment as military attaché. I had been away from troop duty for eleven years, having specialized in Chinese affairs since the end of World War II. I was saturated with intelligence work, I had missed the war in Indochina, I felt I had learned enough about insurgencies, and I wanted to test certain theories I had formed on counterinsurgency warfare. For all these reasons, I volunteered for duty in Algeria as soon as I reached France."[74] Just as military instructors reading Galula in the context of Iraq and Afghanistan were concerned with Algerian history insofar as they could extract generalizable lessons applicable to the post-9/11 wars, Galula himself was interested in developing a generalizable theory of counterinsurgency applicable to any time or place.

In the treatise that follows, Galula separates the phases of counterinsurgency into an initial "mandatory first phase of any counterinsurgency effort," which he titles "struggle for control of the population." Here he writes of Algeria as "a perfect testing ground for the ideas on counterinsurgency and pacification that he had developed through experience and observation in China and Greece."[75] In this initial phase, he describes identifying pro-French colonial subjects through detention, interrogation, and eventual "purging" of rebels from a series of villages. We must also contextualize Galula's sterile step-by-step directions with the food-denial operations, torture, and mass incarceration of civilians that characterized the colonial counterinsurgency.

While this initial struggle for control also included what Galula calls "civic action" projects, including a school and a medical dispensary, projects of militarized development are absolutely central to the second phase, "the struggle for the support of the population." He describes how after "cleaning" a village, "this was the moment for the French to lay the groundwork for a trustworthy local self-government and to launch an intensive program of social and economic improvement."[76] Women and children are key targets of these projects of "civic improvement." "Villages received government funds with which to build roads, schools, wells, and reservoirs. They were persuaded to clean and whitewash their houses."[77] Later in the text, Galula elaborates "a sample process" one of his staff conceived of to win a village's support. The document outlines hiring men for public works projects directly benefiting the villagers (e.g., wells) and benefiting the army and colonial administration (e.g., road construction), using local muleteers for military convoys, and arming the local population.

The Muslim woman is, for Galula, a crucial site of intervention. Summarizing his report for RAND, Galula comments that "the writer even went so far as to initiate the emancipation of the Moslem women, who theretofore had been kept in semislavery, and he was struck by the readiness of their response."[78] After describing the opening of a medical dispensary and a school in one of the villages he was in charge of, Galula reflects on the position of women in his schema. "Reflecting on who might be our potential allies in the population, I thought that Kabyle women, given their subjugated conditions, would naturally be on our side if we emancipated them."[79] He focuses on girls' education, boasting how he ignored protest against his mandate for all girls between the ages of eight and thirteen to attend school in the afternoon. After describing overseeing schools in his area of responsibility, Galula praises how the abundant supply of water in the area allowed the school staff to provide the children with weekly showers. "A minor revolution occurred when the girls were asked to discard once and for all their dirty head scarves, and to clip their hair and wash it; it was contrary to local customs and superstitions. But once the change was made, everybody approved heartily. 'They now look like little French girls,' was the general comment."[80]

This passage highlights the crucial intersection of gender, education, and hygiene that forms a central pillar of Galula's commentary on civic action projects in counterinsurgency. The parallels with the proliferation of commentary on the significance of girls' education in Afghanistan are striking. One must look only so far as popular texts such as *Three Cups of Tea* or the West's fascination with Malala Yousafzai, a young girl in Pakistan's Swat Valley propelled into the public spotlight by her writings against the Taliban's banning of girls' education and attempted assassination in 2012 on her way home from school.[81] In their piece "Feminism, the Taliban, and Politics of Counterinsurgency," published shortly after 9/11, Charles Hirschkind and Saba Mahmood comment on how, following 9/11, "the burqa-clad bodies of Afghan women became the visible sign of an invisible enemy that threatened not only 'us' . . . but our entire civilization."[82] Writing in the same post-9/11 moment, Lila Abu-Lughod makes a related argument about the power of Muslim women, in particular Afghan women, as culturally homogenized symbols for the United States to wage the war in Afghanistan.[83] Apropos of Galula's emphasis on the removal of Algerian girls' headscarves, Mahmood and Hirschkind comment on perceptions of the veil as repressive in the context of its banning from French schools. In this way, Galula haunts the present not only when referenced by architects of ongoing wars but also through the repetition today of older colonial and Cold War legacies under which women's bodies become key sites of intervention.

Galula concludes with four "laws" of counterinsurgency warfare that foreshadow the 2006 *Counterinsurgency Field Manual*. Like Kilcullen's medical rhetoric, Galula's conception of these as laws is professional, hygienic, and authoritative. In the first law, "the objective is the population. The population is at the same time the real terrain of the war. . . . This is where the real fighting takes place, where the insurgent challenges the counterinsurgent, who cannot accept the challenge." In the second law, "the support from the population is not spontaneous, and in any case must be organized," which means accessing the minority of the population that favors the counterinsurgent. In the third law, the "minority will emerge, and will be followed by the majority, only if the counterinsurgent is seen as the ultimate victor," and in the fourth law, "seldom is the material superiority of the counterinsurgent so great that he can literally saturate the entire territory," meaning the counterinsurgent may have to focus on certain geographical areas at a time.[84]

One can see the influence of Galula's thought in more recent counterinsurgency materials. In a memo written for and circulated to all North Atlantic Treaty Organization International Security Assistance Force troops and US forces in Afghanistan, David Petraeus gave his guidance for the conduct of counterinsurgency operations in Afghanistan. Under the first guideline, "secure and serve the population," Petraeus argues that "the decisive terrain is the human terrain. The people are the center of gravity," a phrase practically lifted from Galula's language of "control" and "struggle for support of the population."[85] In Petraeus's 2006 *Military Review* article "Learning Counterinsurgency: Lessons from Soldiering in Iraq," he cites Galula in support of his observation that "success in a counterinsurgency requires more than just military operations." He also cites Galula to argue that "counterinsurgency strategies must also include, above all, efforts to establish a political environment that helps reduce support for the insurgents and undermines the attraction of whatever ideology he may espouse."[86]

As is evident in Petraeus's more recent writing, counterinsurgency's contemporary form relies heavily on historical figures such as Galula and historical case studies such as Kilcullen's. The policy shifts that in the mid-2000s changed the relationship of development to defense grew out of a layering of histories in which Galula's writings on Algeria informed Nagl's thinking on Vietnam, which in turn directly informed the writing team for the 2006 *Counterinsurgency Field Manual*. This layering of history shows that post-9/11 US military doctrine is not new. Yet, what is significant is not only *that* Galula is resurrected to fight ongoing wars but also *how* this is accomplished. Just as Galula wrote of Algeria to extract lessons applicable to other places, when he is taught in military classrooms it is in the spirit of extracting generalizable lessons to be applied to the post-9/11 battlefield. Galula, like Lawrence, is treated as material to place within the skeletal frame of tactics, technologies, and procedures destined for interchangeable locations of war fighting. Given that the US military is referencing occupying powers fighting anticolonial insurgencies, many of the examples instructors draw upon, such as Vietnam and Algeria, come from an occupying force that lost the war. Abstraction allows instructors to claim that whether the battle was won or lost is not significant; the value of the tactic must be identified and stripped of its historical specificity to be added to a tool kit of tactics, technologies, and procedures that can circulate the globe.

This process of military knowledge production speaks more broadly to the changes and continuities of the present imperial moment. Recent counterinsurgency doctrine's place within a longer imperial trajectory is apparent through its direct reference to colonial history. The imperial hierarchy of, for instance, Lawrence in relation to his colonial subjects continues to inform today's military doctrine. Yet, abstraction also erases colonial racism. In place of colonial racial hierarchies, the modern US military is a multiracial force that uses color-blind language to frame its internal composition as a meritocracy in which everyone is "green" (as opposed to Black, white, Latinx, etc.). This color-blind language also offers a racial grammar that uses the implicitly racialized language of "culture" and "civilization" to distinguish the occupied Other.

Institutional Reverberations of Counterinsurgency's Return

The developmental rhetoric of the counterinsurgency and stability field manuals, which took shape through their historical predecessors, provoked a series of institutional shifts that prefigured the entrance of development contractors onto military bases. Policy shifts in this period of the mid-2000s were articulated in the language of a "whole of government" approach to US power abroad. In her nomination hearing to be secretary of state in 2009, Hillary Clinton used the language of "smart power" to promote the deft combination of diplomatic, economic, military, political, legal, and cultural tools.[87] Clinton adopted Joseph Nye's term "smart power," which he developed in 2003 in response to critiques that his foundational idea of "soft power" could alone shape effective foreign policy.[88] While "soft power" was defined as "the ability of a country to persuade others to do what it wants without force or coercion," smart power was a combination of both hard- and soft-power tools.[89] In a speech shortly after this in early 2010, Clinton spoke of the need to "elevate development and integrate it more closely with defense and diplomacy in the field. Development must become an equal pillar of our foreign policy, alongside defense and diplomacy, led by a robust and reinvigorated [US]AID."[90] Clinton coined this as a "3Ds" approach, arguing that "the three Ds [development, diplomacy, and defense] must be mutually reinforcing."[91] Clinton's discussion of "elevating" development to the level of defense was contextualized by massive cuts to

USAID direct-hire staff during the 1990s.[92] Yet the discussion in this period of making development an "equal pillar" to defense and diplomacy was not just a response to budget cuts; it also contained an argument for a particularly securitized brand of development that both harnesses development toward the aim of promoting US interests abroad and institutionally integrates development with defense and diplomacy.

Clinton was not only a key proponent of this securitized development but also embodied a liberal feminist tradition that has celebrated women's ability to rise to powerful positions within the national security establishment, all while remaining uncritical of or, in Clinton's case, actively supporting US imperialism.[93] Clinton prefigures the ways in which militarized development paved the way for the imperial feminism that flourished within female counterinsurgency teams. Her biography, like Samantha Power's, speaks to how militarized development and imperial feminism operated in and through one another.

In her nomination to be secretary of state, Clinton mentioned Secretary of Defense Robert Gates's advocacy of adding resources to chronically underfunded civilian institutions of diplomacy and development. In a 2007 speech at Kansas State University, Gates summarized his position as

> here to make the case for strengthening our capacity to use "soft" power and for better integrating it with "hard" power. One of the most important lessons of the wars in Iraq and Afghanistan is that military success is not sufficient to win: economic development, institution-building and the rule of law, promoting internal reconciliation, good governance, providing basic services to the people, training and equipping indigenous military and police forces, strategic communication, and more—these, along with security, are essential ingredients for long-term success.[94]

Gates emphasized civilian expertise and the need for more funding devoted to "non-military instruments of power." In a move he described as, for some in the Pentagon, "blasphemy," he advocated focusing "beyond the guns and steel of the military" and bolstering diplomacy, foreign assistance, and economic reconstruction and development, which he called "civilian instruments of national security."[95] Gates's words were significant given his own position and budgetary concerns within the DOD. He also drew attention to military tools as insufficient to meet more complex national security needs. Although Gates recognized that his own words might be regarded as blasphemy, those officers I interviewed who were involved in training and response for civil affairs, humanitarian operations, and disaster response echoed his advocacy for civilian tools. One officer who oversaw an army civil affairs training echoed Gates's concern that, in the officer's words, "if your only tool is a hammer, every problem starts to look like a nail," implying that the same "civilian instruments of national security" must be bolstered to rectify this problem.

Clinton and Gates were influential civilian voices within the intertwined "3Ds" of diplomacy, development, and defense. In this same period surrounding the *Counterinsurgency Field Manual*'s release, Reuben Brigety, a former naval officer who went on to work in policy and diplomacy, wrote the influential report "Humanity as a Weapon of War." Brigety begins by describing US Navy Seabees drilling a well in northeastern Kenya. The well turned out to be a humanitarian mission with a dual purpose. In an area populated by ethnic Somalis, the project "shows the face of American compassion to a skeptical population while also giving the military an eye to activity in the area. Winning hearts and minds with an ear to the ground is the new American way of war."[96] Brigety describes the US military's expanding role in addressing basic humanitarian needs of civilians abroad, calling this "one of the most profound changes in US strategic thought and practice in at least a generation."[97] He provides numerous examples of shifts in the organization of the US government, funding streams, defense policy, and attitudes of practitioners. Ultimately, Brigety argues for a concept of "sustainable security" involving "the strategic use of development assistance" in the interest of national security. He provides several policy recommendations to guide civil-military coordination, including what he calls a "national consensus" on development's importance, the "adoption of a National Development Strategy," and a general dispersal and greater institutionalization of development expertise and measurements throughout military and civilian agencies.[98]

Brigety exemplifies a particular argument that the relationship of development to militarism is a policy problem that can be solved through better coordination of institutions, policy, and funding. The argument's popularity at the time he was writing is reflected in the multiple "civil-military coordination guidelines" that civilian development institutions adopted to institutionalize their coordination with the military.[99] From an internal perspective within these organizations, formulated through everyday administrative responsibilities, it makes sense to treat development's relationship to defense as a technical problem. However, the recasting of this problem as a technical one obscures a series of other questions, including the significance of colonial histories in shaping military doctrine.[100]

The remarks of Clinton, Gates, and Brigety represent a particular turning point in militarized development, defined by the years surrounding the release of the *Counterinsurgency Field Manual*. Development discourses within military doctrine were crucial drivers of this turning point, as were the attitudes toward development as, in Brigety's words, "a weapon of war," and in Clinton's concept of a "3Ds" approach. A number of institutions, policies, and funding streams were reorganized, prefiguring the sorts of changes in military trainings I discuss in later chapters. In 2005, USAID established the Office of Military Affairs to coordinate USAID's relationship with the DOD. In 2012, USAID changed the name to the Office of Civilian-Military Cooperation. The office was established in direct response to the shift in policy discourses, specifically the National Security Strategy's demand that "development be a strong and equal partner with diplomacy and defense."[101] The Office of Civilian-Military Cooperation, which hosts military liaisons within USAID, places senior foreign service officers at the Pentagon and the military's geographical combatant commands, develops policy to aid coordination between USAID and the DOD, and facilitates the training of development and military personnel on how they may work with one another. One of this new USAID office's main activities has been to hire and send civilian contractors onto military bases to teach a framework written by USAID, which they describe as "translating" development "best practices" for military audiences.

In 2004, the State Department established the Office of the Coordinator for Reconstruction and Stabilization (S/CRS). The official mission of the S/CRS was to "lead, coordinate and institutionalize US Government civilian capacity to prevent or prepare for post-conflict situations, and to help stabilize and reconstruct societies in transition from conflict or civil strife, so they can reach a sustainable path toward peace, democracy and a market economy."[102] Official statements from the period in which the S/CRS was established describe how the US government previously responded to "stabilization and reconstruction operations" in an "ad hoc fashion" and that the new office was meant to institutionalize policy tools specific to this emerging concern with "stabilization," which notably is mirrored in defense language, such as the *Stability Operations Field Manual*.[103] In 2011, I attended a briefing on Capitol Hill in which Ambassador Robert Loftis, the acting coordinator of the S/CRS, described it as a "surge capacity" for the State Department, a corps of civilians capable of responding to crises of stabilization and reconstruction. Like many policymakers I spoke with in Washington, D.C., the ambassador emphasized his hope that the United States would not become involved in another prolonged conflict such as Iraq and Afghanistan in the future. He saw "stabilization" as a global effort to cut future military conflicts off at the pass, with the ongoing wars serving as material from which to learn. At the same time, he spoke of the unlikelihood of actually preventing US entry into major conflicts of this scale in the future and his hope that the office could retain lessons from the mistakes they had made in the wars in Iraq and Afghanistan, including the need for quicker "civilian uplift," or massive influx of civilian administrators to run the country following military invasion.

This treatment of imperial history—or here ongoing imperial wars—as material to cobble together a tool kit of abstract, technical, depoliticized lessons speaks more broadly to the process of abstraction at work in making military doctrine. The ambassador's cataloging and repurposing of imperial technologies also reveals how this way of constructing US policy abroad (including but not limited to military doctrine) relies on an uncritical approach to history that asks for repetition of past tactics whose technical value will become clear so long as they are wiped clean of their political connotation. The need for such tactics to fit within an existing bureaucratic structure informs how the tactics recycle the same material rather than asking for something new. Loftis's comment on preventing prolonged military occupation also addresses how development, couched in the language of "stabilization," was understood as a sort of conflict-prevention weapon. Institutions such as the S/CRS very much embodied the "smart power" approach captured in Clinton's and Gates's words.

In 2008 Congress established the Civilian Response Corps, overseen by the S/CRS, that drew from different federal agencies to deploy civilian responders with expertise in conflict prevention and stabilization to US embassies around the world. The Civilian Response Corps was another institutional outgrowth of federal institutions' discursive emphasis on "stabilization," a "whole of government" approach, and the "3Ds." The corps has been described as "a kind of international Federal Emergency Management Agency" that would take charge of police, banking systems, airports, and other infrastructure in a context where the state has collapsed or a government has been defeated in a war.[104] Extending from his 2007 speech supporting increased funding for nonmilitary security instruments, Gates became one of the most vocal proponents of the Civilian Response Corps, advocating for an increase in its promised funding. A congressional report on the formation of the new State Department office and response corps names the 2003 invasion of Iraq as exemplifying civilians' inability to fill required civilian jobs. The same report lists peacekeeping operations during the 1990s such as those in Haiti, the Balkans, and Somalia as demonstrating the military's "inability to field adequate numbers of appropriate personnel to perform tasks in the aftermath of conflicts . . . that many defense experts believed would be better conducted by civilians."[105] The Civilian Response Corps was thus established to bridge these dual inadequacies. In 2011 the S/CRS was replaced by the State Department Bureau of Conflict and Stabilization, which continued the work of the S/CRS but pared down the emphasis on state-building postconflict missions, including downsizing the Civilian Response Corps.[106]

These new institutions introduced new forms of funding that blended development and defense. Beginning in 2005, the S/CRS was funded by Congress, providing the DOD with Section 1207 authority. Section 1207 of the National Defense Authorization Act provided authority for the DOD to transfer US$100 million per year in support of reconstruction, stabilization, and security activities abroad. Section 1207 provided this authority from fiscal years 2006 to 2010 and then expired.[107] Section 1207 was introduced to "jump start the S/CRS" by making funds available for interagency projects.[108] The legislation thus came out of efforts within the US government at the time to institutionalize the "whole of government" approach. It was conceived as a short-term temporary measure to fund interagency projects during a time when Congress could not pass a State Department bill authorizing the S/CRS to do emergency and postconflict work involving USAID, the Department of State, and the DOD. Government analysts have also suggested that the Section 1207 authority was introduced because it was easier to obtain funding from Congress in a DOD versus a State Department bill.[109] The program was allowed to expire based on congressional authorizers' expressions that such funding should be directly provided through the State Department budget.[110]

One example of the sort of program that Section 1207 funds were used for was the Haiti Stabilization Initiative, which funded the empty marketplace in Port-au-Prince. The initiative was overseen by the S/CRS from 2007 to 2010. In Haiti, the program took US$20 million of the experimental blended funding to combine the sorts of infrastructure improvement and job creation programs I toured in 2010 with a police training program that was contracted and administered by Dyncorps.[111] The flooded neighborhoods and abandoned economic development sites illustrated a fabric of everyday life largely unchanged by the millions of defense dollars spent on infrastructure and commercial opportunities. The new source of funding did, however, further fuel the contracting machine behind so many development projects in Haiti and beyond.[112] The initiative also amplified the increasing prevalence of references to stabilization and at times even terrorism and counterinsurgency in US government-funded development projects during this period. Contractors leading the tour in Cité Soleil were motivated by the Section 1207 program's own translations of counterinsurgency into development language to present their projects as the "hold" stage of a "clear-hold-build" sequence akin to Galula's and Nagl's advice.

When Section 1207 authority expired in 2010, Congress established the Complex Crisis Fund for USAID, beginning in fiscal year 2011, and the Global Security Contingency Fund, also authorized by the same section of the National Defense Authorization Act, beginning in fiscal year 2012. Like the previous Section 1207 authority, the Global Security Contingency Fund was intended to support joint State Department–DOD stabilization and security assistance projects abroad.[113] Yet unlike the Section 1207 program, the fund has not provoked the same degree of controversy for further blurring the already permeable boundary between development and defense. Instead, the fund seems to have codified what was mired in conflict before. The Section 1207 program caused great controversy in the NGO world. Although it was never intended to be permanent, the program represented the sort of incursion of defense into development that animated the Provincial Reconstruction Teams in Iraq and Afghanistan and Brigety's military "humanitarian" projects in East Africa.[114]

In the words of one think tank member I spoke with in Washington, D.C., the Section 1207 program "puts a bull's eye" on NGOs working in conflict zones by associating them with the military. In 2009 and 2010, I interviewed a series of NGOs in the D.C. area who voiced concern over their shifting relationship to the DOD. The group InterAction, an alliance of almost two hundred NGOs located in D.C., convened a civil-military working group that arose from concerns over the sorts of projects Brigety writes of, such as army civil affairs groups building wells as part of a counterterrorism campaign in East Africa. NGOs vary greatly in perspective on what constitutes an appropriate relationship to the military. At one extreme is Project HOPE, a medical NGO founded by President Dwight Eisenhower's personal physician after World War II that today is staffed by former military physicians. The organization partners directly with the DOD to conduct medical missions aboard floating hospital ships, often with an overt goal of improving local public opinion of the US military and facilitating basing agreements.[115] Doctors Without Borders (Médecins Sans Frontières) sits at the other end of the spectrum, employing a policy of "independence and separation" from military actors to maintain neutrality and impartiality.

Specific to the Section 1207 program and the controversy it incited among NGOs, in 2007 the Section 1207 authority was used to fund part of the Trans-Sahara Counterterrorism Partnership (TSCTP), an interagency program focused on Mali and Niger that designed development projects with the explicit aim of reducing terrorist recruitment. This program focused on Africa, prefiguring the US military's consideration of the African continent as "tomorrow's battlefield" in the latest chapter of the post-9/11 wars.[116] Multiple NGOs were already working in these areas doing related programming. For instance, the international humanitarian agency CARE had recently finished a rural livelihoods, education, and conflict-resolution project for young people in rural Niger. Once the TSCTP and Section 1207 started funding the project's new iteration, the language of counterterrorism became much more pronounced in the request for proposals, sparking concern within the organization over the safety of local staff as well as how this blended funding interfered with their "needs-based" approach and incentivized framing development in terms of strategic counterterrorism.[117] Such concerns caused the organization to turn down the Section 1207 funding even though it had already successfully completed a related project. When I interviewed her in 2009, an employee of the organization described how she had directly experienced a "whole of government" approach to mean that USAID had to introduce DOD representatives to their partner organizations, such as CARE. These fortified linkages between development and defense institutions led to encounters on the ground such as military civil affairs teams approaching the NGO to collaborate with them on local projects in the Horn of Africa. The NGO declined to collaborate, but the staff member expressed concern that even the military's outstretched hand could compromise their image and their staff members' safety. A representative from Catholic Relief Services also recounted in a 2009 interview a similar experience of being offered Section 1207/TSCTP funding essentially to continue work that the organization was already doing in West Africa but couched in strong counterterrorism language. Catholic Relief Services also turned down the funding out of fears similar to those of CARE as well as suspicion that the organization would be asked to inform on its beneficiaries.

I also spoke with Africare, which had accepted Section 1207 funds for related work in West Africa via the TSCTP. This NGO was not ethically opposed to accepting military funding. The representative I spoke with described these blended funds as a potentially valuable trove of future funding that Africare wished to leave the door open to. However, staff members described fissures within the institution. Some members saw the military funding as a valuable resource, while others were hugely suspicious of whether it would introduce the sorts of surveillance concerns that Catholic Relief Services and CARE raised. When a staff member spoke of visiting the Mali program in the early 2000s just before the US Africa Command's establishment (2007), he realized how much interaction his local Malian staff already had with the US military beyond this new funding. The US embassy's Office of Defense Attaché had been funding small development projects, such as microfinance and solar energy, since the 1990s. The deeper roots of militarized development projects in this region also encompass USAID's role as an instrument of national security reaching back to the Cold War. Africare's own experience of Section 1207 funding not marking a sharp break with the past speaks to this longer history that Section 1207 grows out of.

A fourth organization, the Academy for Educational Development, received funding for projects in Chad and Niger through the TSCTP although not in direct relation to Section 1207 authority. The NGO representative I spoke with strongly disagreed with the language of "terrorism" and "recruitment of at-risk youth" but was equally positive about the projects the organization was able to support, which she enthusiastically described as improving opportunities for young people through vocational training, job creation, and construction of youth centers and soccer fields. The project also included a media component that provided equipment and training for community reporters to broadcast different information channels. The grant's language described the media program as "countering extremist messages," but the NGO representative was quick to translate this for me as providing young people with training and opportunities to become local reporters. In the end and against the wishes of some staff, the organization accepted the defense funding and the program's counterterrorism language out of optimism about what the funds could allow them to accomplish. One of the most notable consequences of accepting the funding was that it opened the door for the military to pursue the organization's cooperation on future unrelated projects. For instance, a civil affairs team asked for the Academy for Educational Development's advice on a DOD program in the field. The staff member emphasized how the organization refused to have anything to do with "actual troops," meaning, for example, the civil affairs team implementing this project. She viewed face-to-face contact with uniformed soldiers as entailing larger ethical and practical safety concerns for her organization than those attached to the Section 1207 funding.

What is clear from this variety of NGO perspectives and experiences is how new forms of defense funding constrained the sorts of development projects that could be funded. Some organizations discontinued existing projects because the only available funding came with the requirement to frame, for example, employment creation and media projects in counterterrorism language, potentially endangering staff by perceived (and actual) military alliances. Other organizations embraced the blended development/defense funding with varying degrees of enthusiasm, understanding it as a potentially lucrative source of future program support. This broader institutional and financial climate incentivized organizations to frame development work in the language of counterterrorism and counterinsurgency. The Academy for Educational Development, for example, noted USAID's descriptions of programs that fund the construction of youth centers, soccer fields, and vocation training as "counterterrorism" and the "prevention of recruitment for at-risk youth."[118] If used in the field, this language would alienate some of the religious communities the organization works through, forcing the organization to walk a fine line between implementing effective projects and accurately reporting their work to funders.

Military understandings of development and humanitarianism as weapons of war were fundamental to the post-9/11 revival of counterinsurgency. Defense thinkers actively drew upon the colonial past as they shaped this doctrinal turning point. Such uses of history inscribed the perspective of colonial administrators into post-9/11 military doctrine, erasing occupation's body counts in favor of sanitized tactics, technologies, and procedures. The turning point of the mid-2000s created new institutional and financial linkages between development and defense. New institutions such as the Section 1207 program and USAID's Office of Military Affairs also mark continuities with deeper histories of, for instance, USAID's conception from the beginning as "an arm of political and economic security."[119] USAID was born out of Cold War projects to harness development as a weapon in the fight against communism in the third world. The institutional, policy, and financial shifts discussed here define the contours of key doctrinal turning points in the new imperial wars. Understanding these doctrinal turning points is crucial because they underpin the changes we now turn to in military training. Onto this new terrain step a set of private for-profit development contractors who have laid claim to a slice of the massive post-9/11 spike in defense spending. I follow these contractors onto the bases where they provide the military with counterinsurgency training aimed to remake soldiers in the image of "armed social workers."

THE "SOCIAL WORK" OF WAR
Techniques and Struggles to Remake
Military Labor

The road to Muscatatuck Urban Training Center winds, slow and dusty, through south-central Indiana past farmland, mobile home supply stores, and Baptist and evangelical churches. The rural landscape then gives way to a convoy of armored personnel carriers and tanks making its way between military installations. Muscatatuck is a "theater immersion" facility used to train military personnel as well as civilian institutions preparing for search-and-rescue and hazardous material operations. The facility is linked to Camp Atterbury, an army training installation covering thirty-five thousand acres, about fifty miles northwest of Muscatatuck. A marketing brochure describes Muscatatuck's "full-immersion contemporary urban training environment" as arising from its "unusual origins" in the early twentieth century as the Indiana Farm Colony for Feeble-Minded Youth.[1] The state-run institution confined the very poor along with those deemed "mentally defective," many of whom were transferred from the state's overcrowded jails.[2] The institution fell into disrepair and, amid a tide of sexual abuse and general mistreatment accusations, was ordered to close by the governor of Indiana in 2000. In 2005 the property was transferred to the Indiana Army National Guard, which runs the training facility today.

Elements of the penal colony remain. A gargoyle perches outside of a building the army uses to hold its after-action reports, and rows of decrepit single mattresses line a former dormitory now used to simulate a military–nongovernmental organization (NGO) meeting in Afghanistan. The facility also includes a housing development half inundated with muddy water to simulate a natural disaster as well as a mock Afghan village composed of two rows of prefabricated buildings, painted tan with graffiti scrawled over and populated by actors playing soccer, selling wares, and cooking street food. This layering of US practices mismanaging poverty, mental illness, and other social issues rests just beneath the surface of many military bases.[3] At Muscatatuck, new prefabricated trailers to house contractors are outfitted with flat-screen TVs and shiny faux-leather sofas. The trailers sit atop sedimentations of antipoor social policies and abusive mental health practices. These twin landscapes of military spending and social poverty—replicated across many sites of war making—are linked through national policies focused on imperial reach over social programs that could benefit the poor and the mentally ill.[4]

I came to the Atterbury-Muscatatuck installation to observe a group of development experts contracted by the US Agency for International Development (USAID) to provide a Provincial Reconstruction Team (PRT) with a portion of their predeployment training. The opportunity to shadow these contractors emerged from the interviews I conducted within USAID's Office of Military Affairs, which had managed the contract and authored the training materials. The team I was observing had been at Camp Atterbury for about ten of their seventy-two days of training leading up to their deployment to Afghanistan. They slept in metal bunks (which they called "racks"), ate at the dining facility (which they called the "DFAC"), and were assigned a translator (employed by a private company) who provided them with language instruction and some limited information about Afghan history and culture.

After trainees spent many days in classrooms listening to PowerPoint presentations as well as on ranges undergoing weapons training, the training culminated with a theater immersion activity in the mock Afghan village at Muscatatuck. Although simulation has long been an aspect of military training, the theater immersion simulations used here were historically new in their "dedication to an understanding of theater," or a "system of training that utilizes professional actors, scripts, sets, props, and an audience in a painstaking effort to mimetically simulate war."[5] The mock Afghan villages departed from war games of the past, which often incorporated features and residents of a base's surrounding town to simulate the "enemy."[6] Here, simulations of the Afghanistan War were self-contained on the base, hidden from a civilian gaze. While counterinsurgency has long made claims for the necessity to "know" the civilian population, simulation of the wars in Iraq and Afghanistan presented an unprecedented scale and obsession with hyperreality.

As was the case in other trainings I observed, the development contractors' lessons immediately followed a unit on counterinsurgency warfare. Their instruction mainly revolved around a tool kit designed by USAID to translate development "best practices" into military counterinsurgency tactics, called the

District Stability Framework (DSF). Contractors often had advanced degrees in international development and had worked for various NGOs, the United Nations, and humanitarian agencies prior to becoming DSF instructors. Many of them understood their role on the military base as civilizing and civilianizing the military's death-wielding capacity.

On the contractors' first day, I accompanied them as they drove to the various locations they would use as classrooms over the next several days. After surveying an indoor basketball court and a state-of-the-art auditorium, we stood in a dimly lit trailer furnished with wobbly folding tables and chairs. Sam, one of the contractors, asked where I came from. When I replied "California," he looked disappointed because he was ready with a parable about Florida to explain their work on the base. "These guys," he explained, waving toward the base to signify military personnel, "just want to whack people. But war is not just about whacking people." He asked me what I would do if I did live in Florida and one of my hypothetical children was eaten by an alligator. Before I could answer, he jumped in that most of "these guys here," again referring to the soldiers, would go after the alligator and kill it. But of course this is misguided, because a couple of days later your second kid will get eaten by another alligator. "The problem is the environment," he explained. "This is what needs to be changed, not just whacking people."

Sam positioned himself outside of the "these guys" category he used to refer to soldiers, framing the DSF as a smarter and more effective military tool than "whacking people." He upheld the military distinction between "kinetic" and "nonkinetic," obscuring how the DSF is not separate from but entangled with and enabling of the forms of violence he described. Sam also situated his role within military arguments that "counterinsurgency is not just thinking man's warfare— it is the graduate level of warfare."[7] In the period leading up to the release of the *Counterinsurgency Field Manual*, soldier-scholars played a key role in packaging this form of warfare as more sophisticated, more intellectual, and, most importantly, more effective than conventional tactics.[8] DSF contractors embody counterinsurgency's framing as "the graduate level of warfare." By identifying the problem as "the environment" as opposed to a singular individual in the alligator parable, Sam framed the contractors' tool kit as more comprehensive but also more intellectually difficult than the military approach of "whacking people." Indeed, a primary tactic within the *Counterinsurgency Field Manual* is "the precise calibration of lethal force advocated in *Imperial Policing*," a 1930s handbook for British imperial officers.[9]

Contractors made sense of their role through Sam's divide between the ignorant soldier who approaches every problem with force and the educated civilian who holds the more sophisticated and effective answers. Sam's rhetoric contained political claims for the value that contractors brought into military trainings. As civilians with very different training who are paid to be there, contractors were generally viewed with suspicion by their military audiences. They held a paradoxical role in teaching war to warriors from a civilian perspective. Contractors saw themselves as offering valuable social-scientific tools to win the population's support.

At the same time as contractors narrated their own contributions in terms of the difference between military and civilian perspectives, the empirics of how counterinsurgency doctrine was written reveal the artificiality of this divide. Civilians were certainly important to counterinsurgency's promotion, in particular academics and human rights policy advocates such as Sarah Sewall. Yet this civilian role should not eclipse the cadre of military officers with PhDs, foremost among them David Petraeus, whose "doctorate became more important than his general's stars" in counterinsurgency's promotion.[10] As significant to the military's counterinsurgency tradition is the long history of Special Forces' training in precisely the genre of nonconventional tactics that brought contractors onto this base. Most contractors were aware of these forces, but the binary of sophisticated soldier-scholars versus brutish jarheads was a politically useful claim in a context where contractors' value was in question.

In various ways, masculinity and femininity became mapped onto the binary that contractors used of "soft" intellectual versus "hard" physical military tactics. As Laleh Khalili puts it, "at one level, counterinsurgency itself is presented as the opposite of a more mechanized, technologically advanced, high-fire-power form of warfare. Given that the latter is coded as hyper-masculine, the former is considered feminine."[11] The civilian object of counterinsurgency is also coded as feminine. At the same time, counterinsurgency produces a new form of masculinity that assigns value to humanitarian ideals and scholarship. Sam's example highlighted this softened, more intellectual form of warrior masculinity that Khalili emphasizes as so integral to counterinsurgency.

Contractors were part of a multipronged attempt to attribute value to this softened counterinsurgent masculinity within military trainings. As DSF ambassadors, contractors offered military audiences one articulation of this gendered dimension of counterinsurgency that targets changing civilian social worlds and prioritizes measured force and intellectual labor. Counterinsurgency's weaponization of development into the DSF must be understood as part of a spectrum of military violence rather than a distraction from it. When contractors teach the DSF, they engage in a world-making practice: the categories structuring the DSF become the categories participants then use to make sense of their world and construct interventions. For example, the category of "stabilization" becomes foundational to all other components of the DSF. Military publications define "stabilization" as distinct from long-term development, yet still including certain development "best practices" to restore basic government, public service, and security functions in an area of military intervention.[12]

This chapter follows a PRT as it moved through the world-making practice of DSF training. Contractors generated their own forms of expert discourse that constructed intervention targets as particular objects of knowledge.[13] As trainees moved between the multiple aspects of the DSF, its matrices and technical components came to stand in for the concrete world. All technical solutions were measured against the category of "stabilization," making the category itself increasingly real throughout the training. A dominant strand of literature on expertise emphasizes how expert schemes achieve depoliticization by successfully absorbing critique.[14] In contrast to this emphasis, the very act of teaching the DSF's technical information stirred up conflict within the classroom that could not be contained. Soldiers' critiques of what it is to be, in one trainer's words, "an NGO with guns" sharpened over the course of the training, creating a contentious interplay between soldiers' experiences and contractors' technical world-making practices. In the classroom portion of the training, trainees disdained the valuation of a softer, more intellectually sophisticated masculinity and sometimes rejected the material in its entirety. Instead, they reasserted a combat masculinity through which they had previously defined themselves and their work before being reassigned to more civilian-centric jobs. These were moments when, in Tania Li's words, expert discourse was "punctured by a challenge it cannot contain." Li argues that the emphasis of much expertise literature on political closure disallows understanding of the conditions for this puncture, "moments when the targets of expert schemes reveal, in word or deed, their own critical analysis of the problems that confront them."[15] The military classroom is a lens onto how the subjects of stabilization discourse contest its authority, leaving experts unable to completely render technical their objects of intervention.

Even as I reject expertise literature's emphasis on political closure, my observations of DSF trainings' failures and unintended effects are shaped by James Ferguson's insight into failure as producing significant effects.[16] The gendered and hierarchical relationship between soldier-students and civilian contractors, in which students imagined contractors as schoolmarms, also became the terrain on which associations between combat and masculinity were strengthened. After classroom instruction, soldiers completed a village simulation populated by Afghan role players in which they implemented the DSF's tools. Conflict between the multiple aspects of soldiering came to a boiling point during these simulations. For instance, the security force could not carry out its security mission at the same time as it surveyed village needs with the DSF. Ultimately, trainings did not achieve their stated aim of convincing soldiers to adopt development experts' lessons. They did, however, produce the unintended effect of

more deeply entrenching combat masculinity. If the DSF did not necessarily produce soldiers who could, in Sam's words, change the environment, it did produce a military imagination of soldiers as parental figures responsible for guiding
Afghans into self-sufficiency. This military imagination was itself composed of
imperial characters such as T. E. Lawrence. Drawing on such characters within
an array of linguistic and cultural military technologies, simulations relied on
cultural essentialisms about Afghan civilization that soldiers and trainers used
to understand their work.

Learning Counterinsurgency: Translation, Targeting, and the Language of "Proud Parents"

Sitting in the back of a large lecture hall at Camp Atterbury, I watched as the
PRT's commanding officer gave a PowerPoint presentation on the fundamentals
of counterinsurgency. While the trainers finished familiarizing themselves with
the instructional spaces on the base, the team they were to train was finishing its
counterinsurgency unit. After the PowerPoint presentation, the team watched a
National Geographic documentary about the Taliban, and the commanding officer shared several personal anecdotes of drinking tea with village elders during
his previous deployments to Afghanistan.[17] The documentary, which outlined
key figures and turning points in the Taliban's history leading up to the US invasion, questioned whether the United States could defeat this enemy that was so
deeply rooted in a Cold War legacy. Instructors used film clips to support their
argument for the importance of economic and infrastructural development, essentially the work of the PRT, as an antiterrorism tactic. Pulling from the documentary's material, the commanding officer repeated the quote "If you don't give
somebody a piece of bread, how can he know the difference between democracy
and dictatorship?" The instructor was attempting to imprint the importance of
their economic development work upon the military side of the PRT. Yet most
students were reading news on their phones, sleeping, or browsing the internet
during the documentary and its accompanying lessons. At this point, when students were confronted with a barrage of PowerPoint presentations, they were ex-
hausted from the relentless pace of training. But PowerPoint was also the standard
mode of instruction for a range of topics within military trainings. Students'
minimal attention to this lesson conveyed that they did not accept the argument
the instructor was making regarding economic development work's centrality to
their military role. Instead, the presentation became an opportunity to rest and
recover.

Most of the course involved various lecturers coming to the podium and delivering PowerPoint presentations to the soldiers seated in the auditorium. This format also lent itself to the students' general passivity in relation to the material. Throughout the course, the commanding officer returned to a framework he had developed through a combination of doctrinal reading and his own personal deployment experiences. He drew a triangle on a whiteboard and labeled each point "PoP" (population), "INS" (insurgents), and "GOVT" (government). He scrawled arrows connecting government to population and population to insurgency, arguing that the military's role in a counterinsurgency was to strengthen the population's relationship to government and weaken its relationship to the insurgency.

The commanding officer returned often to the triangle while he lectured. When he introduced the contractors to begin the DSF segment, he referred to the triangle again as a modern-day reminder of the lessons T. E. Lawrence had learned a century ago. "He was on the other side, with the Arabs," the commanding officer said, "making the insurgents powerful to defeat the Turks. His Twenty-Seven Articles, written in 1917—'better let the Arabs do it tolerably than you do it perfectly.' You're there to help, not win the war for them. . . . [I]t has to be Afghans finding their own solutions. *We're not in the triangle.*" By removing himself and those under his command from the triangle, the officer imagined military actors as separate from rather than integral to the cycles of war and foreign invasion that created the "weak" government they were supposed to strengthen. His comment also echoed counterinsurgency scholars such as David Kilcullen in its use of British colonial figures such as Lawrence to build an argument about his team's parental role in relation to civilians under occupation. The commanding officer's lesson of being "there for" Afghan civilians, metaphorically framed as children, as part of an exercise in making them ready to head out into the world on their own was underpinned by pervasive metaphors of family life.

George Lakoff, in his application of cognitive science to contemporary US politics, identified "family-based moral systems" that shape conservative and liberal political conceptual systems. He describes the strict father, who sets strict rules for the family enforced by punishment, versus the nurturant parent, who is caring, protective, and sensitive. The military instructor's description of raising Afghan children used such parenting models from the broader cultural milieu. Soldiers were instructed to adopt the "nurturant parent" role, showing Afghans care in order to shape them as responsible and self-reliant adults.[18] In the military classroom, parental metaphors were overlain by imperial figures such as Lawrence when instructors asked trainees to imagine themselves guiding colonial subjects to independence. Such parental language is a particular iteration of a much longer trajectory of imperialism. But this iteration is different from the colonial impulse Gayatri Spivak described as "saving" the gendered colonial subject.[19] Military actors were not imagining themselves saving so much as *parenting* Afghans into fully independent subjects.

Throughout the course, the commanding officer returned to this emphasis on being there to help and enabling Afghans to find their own solutions. As part of the counterinsurgency course, he gave a lecture to the PRT members on how they must not insert themselves in the triangle, between the government and the population. He drew another triangle diagram, this time with a circle symbolizing a gap between the government and the population. He explained that insurgents were especially skilled at building a link with the population, hence preventing the government from doing so. To explain how they could mentor the government into better establishing this link, he offered his "proud parents concept," which he developed while working as a resident assistant in a college dormitory. He noted that "good parents" allowed their children to make and learn from mistakes, to get out in the world, and to manage alcohol. "The kids who had gotten guidance, they had tried alcohol before. . . . They had learned their lessons; they had been taken care of. They passed. A lot of others went home." He explained how he applied this same philosophy to the PRT's relationship to the Afghan government. "We're giving them the knowledge base they don't necessarily have, helping them with the money, but we're not doing it for them."

The commanding officer's next slide, labeled "proud parents concept," used a solid line to connect the government side of the triangle to the population—the proud parents concept had allowed the government to fill in the gap. He asked his troops to imagine themselves parenting Afghans by teaching them the skills they would need to govern. The parental metaphor also referred to Afghan people as a monolithic group collectively represented as children. Such a statement was continuous with imperial histories of seeing colonized populations as children who are incapable of caring for themselves and thus require the "care" of their imperial overlords.[20] Parental metaphors in this classroom were given meaning through a social evolutionary argument that, particularly since the late nineteenth century, has created evolutionary hierarchies in which subaltern people are evolutionarily "behind" their colonizers as a result of biological and sociocultural deficiencies.[21] Evolutionism was used to justify colonial rule as a form of guardianship to oversee the deficient racialized Other. In imagining the US military in a parental relationship to Afghans, this instructor drew on a racial evolutionary argument for occupation.

Family metaphors were used not only to urge the team members to view themselves as undertaking a certain type of parenting but also to justify how deployment took them away from their own families. After the commander had given a lecture on his proud parents concept, he introduced a lieutenant colonel who had recently returned from Afghanistan and had prepared a lesson on counterinsurgency. "Counterinsurgency is not something that is new," she lectured. "It was used in Vietnam in the Civil Operations and Revolutionary Development Support [CORDS] program, which was based on the so-called hearts and minds theory," referencing the pacification program that, like the Strategic Hamlet and New Life efforts before it, combined warfare and security measures with civic actions and welfare plans designed to produce a new political culture among Vietnam's rural population.[22] The CORDS program must also be placed in relation to the Phoenix Program's detention and "neutralization" of guerrilla supporters, which in practice meant, in one soldier's words who worked in the Phoenix Program, "'uncontrolled violence' that sometimes degenerated into nothing more than 'wholesale killing,'" often for bounty or personal grudge.[23] At the same time as the Phoenix Program oversaw torture through electrocution and the killing of at least twenty thousand Vietnamese people, CORDS "aimed to implement a developmental agenda, ultimately to lay the groundwork for 'village security.'"[24]

As I witnessed many times in military trainings, the lecturer framed Vietnam in a positive light. This presupposed positive attitude toward the Vietnam War was made possible through instructors' laser focus on CORDS without mentioning its relationship to the Phoenix Program. Instead, they argued that CORDS was a sound military strategy that would have seen more success had it been implemented earlier and with more funding.[25] Time and again, I saw military instructors claim that this sound CORDS tactic had to be separated from the "political failures" of the Vietnam War. Lecture settings such as this one, as well as the assumed unidirectional delivery of knowledge from instructor to student in military education, did not lend themselves to a critical reception of material even when its historical accuracy was highly questionable.

The instructor then showed a video that included many interviews with currently deployed US soldiers and marines. One officer interviewed in the film described how "it's hard sometimes to qualify what you do with COIN [counterinsurgency]—that is, how much you impact versus how much you don't. . . . It's really important to see the success of Afghanistan because you come here and you take time away from your family. But it's also important to see how you develop the families here and bring their villages along." In relation to marriage and sexuality, Cowen and Gilbert's discussion of the familial as a significant cultural terrain of militarization is useful to consider here.[26] Just as the commanding officer used the familial to develop his proud parents concept, this soldier then turned the familial lens onto himself, emphasizing the sacrifice of time spent away from his own family as a certain investment in parenting Afghan people into autonomy.

Once the lieutenant colonel had finished her lesson, the commanding officer began to introduce the DSF instructors in the context of the counterinsurgency framework the class had been learning. In concluding the counterinsurgency portion of the course, the commanding officer framed the upcoming unit by describing how "the USAID guy who'll be here tomorrow is the kind of guy who will take over in 2014," the official end of the combat mission in Afghanistan and the beginning of US forces' gradual withdrawal. He introduced the contractor as providing "the method we use to fit things at our level into the COIN shit we've been talking about today," framing the DSF as operationalizing development for counterinsurgency warfare. Contractors also described their role as providing a "translation" of development into a counterinsurgency tactic.

In 2010, I interviewed a number of employees of USAID's Office of Military Affairs, which published the DSF and employed the contractors teaching it on military bases. Sitting in a cubicle inside USAID headquarters on Pennsylvania Avenue while men in suits and military camouflage bustled in and out of cubicles and conference rooms, a civilian employee of the Office of Military Affairs explained to me that the DSF was about "how to gain a rapid understanding of a community for a military audience." His colleague added that USAID had developed the framework to "translate development best practices for a military audience." The colleague elaborated that the framework provided clear criteria to help practitioners in the field decide which school to build or what projects to pursue to achieve stability. He explained that the criteria come from the foundational aspect of counterinsurgency theory having to do with winning the loyalty of the civilian population. To achieve this, the project must address an issue that, first, undermines support for the government; second, increases support for "bad guys"; and third, inhibits the "functioning of normal society." The framework provides a way to direct developmental interventions to the military counterinsurgent goal of winning population support.

The DSF was developed by USAID over a number of years, originating from internal forces in the 1990s that, in the words of one official I interviewed, "recognized the threat to [US]AID's mission posed by violence and conflict." This official proclaimed violence as "the greatest tax on development," citing development economist Paul Collier as reflecting his institution's thinking.[27] What eventually became the DSF was piloted in East Africa and intended to be applicable to situations beyond the post-9/11 wars in Iraq and Afghanistan. By the time I arrived at Camp Atterbury, the framework had become integrated into predeployment trainings, particularly in the Marine Corps, and was mandated for all US government field positions in Afghanistan.

The DSF "translates" by importing language and practices such as "monitoring and evaluation" from USAID's cache of technical tool kits. These appear in the framework that USAID contractors gave to military audiences as an "M&E Matrix" (monitoring and evaluation matrix), which adopts the USAID language of "output indicators" and "impact indicators" conceptualized in the language of securitized development as "stabilization objectives." Likewise, military language, tools, and acronyms are imported into the DSF. One of the first steps of the DSF's initial section, "situational awareness" (itself a military term), is composed of a matrix organized by the two military acronyms, "PMESII" and "ASCOPE" (figure 2). The acronyms, respectively, stand for "political, military, economic, social, information, and infrastructure" and "areas, structures, capabilities, organizations, people, and events." The matrix produced through combining these acronyms is a common military tool used to gather information about an area of intervention, familiar to anyone undergoing the training.

This military language's "translation" into development tools, and vice versa, results in a mash-up of securitized development language. Shortly before the contractors entered the classroom, the commanding officer referred to the PRT's work

USAID FROM THE AMERICAN PEOPLE		PMESII-ASCOPE	
Description		Factors	Relevance
Political/Governance: Political actors, agendas, government capability and capacity	**A**	Key elements of the formal, informal, and shadow systems of government which significantly influence the local population	Why is a factor relevant to the local population? How does it affect stability?
Military/Security: Capabilities in the AO (equipment, mission, resource constraints)	**S**	Key elements that could influence the security situation	Why is a factor relevant to the local population? How does it affect stability?
Economic: Trade, development, finance, institutional capabilities, geography, regulation	**C**	Key elements that influence economic activity in the area	Why is a factor relevant to the local population? How does it affect stability?
Social: Demographics, migration trends, urbanization, living standards, literacy / education level, etc.	**O**	Key elements that describe or could influence traditional social dynamics in an area.	Why is a factor relevant to the local population? How does it affect stability?
Infrastructure: Basic facilities, services and installations	**P**	Effects on the physical infrastructure: sewage, water, electricity, educational facilities, health facilities, and transportation	Why is a factor relevant to the local population? How does it affect stability?
Information: Means of communication, media, telecommunications, word of mouth	**E**	Key elements that facilitate the transfer of information to and among the local population.	Why is a factor relevant to the local population? How does it affect stability?

FIGURE 2. PMESII-ASCOPE Matrix, a military matrix used in District Stability Framework presentations. Image courtesy of the US Agency for International Development.

as "nonkinetic targeting." This weaponized language of "targeting" carried over once the contractors arrived. Contractors referred to the DSF as a "targeting tool," which they expanded to mean, at various points throughout the course, a tool to "identify instability and hit the target," often in opposition to "winning hearts and minds," which was equated with an outmoded, less scientific, and less desirable approach of completing development projects at random. In the first part of his lesson, the contractor Dave commented that he had heard the class talking about targeting earlier that morning before he began his lesson. "Targeting isn't just about who you are seeing through the sight of your rifle. It can be a fourteen-year-old Afghan girl. Or a tribal *shūrā* [consultation]," he espoused from the podium. Dave shared how he too had worked as a civilian on a PRT in Iraq, where his team spent massive amounts of money without being able to concretely show how their expenditure increased stability in the region. To place the DSF within the intelligible and recently used language of targeting, the contractor asked the class, "How do you figure out what you should be targeting and how you are going to have an effect on that target?" The DSF was a presumptive answer to his rhetorical question.

At the heart of the framework the contractors brought to the base was the concept of stabilization. When contractors taught the DSF on military bases, they spent much of the first part of the course distinguishing between "long-term development" and "stability operations." Many contractors had advanced degrees and professional experience in the development sector. Given this background, they emphatically distinguished between "true development," which they understood as the work of USAID and associated institutions, and what they were teaching the military to do, "stability." The *Stability Operations Manual* itself distinguishes between these two categories, defining stabilization as reducing violence and establishing the preconditions for "long-term development."[28] Contractors used this definition when teaching the DSF, emphasizing counterinsurgency as a "subset of stability operations" given that most trainees were going to Afghanistan.[29] However, instructors included other causes of instability in their lesson, such as natural disaster and economic fluctuation.

At the end of their lecture on the concept of stability, contractors used a slide that read

1. Development assistance is NOT stability assistance
2. Needs/Wants are NOT necessarily causes of instability
3. Development assistance is NOT a military task

The slide concluded that "The military should focus on creating the condition—stability—that *enables* development," before stating in bright red boldface, "Stability Operations and Stability Assistance are distinctly different from Development."[30] This distinction between "real development" and "stabilization" informed many conversations I had with employees of development institutions, humanitarian organizations, and various military personnel. Development practitioners were especially anxious to distinguish between the increasing military role in development-type activities—which they categorized as "stabilization"—and their own work, which, by virtue of its long-term, more professionalized character, was "true development."

The key takeaway from this portion of the course was that development was not "stability" and was not a military task. Contractors' definition of "real development" versus military-led "stability" allowed them to logically structure a world in which development professionals were increasingly concerned about military encroachment into various development domains. "Stability" provided an acceptable realm in which military personnel could appropriately participate in development-type activities in a limited way. The category also reassured military personnel that they were not moving too far into the development realm and away from more integral combat-oriented tasks.

Even as counterinsurgency's prominence has fluctuated in formal military doctrine, the notion of "stability" prevails. I returned to some of my field sites in 2017 to investigate whether the DSF was still being used and how the broader language of "stabilization" had changed. Military instructors were adamant that "stability" had become an even more significant aspect of training. The DSF was still being used in military trainings, although instead of relying on private civilian contractors, some military units had developed their own versions of the framework that were now taught by regular military staff instructors. One school had changed the DSF's name to "Stability Assessment Framework," generalizing the lessons away from considering an Afghan district and consolidating how the framework fit into the unit's global mission.

The DSF as a World-Making Practice

Returning now to the DSF's original emergence, once the contractors had laid their foundational concept of stabilization, they moved through the framework's four steps. Repeating the targeting metaphor, Dave urged the class to think of the DSF as "nonkinetic rounds you're sending down range." He flashed a series of PowerPoint slides corresponding to each section of the DSF on two large canvas screens hovering above the podium. He introduced the four steps of the DSF: situational awareness, analysis, design, and monitoring and evaluation. The first "situational awareness" step integrates the military tool PMESII-ASCOPE into a system of gathering information about an area of military intervention. The first step also contains a "Tactical Conflict Survey" used to question villagers about the population, problems, and leadership in a counterinsurgency. Dave used more weapons metaphors to explain how measuring the attitudes of the local population with the Tactical Conflict Survey would allow them to "adjust fire." The contractors' use of weapons metaphors was a form of translation—it provided a familiar framework in which to place the DSF's steps. The various matrices comprising the DSF were not immediately intelligible as a military technology like the physical weapons the teams had also been training with. The DSF was part of a larger intellectual infrastructure in which counterinsurgency used various social science tools, academic participants, and civilians to make war. Counterinsurgency's claim to know the "culture" and "people" of a region play into this imperative whose history is rooted in social science disciplines such as anthropology and geography's role in colonial governance. In framing the survey as similar to adjusting one's fire, the metaphor also attempted to position the military as being well equipped to do the sort of work the survey required.

Dave insisted that soldiers should ask the survey questions verbatim: "Has the number of people in the village changed in the last year? What is the most important problem facing the village? Who do you believe can solve your problems? What should be done first to help the village?" Each question was always followed by "Why?" "Acting natural" was also part of the training. Contractors encouraged the trainees to "be relaxed and comfortable" and to "make small talk," "establish rapport," and integrate the survey into a conversation. The survey information was then to be coded into an Excel database, to be used in the following DSF steps (figure 3).

The second step of the DSF—analysis—used a series of matrices allowing the user to prioritize the local population's grievances, often drawing on survey data. This section emphasized the difference between "needs" and "priority grievances." Dave warned the soldiers, "Don't get dragged into a discussion about wants and needs. Afghans have so many needs. You'll never be able to meet all of them." Instead, he emphasized identifying a "priority grievance" (a need that much of the population agrees on) that is also a key "source of instability." The second step of the DSF was supposed to help trainees distinguish between a source of instability versus wants and needs. Once the concept of a source of instability was established, contractors and written DSF materials referred to it as the "SOI," using military-style acronyms to further codify this abstract concept. The "SOI" category became the central pillar of the logic of the framework. Each component of the DSF was anchored by the concept of "stability," for example, in its reference to whether a particular activity would increase "stability" and how this increase would be measured. As instructors moved through the DSF's four components, the framework's prevailing view of the world made the category of "stabilization" increasingly real—more real, in fact, than social processes in Afghanistan appeared in terms of the

TACTICAL CONFLICT SURVEY

Critical Information - Complete ALL Parts			
Date		Location (Grid)	
Subject Name		Province / State	
Subject Gender	Male Female	District / County	
Occupation		Village / Neighborhood	
Ethnicity/Tribe		Population	
Age *(Check 1)*	"Fighting age" Old (gray hair)	Interviewer Name & Unit	

Question 1: Has the number of people in the village changed in the last year? *(Check 1)*

Increased	*(Go to 1a)*	Decreased	*(Go to 1a)*	No Change		Don't Know		No Comment	

Question 1a: Reason for change in population?

Question 2: What is the most important problem facing the village?

Response to WHY

Question 3: Who do you believe can solve your problems?

Response to WHY

Question 4: What should be done first to help the village? *(1 Answer Only)*

Response to WHY

FIGURE 3. Tactical Conflict Survey, from the District Stability Framework tool kit. Image courtesy of the US Agency for International Development.

language and material available to students. Conversation revolved around identifying the "SOI," then referring to a given social process as the "SOI," making it seem as though various metrics of stability were more real than the concrete world.

Dave taught trainees to input potential sources of instability into an "SOI analysis matrix," which measured the potential "SOIs" against three "instability criteria": whether the issue decreased support for the government, increased support for "malign actors," and disrupted "normal functioning of society," which was defined in terms of local perceptions of normalcy regarding such things as law and order and the circulation of commodities (figure 4). These criteria came directly out of counterinsurgency theory, serving as an example of the sort of translation USAID officials had described. Then, based on whether the potential sources of instability were also "priority grievances," several sources of instability were used as the basis to formulate "tactical stability matrices." The "tactical stability matrix," or "TSM," is another key component of the DSF and made up the next set of slides in the contractor's lesson. Like the other matrices, the questions in the matrix are pregiven (formulated and written through an institutional process within USAID), and trainees were encouraged not to diverge from the exact order, format, or wording of the matrix headers.

The contractors explained the tactical stability matrix as being intended to "guide the development of stabilization activities." The headers of the matrix

USAID
FROM THE AMERICAN PEOPLE

SOI Analysis Matrix

Potential Sources of Instability	Instability Criteria			SOI?	Prioritization
	Does this issue decrease support for the Govt / legit governance? Explain.	Does this issue increase support for malign actors? Explain.	Does this issue disrupt the normal functioning of society? Explain.	Does the issue meet 2 of the 3 Instability criteria?	Is the SOI a Priority Grievance for the local populace?
Drawing from the four Situational Awareness lenses, list all potential Sources of Instability (SOIs)	This determination must be based on known public perceptions – not outsider assumptions! If yes, explain how the potential SOI decreases support for the Govt / legitimate governance institutions	This determination must be based on known public perceptions or behavior – not outsider assumptions! If yes, explain how the potential SOI increases support for malign actors	This determination must be based on local definitions or "normal" – not those of outsiders! If yes, explain how the potential SOI disrupts the normal functioning of society	If the issue meets at least 2 of the 3 instability criteria, it is considered a Source of Instability	For those issues that are SOIs, prioritize them based on whether the SOI is also a priority grievance for the local populace

Priority Grievances: issues or problems that a significant percentage of locals identify as a priority for their community.

FIGURE 4.   District Stability Framework instructional material: Source of Instability (SOI) Analysis Matrix. Produced by the US Agency for International Development and used in military classroom trainings. Image courtesy of the US Agency for International Development.

differentiate "local perceptions" of the cause of instability from "systemic causes," framing the latter as the "true" causes behind local perceptions of instability. For instance, a sample version of this matrix used in the classroom lists "Taliban provides swift justice" as a local perception, next to "formal justice system is slow, inefficient, hard to access" as a "systemic cause." Separating "local perceptions" from "systemic causes" creates a binary in which systemic causes are more "real"—they are the terrain of expertise and the zone of intervention as opposed to the ephemerality of "local perceptions." This framing of systemic causes also relies on the prior steps of the SOI analysis matrix and the Tactical Conflict Survey, both of which provide the data that goes into the "systemic cause" and "local perceptions" columns of the tactical stability matrix.

"Stability" became more real as contractors moved through these steps in the sense that the category came to stand in for the concrete processes in the world it referred to. The logic within the category of stability—as in the three criteria imported from counterinsurgency referenced by the USAID official—also worked to structure the world and direct interventions. The information gathered from the previous steps, then entered into the columns of the matrix, also became more real in this sense as the DSF's user moved between the different steps, each of which relies on the logic of the other steps. Writing of the economy's production as a particular artifact during the twentieth century through new practices of mapping, measurement, representation, and calculation, Timothy Mitchell discusses how the divide between "reality and its representation" becomes an "absolute gap. . . . The question of accuracy or truth could now be cast as the degree of correspondence between image-world and its object."[31] The DSF also tried to define "accuracy" through correspondence to the matrix. But as we will see in the simulation, subjects of this discourse pushed back against its authority at the same time as the framework encountered contradictions it could not contain. Unlike Mitchell's notion of strong correspondence between "image-world and its object," trainings reveal military world making as a contradictory process, a faltering struggle to redefine soldiering.

Another section of this matrix asks the user to state "the conditions that will diminish or eliminate the SOI," which would drive the sort of project the team would design in the next phase. The matrix also identifies "measures of effect," or things the team can measure that would indicate their project has addressed the "SOI." Earlier in the course, contractors spent a good amount of time discussing "measures of performance," or progress completing an activity (they used the example of number of road miles improved) versus "measures of effect" (here the associated increase in regional farm exports resulting from the better roads).

Soldiers discussed which data sources they needed to measure these indicators. They then brainstormed various activities, leading into the third "project design" step of the DSF. Nancy, another contractor, instructed the class on the third and fourth steps. She explained how the third step involved evaluating potential activities that address the "systemic causes of the SOI" identified in the previous step. The potential projects are evaluated in a matrix that asks whether they meet the framework's "stability criteria," which are identified by a series of questions about whether the proposed activity increased support for a legitimate government, decreased support for "malign actors," and increased "societal capacity and capability." Another matrix evaluates potential activities according to USAID's development "best practices" design principles. Finally, projects are screened against available resources, and one is selected. This information is organized in another worksheet. At this point in the course, trainees were given a case study of a fictitious district in Afghanistan and asked to fill in the columns of the SOI analysis and design matrices accordingly. The case study already divides the world into categories such as "tribe" and "ethnic group" that fit within the existing framework. At the same time, the act of extracting information from the case study and placing it into, for instance, the binary columns of "perception" and "systemic cause" makes the matrix's categories increasingly real.

The final step, "monitoring and evaluation," combines donor-centric language emphasizing quantifiable outcomes with counterinsurgency principles to evaluate how the chosen activity has improved "stability." Through another series of matrices and worksheets, the lesson guided the military team in selecting "stability indicators" and associated measurements, which can even be used to create an index representing overall stability, based on factors such as economic health, governance perceptions, "Afghan-on-Afghan violence," freedom of movement, district government recognition, Afghan National Security Forces presence, and security perceptions. The framework's categories drive the ways in which the trainers encouraged their military audience to organize the world. When the instructors modeled how to fill out the cultural matrix based on the case study, each cell was labeled "major cultural groups," "their interests," "cultural codes, traditions, and values," "traditional conflict resolution mechanisms," "traditional authorities," "disruptions to these mechanisms/authorities," and "how spoilers/stabilizing forces leverage these factors" (figure 5). The very format of the matrix demanded short, simple words or phrases in response to these labels. The desired answer to "major cultural groups" in this example was "Pashtuns"; "their interests" were "agriculture and land ownership," and the "cultural codes" were "tribalism" and "Pashtunwali." The technical tool of the matrix forced essentialization of culture. The answer to the question must literally fit in a box.

The DSF was among many new social science counterinsurgency technologies that were just as important to shaping soldiers' thinking and practices as the weapons systems they practiced using during other parts of their predeployment

78   CHAPTER 2

USAID FROM THE AMERICAN PEOPLE			Cultural Matrix
1) Major Cultural Groups	2) Their Interests	3) Cultural Codes, Traditions, and Values	4) Traditional Conflict Resolution Mechanisms
Identify the major cultural and/or tribal groups in your AO	Identify the things these groups' care about or consider to be valuable – both material and intangible	Identify cultural codes, traditions, and values that the major cultural groups live by	Identify how conflicts between individuals and groups have traditionally been resolved
5) Traditional Authorities	6) Disruptions to These Mechanisms/Authorities	7) How Spoilers/Stabilizing Forces Leverage These Factors	
Identify the traditional authorities to whom the locals respect and/or normally turn to for assistance	Describe what new actors or conditions may have disrupted the traditional conflict resolution mechanisms and/or undermined the influence of traditional authorities	Describe how malign actors leverage and/or exploit these cultural factors to their advantage. Consider also how stabilizing forces do or could leverage these factors.	

FIGURE 5. District Stability Framework instructional material: Cultural Matrix. Produced by the US Agency for International Development, used in military classroom trainings. Image courtesy of the US Agency for International Development.

training. The DSF offered a series of abstract categories, such as "stabilization," for soldiers to understand their role in Afghanistan and as the face of the "new" US military at large. Soldiers did not all necessarily internalize these categories and ways of thinking, although some did. A clear effect of this new technology, however, was that it provoked conversation regarding the labor of soldiering in the contemporary moment, with the DSF and its delivery through contractors coming to represent a "less manly" form of war. The DSF problematized pervasive military cultural associations between combat and masculinity by questioning the value traditionally attributed to combat.

The simulation that followed the classroom portion of the course was also an important site of cultural production. At the end of a simulation of this PRT's meeting with Afghan and international NGO representatives (roles played by civilian contractors), the team and role players held a "hotwash," an immediate evaluation of the simulation. One of the Western NGO representatives asked the

Afghan NGO representative if he had done the "I-don't-trust-you handshake" when he was introduced to the PRT members. I had been observing the meeting with Evans, a captain running this part of the simulation. We sat on a decrepit twin bed formerly used by the penal colony, awkwardly craning our necks from behind a wall separating the residential dormitory from the small meeting area where the NGO meetings occurred. The captain proudly showed me the "texture" of a young male role player serving tea, whom he referred to as the "chai boy," as well as the rugs, flags, and photographs decorating the room. This texture, so central to theater immersion simulations, was itself a form of cultural production. During the team's discussion of the handshake, Evans explained to me that there are "three different types of handshakes in Afghanistan conveying varying levels of trust." The Afghan NGO representative, a contractor traveling with the PRT for the rest of the training as a cultural adviser, offered to demonstrate these handshakes. He answered the NGO representative that he had given the PRT commander the "I-don't-trust-you handshake." The group moved on and began to discuss how, in the words of a contractor playing the role of an international NGO representative, "these types of meetings are good for Afghans because they're not naturally good at planning; they need mentorship." The trainer used a social evolutionary way of thinking about Afghans as biologically or culturally "lacking" in areas—here "planning"—that are linked to their underdevelopment and need for parental overlords. It is a racialized and imperial argument about Afghans as a people, rather than a history of serial wars, that explains the need for development. The trainer encouraged the PRT to think of its job in these terms: "When you leave, you want Afghans standing strong and tall." Although the NGO representative was not in the room for the PRT commander's lesson on the proud parents concept, his message to the team fit within the imperial parental framework the team had been taught to operate with in the classroom portion of their course.

Participants in the training referred to the NGO meeting as a "lane," one of a series of elaborate simulations staffed with theatrical sets, role players, and members of the Department of State, USAID, and other US government agencies. A different lane, where the DSF contractors worked, was supposed to simulate a "stability working group," which is a structure the DSF instructors promoted that includes military actors and civilian representatives from local and international NGOs, local government officials, the Department of State, and the Department of Agriculture. In this simulation, a combination of the DSF contractors and Afghan actors played the roles of a USAID stability trainer from Kabul helping the PRT conduct the stability working group; a representative from the Afghan Ministry of Rural Rehabilitation and Development; an Afghan staff member of DAI (Development Alternatives International), USAID's implementing partner and one of the largest for-profit development companies in Afghanistan; a district governor the PRT was supposed to invite to the working group; and a mentor for the Afghan National Police.

The DSF figured prominently in this simulation. The night before, the PRT was expected to meet with the USAID representative to review potential "sources of instability" and work through a preliminary version of the tactical stability matrix to prepare for the meeting. The meeting's end product was a completed DSF tactical stability matrix—the activity was designed to entrench the DSF's thought process into the team's operations. Before the PRT entered the room, the role players rehearsed by introducing themselves and practicing their talking points. The first, an Afghan American contractor acting as the rural reconstruction and development representative, was prepared with extensive handwritten notes from the vignette they had been given the night before. He concisely described how one tribal group felt as though it was being excluded from rural development, that there was prejudice against them, and that this was a key source of instability in the region. In response, a DSF trainer interjected that he had heard older people in Afghanistan take two or more hours to make a simple point that could have been made in two minutes. Before the trainer could finish, a member of the brigade running the training who was acting as the Afghan police mentor smirked that Afghans took hours to "say nothing." The DSF trainer continued: "You know, Afghans tell stories with images. It is sometimes very long but very imaginative as well." The trainers echoed the script the role players had been given, in which the district governor is described as "rather long-winded, which will try the patience of the working group." The commitment to what Evans referred to as "texture" produced a mythical Afghan culture that became real to participants through simulation. As we waited for the PRT to arrive in a convoy between scenarios, Evans chain-smoked as he showed me a dog-eared green notebook from his most recent deployment in which he had written miscellaneous notes on Afghan tribes, language, culture, and custom. The "I-don't-trust-you handshake" and the supposed "long-winded" tendency of Afghans were in this notebook and had clearly influenced how he made sense of the world he encountered while deployed.

Experts made "stabilization" real as they moved through the four steps of the DSF and into simulations. Technical interventions such as matrices rearrange the world of complex political, economic, and cultural processes into a format amenable to technical intervention. As literature on expertise has established, discourse is an embodied practice.[32] But in this literature, experts still rule: "much of the time, they succeed in disguising their failures and continue to devise new programs with their authority unchallenged."[33] However, when students used the matrices, surveys, and various DSF tools, experts could not actually secure a "technical matrix" capable of shutting down political challenges. Rather, military trainees pushed back against the DSF's closed system, sometimes through boredom and other times through overt rejection of counterinsurgency theorists' advice to "practice armed social work."[34]

Classroom Receptions of the DSF

Trainees remained largely passive as they sat in lecture halls watching PowerPoint presentations. One PRT commander instructed his team to remain in "receive mode" during the contractors' initial presentation of the DSF's main steps. While some soldiers took attentive notes, many appeared bored—their eyes glazing over or reading smartphone screens—while others' heads dipped and jerked upright again after unintentionally falling asleep. Some actively challenged the DSF's logic during this portion of the class. On a break between sections of the presentation, a member of the PRT's security force complained that he was good at "do X, Y, then Z, then it's done. But with this training, they're saying sometimes do X, but other times it's Y," conveying the dramatic difference between the job he was trained for and the rather complex social and political questions he was now asked to navigate. More specific to the Tactical Conflict Survey the contractors had previously introduced, the soldier conveyed hesitancy to use it in the field because he feared that it would cause people to confuse him with intelligence collectors and didn't feel equipped to necessarily address the needs that would inevitably come up through the survey questions. "It would be like asking the guy if he was thirsty," he explained, "then saying, 'that's nice. I'm not going to do anything about it myself, but who do you think can best solve your thirst?' Then eventually this guy is going to say, man, you're a dick, and that's not good." The soldier was concerned that asking local populations about their grievances but then being unable to resolve them would further alienate him.

Soldiers' challenges to the contractors' material were leveled not only at the DSF's content but also at times more broadly at the idea that they should be practicing "armed social work." My DSF observations opened into military-only instructional settings, often in trainings where the DSF served a small part. The longest observation I made of this type was a five-week Marine Corps civil affairs training, which included the DSF but also components on humanitarian and disaster response, counterinsurgency, and working with local governments and NGOs. Many marines in this training had been involuntarily reassigned from infantry and artillery to civil affairs, a job focused on interacting with civilians now needed in larger numbers to deploy to Afghanistan.

Victor, for instance, had enlisted in the Marine Corps while he was still in high school out of a combination of economic pressure and genuine belief in the US mission in Afghanistan. "In the military, they gave you a place to stay—you were covered," he explained, emphasizing how taking himself "out of the financial equation" meant that his mom had only his brother to worry about. At the time, the Marine Corps needed to fill infantry and artillery billets. He enlisted in artillery, rising through the ranks to eventually become a noncommissioned officer. We met in the middle of a two-week unit within the longer course in which students war-gamed a disaster-response scenario in a fictitious country. On a break, he dipped into a pouch of chewing tobacco while we stood on a rickety wooden balcony. Inside the portable classroom, Victor's instructor had been talking about how "we don't put warheads to foreheads. . . . We talk to people, develop projects, nonlethal targeting. . . . We don't always need to shoot or kill to get our point across." Victor had been hovering around a folding table, plugging data into various spreadsheets and matrices. This was at the end of a course module in which he was given a description of a disaster scenario in a fictitious country and asked to walk through the steps he would take. The steps came from the Marine Corps Planning Process, the same instrument they would use if they were going into battle.[35] This particular day had been dedicated to the war-gaming step, which meant his group divided into a green cell (good guys) and a red cell (bad guys) and gamed how each would react to their proposed disaster response.

Standing on the balcony, Victor spat into an empty bottle of Patriot's Choice water; its crumpled plastic always stood out to me in a sea of brands that marked the particularity and insularity of life on a military base. He sighed and exclaimed, "My heartache with this is knowin' I'm going from a trigger-puller to a sell-rep." He elaborated through a series of military acronyms how he received the order that he would attend the school we now stood in front of where marines were trained in civil affairs and other nonkinetic operations. He would then deploy to Afghanistan as a civil affairs marine. He ruminated with an angry look that it was likely someone on this very base who reassigned him.

Confused, I asked what he meant by a "sell-rep," to which he replied, "this stuff is about going around and shaking peoples' hands, selling ideas. I'm an 0811. Artillery," he elaborated to my obvious ignorance. "That's large guns that fire rounds at least 3,500 yards. Since I was seventeen, I've been kicking in doors and blowing stuff up. That's all I know." Victor was in his late twenties, having spent the better part of the past decade in artillery. His facial expression blending disdain with resignation reflected the worthlessness he felt in his new civil affairs role. Artillery carried value in terms of one's military career prospects because its status as a primary military occupational specialty satisfied the criteria for promotion. Civil affairs, on the other hand, was a secondary military occupational specialty in the Marine Corps, meaning that spending any length of time in this capacity slowed an active-duty marine's promotion track. Civil affairs did not carry the same associations with combat masculinity as infantry and artillery, jobs that until recently were open to men only. Involuntary reassignment to civil affairs was also alienating in the sense that artillery had become part of Victor's identity, in contrast to the idea of selling something that belonged to someone else.

The course inside the trailer came after the DSF and was taught by a different group of contractors employed by yet another private firm whose subcontractors ranged from ex-marines to Afghan Americans giving lessons on human rights and Afghan culture. Given that the course contained many marines in Victor's position of being involuntarily reassigned from infantry and artillery, it presented some of the most dramatic examples of resistance to course content. While some of Victor's colleagues accepted the notion that "trigger-pulling" was no longer the preferred mode of warfare, many of them shared Victor's anger. The captain sitting next to me—Stern—explained that he had just graduated from expeditionary warfare school, a training and leadership program for Marine Corps officers that focused on traditional war-fighting capabilities. "It's more kinetic than this," he explained, waving his arm around the drab portable classroom. "An exercise like *this* would have taken us two days, and here we are spending ten," he lamented as we prepared for a mock flood response.

Grabbing his hair, another young man Victor usually ate with whom everyone called "Gunny" because of his artillery background, joked that he was "programmed to shoot." He had enlisted in the Marine Corps sixteen years ago when he ran out of work as a welder in rural northern California and spoke often about how he would rather be back in artillery. Stern was also artillery, although as a captain he outranked most of the other young enlisted "grunts" sitting around the table. On a break from the course, when I asked Stern about his background, he dryly recounted, "I knew I wanted to go to college, and I knew it had to be free. So, it was either full ROTC [Reserve Officers' Training Corps], enlist, or Naval Academy." He was in the process of enlisting when he was accepted into the Naval Academy in Annapolis. When I asked why he joined the Marine Corps as opposed to the US Navy, he shrugged and said, "Go big or go home." Stern's last assignment was a bomb-disposal squad in Iraq. When he spoke about going from bomb disposal to civil affairs, he explained the transition as "it's going from 'there's an IED [improvised explosive device], we have to dispose of it,' to 'why'd he put that there?'" or, Victor's friend added from the other side of the table, "what caused him to stop farming and dig that hole?"

Their comments speak to the fundamental contradiction of asking someone who has been, in their own words, "programmed to shoot" to suddenly start thinking in broader terms about what caused someone to shoot at them in the first place, then to intervene without the tool they have been trained in.[36] But the conversation around the table was not only about having one's preferred tool of infantry or artillery weapons replaced with a village needs survey. The DSF and civil affairs material was feminized in military classrooms through its delivery via contractors, its proximity to civilians, counterinsurgency's associations with intellectual labor, and instructors' reliance on binaries between killing versus caring in teaching the material. All of these components of feminization intersected with students' anger at being involuntarily reassigned to a devalued secondary military specialization that would hurt their chances for promotion.

Marines such as Victor often articulated this stew of discontent through a blend of expletive-laden humor, anger, and reference to military violence that pervaded social relations between enlisted men over meals, during physical training, and now during a tabletop exercise. This manner came out as Victor's friend walked by, overhearing the conversation between Stern and me about the transition from working bomb-disposal squad to this course, exclaiming, "I hate this fucking shit. I'd rather get shot at any fucking day." A third student chimed in, saying "I'd much rather be kicking in doors, blowin' up something." Stern sighed, "The good days are gone," to which Victor replied, "they'll be back." "No they won't," Stern said, "this is punishment for Ramadi," framing developmental, civilian-focused work as repentance for the death and destruction that occurred during the Marine Corps' large-scale battles in 2004 and 2006.

The tone and content of this exchange were relatively common during periods when the marines were supposed to be filling in matrices or downtime between course modules. For Victor, Stern, and the other two young men speaking, who had spent their entire careers in artillery, recollection of the "good days" and reference to shooting or being shot at were how they presented themselves as accepting the identity they had been offered since boot camp of "every marine a rifleman." Physical fitness, cursing, and rejecting material that smacked of academia, humanitarian aid, or anything with civilians as a focal point were all part of adopting a certain combat masculinity that was accepted in their social circles and, particularly among the enlisted men, was part of the expected conformity that came with military life. The four men at the table had varied reasons for rejecting the course material, but the trappings of combat masculinity offered them a way to reject the material that was intelligible to peers and superiors alike. Fortifying the existing associations between military masculinity and combat was an unintended consequence of the lesson.

In contrast to Victor and Stern's lament about their reassignment to civil affairs, Sean was one of the only trainees I met during my time at Quantico who had volunteered to join civil affairs. Sean, a young white man, joined the Marine Corps after learning about its involvement in humanitarian relief. He had recently graduated from college in southern California. In chemistry class, he sat next to a reservist who had just gotten back from a two-week trip to Thailand. Sean had always wanted to travel to Thailand, and meeting this reservist introduced a way to get paid to see the world. Sean saw a career in the Marine Corps as a pathway to participating in refugee evacuations, natural disaster responses, and other opportunities to travel and make a positive imprint on the world. He was extremely enthusiastic about the material and took copious notes, making sure he recorded David Galula's laws of counterinsurgency in neat bullet points in his notebook.

After I read my informed consent script to his class on the first day, explaining my interest in militarized development, Sean practically ran up to me, speaking quickly about how "this right here," pointing at the board, "*this* is exactly why I joined the marines and why I'll never get promoted." He spoke quickly about how he thought civil affairs should be a primary military occupational specialty instead of a secondary, devalued one. "*We* can do stuff I can't do with some NGO," he said, continuing that being "forward deployed," or based outside of the United States, meant being closer to and better resourced to handle foreign humanitarian disasters. He recalled how when he enlisted, he told the recruiter to give him any military occupational specialty but begged to be sent to the same civil affairs unit as the student from chemistry class. Later in the course, Sean told me he had made the mistake of telling this story in the barracks the night before—that he had joined the Marine Corps to do civil affairs. All at once the other men started correcting him, that he had "joined the Marine Corps to be a *marine*. First a rifleman, supporting in a civil affairs capacity." Sean elaborated how important the slogan of "every marine a rifleman" was. "Here, it's cool to be a grunt." While the word "grunt" referred to someone in the infantry, it also stood in for the sort of combat masculinity Sean rejected through his interest in literature, his fashionable civilian clothes, and his refusal to adopt casual language that referenced weapons or killing. "They [infantry] are at the center, never to be dislodged. And everyone else is in support of them." Frustrated, he asked me, "How can you convince an institution that *loves* tradition, that's built on killing, that you can't just kill everyone anymore???!!" He drifted off, speaking about how in boot camp he was taught to say "kill" instead of "yes" in response to yes/no questions.

Sean continued to grapple with how to lend credibility to the material they were learning in the course. He was personally excited about the material, staying after class to ask questions and eventually earning the honor graduate title that came with a coin stamped with the civil affairs logo. But his peers constantly reminded him that he needed to think of himself as a "rifleman first." They voiced everything from genuine concern about his career because of his confusion about the vocation of a marine to open hostility that he was ideologically poisoning their ranks. Officers who were to deploy with him complained that they could not trust him. One reservist who was activating to deploy to Afghanistan scoffed that he had heard Sean talk about how he was in a position to change the way people feel about America, to right the wrongs of decades of foreign policy. He complained that he wanted to hear Sean say he joined the Marine Corps to be a *marine*, a rifle-man first. Anything less made him doubt that he wanted Sean by his side in a firefight and even suspicious that Sean would not carry him out if he was injured. Students' disdain for Sean's intellectual agreement with the course blended with personal attacks on his slight stature and the slender fit of his civilian clothes. The same marines who lamented their "punishment" for Ramadi also joked homophobically that Sean was gay, deriding the course material at the same time as they ostracized him. Together, this valorization of being a "grunt" and the rejection of civil affairs was how students reified a preexisting combat masculinity as they refused the course material.

By the time of the final field exercise nearly four weeks later, Sean had grown demoralized. He spent all of his free time reading novels on his bunk, which served as more fodder for his peers to make fun of him for being so intellectual. He no longer sought me out to talk about NGOs and human rights organizations, although his commanding officer asked me to speak to him about alternate careers, such as entering the Peace Corps or USAID, when he got out of the military. Before graduation, a group of instructors had staged an intervention of sorts to try to bring Sean back into the fold by remembering his primary directive to be a rifleman first. They warned him that maybe he should not be a marine if what he really wanted to do was rescue flood victims.

The reactions of fellow marines and instructors to Sean's passion for the course material were ironic—he represented the course's exact priorities. His treatment also revealed the everyday ranks of the Marine Corps' systemic devaluation of key aspects of higher-level doctrine, such as an emphasis on civilians, so-called stabilization including military-led development, and social science tools. The language that the marines used to tease Sean also indicated how gender and sexuality were part of the fabric students used to construct understandings of counterinsurgency. Sean's peers gathered together his skinny jeans, his presumed sexuality, and his interest in literature as evidence of his position outside of the conformist elements of a combat masculinity they had adopted. In rejecting him, they rejected the idea that soldiers should be conducting "armed social work" at the same time as they strengthened their own associations of combat with masculinity.

Contractors as Contradictory Experts

Expert contractors were aware of how most marines felt about the material they were being taught. Through their experiences teaching the DSF and working in other military and humanitarian settings, contractors had also developed their own critiques of the military's role in implementing their material. On drives to and from the base, Nancy and Jane, two trainers, would describe their role as smuggling a "more human" perspective into the minds of their military audiences. On one of these drives, Jane compared her current job teaching the DSF to a previous contract providing Afghan cultural training for a combat training center. A white woman in her early thirties with a background in humanitarian relief, she disdainfully described watching soldiers practice firing very large artillery, which she imagined would decimate the tiny Afghan villages where she had spent time working for the United Nations. The DSF seemed an improvement—more "humane," "sophisticated," and "effective"—than the blunt initial insertions of culture into military trainings. Nancy reminisced about how on Fridays she would go home with local staff and spend the weekend watching Indian soap operas and participating in the rhythms of daily life. She recalled how well she would sleep without the loud sounds of generators running in the fortified expatriate compounds. She and Jane wondered aloud whether in an area like southern California, with a large Afghan diaspora, it might be possible to arrange homestays for civil affairs soldiers and marines with Afghan and Afghan American families living in the United States.

At the same time, contractors were quite aware of resistance to some of the DSF's content. On another drive to the hotel after a ten-hour day on the base, Jane joked, "I wonder if this is what the Vietnam generation felt like," laughing and then clarifying, "it's not that bad. It's not like we're carpet-bombing civilians, but it's pretty bad," referring to her critique of US military strategy in Afghanistan. As we drove away from the uniform beige buildings organized in numbered blocks and wound our way through the flat, brown agricultural land, Jane elaborated that the military was incapable of doing what she had been asking it to do. She described herself as "basically a pacifist" who didn't believe in military solutions to problems except as a last resort. She compared herself to other civilians who got a thrill from riding in military Humvees. "I always think of it as an instrument of death," she reflected on the Humvee. "If you send in the military, be prepared for death and destruction, because that's what you're gonna get." She then described how during her first week working for a PRT in Afghanistan a young girl was accidentally struck and killed by a Humvee carrying members of the PRT to assess an engineering project.

In this way, it was not only soldiers' reactions to the DSF but also trainers' internal critiques of implementing the material that punctured expert discourse. Jane's reservations revealed "the expert" as a category that is far from secure. Her expert status, for example, was made of genuine belief in the technical set of materials she brought along with awareness of the limitations to their implementation. I asked if she ever felt internally conflicted about working for an institution that was responsible for, in her words, "death and destruction" and whose strategy she didn't agree with. "Oh yeah," she responded, "but this train is leaving with or without me on it. You can either critique from the outside or change from within." She explained her pursuit of "change from within" by referring to the time a four-star general participated in her DSF training. She had the ear of the future leadership of the Marine Corps and measured her own success in terms of urging the military to "see the humanity of Afghan people just a little bit." I had also observed this training, which was for a brigade combat team, meaning the trainees were exclusively men and mostly infantry and artillery. Their body language betrayed their lack of interest in the material, which was a required component of their counterinsurgency predeployment training to Afghanistan. Most of their camouflage-clad shoulders drooped forward, and some of their closely shaven heads even dipped and startled from time to time as they drifted in and out of consciousness. Like the dozing members of the PRT in the lecture hall at Camp Atterbury, this brigade combat team also took Jane's lesson as an opportunity to zone out and prepare for components of the course they considered to be more central to their jobs as infantry and artillerymen. To counter this reaction, the contractors invited a four-star general into the class.

The general stood in front of the class and talked about his recent work in East Africa conducting humanitarian assistance. "When I was out in the Horn of Africa," he explained to the class, whose interest had been piqued, "my three sisters were always proud of the HA [humanitarian assistance] we were doing: vetcaps [veterinary civic action programs], medcaps [medical civic action programs], and humanitarian relief, making the village happy and so on. My sisters thought that was really neat stuff. But my brothers looked at me through male macho theory— they were a lot more interested in kinetic phases [violent combat activities]." Using associations of masculinity with combat and femininity with humanitarian relief, the general tried to empathize with the marines that he understood how subscribing to the importance of nonkinetic activities could seem counterintuitive given their prior training. It might even seem "unmanly." Here he channeled the very combat masculinity at work in the civil affairs marines' rejection of the DSF and of Sean, emphasizing the use of force and delegitimizing the form of warfare that DSF trainers promoted.

In response to this delegitimation, the general referred to the "eighty-twenty rule" mentioned in many counterinsurgency texts—that this type of warfare is only 20 percent fighting.[37] Like many instructors teaching related material, he cited defense scholars such as Galula to argue that although this form of warfare might conflict with the gendered valuation of military jobs, historical evidence revealed its effectiveness. In an attempt to still express sympathy with the marines in the room, the general joked that they might write letters home from Afghanistan that said they had three cups of tea and found the source of instability, to which "Mom's going, 'oh, how lovely, he's making a difference.' Dad's saying 'what the hell, I thought he was a mariiiine!!!!!'" The general's caricature of "Dad" resonated with the actual responses of Sean's cohort to his interest in humanitarian response. Through humor, the general urged the audience to both prepare themselves for and steel themselves against such reactions, possibly even inviting the opportunity to educate their fathers about this smarter, if feminized, form of war.

The general tapped into how most members of the brigade combat team sitting in the training had painted the DSF as a feminized form of war their mothers might approve of through its associations with humanitarianism and development. The trainers were also aware of their own feminization. In this particular training, the marines mapped the feminized traits of counterinsurgency the trainers spoke about in the car—the notion of a softer, more humane, and more intellectual side of war—to the trainers' female sex. Trainers themselves became softer, humane, and intellectual compared to the specializations in weapons and combat the team represented. Because of his rank and his references to being a man and a marine who did "humanitarian" work, it was harder for the class to feminize the general in the same way they had feminized the contractors. At the same time as he validated trainees' rejection of the feminized material and feminine contractors, the general insisted that they were learning a more effective mode of fighting war, thus upholding their definition of manliness through fighting (and winning) wars. Trainees interrupted the DSF's expert discourse, itself unstable, through gendered perceptions of the material. Inviting the general to class was one way the contractor attempted to counter this reaction, itself giving rise to more gendered arguments about the value of different military tactics.

Soldiers' reservations about the DSF material and outright rejection of some of the more fundamental principles of the military's stated role indicate how even in the receive mode of classroom instruction, the DSF met with resistance. This resistance was forged out of boredom and anger, the contradiction of asking soldiers trained in infantry and artillery to suddenly perform the role of "armed social worker," and specific concerns about military personnel's ability to implement the framework given the constraints of their job. The DSF represented an attempt to bring the "softened masculinity" Khalili writes of as so central to counterinsurgency doctrine into military training.[38] Yet in practice, soldiers and marines rejected much of the material, often in the language of a more conventional association of combat with masculinity. If the puncturing of contractor expertise began in the classroom portion of the course, it accelerated when the simulation began.

Simulating Stabilization

At the end of the classroom portion of the DSF, I drove with the trainers in their rental cars onto the base, then down a series of dirt roads to a very remote area housing a simulated forward operating base. Mist rose in the early morning off the green sloping hills to either side of us. The forested area seemed peaceful until our gaze was interrupted by clusters of soldiers shooting on the range. In the car, the trainers wondered aloud whether it was strange for their students to listen to them talk about "this soft stuff," then be told to "get out on the range and shoot stuff." While we waited for the trainees to arrive, Jane commented on how much sense it made in stability operations for civilian institutions to try to "work together better" with the military. Shortly after the trainers' rental car convoy arrived at the simulation, a convoy of Humvees appeared carrying the trainees clad in body armor and helmets.

Inside a trailer in this simulation area, a soldier stood in front of several whiteboards filling out the matrices from the classroom portion of the DSF (figure 6). The first part of the simulation revolved around preparing to visit a simulated village by preliminarily deciphering its source of instability using the DSF. The trainees spent the morning filling out the cultural, SOI analysis, and PMESII/ASCOPE matrices on large pieces of butcher paper based on the information they were given in the case study. They filled out the matrices using a packet of information describing a fictitious Afghan village and quickly listed characteristics of the area as "agricultural," "religious," and "low literacy" in the PMESII/ASCOPE matrix. The group then described the importance of honor, revenge, and traditional authorities in the cultural matrix and listed potential sources of instability as high unemployment and lack of irrigation and agricultural opportunity driving men to join the Taliban. In all of these scenarios, the US military presence was never addressed as a potential source of instability. Instead, the military was positioned as outside of these social relations, intervening with the interests of the local population in mind. The matrix format forced single-word answers to describe the area's culture.

During these practical exercises, the DSF's step-by-step technical nature also led to the potential for conflict between contractors and trainees. For instance, in this initial part of the simulation, one of the groups had begun to fill out the *tactical* stability matrix before they had filled out the *source* of instability matrix. A scribe reproduced the charts on a whiteboard and took notes while the commanding officer led the discussion. They talked about the absence of job opportunities and irrigation essential for agriculture as well as a lack of medical care. During the conversation, a PRT member asked, "Is there something we can do to help them help themselves?" They discussed resupplying doctors and clinics to provide local

FIGURE 6.   District Stability Framework training, US army base.
Author photo.

health care and providing education projects for local children. The idea of "help-ing them help themselves" reflected the racial evolutionism and nurturant parent aspect of the commander's proud parents concept covered in the counterinsur-gency section of the course, before the DSF.[39]

The DSF's rigid order combined with the power dynamics giving trainers au-thority over trainees also provided a recipe for conflict. During the discussion of Afghan self-help projects, the trainer complimented the group for its detailed investigation of potential interventions. He also gently reminded them that they had jumped ahead in the DSF's order, essentially discussing projects before going through the steps that the source of instability matrix advised. The matrix in-stituted a logic by which a problem had to contribute to "instability," defined by the key criteria of weakening government support.

Earlier during a small-group activity practicing the various matrices with a case study, I sat with one of the groups, between an army medic and an engineer, at a beat-up folding picnic table in a dark cement cafeteria. The team had jumped to the project-design phase of the framework before going through the SOI analy-sis matrix. Nancy, walking around the room and glancing at everyone's work, stopped to point out that they had skipped over the SOI analysis matrix. Group members rolled their eyes in response. Some expressed frustration with the rigidity of the matrix by mocking the contractor, claiming she had no authority over them or mimicking her high-pitched voice and the hand gestures she used to teach. Their schoolmarmish caricature addressed how they viewed contractors as closer to feminized schoolteachers than symbols of military masculinity such as drill sergeants. When soldiers rejected contractors' lessons, they did so through these gendered symbols such as the female schoolteacher. The matrix itself was not necessarily the aspect of the exercise that students rejected—after all, they had been using matrices such as PMESII-ASCOPE since basic training. Instead, students reacted to the fact the material was delivered via contractors as well as to the "armed social work" ethos of the work they were asked to do. The teacher-student hierarchy between military personnel and contractors was also distinct from other military hierarchies; the civilian and female characteristics of the contractors lent themselves to rejection of a specifically gendered authority.

Nancy announced that they would have forty minutes to fill out the SOI analysis matrix, and several members of the team sighed. One held up the case study and commented, "This paper. I would be pissed to walk into a situation with this information." His colleague voiced concern that a different military entity coordinating civil-military operations duplicated their efforts. Another was frustrated that the team they were going to replace in Afghanistan was using a different framework to collect information about the local area. A third described how they had just been briefed on a number of projects they would inherit as soon as they arrived in Afghanistan, including building an orphanage, a courthouse, and a bridge. They would not have time to fill out all of these charts. They had only a year once they arrived, and they would have to follow their commander's intent.

Until this point, the trainees were filling out the matrices in preparation to go into a mock Afghan village populated with Afghan American role players employed by a private company that set up simulations on military bases across the United States. As the training progressed to the village-simulation component, the team was to leave the forward operating base for the mock village next door. Before leaving for the village, the commanding officer did a mock briefing. The sound of Velcro ripped through the classroom as the team put on their body armor and assembled their gear. Someone called roll, and each component of the PRT—civil affairs, engineering, security, and medics—responded with a guttural grunt. The commanding officer stated that the team's purpose was "to hold a *shūrā* with village elders. The mission is to complete the DSF framework and to confirm that irrigation, security, and health care are the SOIs." His briefing reflected how the village simulation was approached as empirical material to confirm or deny hypotheses generated through the matrices. In this instance, the process of filling out the matrices based on the case study meant that the group had narrowed its focus to irrigation, security, and health care before heading into the village.

During this intensive period of renewed US military interest in counterinsurgency, I was not the only scholar to visit these trainings. Counterinsurgency's manufacture through sinister academic partnerships also presented a unique atmosphere of relative openness to requests for academic observation and marked civilian presence within military trainings. Geographer Oliver Belcher spent one week at Muscatatuck Urban Training Center the year before I found myself there listening to the head of security brief his team on the formation they would take heading into the village. Belcher describes the "circulation of 'culture' within the US military" as "an instrumental activity through which identities are positioned and habitually put to use, like tools, to orient strategic and tactical operations, as well as 'modulate [the] complex environment of insurgent formation.'"[40] Belcher comes to see "cultural knowledge" as part of what Derek Gregory has described as the military's redirection of public attention toward its "non-lethal targeting" and even the "restrained" aspect of counterinsurgency in its approach to killing enemies.[41] Like Gregory, Belcher's analysis unmasks such public-facing military claims as detracting from how "the move to counterinsurgency instead had almost entirely opposite outcomes, insofar as it introduced novel and, in many ways, more insidious forms of violence into the everyday lives of Iraqis and Afghanis."[42]

Belcher's emphasis on the new and insidious forms of violence entailed in counterinsurgency's return is vital to counterbalancing military attempts to redirect public attention from ongoing violence through language such as "armed social work." Yet this interpretation also leaves us operating within the epistemological framework the military has set forth in which there are more and less violent aspects of counterinsurgency (targeted killing versus holding a village *shūrā*), and the less violent aspects are designed to convince subject populations of the military's beneficence. Within this military epistemological framework, allegedly less violent aspects of counterinsurgency are also directed at US public perceptions of the US military abroad. A conceptualization of violence that is adequate to the counterinsurgency practices I describe here must move beyond the imagined boundary between more and less violent attributes. The allegedly "less violent" aspects of counterinsurgency, including military uses of gender and development, may be more accurately understood as violence by other means, often enabling violent events such as raids, targeting, and bombings.

To arrive at this more comprehensive definition of violence, we must look at the aspect of counterinsurgency training that is directed inward, toward those who implement it. Belcher's analysis is based on the final simulation exercise that military teams completed after they had sat in the classrooms I observed. By focusing on the end product of the simulation, we are deprived of understanding how tools such as the DSF are produced. This production is important because it is here that we see relationships between development and military institutions become reworked through, for instance, figures such as Nancy and Dave. On the production side, we see how the DSF's message of "armed social work" is actively undermined by soldiers' own understandings of their jobs as rooted in masculinist definitions of combat. Rather than necessarily changing how war is fought, counterinsurgency seems to have the larger effect of reconfiguring soldiers' understandings of themselves and their work—albeit not necessarily in the ways experts intend—as well as the financial and institutional relationships surrounding them.

Counterinsurgency also necessitated a shift in gendered forms of military labor. Female counterinsurgency teams are emblematic of the "nonlethal targeting" Belcher and Gregory treat as a public relations exercise. Yet the production of these teams—their assembly through training and shifts in members' understanding of their roles—betrays gendered counterinsurgency as being highly integrated into the most violent facets of military combat. Female counterinsurgency teams facilitated violent home raids with one hand and distributed soccer balls to orphanages with the other. The forms of racial evolutionism at work within military trainings prefigure the violence of war's displacement, death, and destruction. Specific to Muscatatuck, the multiple dimensions of training that occurred before the final field exercise insert the banality of PowerPoint into our definition of violence. The numbing effect of how much of this material was delivered in military classrooms is just as significant a component of military violence as the visceral shock of hearing a weapon fired. Rather than a boundary between more and less violent aspects of counterinsurgency, military trainings capture a spectrum of violence that includes the subtle work of PowerPoint in an airless temporary classroom alongside errant bombs. I am not arguing for a flattening of these distinct forms of violence as all the same or, worse yet, reflections of a singular monolithic imperialism. Instead, I am interested in their particularity and how they stand in relation to one another. Examining counterinsurgency's production through these trainings reveals how the various forms of violence on this spectrum *enable one another* and cannot be cleanly separated into more or less violent categorizations.

Back inside one of these portable classrooms, the head of security for the team about to enter the village simulation gave a briefing. He drew arrows on a whiteboard to indicate the formation the team would take walking into the village, then discussed how the valuable Afghan translator would walk next to the commanding officer. The commanding officer instructed me to walk next to him and his translator, both of whom were between two parallel lines of security force soldiers—an inner cordon and an outer cordon—with other civilian contractors and PRT staff.

The head of security concluded by instructing everyone to move to their positions at the end of the journey on foot. Another member of the team prompted a brief discussion on how they needed to get the Afghans to "take ownership." He coached the team to "stress that it's *your* project. Our role in the PRT is just to facilitate it."

The team came back to this theme of ownership many times throughout the day. After the simulation, the commanding officer returned to the ownership question through the analogy of how a person treats a rental car versus their own car, "even if it's a Yugo," because you saved your money for it and purchased it yourself. The conversation recalled the proud parents concept from earlier in the training, with soldiers framed here bestowing upon Afghans a sense of personal responsibility for the PRT-funded project. Getting Afghans to "take ownership" carried the racial evolutionism that painted the occupied population as deficient in ways that required the occupation's oversight. Extending these imperial and parental lessons, the security head also elaborated counterinsurgency doctrine's emphasis on making small talk with villagers. Another officer encouraged the team to "find common ground, talk to them like you would talk to your buddy," suggesting they ask how many family members the villagers have or compare the crops they see growing to those from their home state.

We exited the forward operating base and walked across a berm separating the base from a large grassy field where the village simulation was set up. Large green army tents had been assembled into a cluster to simulate an Afghan village. A role player posed in the middle of the field with a hoe over his shoulder, acting as an Afghan farmer, and two men stood behind a folding table on which they had spread out an assortment of light bulbs, candies, and other small trinkets to simulate the bazaar. Several hundred feet away, three women were crocheting under an army tent. This simulation was part of a network of theater immersion simulations, the pinnacle of which is in California's Mojave Desert at the National Training Center. Used in the 1980s to simulate tank warfare with mock Soviet armies and in the 1990s to simulate the Republican National Guard complete with chemical weapons, the post-9/11 National Training Center housed a dozen working villages populated with Iraqi and Afghan role players going about quotidian tasks such as selling wares and socializing. In 2009, Iraqi role players were contract workers paid twenty dollars per hour with no health insurance or other benefits. They lived in the simulated villages for seventeen days out of each month, sleeping in shipping containers, using portable latrines, and busing back to the garrison to shower every three days.[43]

The simulated village at Camp Atterbury was decidedly less elaborate than those staged at the National Training Center. It did represent, however, the broader turn toward theater immersion simulations employing role players and

FIGURE 7. District Stability Framework training, US army base. Author photo.

sets dressed with certain elements of Iraqi or Afghan culture (figure 7). This particular simulation was typical of those housed on multipurposed military bases where a portion of the base was dedicated to simulation, in contrast to the National Training Center's permanent installation of mock villages and commitment to mimesis.

The commanding officer passed by the simulated bazaar, and his team approached another larger green tent outside of which two role players acting as the village elder's security force questioned the commander. Meanwhile, the security force fanned out to form a perimeter, leaving the commander of the PRT, his second-in-command, his interpreter, the rest of his staff, and observers such as me behind. The role players invited the commander and his team into the tent. More members of the security force established positions in each corner of the tent. The commander confirmed with the village elder that he could take off his vest and helmet. The rest of his team followed suit, removing various pieces of equipment and piling their vests and helmets in the corner.

Huddled near the pile of body armor, the commander introduced himself to the elder as being from the PRT and asked the elder about his health in an attempt to establish rapport. Another soldier introduced himself as an engineer, and the elder enthusiastically commented that "all of our problems are with engineering." The group—about a dozen soldiers and four Afghan role players—then moved to the back of the tent, and everyone sat cross-legged in a circle. Dave,

FIGURE 8.   Provincial Reconstruction Team training, US army base.
Author photo.

Nancy, several other DSF contractors, and I sat on the edge of the circle and listened to the conversation. Members of the security force stood at posts around
the tent. Another group of soldiers, who were out of play, observed the exercise
while kneeling on one knee in a straight line outside of the circle.

A beige army blanket had been laid out to simulate a rug, around which the
staff of the PRT and the role players sat cross-legged on the ground (figure 8). The
four Afghan role players were variously dressed in full camouflage, a track jacket
and khakis, a salwar kameez, and a camouflage vest over a salwar kameez. The
military staff sitting around the circle included the security captain, the civil affairs team captain, a senior medical officer, an engineer, a public affairs officer, and
an executive officer, in addition to the translator and the commander. The role
players began the meeting with a reading from the Koran and a short prayer. The
military personnel clasped their hands together and looked down at the ground
during the prayer.

The Afghan role players passed around a bowl of mints to simulate hospitality.
The host apologized that his house was very poor and there was no place to sit
but the floor. The commander thanked him for his hospitality and asked how
long the elder had lived in the village. The conversation lasted about an hour, with
the commander following a survey from the contractors to determine the village's "SOI." The role players complained that they had held this meeting before;
multiple PRTs had come through the village and made promises they did not keep.

The conversation kept returning to the lack of agricultural opportunity in the area because of irrigation problems. The soldiers planned to come back the following day to inspect the village's canals, which the role players explained had been destroyed by multiple rounds of bombings. The commander concluded the meeting, and his executive officer instructed everyone to "jock up," or put their gear back on.

While the high-ranking officers were discussing irrigation in the elder's tent, the security force had fanned out into the village. Back in the classroom, the students were given a pocket-size laminated card specifically designed to fit in the side cargo pocket of a military uniform. The card contained the four questions from the Tactical Conflict Survey they had learned in the classroom portion of the course. The top of the card had a blank space next to "ethnicity/tribe" and a box to check for either "fighting age" or "old (gray hair)," then the four questions followed about the village's population, problems, leadership, and priorities. Contractors emphasized the centrality of the survey back in the classroom, since many of the other DSF matrices depended on information gleaned from the survey. They reminded the students of David Petraeus's adage—"the people are the center of gravity"—while conducting the survey.[44]

Trainers encouraged the team to assign their security force the Tactical Conflict Survey, since security would fan out into the village while officers conducted key leader engagements inside the tent. However, the security force's training positioned them to take an aggressive stance as they formed a perimeter around the meeting. Some of the security force walked around with their guns drawn, while others lay down in a prone position looking at the role players through their rifle scopes. The role players mocked the security force, mimicking their stance and pretending to look through a gunsight. Some soldiers ignored the part of their mission to conduct the survey, while others aggressively approached role players and asked harshly "Who's unemployed? We want to employ them." Role players would walk away from these aggressive soldiers or make the situation into a joke by offering them flowers or mocking their aggressive stance.

All of the military personnel walked back in formation to the dining facility to complete an after-action report. The staff who had conducted the meeting in the tent talked about how they could have been better at taking off their sunglasses and gloves to appear more at ease. The second officer in command reminded the rest of the team to wear their amber-colored sunglasses in situations such as this so that Afghans could see their eyes. "If you look like you are at home," he explained, "they're going to be more comfortable. Single people do this at bars, and you did it when you were trying to get your parents to let you go to the mall. It's commonsense conversation, but we lose it a lot in this line of work." The same officer also reflected on the importance of making small talk with the local population, urging them to ask about such topics as the kind of tea villagers were drinking or some part of the landscape. He emphasized asking questions in a way that did not feel like interrogation.

Across the cafeteria, the security force was having a different conversation. The head of security addressed the aspect of their mission that involved the survey and engaging local populations, encouraging them to ask questions that would supply additional information. He gave examples such as "is there something we can do to help them help themselves?" or "what was the system like before you had Americans here to rely on?" Another member of the team addressed going on this mission with a security objective: "You've got to look like you're ready for a fight. Aggressive. Ready to go." The contradiction of being "an NGO with guns" was especially apparent here. Contractors had asked a group of military personnel to conduct development at the same time as their superiors instructed them to be aggressive. This tension played out in the village simulation, where the security force interacted aggressively with the role players in line with their previous training and current mission to ensure their team's physical security but totally at odds with the development contractors' objectives.

In the cafeteria, the commanding officer talked about how he might eventually fund the requested irrigation project, but he would not want the village elder to know where the funding had come from and spoke of masking it to look like it came from the provincial government. He explained his thinking in terms of the proud parents concept, which kept resurfacing at various points in the training. The commanding officer explained that "we've been there nine years. We're not going to be there too much longer. They [the Afghans] need to start learning how to do it for themselves." This vision of Afghans as children in need of parental instruction pervaded the training.

DSF trainers came into the simulation offering expert technical solutions to the contradiction of asking soldiers to perform "armed social work." In the classroom, the framework's rigid and technical structure created conflict about how it could be implemented during a military deployment. Soldiers and marines also took issue with its emphasis on civilian interaction over weapons and force, a key counterinsurgency tenet. Frictions sparked over military definitions of masculinity through combat, in contrast to feminization of the civilian-focused aspects of counterinsurgency. Tensions also became apparent between different elements of soldiers' training. In the simulation, soldiers accentuated their critiques of the material as they found components of the DSF, such as the Tactical Conflict Survey, to conflict with other parts of their training and mission.

The simulation also provided a window into how the canals the military team considered building were not nearly as significant an effect of the training as the shifting notions of race and gender within the DSF. As was apparent in Sean's reception, soldiers shaped their critiques through a gendered lens that ultimately reinforced conventional associations of combat with masculinity. DSF trainings provide a window into a faltering imperial hegemony. Contractors embodied counterinsurgency doctrine's "softer," feminized approach to fighting war. Yet soldiers rejected their expert discourse. Instead of accomplishing the transformation of soldiers into "armed social workers," DSF trainings solidified a racial evolutionary framework that imagines Afghans as children in need of US military guardianship until they reach maturity for independence. This framework revives imperial histories such as T. E. Lawrence and introduces newly essentialized notions of Afghan culture. Falling within a spectrum of military violence, PowerPoint-heavy trainings shore up racial and civilizational narratives of Afghanistan that enable bombings, home raids, and the more overt violence of war.

COLONIAL "LESSONS LEARNED"

The Contemporary Soldier Becomes the
Historical Colonizer

As my observations of instruction on the District Stability Framework (DSF) opened into more expansive military-only settings, I attended a Marine Corps brigade combat team's counterinsurgency predeployment training at Camp Pendleton, a large base in southern California. The unit on counterinsurgency was one week long, with the DSF comprising the last half. The training broke counterinsurgency instruction into lessons such as "insurgency and counterinsurgency theory," "traditional village meetings," and "Afghan tribal structure," before moving to the framework's core components. During a break between one of these sections, I spoke with a group of marines who had been sent from their home base to observe and provide insight into this training. We often sat near one another in the section of chairs reserved for contractors, subject matter experts such as the visiting marines, and miscellaneous observers such as myself.

The marines were civil affairs specialists. As we sat together each day, I asked them what civil affairs was and what their jobs entailed, how they understood counterinsurgency, and their perspective on the DSF. Eventually, they suggested that I might as well come see for myself what civil affairs was all about by observing the qualification course they taught at the Marine Corps base and headquarters at Quantico, Virginia. Later that year, I spent five weeks sitting in the back of the classroom of the Marine Corps civil affairs qualification course. I took notes in class alongside other marines, dined with students between classes, and participated in extracurricular outings with marines from the class, such as historical tours of old barracks in the area, visits to military museums and monuments, and watching evening parades celebrating the Marine Corps. For the first four weeks of the course, I stayed in a combination of hotel and sublet rooms outside of the base, and during the last week I slept in the sparsely populated women's barracks for the final field exercise.

Historically, the job of civil affairs troops was to clear civilians from the battle space and offer them compensation for property and life lost as a result of military intervention.[1] Civil affairs was mainly located in the army, with only a small number of reservists in the Marine Corps. Counterinsurgency's post-9/11 revival required military personnel to expand the scale and nature of their engagement with civilians. Civil affairs personnel led emblematic counterinsurgency tasks such as meeting with Afghan village elders, along with more persistent military humanitarian tasks such as responding to a humanitarian emergency or rebuilding infrastructure destroyed by combat.[2] Given this expanding role of civil affairs, the Marine Corps established an active-duty civil affairs group during the wars in Iraq and Afghanistan. To fill these civil affairs billets, some marines were reassigned from specializations such as infantry and artillery, no longer required in such large numbers, to civil affairs. Like the marine on the balcony who lamented that since he was seventeen he had been "kicking in doors and blowing up stuff," marines' resentment toward their reassignment was palpable in snide remarks during breaks; ironic comments about the position of being responsible for, in one student's words, "killing and caring"; and more substantive critiques of course material.

In direct reaction to students who rejected the civil affairs material on the grounds that they were "programmed to shoot," instructors used a variety of historical material as proof that civil affairs had always been a significant part of Marine Corps history. As my research took me to other sites of military instruction, including war colleges populated by officers and counterinsurgency predeployment trainings for enlisted soldiers and marines, a wider phenomenon was apparent that history played a very active role in present-day military instruction. In this chapter, I examine three moments of historical reference in three distinct military trainings to follow how history is used to produce post-9/11 counterinsurgency knowledge. Instructors' historical lessons present starting points at three training sites: the Marine Corps civil affairs classroom, an officer-level war college classroom, and a Marine Corps counterinsurgency training. Each of these nodes opens into greater historical detail of the places, events, and figures driving military knowledge production.

The Marine Corps civil affairs classroom takes us to early twentieth-century US occupations of the Philippines, Haiti, the Dominican Republic, and Nicaragua, all of which inform the 1940 *Small Wars Manual*. A second classroom of officers being trained in counterinsurgency at a war college takes us to mid-twentieth-century British and US imperial wars in Malaya and Vietnam, and a third classroom of combat marines receiving counterinsurgency training takes us to mid-twentieth-century French colonial Algeria. Military instructors reference these histories in relation to today's wars, just as Cold War defense intellectuals referenced early twentieth-century imperial wars. For example, when RAND convened a symposium on counterinsurgency in 1962 with an eye to strategy in Vietnam, participants included counterinsurgents who had fought in earlier twentieth-century contexts of Malaya, Algeria, the Philippines, Kenya, and China. The symposium was republished in 2006 to inform counterinsurgency strategy in Iraq.[3]

Although successive colonial counterinsurgencies provide historical reference for post-9/11 military knowledge production, key historical details are excised from military classroom lessons and documents such as the *Small Wars Manual* in favor of abstract tactics that, modern instructors argue, can travel to any time and place. Haiti, for instance, is a crucial site where small wars doctrine has been produced in the Marine Corps, but when lessons learned in Haiti are codified in the *Small Wars Manual*, the location of Haiti is erased. Uncovering the history animating military doctrine clarifies the violence behind lessons that appear quite abstract in such military texts. Another effect of history's role in military doctrine and classrooms is military instructors' implicit adoption of colonial administrators' perspectives. In military classrooms, this often leads to lectures focused on which tactics were most favorable to the colonial power. Implicit in this analysis is the idea that although the colonial power may have lost the war that the historical example comes from, its tactics still provide valuable lessons for today's conflicts. That argument was especially apparent in the use of Vietnam as an example rife with successful tactics that should be revived. Instructors erased any mention of the population subjected to colonial rule, let alone the tactics' consequences to local lives. Finally, through analysis of Walt Rostow's influence on intertwined US military and development policy in Vietnam, a dense node of connections becomes clear between academic, private, and military institutions that gave rise to the development industry during the Cold War, only to find contemporary resurgence.

Early Twentieth-Century Occupations: Haiti and the *Small Wars Manual*

On the first day of the Marine Corps civil affairs course, Maj. Frank Taylor, one of the staff instructors, towered in front of the class as he shoved a wad of chewing tobacco behind the left side of his lower lip: "Alright," he said as he held up a thick green paperback book, "the *Small Wars Manual*. If you have not read it, read it. It was written back in the 1900s, and it still has relevance today. Trust me. If you get a chance, read it. For those of you who have long flights to Seoul or Japan, take a copy with you and read it." Taylor then gave an overview of the course, preparing the fifty marines in the room for what they would learn over the next five weeks. To introduce civil affairs, Taylor compared the post-9/11 conflicts the United States was embroiled in overseas to the "bad old days" of the Cold War and World War II–era "tank on tank" warfare. His PowerPoint slide read "The difference was, back in the 'bad old days,' we were doing a lot less CMO [civil-military operations] and a lot more fighting. The good news today is we're doing a lot more CMO and almost no fighting." The instructor explained that the "bad old days" the quote refers to were "the Cold War, right? Tank on tank. World War I. Right. Now we have this thing called COIN, [counter]insurgency. CA [civil affairs], CMO plays a larger role in it." He flashed a slide with pictures of the doctrinal publications supporting his point that "stability ops is really the new buzzword now." The slide included joint army and Marine Corps publications on civil-military operations and civil affairs as well as *The US Army Stability Operations Field Manual* and the *Counterinsurgency Field Manual*.[4] Taylor discussed how "this modern complex operating environment means that the Marine Corps must plan and conduct operations using a nonkinetic approach, especially when conducting counterinsurgency operations. . . . Instead of focusing on the force-on-force aspect of operations, which is the Marine Corps' strength, units have been forced by circumstances to adopt a 'softer' way of combating the enemy, focusing on the so-called human terrain of a tribe or ethnic group instead of key terrain such as a hilltop or commanding position."[5]

Taylor asked the class what marine expeditionary units typically got involved with when they weren't in Afghanistan or Iraq. The class muttered together, "humanitarianism," to which the instructor nodded and elaborated that the 2010 earthquake in Haiti was a classic example and that "those [humanitarian responses] are never going to go away. Guess who's going to be the resident experts when those go down?" he asked and nodded toward the class. "So, from a career perspective, you guys are going to have a job. Earthquakes are going to happen. Floods are going to happen. Tsunamis are going to happen. You're going to be involved. The MEUs [Marine expeditionary units] are going to be the 9-1-1 force. The first on the scene." Taylor emphasized that the class needed to be ready to deploy on humanitarian missions "anywhere in the world," not just to the war in Afghanistan. He continually referred to Haiti as an example of the political and environmental disasters that civil affairs marines responded to.

Taylor continued: "03s [the military occupational specialty code for infantry], which is what I am, know how to shoot things and break things. It's what we've been trained to do since TBS [basic training]." He was responding to the senti-ment in the classroom that, as one student previously put it, "I've been pro-grammed to shoot." During breaks between classes, students would regularly discuss how their previous trainings conflicted with their new training in civil affairs. To alleviate this tension, students and instructors alike used humor to mediate their skepticism. For example, another instructor joked to the class that when he first heard of the civil affairs military occupational specialty, he thought to himself, "first you want me to kill them, now you want me to fucking take care of them?! Make up your fucking mind!" His comment focused on the job of man-aging the civilian populace. It also responded to a similar critique students lodged at counterinsurgency's emphasis on establishing rapport with local populations and minimizing civilian casualties, both of which could conflict with the "force protection" mandate of protecting one's own troops. Instructors also used humor to respond to students' antagonism toward the course's "nonkinetic" approach.

In addition to using humor, instructors emphasized civil affairs' complexity to convince students of the course material's value. Taylor, who had described him-self as trained in shooting and breaking things, said, "This. This CA, this CMO thing," gesturing toward the screen projecting his PowerPoint slides, "it's hard. It's what I refer to as three-dimensional chess. . . . There's not going to be immediate impact." Taylor continued, as he and his colleagues often did, to compare the ma-terial he was teaching to kinetic military tactics, such as firing a weapon. "If I put a round down range and I hit the target, I get immediate feedback. But not with CMO. We're going to talk about building schools, we're going to talk about dig-ging wells—whether that's the appropriate thing to do. This is a thinking man's, a thinking lady's game," echoing military promotions of counterinsurgency as the "graduate level of war."[6]

Taylor scrolled through various slides describing different components of civil affairs. Instructors emphasized the complexity of the job but also historical pre-cedent. "We've been doing CMO since the beginning of the Marine Corps," he read from a slide, listing off Nicaragua, Haiti, and the Dominican Republic, re-ferring to the early twentieth century, as well as the Vietnam War; Kosovo, Bos-nia, and Somalia in the 1990s; Iraq and Afghanistan today; and Haiti again after the 2010 earthquake. He lingered on the example of Haiti because several mem-bers of the class had been deployed in the earthquake response and again very recently on a medical outreach and training mission.

Taylor projected a slide onto the wall behind him that contained a picture of the *Small Wars Manual* overlain by an old black-and-white photograph of two marines and two Latin American members of a local military, along with re-cent color photographs of marines interacting with women and children in an unidentified African country and an unidentified Asian country. The slide read

"The Marine Corps has been engaged in CMO since the beginning, providing stability and security, raising the overall standard of living in areas of war and conflict. . . . The Corps protected American citizens and business interests by intervening in the Dominican Republic (1916–1924), Haiti (1915–1934), and Nicaragua (1912–1933). In addition to providing stability and security during these 'Small Wars,' Marines developed CA doctrine 'on the fly' as they built roads and schools, taught local citizens how to become civil servants, and raised the overall standard of living of these countries."

In response to students' reticence to transform themselves into "armed social workers," instructors called upon colonial history to serve as a positive example of the nonkinetic work the Marine Corps had always done. The argument was historical but also geographical, as instructors reminded students of the necessity to be prepared for places that were not Iraq or Afghanistan. "We're here to teach you CMO, but not just for Afghanistan," Brooks, another instructor, explained. "We're here to teach you to go anywhere in the world, for any type of mission; you could be in Haiti, in Panama, anywhere in the freakin' world." Taylor's geography of going "anywhere in the freakin' world" was also an identity claim that marines are defined by their seamless circulation between locales, from Iraq to Panama, and that this circulation included "stabilization" as much as it did traditional battles.

Instructors actively drew upon history in military trainings as evidence that the work of interacting with civilians, managing local police forces, running elections, and building infrastructure has always been a significant aspect of military intervention. Such uses of history were part of the identity claims Taylor and his colleagues made, that true marines had always been defined by their participation in stabilization work and their travels between the far-flung, often forgotten sites of US imperial interventions, such as early twentieth-century Central America and the Caribbean. Students in the course were invited to imagine themselves through such identity claims—as "true marines" who do the work of civil affairs because this is what marines have always done, and now this is who they are too.

Instructors used history to defend their identity claims, reacting to students who resisted reassignment to civil affairs. Given that so much of small wars history takes place within the Marine Corps, history presented an especially powerful antidote to marine trainees' resistance. Likewise, many of the key figures available to instructors through biographies and popular military lore—such as Chesty Puller and Smedley Butler, who exemplify the sorts of lessons instructors wanted to legitimize—were themselves marines.[7] Much of the history used in training contexts came from the early twentieth-century occupations of the Philippines and Caribbean and Central American countries such as Nicaragua, Haiti, and the Dominican Republic.

After showing a series of films set during the Vietnam War, nineteenth-century US westward expansion, and early twentieth-century British occupation of Africa, Taylor proclaimed to the class,

> The point I'm trying to make, marines, is this. These events that are being depicted in the film over a hundred years ago—so, what we're seeing is one hundred years later, here we are, Westerners again. We're not the British in our shiny red uniforms but Westerners in a foreign land, a Muslim land, and we're doing these same things. So these currents of strategy—we can go back and see how people have dealt with them in the past. This stuff is timeless. It doesn't go out of style. So events that are occurring in the video are the same events that are occurring when you're over there in Afghanistan or wherever you may go around the world.

This early twentieth-century history also informed many of the lessons in the *Small Wars Manual*, which formed the basis of the 2006 *Counterinsurgency Field Manual*. After his colleague, Brooks, finished his component of the lesson, Taylor jumped in to explain that he was using historical texts because "we keep going back to history, marines, because this stuff doesn't really change." Brooks continued: "OK, marines. Now, we've talked about Sun Zi, and how things don't change. . . . Everything that comes out of this class is going to come directly from this text," holding up the *Small Wars Manual*. Brooks asked how many marines had read the manual and if anyone could comment on it. When few hands went up he said, "If you're going forward, have this text with you. If you are going to conduct any sort of small wars operation, you need to have this." Taylor concluded with a story from his deployment to Iraq in 2004:

> We had just finished clearing the city [Fallujah]. We had been through the assault phase. We were now in the rebuilding phase. And the battalion commander has us all sitting down and he was telling us, "Now we're being tasked with conducting elections." And he was very upset about that. He was like, "It's not a Marine Corps task; the State Department should be doing it. We don't do this." And I leaned over to my team leader and I said, "Sir, *Small Wars Manual*." And he raised his hand and said, "Sir! Uh, it's in the *Small Wars Manual*." The battalion commander was really impressed—he didn't know that. . . . So with the *Small Wars Manual*, we figured out how to conduct elections. So anything you're looking for, you're probably going to find it here. Again, everything we say in this class is going to come directly from our *Small Wars Manual*.

Taylor drew attention to how in 2004 his superiors, unaware of historical precedent, were resistant to civil affairs tasks. The *Small Wars Manual* provided historical examples that validated marines running an election. That historical text born out of early twentieth-century US imperialism formed the basis of the civil affairs curriculum. The Marine Corps drafted the first edition of the *Small Wars Manual* in the 1930s, using material from occupations of the Philippines, Central America, and the Caribbean in the early part of the twentieth century as well as a British colonial handbook on imperial policing.[8] Laleh Khalili notes the 1940 manual's resurrection in the context of Latin American counterinsurgencies in the 1980s, "providing a thread that connected the Indian Wars of the nineteenth century to US asymmetric warfare in the twentieth."[9] At the time of the first US occupation of Haiti in the early twentieth century, prevailing small wars doctrine came from British military strategist C. E. Callwell, who believed that "only punitive methods designed to inflict casualties and economic harm" were effective when dealing with the "lower races."[10] However, US press coverage of the marines' brutal suppression of the 1919 Haitian rebellion and the associated Senate investigation caused the Marine Corps to depart from Callwell and emphasize "a minimum loss of life and property and by methods that leave no aftermath of bitterness or render the return to peace unnecessarily difficult." Taken from lessons learned in Haiti, this exact line appears in the 1935 *Small Wars Operations*, the basis of the 1940 *Small Wars Manual*.[11]

The final edition of the *Small Wars Manual* was published in 1940, just before US troops entered World War II. Although the Marine Corps reprinted the *Small Wars Manual* while it fought counterinsurgencies in Latin America in the 1980s and integrated it into curricula during 1990s interventions in Iraq, Somalia, Kosovo, Bosnia, and Rwanda, the manual was largely forgotten until a team of writers convened to produce the 2006 *Counterinsurgency Field Manual*. The counterinsurgency manual's authors revisited the US history of small wars as well as histories from British colonial Malaya to Greek suppression of communist insurgency in the 1940s and to French colonial Algeria.[12] Although these histories directly informed military doctrine, one striking characteristic of the *Small Wars Manual* is the absence of specific places and historical events. Rather, the manual abstracts history into tactics, erasing specific times and places that produced those tactics.

The abstraction of place is symptomatic of a military definition of politics at work in the classrooms I observed, where civilians are in charge of the political domain and military identity takes shape through its separation from politics. "Politics" is where the win/loss column of various wars is decided, and this is not the military's concern. In the context of not having won a war in some time in the sense that victory was celebrated in World War II, the rhetoric of winning and losing has disappeared from military trainings. The military's job is to find tactics useful to its role of carrying out orders from the civilian domain. In place of winning and losing enters the much more nebulous and less quantifi-able goal of stabilization, without a clear beginning or end. This military defini-tion of politics informs the treatment of history as neutral material from which to freely extract tactics, even if they came from a conflict, such as Vietnam, widely regarded as a national disgrace.

One of the most influential sections of the 1940 manual is its lengthy section on psychology, which is framed by the difference between regular and small wars, with small wars requiring the study of psychology. Like the concepts of government and civilization, psychology is highly racialized, mapping "racial and social characteristics" to particular approaches for interaction.[13] The section mentions a nameless indigenous population, treating knowledge of the interi-ority of the "native" mind as part of military strategy. Psychology also refers to the mind of US troops. The manual argues that in contrast to conventional war-fare, in which "hatred of the enemy is developed among troops to arouse cour-age," small wars rely on "tolerance, sympathy, and kindness" toward the population.[14] The very same paragraph notes, however, that "there is nothing in this principle which should make any officer or man hesitate to act with the nec-essary firmness . . . whenever there is contact with armed opposition."[15] Taylor and Brooks echoed this tension between sympathy toward the population and preparedness to enact lethal force.

True to the instructor's words that "everything we're going to learn in this course comes from the *Small Wars Manual*," the civil affairs course mirrored the manual's sections on psychology and "attitude and bearing." While giving a lesson on the civil affairs motto, Brooks used the catchphrase "be polite, be professional, be pre-pared to kill," echoing the manual that troops must be psychologically prepared to fight with tolerance, sympathy, and kindness even as they are prepared to kill.[16] Instructors used history as evidence that being polite had always worked in tandem with being prepared to kill. This evidence was important in the context of how ma-rine students received the three parts of this motto. Watching a student in the front row spin a water bottle on the table with a bored look on his face during this sec-tion of the class, Brooks joked, "Hey, I see you there, spinning that bottle, going 'bullshit,'" to which the classroom erupted in laughter, "but," Brooks continued in a more serious tone, "we're gonna get you there." He then told a story about teaching this class on another base. Brooks crossed his arms over his chest and leaned back, glaring down his nose to demonstrate the stance of the marines in this class who wanted nothing to do with the civilian focus. "Down there I asked a devil dog, I asked a young lance corporal to read this slide," referring to the one he used on this day with the civil affairs motto. "You know what he said? 'Be prepared to kill,'" leav-ing out the first two parts of the motto on politeness and professionalism. "He didn't even see the first two bullets!" Brooks exclaimed to hearty laughter.

The instructors called on famous historical marines such as Mike Edson, Chesty Puller, and Smedley Butler in response to students' dubiousness. Here the instructors harnessed marines' own understandings of themselves as occupying a place within a lineage of imperial masculinity. Yet instructors also emphasized the centrality of stabilization work to this lineage. Butler and Puller were formed through their deployments to Haiti during the same early twentieth-century period as Edson's deployment to Nicaragua. The production of the 1940 *Small Wars Manual* can be traced back to the early 1930s, when Harold Utley, a Marine Corps major, established a small wars curriculum at the Marine Corps headquarters at Quantico. Utley was advised by Merritt "Red Mike" Edson, a marine who led patrols up Nicaragua's Río Coco from 1928 to 1929.[17] Edson delivered a series of lectures based on his Río Coco patrols at the Marine Corps Basic School in Philadelphia. Based on Edson's lectures and recollections and letters shared personally with Utley, Utley codified the Río Coco patrols into a series of articles in the *Marine Corps Gazette* in 1931 and 1933. Through this circuitry of military knowledge production, Edson's patrols in Nicaragua became a template for the 1940 *Small Wars Manual* and informed the 2006 *Counterinsurgency Field Manual*.[18] The nine hundred–page predecessor to the *Small Wars Manual* (1940), *Small Wars Operations* (1935), included Edson's lessons alongside older classic writings on small wars such as Callwell's.

Through this colonial geography, the 1935 document codifies US military small wars doctrine for the first time. It also defines, for the first time in US military doctrine, the term "small war," emphasizing its "political" nature that combines diplomatic with military power. Policing and devolving responsibility to "native forces" are also key aspects of this early rendition of small wars doctrine.[19] Much of the 1935 manual's length comes from its extensive appendices that support doctrinal lessons through reference to historical instances of small wars. The first chapter, for example, examines historical examples of Marine Corps invasions to protect US property, persons, and interests (including basing interests) and presents excerpts from military proclamations during periods of Marine Corps occupations in Haiti (1915), the Dominican Republic (1916), and Nicaragua (1926).[20] These lengthy historical appendices disappear in the 1940 manual, erasing the early twentieth-century historical geographies of US intervention that inform its lessons.

In Utley's series of articles that prefigure the *Small Wars Manual*, Haiti receives as much attention as Nicaragua if not more. Utley writes of the atrocities committed in 1920 during the antioccupation uprisings. After describing the machine-gunning of a hillside populated by peasants in the north of Haiti, Utley writes, "But that particular moment was not one in which to lay ourselves open to the charge of bombing 'innocent' inhabitants, no matter how justified the act might be under the Rules of War."[21] Directly acknowledging public outcry over Marine Corps atrocities in Haiti, Utley wished to prove a larger point that "measures justifiable in a regular war [killing civilians], tactically sound, and probably the most efficient available, must frequently be eliminated from the plan of campaign as not being in accord with public policy in the existing situation." In the second part of this series, Utley uses examples from campaigns in both Haiti and Nicaragua, in which patrols became lost, as evidence of the need for better maps as well as the sort of "cultural knowledge" that the *Counterinsurgency Field Manual* emphasizes.[22]

The brutality of, for instance, machine-gunning civilians did not disappear from counterinsurgency in practice.[23] The gulf between rhetoric and reality only becomes more apparent as we examine how these lessons learned translated into practice during the American war in Vietnam. Acknowledging this gulf, I wish to emphasize how Haiti is central to the geography of military learning about how counterinsurgency can weaponize development and humanitarianism. Haiti's closely intertwined history with the United States makes it a key reference point in the identity work within civil affairs military classrooms, where marines are asked to step into the "armed social worker" role that instructors claim has long defined them. Particularly in the Marine Corps, which has composed much of the response force to the multiple US military interventions there during the twentieth century, Haiti is a common reference point when instructors come up with examples of small wars interventions or humanitarian response. The US Marine Corps occupation of Haiti from 1915 to 1934 is a key event in the history of development as a counterinsurgency weapon. Following the same 1919 peasant uprising Utley mentions, US military strategy in Haiti began to incorporate public health and education.[24] One element of this revisionist strategy of rule was an education program that offered Haitian students training in agricultural and vocational fields. Contrary to the program's intent to suppress protest, it fomented a student uprising that grew so large that it prefigured the end of the US occupation. A change in student scholarships originally sparked the uprising, but outrage at colonial officials' racism and the occupation's emphasis on plantation agriculture fueled a national uprising.[25]

Historian Frederick Cooper has made a related point that French and British governments in the 1940s attempted to use development to win consent of colonial subjects following a series of strikes in the African and Caribbean colonies in the 1930s and 1940s.[26] For Cooper, development's origin story is located in a history of colonial counterinsurgency, where development emerged as a mechanism to control and retain the colonies in the face of anticolonial rebellion. At the same time, the language of universal rights became available through development's implementation in the colonies to trade unionists and political leaders who could now use this language to make claims intelligible in London and Paris. In Haiti as in the cases Cooper examines, development was intended to strengthen the bonds of foreign occupation, but in practice it provided the tools for its dismantling. In inserting Haiti into this origin story, I move the periodization of militarized development back to the 1920s, pointing to the early twentieth century's colonial small wars as essential to understanding the history of militarized development.

A more expansive geography of US intervention in the early twentieth century certainly informs the historical material that went into the civil affairs course. Instructors also referred to the Philippines as well as the broader geography of intervention in Central America and the Caribbean. But Haiti's role in the production of small wars doctrine, tactics, and training is especially significant for several reasons. First, the early twentieth-century history of development's role during the late occupation years is central to the sort of understanding Cooper provides of development as growing out of colonial counterinsurgency. Yet Haiti is largely missing from the historiography in this area. This absence continues a long-standing erasure of Haitian history.[27] In the face of such historiographical erasure, it is especially notable that Haiti plays a significant role in military trainings such as the Marine Corps civil affairs course. The multiple layers of US intervention in Haiti provide context for significant military attention to the country as a historical case study. Haiti punctuates the history of small wars and stabilization right through to its use in a military classroom in 2012 as exemplary civil affairs work. Instructors frequently used Haiti to demonstrate the "sort of place" where civil affairs marines could be deployed. Haiti was present through a group of reservists in the course who had recently spent several weeks there on a medical humanitarian mission. One of the instructors had also deployed on a similar medical mission to Haiti several years before, and others had responded to the 2010 earthquake. These multiple threads of interconnection signal the ongoing ties that bind Haiti to the United States, some of them sewn in the early twentieth-century occupation period.

As the only nation born from a revolt by enslaved Black people, the Haitian Revolution is a powerful symbol of antiracist, anticolonial liberation.[28] The country's position as a Black republic of self-liberated formerly enslaved people at a time when transatlantic slavery fueled the global economy meant that it bore the entire racist weight of slaveholding imperial powers. France refused to recognize the nation's independence until Jean-Pierre Boyer, one of Haiti's early presidents, agreed in 1825 to honor the indemnity that the French leveled to repay the former colonizers for the life and property lost in the revolution. The United States refused to diplomatically recognize Haiti until the dying gasps of slavery in its own territory in 1862. This history of Western powers ostracizing the island nation produced the image of racialized deprivation most service members had been exposed to in news segments that so frequently refer to the country as "the poorest nation in the Western Hemisphere." Closer still to marines' experience is how racial attitudes in the United States informed those of the marines during the early twentieth-century occupation.[29] Haiti's history of race and empire is woven into the fabric of military instructors' identity claims and construction of various tactics. At the same time, the actual place of Haiti— and with it much of this history of race, slavery, and imperialism—is transformed into an abstract space in military classrooms.

As in Gregory's discussion of how military performances of space reduce opponents to "objects in a purely visual field," Haiti becomes "Haiti," a placeholder for whatever "heart of darkness" the marines are summoned to where they will manage their "new-caught sullen peoples, half devil and half child."[30] The civil affairs training emphasized the interchangeability of tactics from place to place and time period to time period. In an entry in the *Small Wars Journal*, "Lessons from a Military Humanitarian in Port au Prince," a Haiti earthquake responder and field artillery officer enumerated military capabilities that, he argued, were interchangeable between counterinsurgency and foreign disaster relief. "Foreign Disaster Relief (FDR) is counter-insurgency (COIN)," the author argues, "only no one is shooting at you (yet)."[31] This argument about the interchangeability of tactics from Haiti to Afghanistan, from humanitarian response to counterinsurgency, was reflected in the civil affairs course. Recall the instructor's warning to the class: "We're here to teach you to go anywhere in the world, for any type of mission." Such interchangeability relies on an imaginative geography that erases differences between places and links large parts of the globe through a colonial vision of savagery.[32] Imperial subjects from Haiti to Afghanistan are grouped together through their poverty as well as their classification as racial Others. This homogenization allows military instructors to make claims for the smooth military geography that accommodates an abstract set of tactics "anywhere in the world."

Learning Counterinsurgency: Vietnam and Malaya

At the highest echelon of military training is the network of five war colleges operated by the US Army, the US Air Force, the US Navy, the US Marine Corps, and the Pentagon (the latter through the National Defense University). Students at these schools are mainly senior military officers and some civilians completing master's degrees in strategic studies. Widely understood as intellectual factories of the various branches of the armed services, these sites are home to many of the military's "organic intellectuals."[33] I observed two series of lectures at two different war colleges during my fieldwork. One series, part of a strategy and policy course, focused on the Cold War in Southeast Asia, homing in on Malaya and Vietnam and, to a lesser extent, the Philippines. The class had been assigned to read the Briggs Plan, which was written in 1948 by Lt.-Gen. Harold Briggs and provided the template for the "New Villages" that the instructor held up as a successful if brutal model of population and food control. The plan facilitated the mass deportation of tens of thousands of Chinese Malay, if not more, to China; established military control of civilian institutions; and forcibly resettled over one million people into New Villages surrounded by tall barbed wire and "regrouping" areas near tin and rubber plantations.[34] Projecting a somber black-and-white photograph of one of the carceral villages, the instructor jokingly referred to the "lovely gated communities" the British used as a mechanism of population control. The lecture emphasized the importance of insurgent access to food and the general population, framing the New Villages as an effective way to cut the insurgents off from the population and enable rice rationing. British strategies in this climate, as in other colonial referents, were generally regarded as successful, including not only forced villagization but also amnesty and cash reward programs for naming insurgents.[35] The military instructor's detached perspective on British counterinsurgents' strategies as "successful" and worthy of replication was echoed more broadly in the treatment of Malaya, particularly the forced villagization program, as a template for counterinsurgency strategy in Vietnam. Military instructional messages about Malaya as a successful template worthy of replication could not differ more from critical academic perspectives that the counterinsurgency's "success" can only be attributed to massive coercion, detention, deportation, and resettlement as well as a repressive security apparatus and New Villages that remained in place beyond the emergency.[36]

In the war college classroom, another instructor lectured on Malaya before turning to Vietnam. The second lecturer emphasized how population control had "worked well" for the British to crush the insurgency but conceded that from today's perspective, the New Villages were a human rights violation. This lecture was framed differently than the previous discussion of tactics, this time focusing more on how the conflict shaped geopolitical concerns for what the lecturer called the "liberal great powers," arguing ultimately that the outcome in Malaya protected British interests. As in the marine history lesson, the instructor here implicitly adopted the colonizer's perspective, leading to an analysis that favored the colonial power's interests. This lecturer also used a photograph of a New Village, this time overlaying the image from Malaya with the quote "create a desert and call it peace," referencing the "Roman model of COIN." The instructor's point was that people living in a New Village, going through twice-daily body searches, would not call this reform. At the same time the lecturer wished to get across her point that "successful COIN is ugly," meaning that counterinsurgents do what they must to secure victory. She discussed the necessity to reduce the expectation of whether counterinsurgency could actually achieve developmental or democratic goals, instead emphasizing a more conservative goal of securing colonial power. After using Machiavelli's quote that "a prince who wishes to maintain the state is often forced to do evil," the lecturer made the point that this might be an attractive approach for US partners, although it is not one she would advocate for the United States to pursue directly.[37] Because the course was in a massive lecture hall seating at least two hundred students, it was difficult to measure how the students received her argument. Students mainly took notes and listened quietly to the material. When I asked them during the break about their thoughts, they spoke generally of how the material was "interesting" without necessarily noticing and certainly not questioning its colonial viewpoint.

The next unit moved to Vietnam. Before departing from Malaya, however, the instructor made the point that the Malayan case, though relinquished to the dustbin of history, must be understood if only because the New Villages informed the forced villagization strategy in Vietnam of strategic hamlets. Lecturing initially on the 1945–1954 period in which the French fought to retain Indochina, the instructor focused on the role of Charles de Gaulle's Gen. Philippe Leclerc, the same French military figure Frantz Fanon engages with throughout his writings on the Algerian revolution.[38] In contrast to the sinister place Leclerc occupies in Fanon's writing, the military instructor referred to Leclerc in a laudatory fashion, calling him a "master of intrigue" and admiring his creativity in getting so close to capturing Ho Chi Minh. Again, the lecture's French colonial perspective erased the Vietnamese population. Implicit in the argument, as in discussions of colonial wars from Haiti to the Philippines to Malaya to Algeria, was that the colonial power may have ultimately lost, but its tactics are valuable and can potentially be repackaged for today's wars. Recuperating this value depends on a way of understanding defeat in war as part of an experimental science in which tactics and politics can and should be separated.

This way of understanding separates military identity from the political domain, associated with civilians, leaving military instructors to analyze historical tactics they claim can be separated from civilian politics. The instructor clarified that it was not for inadequate tactics that the United States lost the war in Vietnam. Instead, geopolitical factors—in particular Mao Zedong's rise allowing the retention of the Viet Minh—precipitated US defeat. The lecturer used as evidence that French colonial counterinsurgents had succeeded operationally in expanding French control but that the United States confronted a different geopolitical terrain in the context of the Cold War. This was a common argument in other military instructional contexts I observed—that one must separate politics from tactics to extract military tactics that still remained useful even though they may have been discovered in the context of a war whose US soldiers were instructed to "kill anything that we see and anything that moved."[39]

The scale of atrocity, the systemic dehumanization of Vietnamese civilians, and the proving ground of advanced technologies capable of horrific violence are all laid bare in historian turned investigative war reporter Nick Turse's *Kill Anything That Moves*, which draws on secret Pentagon archives and interviews with US veterans and Vietnamese survivors. Despite the popular conception of the My Lai massacre as the work of a "few bad apples," Ronald Ridenhour, the soldier who exposed My Lai to the public, himself described the event as an "operation, not an aberration," in the context of widespread murder of Vietnamese combatants in the manner that has become associated with My Lai.[40] And yet, in the classrooms I observed, most military instructors completely set aside this criminal violence, instead framing war as a science they must perfect through analysis of its component parts. Whether the war is won or lost is less relevant to this "scientific process" than the need to remove particular tactics from their political and historical context to assess their potential in the broader science of war.

A key reference for the war college course was RAND's 1962 counterinsurgency symposium. Proceedings from the symposium describe its intention "to distill lessons and insights from past insurgent conflicts that might help to inform and shape the US involvement in Vietnam and to foster the effective prosecution of other future counterinsurgency campaigns."[41] Participants in the symposium were high-ranking military officers and members of RAND and the Defense Advanced Research Projects Agency from the United States as well as France, Britain, and Australia. The published symposium outlines a moderated discussion between figures such as David Galula; Frank Kitson, a British lieutenant colonel who fought counterinsurgency campaigns in Kenya and Malaya; and Edward Lansdale, a US Air Force officer and former intelligence operative who advised the Philippine government during the Hukbalahap rebellion and undertook a number of roles advising South Vietnamese government officials and conducting psychological operations, intelligence, and counterguerrilla campaigns in Vietnam.

Galula was one of the most vocal participants in the forum, his experience from Algeria coloring many segments of the discussion. To the discussion of "primary objectives" in a counterinsurgency operation, Galula added a lengthy description of a troop formation he used in Algeria to clear an "infested area" of guerrillas.[42] The group discussed issues such as insurgent food access and the rule of law and legality in maintaining the colonial power's appearances. A comparative approach framed the discussion between experiences from Malaya, Algeria, and the Philippines with an eye to extracting tactics that might also be effective in Vietnam. The RAND symposium further exemplifies how military doctrine is produced by reviving colonial and Cold War histories whose trajectory was in turn shaped through the study of wars that came before. The symposium also demonstrates the web of connections between defense, government, and academic knowledge that continue to shape war.

During the Cold War, Walt Whitman Rostow prefigured the coming together of academic, development, and military worlds that defines the security apparatus today. A professor of economic history at MIT, Rostow worked as President John F. Kennedy's deputy assistant for national security affairs before rising under the Johnson administration to national security adviser in 1966. Rostow provided Kennedy with the rhetoric of launching a "Decade of Development" with the US Agency for International Development's (USAID) inauguration in March 1961.[43] He also had a heavy hand in Kennedy's Alliance for Progress in Latin America, providing seven of the alliance's twelve goals, and economic theories that served as "the intellectual scaffolding for the entire program." At the same time as Rostow was acknowledged in the period as a champion of third world development, he was, in diplomatic historian David Milne's words, "the most hawkish civilian member of the Kennedy and Johnson administrations," advocating for the bombing of North Vietnam with increasing intensity and the deployment of combat troops to South Vietnam while he played a central role in the establishment of USAID and the Alliance for Progress.[44]

These two seemingly contradictory sides of Rostow's career were held together by his fervent anticommunism, visible in the title of his famous work *The Stages of Economic Growth: A Non-Communist Manifesto*. A theory of economic development, which informed USAID's birth and early postwar development programs such as the Alliance for Progress, promoted the infusion of capital into third world societies to push them past what Rostow conceived to be the "danger zone" of a country's susceptibility to communism. Alternately, communist societies must be met with US military might. Rostow greatly admired the US military and advocated for its increasing role in promoting economic growth.[45] His intellectual corpus is one of the clearest examples available of a theory of third world development that works hand in glove with military force.

Rostow embodied the ways in which development as the industry we know today took shape through its inseparable relationship to militarization during the Cold War. His firm intellectual imprint on USAID's institutional formation is apparent in the scale of expenditure on militarized development programs during the Vietnam War. "During FY ending in June 1964, AID provided $82 million in building materials, medical kits, school equipment, livestock, pesticides, and food in conjunction with the strategic hamlet program in addition to the $215 million for military equipment, services, and supplies."[46] *The Stages of Economic Growth* became a "clarion call" for anticommunist US aid.[47]

The Strategic Hamlet Program, figuring prominently in post-9/11 war college curricula, was a practical application of Rostow's ideas writ large, the operationalization of what Samuel Huntington, writing of Vietnam in *Foreign Affairs* in 1968, argued was the solution to the fact that "societies are susceptible to revolution only at particular stages of their development.... The effective response ... is ... forced draft urbanization and modernization which rapidly brings the country in question out of the phase in which a rural revolutionary movement can hope to generate sufficient strength to come to power."[48] The Strategic Hamlet Program removed peasants from the Vietnamese countryside, often at gunpoint, and resettled them in settlements within a fortified perimeter, often forcing them to construct new homes using their own materials. Forced relocation occurred after the military cleared the area of insurgents, setting up the logic whereby anyone outside of the strategic hamlet was considered no longer a peasant but rather a potential insurgent. The Strategic Hamlet Program attempted to stem insurgent access to food and the general population. But it also tried to create a new sense of nationalism toward the South Vietnamese state through civic action projects, such as roads and bridges constructed by the South Vietnamese army. The program's emphasis on changing the mindsets of peasants living in the villages adopts Rostow's argument that a certain mentality is associated with the economic conditions for growth.

The concept combined strategies previously pursued by the French colonial government, the US-backed government of Ngo Dinh Diem in the late 1950s, and knowledge accrued through colonial histories in the Philippines and Malaya. In fact, the head of the British Advisory Mission to Vietnam was Robert G. K. Thompson, who had implemented the New Villages during the Malayan Emergency and whose writings students read in the war college class I observed. Drawing directly on his experience fighting the insurgency in Malaya, Thompson advised the US-backed Diem administration in South Vietnam on developing a similar program of forced villagization. A parallel line of colonial influence was at work via Rostow's advice to Dean Rusk, Kennedy's secretary of state, that the type of agrarian resettlement combined with civic action and relentless use of force in the Philippines during the Hukbalahap rebellion of the early 1950s provided a useful template for actions in Vietnam. Thompson's and Rostow's recommendations also resonated with the longer history of US colonial counterinsurgency in the Philippines in the early twentieth century, which ruthlessly employed concentration camps accompanied by the systematic destruction of anything outside the "dead line" bordering the camp.[49] The ways in which Thompson and Rostow drew on colonial histories from Malaya and the Philippines are representative of the broader historical influences on contemporary counterinsurgency.

John Nagl's influential counterinsurgency writings, which also figured prominently in the war college curriculum, provide a more recent rendition of this same pattern of military intellectuals looking to colonial and Cold War histories to produce doctrine for the post-9/11 wars. Nagl uses British general Gerald Templer's voice throughout, admiring his "energetic personal leadership" and "organizational ability."[50] Nagl profiles some of the tactics Templer adopted in the face of the insurgency, including a twenty-two-hour daily curfew, cutting rice rations, and closing schools as collective punishment directed at towns suspected of harboring insurgents. One of Nagl's richest sources is Templer's papers at the British National Army Museum, and he enthuses about being only the third researcher to gain access to them.[51] This source also includes a series of letters between Templer and British colonial secretary Oliver Lyttelton, whose significance Nagl argues would be "difficult to overstate." Nagl adopts the words of these colonial figures as his own to narrate the Malayan Emergency, adopting the colonizer's perspective in the process. Instructors in the war college classroom resurrected the same voices of Templer and Lyttelton, emphasizing, as Nagl does, how the tactics these historical figures offer are "the first step to any real progress in counterinsurgency."[52] The war college lectures on Malaya in turn discussed the same tactics Nagl mobilizes through Templer's and Lyttelton's writings, including programs offering large cash rewards as bounties for insurgents surrendering themselves, informing on fellow insurgents, and even leading raids against former comrades. War college instructors also used Nagl as a key source on food-denial operations as well as the British army's "effective" policing of the New Villages in which he outlines new methods of patrolling and tracking generally regarded as innovative in both his writing and the war college classroom.[53] Citing a contemporary source, Nagl emphasizes the need to coordinate police and civil authorities, a point echoed in post-9/11 military classrooms.[54]

Alongside lessons from Malaya, Rostovian ideas of modernization informed many aspects of the US counterinsurgency strategy in Vietnam, including the Civil Operations and Revolutionary Development Support (CORDS) program. A report developed for that program in 1969 to guide civic action programs in support of pacification demonstrates both the influence of development as modernization throughout this period of the Vietnam War and the difficulty troops faced implementing this strategy. The report is reticent to recommend specific development programs and mentions throughout how development may have been the objective in military doctrine, but "this is not what is happening" on the ground. "In the harsh light of day-to-day military events and under the pressure of extreme complexity, development concerns recede into the background and the defeat of the enemy's combat units becomes the objective. *The ineluctable relationship between security and development is ignored.*"⁵⁵ The report goes on to challenge a Rostovian theory of economic growth, instead proposing changes in "habits, attitudes, and motivation" of the Vietnamese people and government.⁵⁶ Written by marines at the height of the CORDS program in Vietnam, this report addresses how, although Rostow's ideas may have been influential in shaping policy in Vietnam, military personnel closer to the ground have always pushed back against the notion of development as a weapon of war. Here, a governmental argument instead emerges regarding the necessity to change the character, behavior, and attitudes of the native population.⁵⁷

Visible in the writings of defense luminaries such as Nagl as well as in the lectures of war college instructors, Vietnam and Malaya are key sites of post-9/11 military learning about counterinsurgency. Taken together, they also exemplify how each paradigmatic example of counterinsurgency was shaped by reference to its predecessors. In Rostow's writings in particular, we see how such knowledge about counterinsurgency is shaped by a nexus of academic and defense institutions that together gave rise to the international development industry we know today. Rostow, Nagl, and their contemporaries breathe new life into the words of colonial figures such as Templer, Thompson, and Lyttelton, who in turn inform military instructors in the post-9/11 era.

Gendered Counterinsurgency in Algeria's "Savage War of Peace"

Before the DSF contractors arrived at Camp Pendleton, a group of Marine Corps trainers and civilian contractors were giving a series of lessons to a brigade combat team on various aspects of counterinsurgency. The lessons included the theory and history of counterinsurgency, background on the Afghan National Army, working with interpreters, and managing civilian casualties. Jones, one of the marine instructors, was the only female marine in the room. As part of the lesson on "intelligence in counterinsurgency," she gave a lecture titled "Why Consider Women?" and asked the class to consider the influence that women in "traditional societies" hold over their sons. Invoking motherhood, she explained this influence to determine "whether a man picks up a shovel to dig a hole for an IED [improvised explosive device] or for an irrigation system." Asking the students to think about their own home life, she read the phrase "if mom's not happy, no one's happy," then asked them to raise their hands if this was true in their home. She then urged the class to think about this phrase on a societal level, citing studies that show women's access to health care, involvement in government, and education as predictors of "state security and stability."

Jones projected a slide featuring an excerpt from David Kilcullen's "Twenty-Eight Articles." Article 19 begins with the advice, in boldface, "engage the women, beware of children." Here Kilcullen argues that "in traditional societies, women are hugely influential in forming social networks that insurgents use for support. Co-opting neutral or friendly women, through targeted social and economic programs, builds networks of enlightened self-interest that eventually undermine the insurgents. You need your own female counterinsurgents, including interagency people, to do this effectively. Win the women, and you own the family unit. Own the family, and you take a big step forward in mobilizing the population."[58] Kilcullen mobilizes an imperial notion of possessing a foreign people, discussing "winning" and "owning" the population. The metaphor of "ownership" targets women and their families as the primary subjects of occupation upon whose domination the rest of the population follows. Women are central to this modern imperial narrative, yet in contrast to Gayatri Spivak's notion of British colonialists "saving brown women from brown men," here the US military imagines Afghan women as potential agents of the counterinsurgency message to trust the occupation and share intelligence.

An appendix to the 2007 *Counterinsurgency Field Manual* uses almost exactly Kilcullen's language, adopting his message to build "networks of enlightened self-interest" through women's support, but it takes the argument one step further, arguing that "female counterinsurgents, including interagency people, are required to do this [build networks of 'enlightened self-interest'] effectively."[59] Such doctrine adopts a twisted, militarized liberal feminist rhetoric of "enlightening" women who live under occupation. US servicewomen are key to bringing local women into "enlightened self-interest." Using these counterinsurgency classics, Jones began to describe how her unit in Iraq's Al Anbar Province undertook various "civic engagement" projects to build rapport with local women and influence their perceptions of the occupation and level of support for the insurgency. Such efforts in 2005–2006 grew into the Marine Corps' Iraqi Women's Engagement Program that prefigured the much more expansive female engagement teams (FETs).

In 2011 the Army Center for Lessons Learned published the *Commander's Guide to Female Engagement Teams*, which recognized the teams' widespread use in the field without great consistency in their composition, training, and use among brigade combat teams in Afghanistan.[60] The document was part of a broader attempt during this time to codify the concept of "female engagement" and develop more consistent training. As part of the background it provided, the authors discuss the French colonial army's use of teams that resemble modern-day FETs. This contemporary army document describes *équipes medico-sociales itinérantes* (mobile medical-social teams, EMSIs) used as part of the

French pacification campaign during the Algerian war of independence (1954–1962). As previously discussed in relation to Galula, Algeria was a primary historical reference for the *Counterinsurgency Field Manual*'s writing team. Shortly after the 2003 invasion of Iraq, Alistair Horne (historian of the Algerian war of independence) wrote that "at the time of writing, one feels that Bush's Washington (and Blair's London) also went blindly into Iraq—and into collision with the Islamic world—without the kind of necessary preparation, where study of Algeria in 1954–62 might have helped."[61]

In the 2006 preface to *A Savage War of Peace*, Horne outlines three areas where Algeria's resonance is especially pronounced: first, in relation to the effectiveness of insurgent attacks on native police loyal to France destroying police morale; second, parallels between Iraq's porous borders with Syria and Iran and Algerian rebels' ability to use Tunisia and Morocco; and third, the role of torture in both contexts.[62] Electrodes fastened to genitals, dangling suspected insurgents by their feet and plunging their heads into water, and the apprehension and interrogation of large portions of the population all became institutionalized practices within the French army in Algeria.[63] Details of this torture spread back to metropolitan France, ultimately undermining the case for a French Algeria. In the words of Albert Camus, writing of the French army's proliferation of rebels in reaction to acts of torture committed, "it is better to suffer certain injustices than to commit them. . . . [S]uch fine deeds would inevitably lead to the demoralization of France and the loss of Algeria."[64] Henri Alleg, a European Jew and editor of Algeria's communist newspaper *Alger Républicain*, was detained and interrogated by Gen. Jacques Massu's paratroopers for an entire month during the summer of 1957. Writing in explicit detail of what electrocution felt like while under interrogation, Alleg's publication of *La Question* provoked metropolitan France to reckon with its use of the same torture techniques that had so recently been condemned under Nazi Germany. The torture of someone of European heritage such as Alleg sparked revulsion in metropolitan France.[65]

Institutionalized torture, forced villagization (*regroupement*), cataloging of homes, and imprisoning insurgents were shared techniques used between Algeria and other colonial wars of pacification. Vietnam was a dense node of circulation between colonial encounters, with North African troops who had served with French expeditionary forces in Indochina allegedly applying lessons in Algeria that they had learned in Viet Minh prisons.[66] French military theorists similarly looked to the Indochinese War for lessons applicable to the North African front. Such lessons as well as experiments with social policy were distilled in the French army's Center for Training and Preparation in Counter-Guerrilla Warfare, which began operations in March 1956.[67] Officers called for active duty completed a program in pacification and psychological warfare. Under the instruction of a French colonel imprisoned by the Viet Minh, they also read the writings of Mao Zedong and other theorists of Marxism and armed revolution. In the time between Horne's original insight that Washington could stand to learn from the Algerian revolution and the height of counterinsurgency's influence within the US military, practitioners indeed began to pay closer attention to the Algerian case. *A Savage War of Peace* appeared on military reading lists. Historical referents such as Vietnam and Malaya were recycled alongside lessons in pacification, such as the French army's insight that "the object of struggle was support of the people and not conquest of terrain."[68] The EMSIs' appearance in contemporary military doctrine is but one refraction of the US military's process of learning from Algeria, which began with the 2003 screening of the film *The Battle of Algiers* and expanded into a more systemic study of tactics to be redeployed to the post-9/11 battlefront.

Algerian sociologist and scholar of torture Marnia Lazreg writes of the EMSIs in the context of what she names a "military feminism" rooted in French colonial notions of Algerian women as "oppressed." "The rhetoric of 'women's emancipation' purported to liberate women (from their cultural norms deemed beyond the pale) just as it sought to 'protect' them from the FLN [National Liberation Front]."[69] Lazreg writes of how military strategists became increasingly interested in developing a "military feminism" they could use tactically as they realized women were supporting and fighting on the side of the National Liberation Front. "Military feminism adjusted antisubversive techniques of psychological action to focus on women as the molecular units of the population friend-enemy."[70] Although Kilcullen does not seem to have read Lazreg (he does not cite her), his writings in "Twenty-Eight Articles" of co-opting women to "win the family unit" deeply resemble the French army's military feminism.

The EMSIs were first piloted in March 1957 as part of the French army's pacification strategy in Orléansville. French forces considered the teams a success because they coincided with the National Liberation Front's military defeat in this area and led to useful intelligence for French forces. After this point, the program increasingly recruited Algerian women to serve on the EMSIs. The teams were eventually composed of 1 medical doctor, 1 European assistant (a woman), and 2 Muslim assistants (both women). At the height of the program in 1961, the EMSIs employed 690 women on a total of 223 teams.[71] Although they provided medical and educational assistance to Muslim women, these forms of assistance were always tied to psychological warfare by the French army. Medical care, social assistance, and education programs meant access to the female population, who could then be surveilled and potentially used as an intelligence source or whose opinions about maintaining a French Algeria could be swayed. This psychological warfare aspect of the ESMIs is evident in instructions from the French military command that the teams should not lose sight that their "'real objective' was to use sociomedical assistance as a medium through which to 'make contact with women,' that is to say, 'to know, inform, educate, organize and guide them' in preparation for their acceptance of the 'most French solution to the Algerian problem.'"[72] Lessons on hygiene, a common EMSI activity, included messages about France's benevolence in Algeria and commitment to civic rights, which were contrasted with native Algeria's gender inequality.[73]

The EMSIs' main achievement was a series of public military unveilings of Algerian women, which took place in May 1958 in major cities across the country. The EMSIs played a large role in disseminating propaganda and information leading up to the public unveilings. They also organized women's groups to cement messages of women's liberation as possible only in a French Algeria. In his essay "Algeria Unveiled" in *A Dying Colonialism*, Frantz Fanon describes the tremendous significance of the Algerian woman's veil in the eyes of the colonizer, how the "woman who sees without being seen frustrates the colonizer."[74] Here he examines strategic uses of both the veiled and unveiled woman's body to transport weapons, identity cards, and other materials to support the National Liberation Front. Writing of the veil's "historical dynamism," placing it at the center of a "new dialectic of the body and of the world" central to revolutionary women, Fanon analyzes how "removed and reassumed once again, the veil has been manipulated, transformed into a technique of camouflage, into a means of struggle."[75] He documents the colonial administration's establishment of a "precise political doctrine" that evolved from an earlier simple formula that identified "winning over" women as the first step to societal conquest: "If we want to destroy the structure of Algerian society, its capacity for resistance, we must first of all conquer the women: we must go and find them behind the veil where they hide themselves and in the houses where the men keep them out of sight."[76]

In his descriptions of public unveilings culminating in the EMSI's propaganda component, Fanon depicts participants in the unveilings as coerced: "servants under the threat of being fired, poor women dragged from their homes, prostitutes, who were brought to the public square and *symbolically* unveiled to the cries of *"Vive l'Algérie française!"*[77] This observation of impoverished women coerced into public unveiling is supported in other scholars' findings from the period. Lazreg, examining archival photographs, describes how some of the women publicly unveiled appeared poor by their modest clothing, although this was not the case for all women.[78] One of the women publicly unveiled in Constantine was a student whose brother was in detention and would have been killed had she not participated in the ceremony. She had never before worn the veil but was coerced by the military to put it on, then publicly unveil herself on the official podium at the ceremony.

Fanon's writings on unveiled women as "test women" capture colonial attitudes seeking to uncover "the flesh of Algeria laid bare"—the "aggressiveness"
of the occupier, seeking to achieve, with every woman's face uncovered, "an Algerian society whose systems of defense were in the process of dislocation, open
and breached."[79] At the same time, he draws on his psychoanalytical work with
Algerian women who had unveiled for a number of reasons.[80] Writing from female patients' perspectives, he describes how the veil "protects, reassures, iso-
lates," and without it "she has the impression of her body being cut up into bits,
put adrift; the limbs seem to lengthen indefinitely. . . . The unveiled body seems
to escape, to dissolve."[81] Fanon represents the Muslim Algerian woman's experience of unveiling as corporeal and metaphysical, forcing the woman to "in-
vent new dimensions for her body" and to cope with "the anxious feeling that
something is unfinished, and along with this a frightful sensation of disintegrat-
ing."[82] Fanon's writings from this period address the psychoanalytical consequences of French military and cultural policies, underscoring the need to
develop new forms of personhood in the postcolonial era.

While the EMSIs viewed fighting the veil as "on par with getting rid of 'flies,'
'ticks,' and 'lice,'" modern female counterinsurgency teams adopted the veil to
gain access to Afghan women.[83] The 2011 *Commander's Guide to Female Engagement Teams* spends a portion of its "best practices" section discussing the veil.
The document's ambivalence on servicewomen veiling reflects the military's internal controversy over this issue. At every training I observed, the issue of
whether or not servicewomen were going to veil on their deployment came up
informally during the less structured components of the training. For instance,
during an Afghan dinner—an event that came at the end of most trainings—men
and women were separated into different sections of the room. A State Department employee struck up casual conversation with one of the Afghan interpreters, who complemented the purple floral scarf she had wrapped loosely around
her hair and over her shoulder. The State Department employee, a white woman,
mentioned that she had been advised by colleagues to wear a veil during her mission for reasons of "cultural sensitivity." She asked a nearby female soldier, a
member of the same Provincial Reconstruction Team, whether service members
also veil, to which the soldier recoiled, explaining that nobody could force her to
wear this symbol of women's oppression and that it was not an official part of
military uniform.

Later into the Afghan meal the soldier, Dawn, explained to me how as a Black
woman she had worked hard to get to where she was, and it was especially offensive that she was asked to—in her words—"degrade" herself by adopting the
veil. Many members of the FETs and cultural support teams I interviewed did
wear a veil while on patrol. Although my sample size was not large enough to

make general claims, there was a strong racial difference in who adopted or re-jected the veil, with women of color more often placing the veil as Dawn had in a frame of oppression they had long been maneuvering within. Servicewomen de-cided whether or not to veil through the lens of their own experiences of racism and sexism within the military, considering how they would be perceived not only by Afghan civilians but also by other soldiers. They often framed the veil, reflect-ing military trainings on Afghan culture, as static and oppressive and with the sort of anti-Muslim tone and colonial vision that scholars of veiling have argued denies Muslim women's agency and does not reflect their lived experience.[84]

On the one hand, the *Commander's Guide to Female Engagement Teams* warns that "headscarves are not a necessity for good relations with locals" and that they might actually identify the FETs as female and make them ideal targets for the Taliban. On the other hand, "patrolling with headscarves on under helmets will identify Soldiers as female when they enter a house or stop to search a woman, and they will not be mistaken for men by people watching from the sidelines."[85] The best practices settle on recommending headscarves in "olive drab, black, brown or multicam" and in particular circumstances, such as when women are inside visit-ing a compound (as a sign of trust, along with removing their helmet, protective vests, and eye protection) as well as in the case of "very short-haired, darker skinned, African-American female Soldiers" who, the document warns, are most likely to be mistaken for men given that "a vast majority of rural Afghans have never seen persons of African descent and may unintentionally assume that they are men (especially in uniform and carrying weapons)."[86] The document expresses concern that Afghan civilians would confuse Black servicewomen as men, reveal-ing how the authors thought of Afghans as unworldly, backward, and naive. In the lessons learned document, one can see the ambivalence of recommending that servicewomen veil while recognizing its strategic value. Fanon's insight into the fluidity of the veil in French Algeria continues to be relevant, though the US mili-tary now deploys the veil's use in the language of "cultural sensitivity."

When the Center for Army Lessons Learned wrote the *Commander's Guide to Female Engagement Teams* in 2011, EMSIs were summarized as "supporting pac-ification efforts aimed at isolating the insurgency from the Algerian population. EMSI engaged with Algerian women to enhance their living conditions and to improve France's reputation. EMSI included social workers, nurses, and educa-tors, and their primary tasks were fostering girls' education; teaching child care, cooking, and sewing techniques; and conducting other efforts necessary to assist the women of Algeria."[87] Overtly adopting the perspective of the French colonial counterinsurgents, the army document admires "the success of EMSI" based on positive reviews by the French Special Administration Section that the teams were "one of the most efficient ways to engage the population."[88] Echoing Kilcullen's advice to "win the women" as a step toward winning the population at large, the document adopts French units' framing of women as "enablers." It takes the perspective of French troops, adopting a colonial perspective mirrored multiple times over in such instances as war college instructors reviving colonial figures from Malaya and Vietnam to teach counterinsurgency for the post-9/11 wars.

In adopting a French colonial counterinsurgent interpretation of the EMSIs, the US military document takes at its word colonial statements that the EMSIs' "primary task was fostering girls' education." This runs contrary to the academic literature's findings of education (or any other allegedly humanitarian program) as a means to access Algerian women to influence their favoritism toward remaining a French Algeria. Central to this message was a colonial feminism in which women's liberation could be achieved only through continued affiliation with the metropole. The emphasis on education, among other developmental programs, was prevalent in an Obama-era White House promotional video featuring commentary by US Army and Marine Corps FET participants as well as Jill Biden. The video opens with the voice of a young servicewoman reflecting, "We are actually changing people's lives. We actually have a hand in what is going on over there, and we can do great things." Over images of Afghan children going to school and receiving medical treatment and servicewomen sitting cross-legged with Afghan women and children, Jill Biden's voice explains how the FETs are there to help Afghan women access health care and education and to support small businesses.[89] Such representations of the FETs carry over from French colonial Algeria the notion of providing Muslim women with access to health and education that are available from the metropole only. A second element of the EMSI that reverberates through post-9/11 gendered counterinsurgency is the idea that the military teams served as a model of Western women's liberation.[90]

Some FETs' adoption of the veil distinguishes them from EMSI references to unveiling as akin to "getting rid of lice and ticks." Yet beneath this apparent difference, women from Western military powers are still held up as models of what colonized women could be if only they adopted the colonizer's practices and mentality. Such "benevolence" is visible in the White House video. It was also evident in the commentary of Donna, a FET member I interviewed. She described how she was looking at pictures of herself in Afghanistan and came across one of a young boy who had laid his hand on her medical pack and was resting his head against her body. She recalled, "You know that they looked up to us at that moment. They knew that we were there to do good things for them." Donna poignantly recalled the old photograph, describing the position of the boy's head as though she could still feel the surge of emotion and warmth of his tiny frame draped across her. Donna performed the emotional labor of soothing and calming Afghan women during her deployment. Her recollections

through this photograph also speak to the emotional rewards some women garnered from these missions, particularly those involving interaction with local
children. Donna's experience being on the receiving end of what she interpreted
as a gracious look in this child's eyes molded her view of the FETs as benevolent
and of Western military women as models of desirable behavior and moral traits.
This pattern of modeling is directly linked to French colonial technologies of
providing "examples" of desired traits the colonized might adopt that would support the "French solution to the Algerian problem." A colonial document describes the effort this way: "To make contact with the women's world in order to
know it, to inform it, to educate it, to organize it, to guide it, in order to prepare
it first to adopt and then to truly live the most French solution to the Algerian
problem. In time, the EMSI need to make contact with the woman's world, which
needs to know, through concrete examples, the modern future that France is
proposing."[91]

Kilcullen's influential version of such recycled colonial technologies, which sees
"winning" Afghan women as key to the counterinsurgency's success, uses the language of enlightenment to describe convincing local women to share intelligence.
Military discourses imagine women—their own soldiers as well as occupied
subjects—not so much as passive, voiceless victims to be "saved" rather as active
participants in the counterinsurgency effort. This co-opted and militarized feminist rhetoric of empowerment merges with the parental metaphors we saw in the
DSF training. Together, these different military understandings of the occupation—
parenting Afghans into modernity through development projects and "winning"
Afghan women over to support the counterinsurgency—form some of the contours of a post-9/11 military humanitarianism and imperial feminism.

DSF contractors embodied this military humanitarianism by bringing to life
structural changes in financial, institutional, and policy shifts post-9/11. DSF
trainings did not convince soldiers of the imperative to become "armed social
workers," but they did entrench racial evolutionism and associations between
combat and masculinity. Military instructors actively using colonial history to
make present doctrine form another strand assembling military humanitarianism and imperial feminism. Military uses of history erase the colonial violence
that accompanied examples such as the Vietnam War–era CORDS program as
they amplify colonial voices. DSF contractors revive the nexus of academic, private, and military institutions so apparent in Rostow's life trajectory. One distinctive attribute of the new imperial feminism is the story it tells of US military
women as models of liberated feminist empowerment. The revival of a colonial
military feminism out of the Algerian model grows to full scale in the post-9/11
FETs.

The colonial perspective apparent in the *Commander's Guide to Female Engagement Teams* is magnified in recent examples such as the White House promotional video and Donna's recollections of looking at old photographs and coming to understand herself as a model of imperial benevolence. However, the narratives that servicewomen provide of their deployments and the meaning they associate with the work paint a more complex reality in which servicewomen, themselves forming a vector of imperial feminism, are also marginalized by a whole range of military practices. It is insufficient to frame servicewomen through an understanding of the military unilaterally rejecting women's presence. Instead, servicewomen's experiences of repression while framing themselves as imperial liberators paint a complex picture of co-opted feminist language that celebrates the inclusion of women in combat at the same time as it reinforces gender stereotypes. It is to this picture we now turn.

SOOTHING OCCUPATION
Gender and the Strategic Deployment
of Emotional Labor

Edith deployed to Iraq as a supply clerk supporting an engineering battalion in 2003. She was posted on a remote base in Ramadi. Her regular job as a supply clerk consisted of ordering supplies, keeping track of inventory and equipment, maintaining weapons, and making sure the commander was aware of the battalion's inventory. For the first three months of her deployment, she bathed with a makeshift shower constructed out of an inverted water bottle perched on top of a pallet while her "battle buddy" shielded her from view with a poncho liner. Edith's name was on a list her commander kept of all women who could be pulled from their regular duties and temporarily attached to units carrying out home raids or traffic-control points. These teams of female soldiers became known as "Lionesses."[1]

From its inception in 2003, the Lioness program continued to assemble all-female teams in an ad hoc manner: an officer in charge would pull servicewomen from mainly support roles such as supply clerk, cook, and mechanic and temporarily attach them to combat units. The language of being "temporarily attached" was significant because military policy banned women from being directly assigned to combat units below the brigade level. In practice, however, the Lioness teams conducted house-to-house searches and patrols to search women and children. In this capacity serving mainly alongside infantry units, Lionesses found themselves in combat situations they had not been trained for. Many, including Edith, suffered combat injuries. However, because they were not technically part of combat units, women such as Edith were often unable to prove the connection between their injuries and military service and were thus denied medical care.

Drawing on the experiences of Edith and her cohort, in this chapter I examine how counterinsurgency relied on understandings of female soldiers as the emotional experts of war. Female soldiers deployed emotional labor when they calmed residents down during a night raid. When deployed on home raids, members of female counterinsurgency teams describe their job as being to separate out women and children and, before searching them or trying to extract information from them, "calming them down." Female soldiers were also valued for their ability to access the household, which counterinsurgency theory understood as a key terrain of war fighting. There was a strong intelligence-collection component to counterinsurgency's gendered uses of emotional labor. Although official military rules make sharp distinctions between who is allowed to collect intelligence and who is not, in practice members of female engagement teams (FETs, a program from 2009 onward that grew out of the Lioness teams) accessed information that certainly overlapped with or entirely consisted of intelligence collection. This focus on intelligence collection marks a departure from the focus in scholarly literature and popular media coverage of female counterinsurgency teams on their alleged humanitarian activities such as distributing relief supplies. Analysis of what happens within military institutions shows a dimension beyond military rhetoric that draws emotional labor, combat, intelligence, and humanitarianism together in a more extensive formation than is apparent from the military's own statements. I examine here how counterinsurgency relied on ideas of women as being "naturally" more skilled at performing emotional labor to "soothe" the subjects of occupation as well as collect intelligence used to execute violence.

Gendered Counterinsurgency and the Strategic Deployment of Emotion

Military valuations of emotion draw on a long popular and academic history of viewing women as the "emotional gender."[2] Gendered counterinsurgency's emotional labor provides an occasion to revisit an older strand of feminist scholarship on gender and emotion. In their various iterations as Lioness teams, FETs, and cultural support teams, female counterinsurgency teams weaponize emotional labor to calm the subjects of a home raid or gather military intelligence. But such deployments of emotional labor are also linked to forms of devaluation, such as equipping female service members with insufficient training that exposes them to additional physical risk, all while the (mis)treatment of their injuries by Veterans Affairs (VA) was colored by their combat's invisibility. Female counterinsurgents use the rhetoric of emotion to give meaning to their work and to explain their labor of alternately searching, calming, and collecting intelligence from Afghan civilians (figure 9). This rhetoric militarizes two feminist conceptualizations of emotion that, on the one hand, explore emotion's association with irrationality and negativity and, on the other, positively value emotion as the core of human life.

Since emotion overdetermines female counterinsurgents' narratives, it is necessary to distinguish between the specificity of this emotion and affective labor, usually defined in relation to Hardt and Negri's distinction between the new "informational economy's" dependence on "immaterial labor" as opposed to an economy formerly dependent on material and durable goods.[3] Existing studies of FETs have explored the emotional and familial dimensions of soldiering associated with gendered counterinsurgency in terms of affective labor. Elizabeth Mesok, for example, theorizes women's experiences on Lioness teams and FETs in terms of "affective technologies of war," which she defines as "the militarized performance of affective labor."[4] This particular strand of thinking on affect draws on feminist critiques of Hardt and Negri's naturalization of the gendered distinction between categories of labor, the problematic binary of immaterial versus industrial labor, and the erasure of earlier feminist literature rethinking emotion.[5] My analytical approach departs from affect, instead returning to Arlie Hochschild's notion of emotional labor because emotional labor more closely reflects female soldiers' own narratives. Just as Hochschild emphasizes female workers' management of their feelings in order to outwardly display emotion conducive to job requirements, female counterinsurgents describe managing their own emotional responses to the experience of breaking down a family's door in the middle of the night. Alongside this emotional self-management, servicewomen discuss deploying an emotional adeptness that allows them to access information valuable to military targeting. Servicewomen's narratives point to the relevance of some older feminist critiques of emotion, which have been eclipsed by more recent preoccupation with affect.

In her exploration of emotion as a "master Western cultural category" that contains unspoken assumptions, Catherine Lutz writes that "emotion occupies an important place in Western gender ideologies; in identifying emotion primarily with irrationality, subjectivity, the chaotic and other negative consequences, and in subsequently labeling women as the emotional gender, cultural belief reinforces the ideological subordination of women."[6] Relatedly, she argues that calling women "emotional" is also often an assertion of their inferiority, given emotion's general cultural devaluation.[7] Military praise of women's emotional capacity is jarring when read against this broader cultural phenomenon because it rubs against the grain of the general cultural devaluation of emotion and, with this devaluation, of women in relation to men. At the same time, there is a secondary direction to this grain by which emotion is positively valued in contrast to estrangement and alienation.[8] This source of contradiction in societal views of emotion plays out in counterinsurgency warfare, where relationships with local populations are crucial to the counterinsurgency force's ability to get information about its enemy and gain favor with civilian populations.

Feminist responses to cultural conceptions of women as emotional and the simultaneous devaluation of emotion place emotion within a "social view of power."[9] Feminist literature reframed emotion as a social fact, moving it out of the purely individual, psychological realm and reconceptualizing it as "implicated into the play of power and the operation of a historically changing system of social hierarchy."[10] One example of such feminist work reclaimed emotion as a source of value. Such work has embraced women's association with emotion, for instance, Susan Griffin's linkage of women's repression with the repression of nature and the opportunity to reclaim power through the "untamed nature" of women's inherent emotional superiority.[11] Working against a broader cultural devaluation, such work asserts the value of emotion, embracing women's association with nature and emotion. Another vein of related scholarship retains the idea of emotion as a source of feminine value but reframes how emotion "becomes female" through social learning.[12]

Military ascriptions of value to emotion and to women's association with emotion represent an unexpected chapter in attempts to reclaim emotion as a valuable yet still inherently feminine skill. Unlike the feminist literature, military arguments are not coming from a political project of recognizing and valuing women's labor. Instead, their valuing of emotional expertise comes from a strategic purpose, often having to do with extracting information from civilians in stressful and dangerous situations. Importantly, the collection of such materials is tied to the potential for lethal targeting and detention. Here, emotional expertise gains its value through interaction with the Afghan woman and child, whom soldiers and training literature describe as having emotional outbursts during home raids. While Afghans' "emotionality" is part of a military imagination of this population as generally deficient, the emotional expertise of female soldiers is reclaimed as valuable and its association with women is retained, suggesting a specific military valorization of emotional femininity that is distinct from available analytical categories.

Alison Jaggar's idea of women's "epistemic advantage" offers some insight into military practices that echo the broader cultural feminization of emotionality.[13] Perhaps in parallel to Jaggar's reframing of women's emotionality as a skill in political analysis, we can conceive of military arguments for women's emotionality as a skill in warfare. Here women's emotionality is considered not only an epistemic advantage, as in Jaggar's argument, but also a tactical advantage. Counterinsurgency has co-opted feminist language such as Jaggar's valuing emotion, with some important differences. In addition to the obvious difference that military arguments for emotional value come out of a very distinct political project from feminist interventions, it is striking that such an argument now comes from an institution that scholars have generally considered to be essentially masculinist.[14] Cynthia Enloe has theorized women's integration into such a masculinist institution as always refusing to destabilize its masculinist character. Military valorizations of emotionality leave fundamental forms of military masculinity untroubled by relying on the same gender essentialisms that protect the masculinist character of military institutions. By laying claim to emotional expertise as the cornerstone of their contribution to combat teams, female counterinsurgents leave combat masculinity untroubled by doing the emotional work themselves instead of requiring men to perform it. At the same time, gendered emotional work's *centrality* to counterinsurgency departs from the trend Enloe maps out, making room for feminized, if still essentialist, valued military traits.

Alongside popular and academic conceptions of emotion as written into a female genetic code, the family has become increasingly conceptualized as an "emotional unit" and, with this, strongly associated with women's domain.[15] Counterinsurgency represents a confluence of ideas about gender, emotion, and the family unit. This confluence is visible in Kilcullen's writings, particularly when he equates "winning" the women with "owning" the family unit and identifies the family unit as crucial to fighting counterinsurgency warfare.[16] Such a perspective continues from a long history of women's family work supporting US military power abroad. During the post–World War II period, for instance, military family members living on overseas bases came to be understood as "unofficial ambassadors" of military Cold War objectives.[17] Military officials came to see American family members' interaction with local populations in occupied Germany and Japan as crucial to the maintenance of US hegemony abroad. Military wives also understood themselves as performing the role of "unofficial ambassadors" through charitable events, educational institutions, and activities that generally revolved around interaction with local residents. Women's latent association with the family unit more recently, in the context of being able to interact with the families of occupied Iraqi and Afghan populations, grows out of this much longer military exploitation of reproductive labor. Yet the emphasis on the female soldier as the executioner of this strategy is a unique departure from the more prominent historical use of military wives to smooth the tensions of military occupation. Across time periods, the military has used women's association with the family unit to further military goals, especially through interaction with local families. This ascription of value to a nexus of emotion-femininity-family is apparent in the experiences of women who served on female counterinsurgency teams.

Team Lioness: Marginalization and the Rhetoric of Emotion in Early Gendered Counterinsurgency

As the Lioness teams became more widely used from 2003 onward, the army requested that commanders compile lists of women who could be assembled into Lioness teams as required by other units. For example, one servicewoman I interviewed who was a Lioness during this early period was informed sporadically by her commander that a different unit needed a Lioness (she used the phrase "needed females"). The team could be asked to search women at a traffic-control point, join an infantry battalion as they went on home raids, or go through a village searching for information by knocking on doors. The Lioness team usually consisted of two servicewomen temporarily pulled from their regular jobs and attached to a combat unit. They received minimal if any additional training before joining the combat unit for the duration of the mission before returning to their regular jobs.

Edith served on one of the first Lioness teams in Iraq. Diminutive and friendly, she cited her unthreatening demeanor as an asset to her time as a Lioness (she was just over five feet tall). Having originally joined the army in August 2000, she explained her decision to enlist as part of her determination to disprove the stereotypes she encountered growing up that, in her words, "being a Hispanic female, I wouldn't do much." She wanted to attend college to become living proof that these stereotypes were wrong. Because her parents could not pay, enlisting in the army was an attractive way to access the GI Bill. Reiterating the racial diversity of the armed forces, she recalls that "we were white, Black, Hispanic, Asian. We were a mixture of a little bit of everything. . . . We were all soldiers. In the military, you were just rank and last name. As long as you did your job, you were good to go." Echoing a phrase I heard often in my discussions with service members about race, gender, and ethnic diversity that "we are all green," Edith used a certain multicultural understanding of the armed services as more racially equitable than society at large. She compared the experience of being judged fairly according to merit within the military to the bald-faced racism she experienced living in the US South, where she described being passed over for jobs she was qualified for and the constant feeling of being looked down upon.

In Iraq, Edith was sent on so many missions that she could not recall an exact number, but in our conversation she remembered periods of time when she went on Lioness missions every day. The missions varied, but she typically went out at night with a unit whose goal was to search for information or weapons or, in her words, to "pick up bad guys." The team would also gather information from family members, neighbors, and local residents. "My job as the Lioness there," she explained, "was to talk to women and children and try to get information, especially from the women. I would try to keep them calm. The children, we would give them candy and toys. Not to con them into talking to us but to try to get them to be a little more comfortable so they're not so scared, just to let them know we were there to be friendly. We were not there to hurt them." This official capacity of the Lioness teams exemplifies the intersection of information and intelligence gathering with the emotional labor entailed in deployment as a Lioness. Edith understood her job as "comforting" and "calming" women and children. She used the rhetoric of emotion to describe her value to her team and specifically to the military objective of collecting information. Products of "comfort" and "calm" were linked to the military objective of collecting information about people and weapons involved in the insurgency.

Most members of Lioness and other gendered counterinsurgency teams I interviewed equated femininity with the ability to do this emotional work. Even more specifically than the broader category of emotional work, Edith classified this work as "having compassion, sensitivity, understanding." "Having a family"—usually shorthand for having children—was also part of how team members understood the "epistemic advantage" they brought to the battlefield.[18] Edith framed the desired trait of a Lioness as "to understand how it is to have a family: to show sensitivity, to make sure women and children understand you're not there to hurt them, just to get information." Edith's emphasis on the emotional expertise she brought to the Lioness team from her own experience raising children resonates with feminist scholarship on emotion that has reclaimed feeling as a renewed source of value.[19] In particular, Sara Ruddick has developed a vocabulary for a sort of "maternal thinking" similar to what Edith references in which women's (and by correlation mothers') emotions are shaped through the work of parenting.[20]

Ruddick's argument is problematic for its reliance on what Lutz calls a "cultural logic of engendered emotion" that, in this case, uses biological processes to naturalize the gendering of emotion as female.[21] At the same time, this is a popular view—and one Edith used—of women as more emotionally sensitive and compassionate as a result of their own caregiving roles. Ruddick uses these associations of feminine emotion as the basis for an antiwar standpoint, arguing that there is "a contradiction between mothering and war."[22] Edith's use of such "maternal thinking" to make sense of and give value to the work she performed as a Lioness demonstrates how there is nothing fundamentally contradictory about women's roles as mothers and their position toward war. In this case, the engendering of emotion was used to facilitate military violence by dampening the reaction to a home raid, a body search, or a traffic-control point.

Lionesses such as Edith also recalled emotional labor in the sense Hochschild wrote about as workers' management of their own emotions in order to create outward displays that were conducive to doing their jobs.[23] Edith recalled her own revulsion at breaking down families' doors in the middle of the night. Her recollections of the actual experience of going on home raids redefine what is meant by the military gloss of "calming" women and children. "You were just thinking—you're busting into someone's house at two, three o'clock in the morning. You're scaring the living daylights out of these people. And you were just like, wow, imagine myself in their situation. I would go bonkers. Forget about wanting information. Come back during regular business hours! To have a family, have a spouse and kids—imagine how the kids felt. They were scared completely shitless. A kid doesn't know what's going on if their families are being taken away."

Her description draws attention to the chaos and emotional damage entailed in what is often described in military documents and by participants as the work of "calming civilians." During the same year (2003) Edith was out on these raids, Riverbend, a twenty-five-year-old Iraqi woman blogger, wrote of waking up "jolted into reality with the sound of a gun-shot, explosion or yelling. You sit up, horrified and panicked, any dream or nightmare shattered to oblivion. What can it be? A burglar? A gang of looters? An attack? A bomb. Or maybe it's just an American midnight raid?"[24] Riverbend captures the visceral terror of being ripped from sleep to a fear for one's life. These are the very raids Edith was called upon to separate and "calm" women and children. Riverbend responds to the occupation's framing that "the raids are for YOU! But the truth is, the raids only accomplish one thing: they act as a constant reminder that we are under occupation, we are not independent, we are not free, we are not liberated. We are no longer safe in our own homes—everything now belongs to someone else. I can't see the future at this point, or maybe I don't choose to see it."[25] Night raids mark the existential violence of perpetual insecurity, including within the confines of a home whose walls can be breached at any time.

Edith's account of terrifying Iraqi families also betrays the emotional work she had to perform on herself to fulfill her job requirements. She reasoned that at risk of being disciplined, she had to regulate her own emotional response to her assignments. "It was hard, but we *had* to do it. We had no choice." She needed to follow orders to keep her job. "I got bills to pay. I need my paycheck." Edith operated with fragments of competing ideologies in mind: her official military capacity to "calm down" women and children encountered in home raids as well as her lived experience imagining what it must be like for these populations when her team raided homes in the middle of the night. Although they were rarely intended in this way, interviewees' repeated references to "calming women" could also refer to their own experiences of self-regulation.

Edith's description of her job names the emotional labor that Lioness teams performed in a context of relative invisibility and institutional disrespect. Her marginality was captured in her recollection of poor training and an incident when she was left behind by a field artillery unit she was attached to while supporting a traffic-control point. The unit went through the town after the mission and handed out fliers. "I got left," Edith recalled. "Everyone else was a lot taller than me. And they kind of left me. You have all this weight on you, and that kind of slows you down." She recalled the incident as an accident but also attributed it to a lack of training. "We were not really ready for it," she explained. Her unit had three months' notice before it deployed, during which she recounted getting families ready—sending children to live with relatives, getting the house packed up, and ordering and shipping supplies. Because she did not join a Lioness team until she was already deployed, the preparation for her missions as a Lioness occurred only in the short amount of time leading up to the particular missions she was required for.

Inadequate training, particularly in the early iterations of the teams, is a common theme in some of the policy literature on early female counterinsurgency teams. It was also a common experience that servicewomen cited in our conversations. Since a Lioness such as Edith would be temporarily attached to different units for each individual mission, her lack of integration into the field artillery unit she was attached to intensified the issue of inadequate training. A more extreme example of this situation is reflected in the documentary *Lioness* when one of the characters, Shannon, was sent on a Lioness mission with a fire team, the portion of the unit that goes first into battle.[26] The team was to conduct a search operation, in which the Lionesses typically searched women and performed the sort of emotional labor Edith described. Shannon recalled an insurgent attack during the search operation followed by a flurry of shooting on all sides. She described being left behind by the fire team—all of a sudden, she was the only one on the street. The fire team had used hand signals that were standard among marines but unknown to Shannon, who was from the army.

Another aspect of Edith's marginality was manifest in the physical ailments she experienced as a result of her military labor and her corresponding mistreatment within the VA medical system. Injury and combat invisibility, compounded by VA practitioners' disregard, distinguished this first phase of Lioness teams. When Edith returned from her deployment, she noticed a constant ringing in her ears (tinnitus) as well as difficulty hearing in general. She avoided saying anything to her command, fearful that, especially as a woman, she would be perceived as trying to get out of the next mission, the next deployment, or the military. "I wanted to do my job. I just didn't want to be labeled," she explained when I asked if the hearing loss was noted in her discharge paperwork (it was not). As the hearing loss became more noticeable, she sought help at a VA medical center. She was tested and diagnosed with hearing loss and tinnitus at the center but was also told there was nothing the VA could do for her, since the injury was not considered "service connected," or directly caused by her military service.

Edith attributes her hearing loss to her work as a supply clerk and especially as a Lioness. So much ordnance was being used during her deployment that she would regularly run out of supplies. Her job as a supply clerk involved maintenance on vehicles in enclosed spaces, which meant a very high noise volume given that multiple vehicles were being run at once. As a Lioness, she went out in open vehicles and described how "sometimes we had to move fast. We didn't have hearing protection. When you have a cannon going off next to your ear, hearing protection isn't going to work." When she described the sorts of missions she went out on as a Lioness to the VA service provider, she was told that supply clerks do not go out on missions like that: "why would they be needed?" When Edith previously described "calming" women and children, she used the rhetoric of emotion to claim visibility and legitimation for forms of her labor that were completely disavowed by the VA, with dangerous consequences for her physical and mental health.

When veterans enter the VA system, they must provide evidence that their complaint is connected to their military service. There are a number of ways to make this connection. During the period Edith sought VA services (before legislative changes in 2010 concerning post-traumatic stress disorder [PTSD]), veterans had to prove three things: first, their current condition; second, an event or entity that caused the condition; and third, a nexus that tied the current condition to the event, such as a doctor writing in a report that a veteran's leg had been amputated because they stepped on a bomb.[27] For the first wave of veterans from wars in Iraq and Afghanistan, these criteria meant that they often faced difficulty in identifying an event that definitively caused their PTSD. Journalist and author Aaron Glantz extensively documented the VA's practices during this period, laying bare a process designed to "ferret out veterans trying to cheat the system, rather than compensate soldiers injured in the line of duty."[28]

Glantz gives the example of a veteran applying for compensation for PTSD being required to submit a twenty-six–page form, including an essay detailing the terrifying events leading to the onset of mental illness. The process of proving service connection is incredibly onerous, requiring veterans to file Freedom of Information Act requests from the Pentagon and the VA to obtain their own service records and pay to hire private specialists to get injuries legitimately evaluated. At times, veterans must go through a lengthy appeals process or, if their claim is approved, undergo another layer of compensation and pension medical examination (fraud detection), then wait for a claims adjudicator with no medical training to rate their disability.[29]

Changes in VA policy since that time now permit deployment to a war zone to count as what was formerly a qualifying event causing the onset of symptoms, assuming service members had reasonable fear for their lives at any point during the deployment.[30] Yet a VA inspector general report found a 30 percent error rate in the processing of VA claims, which was almost entirely attributed to the biases of the VA clerk processing the claim, such as assuming one's job (e.g., supply clerk) or gender limited that veteran's exposure to combat.[31] Edith's experience thus represented broadly problematic VA practices during the post-9/11 period. While VA exclusions were broad in the sense Glantz documents, a more specific pattern also emerges in relation to women such as Edith who suffered injuries when they were pulled from their regular job and sent on Lioness missions.

Because of the public advocacy Edith had done for women veterans' health, I was familiar with her story of being denied hearing aids by the VA and contacted her. She did eventually—and ironically—receive hearing aids through the private sector because her spouse, still in the military, had military health care (TriCare). In the process of sharing her experience as a Lioness and within the VA, she was also forthcoming about the PTSD she suffered as a result of her exposure to trauma during Lioness missions. She experienced nightmares after she came home, and certain things would trigger traumatic memories, such as the sound of fireworks reminding her of explosions and receiving gunfire. At the time we spoke, she still had difficulty in crowds. This especially bothered her because it limited the places she could take her young daughter. Realizing that she needed help, Edith sought out mental health services at the VA. Edith recalled her PTSD screening and the clinician's questions and comments: "What did I know about combat? What did I know about what goes on out on the battlefield? You're a woman, a logistics clerk. You wouldn't have seen combat," again erasing the emotional labor Edith described as quite central to the combat mission. She asked the male clinician a series of questions about his deployment, only to realize that he was in the staff section of an infantry unit and went off the base two to three times during his deployment. "I was outside the wire on an almost daily basis," she recounted with indignation in our conversation. "If I wasn't on some type of [Lioness] mission, I was on convoy. I did not get to sit in the office all day in the AC [air-conditioning]. My makeshift office did not have AC."

During this early period of Lioness missions, Edith recalled, there was tacit discouragement from her command of speaking too openly, especially outside of the military, about Lioness missions. After all, military policy technically prohibited women's participation in the sort of ground combat Edith and many of her fellow servicewomen were drawn into. One effect of the deliberately quiet nature of the early Lioness programs was that VA clerks such as Edith's were unaware of women's proximity to combat. Given the absence of a front line in the wars in Iraq and Afghanistan, men and women in logistics and other support specializations were also drawn into combat, making this experience not unique to women on

Lioness teams. Lionesses, however, exemplify a particular contradiction of being both valued precisely because they were women and marginalized for the very same reason. One advocate for women veterans' health explained in a private conversation that she had observed through advocacy in this area that clerks and practitioners such as those Edith interacted with were often male Vietnam War veterans who imported their own experience and assumptions into interactions with patients.[32]

Edith's experience at the VA discouraged her from seeking further treatment. "I felt so bad," she explained. "I was out there with my team. I was out there working and doing what I had to do." After the VA clinician asked "what she knew about combat" at the end of an hour-long session, Edith stopped seeking treatment for her PTSD for several months until she participated in a VA women's summit and was informed that she should not have been treated this way. After getting help through an advocate, she eventually did access treatment by returning to the VA and obtaining a different service provider.

Edith's attempts to get PTSD treatment within the VA system indicate the invisibility of Lioness' labor as well as a more widespread gender bias within military medicine. A VA inspector general report found that lower proportions of women veterans are diagnosed with PTSD and traumatic brain injury (the signature wounds of the US wars in Iraq and Afghanistan) and that the Veterans Benefits Administration denies women veterans' disability claims for PTSD more often than claims by men.[33] The veteran advocacy organization Swords to Ploughshares has found that women who have been physically injured are more likely than men to suffer PTSD, which makes their more frequent denial of PTSD disability claims even more concerning.[34] This organization has argued that higher disability denial rates and lower diagnoses rates are related to the assumption that women do not serve in combat.[35]

Combat invisibility and injury defined the first wave of gendered counterinsurgency under the Lioness program. Edith's experience also speaks to how breaking down barriers to women's integration into combat units happened through exposure to injury. The lack of training evident in her account heightened her exposure to injury during missions. This was especially apparent in Shannon's account of getting left by the fire team she was attached to, unaware of the hand signals its members were using. Edith's labor was given new value with the advent of Lioness teams. She was no longer an interchangeable supply clerk but instead was a soldier whose female status, in the eyes of her military command, gave her the unique ability to access and calm Afghan women. She understood her own experience as a mother as equipping her with the emotional expertise needed to calm the subjects of occupation. The rhetoric of emotion was also a way to lend visibility to labor that was erased through the unofficial, ad hoc nature of the Lioness program,

FIGURE 9.   A female engagement team member questions an Afghan boy during a vehicle interdiction. Image courtesy of the Defense Visual Information Distribution Service.

which also exposed Edith to additional physical and psychological harm. Exacerbating this additional harm, official VA policies and unofficial VA and popular assumptions of women's relationship to combat prevented Edith from accessing treatment for medical conditions caused by her military service.

Female Engagement Teams: Emotion as an "Epistemic" Military Resource

In February 2009, a team of female marines and a female interpreter called themselves a "female engagement team" as they completed a cordon-and-search operation in western Afghanistan. This team, and what would grow into the larger FET program, performed a searching function similar to what the Lioness teams undertook in Iraq at the time. The FETs were partially based on the Lioness program, but military literature on the teams uses the word "engagement" to draw attention to how they distributed humanitarian relief supplies to Afghan women in their homes.[36] In practice, "engagement" meant that FETs built medical clinics, spearheaded education projects, and visited orphanages in an effort to improve the military's public image. Here FETs sought to draw support away from the insurgency and develop relationships with civilians who might supply information valuable to the military occupation.

By late 2009, the International Security Assistance Force commander required all military units to assemble and deploy FETs. From this point onward, the military used the term "female engagement team" to describe all-female military teams assembled to do a variety of counterinsurgency tasks.[37] With the formal establishment of the FET program, we also see a shift in how the military emphasized emotion and how that affected women involved. Women such as Edith described their ability to calm civilians down amid a violent home raid, while FET participants were more overt in their specific emphasis on emotion as an intelligence-gathering asset. Their emphasis on emotion as a resource to gather intelligence valorizes female emotionality in a way that mirrors some feminist theorists' treatment of emotion as an "epistemic resource"; however, in sharp departure from theorists such as Jaggar, who argue for female emotionality as containing the seeds of new critiques of power, military valorizations of emotion aim to further entrench occupation.[38]

The Iraqi Women's Engagement Program was an informal and largely undocumented program undertaken by the US Marine Corps in 2006 that featured female marines discussing "factors of instability" with Iraqi women through sewing projects, medical clinics, and the requisite cups of tea.[39] The program and its elements that filtered into the FET program shared similarities with the District Stability Framework's use of the category of "instability" as well as its emphasis on using development projects to mitigate the causes of instability established by the framework.

Military documents discuss the FET program evolving from the ad hoc assembly of women temporarily pulled from their regular jobs with little additional training to, by 2010, a more institutionalized and trained dedicated full-time force to support battalion and company commanders. One such document estimates that during the last half of 2009, ad hoc on-call FETs (as opposed to those permanently assigned) conducted seventy short-term "search and engagement missions" in Afghanistan.[40] The first platoon of full-time Marine Corps FETs was deployed to Afghanistan in March 2010. Interviews with women who served on FETs during this period suggest that while dedicated full-time FETs may have existed, their ad hoc and partially trained iterations were more prevalent. Military efforts to institutionalize FETs in the form of training and dedicating full-time teams does, however, speak to certain factions of military leadership recognizing feminized emotional labor's value to the sorts of home raids, house-to-house searches, and other missions the military engaged in.

When the army published the first *Commander's Guide to Female Engagement Teams* in 2011 to codify knowledge of the FET program, it outlined how FETs should be organized, recruited for, and trained. The guide includes reading lists of popular and historical books about Afghanistan as well as some films. It also discusses the variation in training leading up to this publication, with marines receiving four months of formalized training compared to the army's one to two weeks. The document states that army training became more formalized after June 2011, ranging from three to fourteen days, although interviews with trainers and team members suggest that this was far from uniform.

Courtney was one such interviewee. Having recently graduated from West Point, she was preparing to deploy to Afghanistan as an officer in 2011, precisely at the moment when the army issued an "all army activities" statement that anyone deploying to the Operation Enduring Freedom theater was required to have a FET. Courtney summarized the army directive: "If you were deploying to the OEF [Operation Enduring Freedom] theater, you will have a FET—nonnegotiable—you will have one." This was "accompanied with zero guidance on who would make up these teams, what these teams were supposed to do, how they would be equipped, how they would be trained. It was just 'you will do this.'" The institutionalization of gendered counterinsurgency over time grows out of a military tendency to necessitate acronyms, manuals, and other bureaucratic forms when any idea, such as "engaging women," is implemented. It also signals internal anxiety within the military over the necessity to improve relationships with local populations to prevent accelerating the insurgency.

Courtney was preparing to transition out of her unit when her brigade commander asked if she would be willing to take on the role of assembling and being the officer in charge of a FET. She was excited about the opportunity because she was in the process of applying to the cultural support team program, which was training its first classes during this same time. Many of the female officers I spoke with, particularly those who had graduated from military academies, expressed similar excitement at an opportunity to create something new and to promote women's equality in the military. Courtney saw herself as a feminist blazing a trail for women's equal pay and equal rights within the military. She represented a particular strand of military liberal feminism concerned with the equal rights of US servicewomen. This strand either considered US military presence to be an improvement for women living under occupation or bracketed out entirely the question of what foreign military intervention meant for local women.

The *Commander's Guide to Female Engagement Teams*, which Courtney located through a Google search, was the only official document she could find to refer to while she put together the FET. The guide is a window into how the army conceptualized servicewomen's value, with access to information featuring as paramount in the FETs' purpose. The guide describes a "triangle of knowledge" several times "that must be targeted for information collection" and differentiates the triangle according to the type of information men, women, and children are privy to: "In Afghanistan, we observe rather consistent themes. Men interpret information and tell you what they think you want to hear. Women see and hear what goes on behind the walls. Children run free in the community and see, watch, and are involved in nearly every activity in the community."[41] Women are understood here as a more authentic source of information and thus a coveted intelligence source. To access this source, the guide provides a list of questions that servicewomen can ask Afghan women ranging from "what is the biggest concern for your family/village?" and "is the population in this village changing?" to "who do you think can help you?" and "what is your typical day like?"

In addition to civilian women being seen as a valuable intelligence source, FET materials consider the moral role of women as holding the potential to influence an insurgency's outcome. Another army source describes the teams' intent to "build relationships with Afghan women to earn their trust and give women confidence in the local government," where the "desired end state is to influence families/communities to disavow the Taliban, influence other women, and demand basic services from the local government (with coalition force support)."[42] This goes beyond conceptualizing women as an untapped intelligence source and reaches into the expansive domain of counterinsurgency as a war for the population's approval.[43]

Much of the popular media coverage of the FETs emphasized their humanitarian and developmental activities, such as medical outreach and microfinance.[44] This coverage took at face value the military's own claims that these were the primary tasks of female counterinsurgency teams and that their main objective was to sway local popular opinion in favor of the occupation, or "win hearts and minds" in military parlance. Prominent academic critiques of counterinsurgency, themselves drawing on such media coverage, perpetuate this assumption that counterinsurgency's humanitarian rhetoric aims at securing local consent to foreign occupation as it also attempts to sway domestic public opinion.[45] However, a much more important aim of these programs was related to intelligence collection and combat. Gendered understandings of emotion as a weapon that female soldiers could deploy to collect intelligence or silence a home raid were a far more significant aspect of these programs. Certainly, materials from multiple trainings reference FETs' support of midwifery education and clinics as well as medical outreach and visits to local orphanages and schools. Yet taking these projects at face value obscures the teams' intelligence purpose and combat function. Female soldiers' narratives and a deeper look into program documents instead show how violence was perpetuated through gendered understandings of emotion as an "epistemic [military] resource."[46] This violence was projected outward, toward civilians such as Riverbend, and inward, as was manifest in Edith's PTSD.

In interviews, former FET members described how a humanitarian activity such as a hospital clinic served the dual purpose of interviewing those waiting for medical services and gathering "atmospherics." A public affairs officer I interviewed who was previously assigned to publicizing the FETs clarified some of the structural reasons for their documentation as humanitarian. She explained that she was forced to delete photographs of women doing anything that violated combat arms restrictions, thus skewing media coverage to feature female counterinsurgents engaged in humanitarian outreach. Angry and exasperated in her recollection of the order, the public affairs officer understood this erasure as part of why the public so misunderstood the role that women such as Edith had played in the wars. At the same time, allegedly humanitarian locations such as a medical clinic, which could be officially documented and promoted by public affairs, were rich sites for intelligence gathering. Military documents such as the *Commander's Guide to Female Engagement Teams* imagine servicewomen as "naturally" more equipped than their male counterparts to gather "information," "intelligence," and "atmospherics," variously termed.

This imagination of women's superior intelligence-collecting capabilities goes beyond claims for women's unique ability to access other women and considers intelligence collection a natural ability that can be mapped onto sex. For example, the *Commander's Guide to Female Engagement Teams* states that "anecdotal evidence shows that Pashtu men often feel more comfortable opening up around American women than American men and see American women as sort of a third gender."[47] The same document talks about ancient Persian queens wielding political power "behind closed doors," listing FETs as a way to gain access to those conversations. The reference to Persia again creates an imaginary ahistorical Afghan, stating "we are still in Persia" as if nothing has changed. The reference to Pashtun men's increased comfort level around American women is an expression of the argument that the mere presence of servicewomen will cause Pashtun men to open up with information that may contain valuable intelligence.

Exemplifying this way of thinking, a male Special Forces commander I interviewed about the program described what he called the "intelligence value of having females on a raid site to secure, separate, and calm." His team had come to recognize that when a FET separated and calmed Afghan women, this interaction could also be an "information operations" mission to "tell women the truth that 'we are females just like you. We understand your concerns. This is why we are in your village. We're not here to rape and kill. We're here to try to help against the people persecuting you.'" Tying this feminized calming presence to the collection of information, the colonel also described the sort of information FETs were privy to such as the last time the Taliban were seen in a village or when an attack was supposed to happen, which the unit could then confirm based on what others had said. The *Commander's Guide to Female Engagement Teams* echoes a similar intent of the teams: "Part of the mission is to search women. But, as the word 'engagement' suggests, this really is about building relationships with Afghan women from whatever tribe is in your area of operations (AO). . . . It is about reassuring local women that US intentions are good and that the United States is there to protect them. The moment the FET walks into a village wearing headscarves and politely approaching local families, the FET is already sending a powerful and positive message."[48] Informing this military text's representation of a "powerful and positive message" is a series of arguments about female counterinsurgents as being predisposed to representing themselves as a peaceful, calming presence capable of developing relationships with civilian populations. Women's labor is marked as distinctive in its emotional quality, in contrast to the relative unremarkability of male soldiers. But rather than accepting the FETs according to the *Commander's Guide to Female Engagement Teams'* description of sending a "powerful and positive message," we must understand them as a form of violence that operates through gendered notions of emotion in combat.

When the Special Forces commander tethered intelligence collection to FETs' emotional labor of calming Afghan women, that connection ran much deeper than his own unit's experience. An article written for the army's website quotes an officer getting ready in 2011 to deploy on a FET who explains to the public affairs officer interviewing her that FETs' "primary purpose is intelligence gathering from Afghan women."[49] The statement and its publication on the army's website contradicts other official military statements that go to great lengths to delineate the gathering of "atmospherics," understood as information in general, versus the collection of intelligence, which carries a more specific meaning and is officially restricted to trained intelligence operators. An article in the *Marine Corps Times* similarly quotes a FET trainer who was interviewed. "'Women are invited into homes almost categorically.' This access can lead to important intelligence. '[Afghan] women observe key terrain every day. . . . These women know who's supposed to be in their village and who isn't.'"[50]

Beth's deployment reflected a similar focus on intelligence gathering. She went to Afghanistan on a FET in 2010. After her partner was injured and sent home, Beth was the only woman assigned to an eighty-person troop and was among a handful of other women—flight medics, pilots, counterintelligence operators—stationed on the same forward operating base. She lived in her own containerized housing unit (essentially a repurposed shipping container) sandwiched between housing for men in the unit. Beth spent most of her time "outside the wire" on FET missions. In an interview, she spoke of the need to "sell" the Special Forces operators on the base on the capabilities the FETs could offer them. "We can speak to females because male soldiers can't, but our capabilities go farther. Just like any other HUMINT [human intelligence] going out, we always steer clear of saying 'collect,' but essentially that's exactly what we were doing," she explained, referring to her interpreter's security clearance level and recording device. She gave several examples of FET missions she went out on, describing their purpose as "eliciting information" and passing this information to the Navy SEAL and counterintelligence teams with which she worked.

Beth's discussion of her unique access to "information" redeploys a warped version of an argument that feminist theorists of emotion have made for recognition of how observation and emotion shape one another. Jaggar has influentially argued for emotion as an "epistemic resource" that does not just shape knowledge in a way that is obscured by Western dichotomies of reason versus knowledge but is in fact fundamental to the creation of feminist social theory.[51] Beth and Edith both rely on an understanding of women as more capable of using emotional sensitivity to calm civilians down and gain access to information. This understanding is not altogether different from Jaggar's argument that women's socially assigned roles as caretakers requires emotional expression and that this emotionality should be considered a strength.[52] Where Jaggar develops an argument regarding the possibility for what she calls "outlaw emotions" to enable critiques of the status quo, Beth's argument is rather different regarding her "epistemic advantage" of being able to access certain information her male counterparts cannot. Yet her access to this information is not "outlaw" in the sense Jaggar suggests. In fact, it further entrenches status quo power structures of violence by promoting the US occupation.

Beth also spoke of the "advantage" that FETs brought through their access to children. In contrast to defense officials' guidance to "harden your heart and keep the children at arm's length," Beth and other interview subjects cited children as valuable sources.[53] "We found that kids are terrific sources of information. . . . They're a lot easier to read. We were in a village we knew had been a bed-down location for high-value targets and also places where they manufactured IEDs [improvised explosive devices] and then would go out and disperse them." She explained how part of an improvised explosive device is made up of rods from batteries and that throughout her patrol they had stumbled on a few. "We were always equipped with pens, pencils, and pads of paper because the kids would eat that stuff up." In exchange for such goods, "kids would pick up rods. Kids would find a few and we would say 'oh, bring me more, tell your friends.' We set a record for 120 rods found in one day. That told us they manufactured this stuff [improvised explosive devices] there."

Beth used this story as an example of her FET's victory in demonstrating its value to obtain intelligence, proudly recalling how after this mission the SEAL team she was attached to adopted a similar strategy. She also brought the example up in recalling what she referred to as the more "devastating" aspects of the mission. She explained how they were able to do this operation because senior men from the village had gone away to do a "key leader engagement" with the male soldiers. "When the meeting dispersed, you could see the frantic 'what are you doing?!' and the men began throwing rocks at the kids. You feel bad, but you need to survive." She continued ambivalently, seeming to search internally for a way to square her own emotional response with the mission. "You have a mission at hand. Maybe it's manipulation. Maybe it's survival." Similar to Edith's emotional labor of regulating her own reaction to night raids, Beth too performed emotional labor to filter out her ethical questions about the risk she exposed children to by using them as an intelligence source.

FETs deployed emotional labor in multiple directions: in relation to the subjects of military occupation targeted for intelligence collection and, internally, to suppress soldiers' own reactions to the emotional disturbance entailed in a home raid and in the exploitation of children's access to intelligence materials at the expense of their safety. Emotional labor also took on different valences depending on its application, with Edith's emphasis on "calming" the subjects of a night raid differing from Beth's memories of the intelligence sources she was able to access. Intelligence collection proved to be one area in which FET members described their value as coming from unique emotional capabilities available to them as women (or, in the case of the male Special Forces commander, available to those under his command). Both of these examples echo a strain of feminist theory (Jaggar and others) that emphasizes emotion as a source of feminine value, but in contrast to feminist theories aiming to disrupt prevailing power relations, FETs use a liberal feminist language to entrench imperial violence.

Rochelle's Journal: Imperial Feminism and the Rhetoric of Emotion

Rochelle, a white woman in her late twenties when we met in 2017, came from a midwestern town with a population of 2,500. Tucking her hair behind her ears, she recalled how her high school had a graduating class of 56. The military was an avenue out of her small town to experience something different. Although she had a cousin who was a marine deployed to Iraq while Rochelle was in high school and one of her grandfathers had also served in the army, she had never really thought of joining the military until West Point began recruiting her for her track abilities. She visited West Point and was swept away by the campus and, in her words, the feeling of "purpose" a military academy provided. "I wanted to—I guess like any young person—get out there to make your mark on the world. I wanted to make a difference. And I wanted to get out of my small town and experience the world. It's very purposeful, and I think that's what I was really seeking at that point, was just bringing purpose to my life, to have that driving force." After graduating from West Point in 2009, Rochelle was commissioned as an army officer trained in transportation logistics, a specialization she described as a way to be "part of the action, part of the war that was going on when, as a female, options are limited when it comes to combat. But convoys had to go out; people needed supplies." In 2010 she deployed as part of a FET with a field artillery battalion.

I interviewed Rochelle initially, then we stayed in touch about my project. After our interview and subsequent conversations, she generously shared journals and correspondence she had kept during her deployment. Her memories of serving on a FET amplify Beth's emphasis on servicewomen's emotional labor as primarily geared toward accessing information that could be useful to the military occupation, which she describes through the terminology of "atmospherics." Feminized emotional labor brought access to the Afghan home and family, with the trope of family gaining further definition through Rochelle's deployment with her own husband. In addition to the emphasis on calming Afghan civilians and having unique access to intelligence, Rochelle also used the rhetoric of emotion to develop an imperial feminist language that exoticized the Afghan Other as it painted the female soldier as a liberated model of women's empowerment.

In Afghanistan, Rochelle was attached to a field artillery battalion that was taking over from an infantry battalion. The shift meant that the artillery battalion, which was trained in firing large weapons over long distances, was doing things outside of its expertise, such as door-to-door, village-to-village missions. During these missions, soldiers went from house to house gathering information from villagers and looking for weapons. FETs were becoming more institutionalized in the army at the time, and Rochelle's commander brought the idea to her of assembling a FET. She was excited about it, describing how she "took it and ran with it. I have always been very interested in other people's cultures. And being able to get out of the security of the forward operating base and take part in the missions my fellow soldiers were going to be taking a part of and really feel like I was needed and contributed a lot to it" were all reasons she was enthused about the program. In our conversation, she framed her work on FETs as akin to the alternate career she had considered before attending West Point of becoming a therapist, a job she defined as "helping other people." Expanding on how military service had always "called" to her, "whenever you think about the war, all we're out there trying to do is the right thing. It called to me. And that's kind of the same way I felt about the female engagement teams, especially as it started developing after we deployed. I just hope that the skills and training and all that affected at least one person in a positive way." The rhetoric of emotion was here a way to talk about positively changing the lives of others. It also gave meaning to military service as a self-sacrificing job that was about improving people's lives abroad while also protecting US citizens domestically.

Rochelle applied this parallel with therapeutic work to her self-described leadership style of making those under her command "feel cared for" and observing that "people come to you with their issues or their problems, and they're just looking for somebody to provide advice or just listen to them." In our discussions, Rochelle frequently used the language of caring, directing the work of care to both her own military team and the Afghan civilians whom FETs interacted with. Discussing the foundation of trust her leadership relied on, she talked about how, "as a good leader, you've got to cultivate the sense of belonging and caring. Nobody is going to want to follow you anywhere if they don't believe in you and what you do, because there are a lot of times that we have to do things that we don't believe in. We have to follow orders that we don't want to follow." She described how her convoy had gotten lost during a mission and, with tensions running high, one of her US soldiers nearly came to blows with an Afghan National Army member (both men). Based on the trust she had previously established with the US soldier, she was able to talk him down and convince him to walk away. Rochelle's language of emotional maturity placed her in contrast to the two hot-headed male soldiers and in particular the Afghan who, unlike the US soldier, did not benefit from a woman's friendship to gracefully extract him from a volatile situation. Emotion here was an "epistemic resource" but directed toward the male troops with whom women were deployed, as opposed to Afghans from whom the military was trying to extract intelligence. This example also points to the various ways that military rhetoric of emotion describes situations in which emotion is strategically valuable to achieve a particular outcome or set of information. Such strategic manipulation of emotion stands in contrast to dominant cultural narratives of emotion as an authentic reflection of one's humanity.

In her journals and letters home, Rochelle described the monotony of the time she spent on the base. She wrote of waking at 6:00 a.m., 6:30 on alternate days, to the feeling of "ice sitting in the air" once winter had set in. In these records, she mentioned gathering her clothes, helmet, running belt, and things she needed to shower and shoving them into a backpack she referred to as her "assault pack." She then walked to a series of trucks housing a small building with three toilets and three shower stalls. She described being able to walk across the length of the building in five steps, meaning showering became a race because the occupant was in full view of everyone outside each time the door opened. Many women I interviewed felt it was necessary to describe showering in detail, often in an attempt to convey their spartan living conditions as well as to draw attention to the increased visibility and physical vulnerability they experienced while attending to basic physical needs such as using the toilet and bathing.

As a staff member working on a more established base, Rochelle's access to hygiene was better than most, but she still painted a picture in letters to family of showering in broken stalls by crouching next to the faucet and throwing water on herself. In response to my questions about her concern in her journals of someone seeing her shower, she explained that male and female facilities were separate, but she would take precautions such as never showering at the same time each day and informing the male soldiers she trusted in her tent when she was going to shower and when to check on her if she had not returned. For part of her deployment, Rochelle had a "room" constructed out of a partition that separated her area from the rest of a large tent where men slept, while at other points she slept on a cot in an unpartitioned tent with several other women.

Despite growing public concern at the time about sexual assault within the US military, Rochelle's concern for her physical safety while showering did not involve US soldiers but instead a group of Jordanian soldiers stationed on the same base.[54] Some fellow male soldiers were supportive of her concern, while others thought she was "making a big deal out of nothing."[55] To protect herself, she tried to always travel with one or two other soldiers, which led to rumors of relationships between her and anyone she was consistently seen with. At one point during her deployment, evidence came to light that she was being stalked; an interpreter turned in a written schedule he had found that tracked her movements. When she retold the story, the written schedule vindicated the precautions she took even at the skepticism of some of the men on her unit. Rochelle's experience of taking precautions to physically protect herself from male soldiers recalls what some feminist scholars have called female "bodies being viewed as foreign within an institution that embodies masculinity and virility."[56] Although many women I interviewed were eager to share experiences of gender discrimination and sexism in general throughout their military careers, they also emphasized how the *foreign* male troops they worked with as part of the International Security Assistance Force displayed even more horrendously inappropriate behavior. Foreign male troops' indiscretions were distinctly racialized in these narratives—for instance, attributing the Jordanian soldier's sexism to his foreign culture—while sexism within the US military was not attributed to the soldier's racial or cultural origins.

Rochelle describes the disorientation of being on the base, where "everything is gray and dusty. Large cement barriers line every gray dirt road. The same tent is used for every building—tall with a rounded top." One-room windowless wooden buildings and dented containers fill the spaces between the tents. "The sound of helicopters coming in and going out bounces off the barriers until you can't tell where exactly the sound is coming from." After showering, Rochelle walked for ten minutes through this landscape to her office. Here she reflected that "it is really hard to remember that I'm in a war zone sometimes," chronicling how she arrived in the office around the same time most days to prepare the same reports. "If it wasn't for the random incoming rounds I wouldn't know here from [Fort] Polk [military base in Louisiana]. On the really busy days I hardly leave my office. It feels like the same day every day." She emphasized how she loved her job but, as a staff officer, "I hate being in the office away from the action. At least tomorrow I get to go out on a VMOP [veterinary and medical operations program], a medical support mission to one of the surround[ing] villages. We provide basic medical support to whoever shows up. So that will help the drag. But I really need to start getting out there because that is when I really feel like I'm doing something. Well something other than staring at a computer screen for eighteen hours every day."

Like many of the women I interviewed, Rochelle described the FET missions as a way to break up the monotony of what otherwise, in her words, felt like the movie *Groundhog Day*, in which the protagonist is doomed to wake up and repeat the same day again and again. In other interviews I conducted, female marines spoke of the FET as a way to get off the base and feel like they were "doing something." This was amid the drudgery of waiting, preparing presentations, and arranging logistics—often less discussed but very prominent parts of a military occupation. Rochelle wrote in her journal how she and several others were the only ones in her staff division who regularly left the base. FET participants often framed the opportunity to get off the base as a welcome interruption to the boredom they experienced as a very real part of war making. It was also an opportunity to fulfill some of the fantasies service members carried with them on deployment of improving the lives of civilian populations. Rochelle's journals also show how her own personal experiences contradicted some of the impressions she had received from military cultural awareness trainings of Afghanistan as being populated by helpless, universally oppressed women.

Rochelle wrote in her journal and described during her interview how humanitarian aspects of the FET such as medical relief infused deployments with personal meaning. Her description is similar to what Didier Fassin refers to in relation to humanitarian reason as "moral sentiments," or "emotions that direct our attention to the suffering of others and make us want to remedy them."[57] In a parallel fashion to how aid workers and other humanitarian benefactors are often discussed, such moral sentiments served as powerful motivators for many servicewomen to join and carry out FET missions. Such sentiments serve as a reminder that FETs' humanitarian dimension cannot be dismissed as propaganda alone. They also structure female counterinsurgents' own meanings of their deployment as in part concerned with the liberation of Afghan women. In media accounts, FET members speak of their belief in "giving Afghan women hope," "getting Afghanistan back on its feet," and "making sure women's needs are met," suggesting that this was a more powerful narrative that gave meaning to women's participation in counterinsurgency.[58]

Rochelle was the officer in charge of FETs during her deployment, meaning she led every FET mission within the brigade. She assembled the teams, selecting women she felt could "hold their own" to prove the strength of this new program. She trained them as well, drawing on the expertise of her interpreter, Maryam, whose skills she lauded and with whom she remained close at the time of our first interview. Rochelle also participated directly in a number of missions. When we spoke, she divided her team's missions into two categories: the first consisted of accompanying the platoon out on patrol to search for weapons or any other suspicious materials or information, and the second involved meetings and events with Afghan women. For the first category of mission, she told of the area in which she was deployed as one of "known enemy activity" and explained that the patrols were also a way for the International Security Assistance Force to show its presence in the area. Along with the platoon, the patrol consisted of Rochelle, Maryam, and at times another FET member. The platoon of US and Afghan soldiers would approach an Afghan home and ask if Rochelle could speak with their wives, sisters, daughters, or any other women who might be inside. She would then go into the home while US forces did security outside. Rochelle recalled speaking with women in their kitchens while they prepared food, asking questions such as "Do you feel safe in this area?," "Have you seen any activities we can do to help you?," and "Are there weapons here?"

In her journals, Rochelle chronicled these sorts of missions in greater detail. She was deployed with her husband at the time, an occurrence replicated in several other women's interviews. In a unique set of circumstances, Rochelle acted as the FET to her husband's infantry company to "smooth their interaction with the locals and make it easier for them to enter into households" during patrols. She wrote in her journals of being incredibly nervous about her position not only as the sole woman working with an infantry company but also as the wife of the company commander. On the particular mission she documents, the infantry company was searching for weapons storage sites. She recalled running over and over in her mind the protocol for loading into the helicopter, "how to fasten my belt, how to load off the bird. Checking and rechecking my gear. And mainly trying not to look nervous in front of the soldiers and trying to calm myself down. . . . I wanted to do everything right, and I wanted everyone to see that

I was doing the right thing as a way of proving that I was a good soldier and could fit in with them." The experience of being the only woman on a combat arms company or some other space in which female bodies are considered "foreign" was a common experience among FETs and often manifested itself through additional pressure to model women's capabilities.

One aspect of military occupation the FETs allowed, which came with the increasing prevalence of FETs during Rochelle's deployment, was the transformation of the Afghan home into a key invasion site. "One very vivid memory that I have was walking in, not realizing it, to a woman that had maybe given birth five hours ago," Rochelle wrote. "And she was there, surrounded by all her female relatives. That was a very short conversation because I felt like I needed to let them be." In an instance Rochelle herself recalls as an extreme invasion of privacy, this experience exemplifies the vulnerability of the most intimate experiences, now transformed into objects of security surveillance. Soldiers' recollections of such experiences vary from a certain matter-of-factness that this was their mission and they did not have a choice to the horror Edith expressed at breaking down doors in the middle of the night and terrifying children. Rochelle forged an explanation for the events out of ideas about Afghan masculinity: "Men [in Afghanistan] are in the director's seat. They're the one who drives the family. But what a lot of people don't realize is that they don't hold moments like that [birth] as high as they should, or I feel like they should." Her explanation exonerates the military occupation, treating it as necessary and immovable. The reason for the unfortunate invasion of privacy then comes from the men of the household failing to keep extraneous people out of this most important event, with the story demonstrating the shallow moral depths of Afghan men in general.

FET members used the notion of family, particularly when it included children, to conceptualize their purpose. Immediately after her comment about Afghan men as undervaluing key moments such as birth, Rochelle continued, writing that "women are the ones who are raising the children, who are influencing them. I always felt like if you can reach the children and help influence how they see the world, and have a broader view of what life is like, then that's where the real success is." The theme of children and the familial more generally came up frequently in conversations with former FET members, often in terms of making the Afghan family or home a target for military intervention.[59] FET members often mentioned women as a conduit to children who, as in Rochelle's comment, were seen as the greatest hope for shifts in cultural and political attitudes. Servicewomen's own familial status—as married or as parents—became further currency through reference and display of photographs in interactions with Afghan villagers.

Rochelle emphasized how the quality of her access to Afghan men was at times strategically more useful than the access her male counterparts experienced. She described Afghan men's fascination with her blond hair and blue eyes, which translated into men wanting to come over and see her. In her journals, she wrote of wearing a headscarf to delineate herself as a woman. "They didn't necessarily see me as a soldier, so they were freer in talking to me. A lot of times I could get more information out of them. Like the location of the enemy." She described an instance in a village when the male soldiers were unable to get information about Taliban who were known to be active in the area but would disappear when the soldiers arrived. Within fifteen minutes Rochelle was able to get information (from male villagers) that the Taliban had fled to a nearby hillside as soon as they saw the patrol coming, identifying their location as well as what had happened. She explained this as an effect of how "the male population didn't necessarily see me in an authoritative role or a role where I was an actual soldier and could do things like the men could do." Her account reflects the FETs' emphasis on gathering information and contributing to intelligence collection, which stands in contrast to military and popular media emphases on the FETs' humanitarian activities.

Rochelle's recollection of not being seen as a soldier resonates with the message in FET training materials that female soldiers provide "different insights in regard to what they see happening around them in the local community."[60] The *Commander's Guide to Female Engagement Teams* emphasizes FETs' ability to engage Afghan men as well as women, arguing that Afghan men interact differently with female versus male soldiers. Such a claim lumps together the category of female soldiers into a coherent unit and argues that it is on the basis of their sex that they are able to provide these "different insights." It is unclear in the guide exactly what these "different insights" might be, but other military documents and conversations with commanders referred to the perception that the ability to speak with both men and women alone meant that female soldiers were better equipped than men to keep a pulse on the "atmospherics" of a particular village.

A Special Forces commander I interviewed attributed FETs' ability to obtain such atmospherics to biological sex. "There's something to the saying men are from Mars, women are from Venus. Men look at things in scientific black and white. Females bring a different perspective to the fight that Mr. Male Macho Meat Eater's not going to give you. More perspective on the battlefield is not a bad thing." I asked him more about the skills he associated with his female team members, which he elaborated as women's ability to get "true atmospherics on the battle space quicker than men talking to an elder." He described how if women had a medic with them it was easy to "break down barriers and just start talking," and he contrasted Afghan men "putting on bravado, poking their chests out, protecting their village" versus women who did not put on a front. The officer made claims for female soldiers' ability to interact with Afghan men and women in a way he described as more "genuine" than male soldiers, leading to the potential for better information.

The idea that women were better at calming civilian populations was pervasive, as was the notion that women could get more or different types of information. Multiple official documents, including the *Commander's Guide to Female Engagement Teams*, describe how locals perceive female soldiers as "there to help versus there to fight."[61] Many of these documents reference a former FET member turned marine trainer's writings that "female service members are perceived as a 'third gender.'" The author elaborates how this "third gender" status "allows us access to the entire population, which is crucial in population-centric operations."[62] This trainer's use of the term "third gender" is striking, given its meaning in gender studies literature in relation to societies with nonbinary gender practices, or behaviors outside of dyadic male-female norms.[63] The trainer's use of the term here, however, is more in reference to the US female soldier's placement in Afghan society as distinct from both Afghan men and US male soldiers.[64] The trainer argues that women on FETs become a "third gender" by adopting both the dyadic "masculine" trait of carrying a gun and the dyadic "feminine" trait of domesticity. Rochelle's experience of being seen as a pseudosoldier marked by feminine difference reflects this strategic positioning that contained such value for intelligence collection. By maintaining the masculine-feminine dyad, such gendered deployments of traits that can be mapped onto this dyad uphold normative gender traits and assemble a "third gender" identity that can be adopted to gain strategically useful information. Military uses of the term "third gender" refer to a soldier who is biologically female yet maintains "male" attributes of dress in terms of military uniform, weaponry, and power. This particular use of "third gender" leaves the masculine-feminine binary untouched. At the same time, it plays into the construction of an imagined Afghan who is so ignorant as to be unable to dissect gender binaries.

If accompanying male patrols was one type of mission, Rochelle's second category involved meetings and events with Afghan women, including visits to girls' schools, monetary donations to build or improve girl's schools, and donations of books and toys—activities she referred to as "improvement and welfare." Such projects focused on improving opportunities for income generation. Rochelle recalled a meeting she held for Afghan women during which they discussed techniques for sewing, crocheting, and dehydrating food, all of which she described as "socially acceptable" ways to make money. To explain the income-generation component and why it would be considered linked to the objectives of a military occupation, Rochelle told the story of a woman she met during one of these meetings who had no way to generate income. "Her oldest was in his teens and had been approached by the enemy and offered money to lay roadside bombs as he was paving the roads. And of course she said he didn't take it. . . . But it gave me a better understanding of how these women need the ability to support their family. If they can support their family and they can get legitimate income coming in, then the enemy wouldn't have such a strong foothold."

Rochelle's is a fairly explicit argument for a direct link between poverty and extremism. This link mirrors the official development rhetoric that underdevelopment creates populations vulnerable to terrorist recruitment. In the words of the US Agency for International Development's Countering Violent Extremism Program, "many of the drivers of violent extremism and insurgency are development challenges. Indeed, factors such as socioeconomic inequalities, repression, corruption, and poor governance often create an enabling environment for radicalization and violent extremism."[65] On the defense side, the 2010 National Security Strategy reflects similar language: "to advance our common security, we must address the underlying political and economic deficits that foster instability."[66] This language suggests a broader terrain of funding, institutions, and development rhetoric and practices explicitly linking development objectives to fighting terrorism. In Rochelle's case, this link had material consequences. She observed from these meetings that women's lack of opportunities to generate income was linked to their support for the Taliban, so she advocated projects to support income generation and education for women.

In one of her accounts, Rochelle described traveling in a convoy to a village when a captain requested that she meet with the head of a regional women's *shūrā*. "So out the gate I went, headscarf and pistol. I went into town, and I can tell you that the Afghan men were not used to seeing American women (let alone soldiers) in scarves. It was really neat to see their reactions," describing how strange looks gave way to welcoming smiles. Most women I interviewed donned headscarves when they went out on FET missions, explaining it as a way to be both "culturally sensitive" and "identifiably female." Rochelle, like most women I interviewed, understood the veil as a symbol of women's repression at the same time as her actual experience interacting with veiled women complicated this understanding. One of the most striking things about Rochelle's journals was her shock at who was "under the burka." Upon encountering two women involved with the *shūrā*, Rochelle recounted how "the taller of the two walks up to me and flips open the front half over her head. And there stands a woman I could have met in Anywhere USA. She wore heavy eye makeup and lipstick. Her hair (that I could see, she wore a scarf under her burka) was done in a New Jersey bump. . . . And she came with a wide smile and a knock-off designer purse! She wore black heels with fishnet stockings." In the journal, she described other women she encountered with similar surprise at the fashion and modernity beneath the burka. There was also an element of delight at being "let in" to a secret world hidden from the male view. The journals betrayed the difficulty of maintaining the assumptions Rochelle carried to Afghanistan, often originating from superficial "cultural sensitivity" predeployment trainings, of women as one-dimensional repressed figures whose lives were untouched by modernity.

During this same mission, Rochelle wrote of meeting with Afghan women villagers eager for opportunities to generate income. One woman from a smaller village turned to her and said, "We don't want gifts or money, we want to learn to take care of ourselves. To raise chickens, cows, plant gardens, learn to sew, jam, anything that we can use to sustain our families." With clear admiration for this woman, Rochelle described how the village she had come from had been inundated with "night letters," death threats from the Taliban in retaliation for speaking with American troops. "But this lady came in spite of the threats in order to help her family and her village. How brave she is!" In this journal entry, Rochelle went on to describe how the meeting shaped the FET's projects for the rest of the deployment as the team focused on visiting outlying villages such as this woman's and support for agricultural and handicraft projects that would generate income. Rochelle was excited about being able to do this, exclaiming how blessed she felt to have met these women who gave her the project ideas. "Every step they take could very well mean their lives but they keep going anyways. How could you not want to help?"

Rochelle's language of admiration, nobility, and courage throughout her descriptions of Afghan women echoes notions of the (post)colonial subject as a "noble savage." Scholars of poverty and disaster have pointed to the use of phrases such as "resilience," particularly those repeated in popular media coverage of global poverty, that enable racist narratives of certain populations having an "exceptional ability to suffer."[67] Rochelle's use of such language not only exoticized the suffering other but also drew attention away from the forms of suffering caused directly by the military occupation, instead emphasizing the ways in which women in particular have "always" experienced suffering and confronted hardship with courage and ingenuity.

Rochelle built a related narrative that located Afghanistan as "backward" in historical time. Many FET members and other military personnel I interacted with described Afghanistan as being "back in time," including similarities to biblical times and the Stone Age. In an entry about a *shūrā* she participated in following up from her original meeting about livelihoods with Afghan women, Rochelle similarly reflected, "For years, I have always wondered what it would be like to live in the Stone Age[,] and now I know. I see it every day all around me. People walking around in clothes that haven't been washed, ones they have worn for years. Children with hair white from days of dust build up. Six-year-old girls carrying around their baby brothers. Eyes that tell a story of years of hardship. Houses made of mud and wooden poles, squares cut out for windows. Dirty misshapen feet." The imagery of dirty, misshapen feet evokes the colonial trope of hygiene historically used to justify intervention on behalf of a racialized people framed as unable to take care of themselves. In our interview, Rochelle described the villages she visited as "like going to the Stone Age," giving the example of mud houses and outdoor kitchens composed of four walls surrounding a metal bowl over a hole in the floor with an open fire. Her description removed Afghan people from their actual historical and geographical context that was shaped by the ongoing military occupation as well as US-Pakistani intervention that saw the active importation of weapons and extremism to the region during the Cold War. These geographical linkages are a far cry from the isolation that many soldiers describe in Afghan society.

In letters to family, Rochelle set up Afghan villagers not as pathetic victims but instead as heroic. "America has this way of looking at countries such as this one and sees poor uneducated creatures incapable of life. DO NOT be mistaken, these are people who live their lives and find happiness in them. They may not know how to read or write but they have survived here for years." She compared the integrity and ingenuity of Afghans to the many Americans she imagined who would never be able to survive the conditions she had observed in Afghanistan, ending her entry with a proclamation of love for the people she had come to know during her deployment. Rochelle expressed in these letters her desire to convey "how innovative these women are" as well as their selflessness and their ability to smile, joke, and "find joy" amid massive hardship. "They humble me and I will forever carry them in my heart," she proclaimed, repeating feelings of commitment and hesitation to leave unfinished missions when her deployment time expired. She juxtaposed her pleasant experiences being served tea, sweets, and new foods in the company of women and children she remembers looking like "full-sized dolls" to the experiences of her male counterparts being served undercooked goat meat in their meetings. Her letters home painted a romantic picture of raising children—imagined as inanimate yet endearing "dolls"—through a "village mentality" of older children helping younger children and everybody looking out for one another.

In our interview, Rochelle spoke of how her time on a FET gave her a greater perspective about what caused villagers to support the insurgency. The experience left her with the impression that "a lot of the [Taliban] organization is people without hope. They're caring for their families and doing the best they can with the opportunities that are presented to them. Unfortunately, a lot of those opportunities are very violent." Her journal displayed a similar empathetic understanding of what is more often in military doctrine described as "the enemy." At the same time, she presented an individualized argument about Afghans needing to make change for themselves, again in a way that is not dissimilar from aid workers' narratives lamenting the need for their beneficiaries to "take responsibility" and "pull themselves up by their bootstraps."[68] Rochelle wrote, "I am just here to help show them a better way. The rest is up to them." The notion of "showing them a better way" imagines the military as deployed to both serve a military objective and model certain behaviors to occupied populations. Rochelle talked about how she knew very little about Afghanistan before she was deployed. Her perspective of Afghan society was formed mainly through her relationship with her interpreter as well as information gleaned from military reading list material, such as *Three Cups of Tea*.

Early iterations of female counterinsurgency teams (2003–2010) valorized servicewomen's emotional labor. At the height of counterinsurgency's popularity within the US armed forces, this form of warfare's emphasis on civilian relationships was carried out through emotional labor. Edith, Beth, and Rochelle allow us to examine how the military ascribed value to and institutionalized that emotional labor. For Edith, military emotional labor was directed at calming down the subjects of a home raid. It also exposed her to heightened risk of physical injury, given that early iterations of female counterinsurgency teams were not trained for the sorts of missions they were sent on. Beth's story indicated how military emotional labor was categorically tied to intelligence collection, deploying a version of Jaggar's emotion as "epistemic resource" warped to military objectives.[69] This manipulation of certain feminist language—for instance, Jaggar's understanding of emotion as an "epistemic advantage"—allows FETs to frame themselves as a feminist force both within the military and toward Afghan society at large. A more critical eye toward emotional labor, which Hochschild enables, asks what forms of labor and exploitation go unrecognized *because* of their emotional character.

When female counterinsurgents perform emotional labor that has now become a military "epistemic resource," their labor is often tied to intelligence collection and, by extension, military violence such as detention and targeted killings. Imperial violence is constitutive of new military claims for the value of women's emotional labor. Gendered counterinsurgency's perpetuation of military violence also undermines popular and official narratives of female counterinsurgency as "softening" warfare and attempting to win consent to occupation through medical clinics and schools. Instead, the connection to intelligence exposes the bond between emotional labor and violence. It also provides a conceptually challenging twist on broader societal dichotomies of emotion that gravitate between devaluing emotion and caring work and elevating emotion to the core of human being.[70]

Military praise of the benefit that female counterinsurgency teams offer does not fit neatly within either of these dichotomous understandings of emotion.

On the one hand, military arguments for women's "innate" emotional expertise to calm violated civilians or access certain types of information value emotion, but only insofar as it serves a strategic purpose and further entrenches occupation. In this way, such military arguments are at odds with existing feminist critiques that reclaim emotion as containing the seeds to destroy the status quo. On the other hand, military celebrations of feminized emotional labor rely on a manipulation of emotion, visible in Beth's recollection of using children as an intelligence source, in contrast to the notion of emotion as a source of authentic humanity. In this way, the forms of emotional labor I have explored here provide a new conceptualization of emotion as a weapon of war. This weaponization of emotional labor reinscribes the idea of women as the "emotional gender" as it uses feminist rhetoric to shore up imperial violence.

In Rochelle's interviews and journal entries, we see how military emotional labor carried with it aspirations to improve the lives of Afghan subjects. Here emotion is also directed toward Afghan women and children, who Rochelle admired and romanticized while using moral sentiments in her attempts to improve their lives. Her narrative begins to assemble an imperial feminist framework that imagines servicewomen as models of liberated Western womanhood who can "enlighten" the imagined Afghan woman into supporting the counterinsurgency and liberating herself to be more like the Western woman. This central aspect of the new imperial feminism—military imaginations of servicewomen as global ambassadors for women's rights—deepens as the earlier Lioness teams and FETs grow into the special operative cultural support teams discussed in chapter 5. Emotional labor became even more closely sutured to violence when special operations seized upon gendered counterinsurgency to raid homes and pursue intelligence. Servicewomen used a liberal feminist language of equal rights and equal pay to frame themselves as trailblazers for military gender equality. At the same time, this became an imperial feminist language as servicewomen came to understand themselves as models of modernity and liberation. Servicewomen's understandings of themselves as models for Afghan women and trailblazers for equal rights must be held together with the violence they perpetuate through, for instance, home raids, and the violence they experience as they are denied veteran benefits and abused within the military.

5

A NEW IMPERIAL FEMINISM
Color-Blind Racism and the Special Operation of Women's Rights

In 2010, US Army Special Forces began to select and train women for cultural support teams (CSTs). Unlike the Lioness teams and female engagement teams (FETs), the CSTs were assembled through a competitive screening and selection process from a pool of applicants. A *Washington Post* reporter observing the second CST training in 2011 refers to the assessment and selection of the team as "100 hours of hell."[1] Several CST members I interviewed repeated this language of "100 hours of hell" as a point of pride, emphasizing the program's greater selectivity compared to the earlier less formalized iterations. After completing the physically rigorous selection process, women underwent six weeks of training at the JFK Special Warfare Center and School at Fort Bragg Army Base in North Carolina. A parallel program existed within the US Marine Corps, which attached CSTs to marine special operators. Women were trained on weapons and combat techniques they were largely unfamiliar with given their prior military jobs. They were given elements of special operations training, such as questioning, driving, field survival basics, and hostage and detainee operations; and a condensed cultural and linguistic training in which civilian contractors and linguists provided several hours of instruction on Afghan culture and language. This training was even more compressed than other military trainings due to the six-week total timeline, and the cultural and linguistic components mirrored the essentialist and minimalist approach taken in other military trainings. For instance, slides for one CST training listed in bullet points "stories of deprivation, stories of abuse, and signs of frustration, fear and desperation" as a description of Afghan society. There is no mention of the historical and structural economic factors behind these stories. As Rochelle's journals displayed, female soldiers found that the one-dimensional depiction of Afghan society they arrived with did not prepare them for their interactions with Afghan people.

As Special Forces established multiple full-time CSTs whose members had been screened, competitively selected, and trained more extensively than their Lioness and FET predecessors, they institutionalized gendered counterinsurgency in a way the military had not previously undertaken. The greater formalization and institutionalization of gendered military labor reflects how, within Special Forces, emotional labor was recognized and valued as enabling military tasks from home raids to intelligence collection. By 2010, team members and trainers also recognized that commanders in the field were increasingly requesting female counterinsurgency teams to accompany their missions. Once deployed, CSTs were generally used to support missions with US Army Rangers or Green Berets. More documentation is available of Ranger assignments, in which a common task was to accompany raids of Afghan homes and play the role of separating, searching, and questioning women and children. Most policy literature on these teams and conversations with those involved refers to women's innate ability to "calm" or "soothe" groups of women and children whose homes were raided, most often at night. The ability to soothe and calm served a strategic purpose because noisy protest from a household alerted the entire area to the raid. When CSTs were attached to Green Berets, these assignments revolved around special operative village stability operations (VSOs).

Special Forces developed the VSO strategy in Afghanistan by studying the history of Civilian Irregular Defense Group during the Vietnam War, which grew out of military advisory groups training, advising, and assisting the South Vietnamese army.[2] The program consisted of Special Forces soldiers occupying a village in order to train a local "village security force."[3] In the VSO program in Afghanistan, Special Forces aimed to establish a "foreign internal defense force" within Afghan villages to counter the Taliban. In the program's pilot version, CSTs were used with the intention of convincing Afghan women to encourage male family members to join the foreign internal defense forces.[4]

Women who served on CSTs have become cultural icons of a military feminism focused on women's ability to do the same jobs as male soldiers. Policy discussions leading up to women's integration into all combat jobs and popular cultural products such as the best-selling book *Ashley's War: The Untold Story of a Team of Women Soldiers on the Special Ops Battlefield* used CSTs to indicate progress toward military gender equality.[5] This new imperial feminism is reflected in servicewomen's understandings of themselves as models of liberated Western modernity and empowerment for Afghan women. Women defined their modernity through a sense of sexual freedom, which they used to frame interactions with Afghan men to dovetail with military intelligence gains. As CSTs' perceptions of themselves as ambassadors for women's rights became a powerful driver of their experience, they also found that increasing participation in previously male-only combat roles was tempered by their relegation to the gendered role of emotional expert. Female soldiers were considered "natural soothers" of tensions unleashed by violent home raids.

A new imperial feminism frames female counterinsurgents as ideal candidates to save brown women from brown men.[6] In contrast to the Lioness teams and FETs discussed in chapter 4, whose racial diversity reflected the diversity of the armed services at large, the women I interviewed who had served on CSTs were all white. Although I was not able to access demographic data on the composition of the CSTs (it was not clear if these data were kept), the documented white composition of special operations was certainly reflected in my small data sample of CST members and in general perceptions from within the military of the special operative teams. The military officially insisted on "color blindness," asserting that all soldiers are "green." Color-blind multiculturalism at once hides everyday and deeper historical practices of racism and white supremacy within the military as it enables arguments that a modern, multicultural military can liberate the imagined Afghan woman. Imperial feminist practices that further entrench racism and essentialized gender roles, even as women are integrated into combat, are linked to the image of the Afghan woman as a one-dimensional oppressed figure who must be saved. These interlinked workings of a new imperial feminism in domestic and foreign spaces challenge any notion of the post-9/11 wars as promoting a feminist agenda that liberates women abroad as it signifies gender equality within military ranks.

"We Are All Green": Race and the Language of "Military Multiculturalism"

In contrast to Edith's description of inclusive liberal multiculturalism in the military, where she was evaluated on the basis of her merit alone, Claudine recalled her experience at West Point as more overtly colored by race. Born in Miami to Haitian parents who fled the Duvalier dictatorship, Claudine enlisted in the army in her senior year of high school after she was rejected from the college she applied to. She saw the army as an opportunity to buy some time and gain access to the GI Bill to eventually continue her education. As an enlisted soldier, she was admitted to West Point after several years of service, joining the proportionally tiny number of Black women to graduate from the military academy. In 2016, West Point had graduated 357 Black women in its 114-year history. That year, 16 of the 18 Black women graduating from the class of over 900 at West Point raised their fists in an otherwise traditional graduation photo. An internet firestorm and an official investigation ensued, in which the women were accused of violating the Department of Defense rule banning political activity for those in the armed forces.

Claudine understood the photo as a reflection of how "African American females are a really small percentage of the population [at West Point]. They cleave together as a way to make it through. There are educational gaps, knowledge gaps. The idea that the community is there to uplift and support so you don't feel like you're a fish out of water. There is a generational weight in terms of if you're a first-generation college student in your family—just different things—so they come together to try to make it through West Point." She experienced racism at West Point veiled in the language of "culture" and "tradition," for instance, when a group of white cadets smirked under their breath to "turn that crap off" when a group of Black cadets gave an officially sanctioned dinner performance of a rap version of a traditional West Point song "The Corps."

For Claudine, sexism at West Point was a more overt experience. She described running from her class to get to lunch in the ten minutes they were allowed. "I had my arms full of books, and my backpack was full. I was running from class to get to our lunch formation; freshmen are not allowed to use the elevator. My arms are full. I'm running to the door. I realize it's going to be hard to open it because my arms are so full. I see a guy and I'm like, 'OK, he's going to open it,' and I smile and go, 'thank you so much,' and he literally slams the door in my face and he says, 'you're a female. You want to come here—you can open up your own goddam door.'"

Claudine graduated from West Point and later returned as an instructor. Upon her return, she sought to provide the sort of mentorship that she relied on as a cadet. As Claudine and many Black female cadets at West Point recall, the gospel choir was an important node for this mentorship. Sakima Brown graduated from West Point in 1998; her class included only eight other Black women. Brown described how "there were times we would sit at a table, and if there were more than two or three African Americans it was a problem . . . [p]eople would come over and ask, 'What are you guys doing?'"[7] The choir was, as Brown describes, "the only place you were allowed to be together, and it was once a week for two hours. During that time, you could talk about what was going on. It was the only place we were safe being together."[8] In response to the controversy surrounding the 2016 photo, Mary Tobin, a 2003 West Point graduate, described how "we don't talk about the microaggressions that minority cadets experience every single day. We don't talk about how many times we have to let racial slurs or crass racial jokes roll off our backs because all we want to do is graduate. I don't talk about how as a Black female leader within the Corps, I was told time and time again that I was a good leader because I was 'not like the rest of them.'"[9] Another veteran—a Black man who had attended West Point in the 1980s, described how Black cadets were spread into different housing units to "maximize [other students'] exposure to Blacks," writing that "the Army and Academy had an extra measure of expectation of the minorities of the nation who attended, to help the military to sort out their racial problems, while not so much helping the minorities sort out theirs."[10]

Even in the context of such overt anti-Black aggression at West Point, Claudine and many of her colleagues emphasized the military's color-blind approach to race. Speaking about her own mentors, she explained, "I always had good leaders when I was enlisted that always taught me how to advance myself. They never made it about race or anything. Just focused on how I was a junior soldier who was willing." Like Edith, Claudine understood the military as a meritocratic institution in which assumed neutral measures such as tests provided color-blind opportunities for success for those who try hard and do their jobs.[11] A key part of her experience was managing her own image, particularly when she entered a leadership position, to be seen as treating all cadets equally without regard to color. When Claudine wanted to become involved with the gospel choir upon her return to West Point, her mentors cautioned her that "you have to be careful not to show too much favoritism or partialness to your own race so the perception is not that you are partial to your own race. We have this phrase in the army that 'perception is reality.' Even if it's not your intention, it can be perceived this way." When she returned to West Point as an instructor, Claudine spoke of the particular way she had to make sure she was seen. She couldn't be socializing with or offering mentorship to Black cadets only and was careful to not be perceived as "grouping together" or "gathering together" with other women of color.

Catherine Lutz considers how, from the Cold War to the present, "the African American soldier has been a powerful symbol, his uniform a claim to full citizenship, in a sense to 'uniformity' with whites." At the same time, this figure remained, for many, "an oxymoron, at least, and an explosively dangerous error, at worst, and a challenge to the system on its own terms."[12] The West Point photo represents a more recent moment when the "explosively dangerous" quality of what Black soldiers have historically represented again became apparent. Even if the raised fists were not "political" in the sense Claudine discussed of representing Black power, the need to "cleave together" was itself a response to the racial disparities within elite military institutions such as West Point. The photo was dangerous because it poked so many holes in the story the military tells about itself—summed up in the adage I heard dozens of times on military bases—that "we are all green."[13] A reference to the olive drab green of some military uniforms, the assertion that everyone is "green" (not Black, white, Latinx, etc.) is an argument that race, articulated here as color, is not significant in the military. It is also a story about the military as a meritocracy: that everyone is treated the same regardless of their race and that promotion and success are the direct result of merit alone.

From my experience interacting with hundreds of military service members during this study, I found the narrative of color-blind liberalism and merit-based promotion to be widely internalized across military services. Military color-blind liberalism is not entirely different from what Eduardo Bonilla-Silva described in a different moment as a "frame of abstract liberalism." It is one of multiple frames of color-blind racism that, specific to its liberal frame, uses "ideas associated with political liberalism (e.g., 'equal opportunity,' the idea that force should not be used to achieve social policy) and economic liberalism (e.g., choice, individualism) in an abstract manner to explain racial matters."[14] In this way, a specific military iteration of color-blind racism comes into view in which race is discussed and understood through such liberal frames. The language of "culture" and "civilization" is also part of a color-blind frame of racism used in relation to foreign populations living under US military occupation. One effect of the internalized narrative of color-blind, merit-based "equal opportunity" was a general sense that race should not be discussed overtly within the military. This stood in stark contrast to the willingness I encountered, not unrelated to my own positionality as a white woman, to discuss gender.

Overt conversations about race were a threat to the story of everyone being "green" and were avoided at all costs in the military settings I observed. The distribution of racial diversity across military rank and services undermines military narratives about racial equality. Directly relevant to the CSTs, the US military's special operations is less racially diverse than the armed forces at large. The fact that African Americans make up 17 percent of the 1.3 million members of the armed services is commonly cited as evidence of the armed forces' diversity. Demographic data collected by the Defense Department show that Black women represent nearly one-third of all women in the armed forces, which is twice their percentage in the civilian female population.[15] Yet, while 18.5 percent of enlisted soldiers are Black, this number shrinks to only 9.4 percent of the officer corps, and the lack of diversity becomes more apparent with increasing rank.[16] The US Special Operations Command has become increasingly concerned about diversity. Joseph Votel, its commander, spoke publicly in 2015 about how the Special Operations Command "needs diversity. We need people of color, we need men, we need women to help us solve the problems that we deal with today."[17] As one CST trainer put it to me, special operations is "notoriously white," with Black service members comprising only 2 percent of Navy SEALs, 4.5 percent of Green Berets, 0.6 percent of the Air Force's pararescue jumpers, and 1 percent of total Marine Corps special operators.[18]

The military often argues for more diversity within special operations as strategic, that racial diversity will allow special operators to more smoothly integrate themselves into future "hot spots," particularly in Africa and Latin America.[19] This fits conveniently with official military narratives about how the military has historically provided more career opportunities and upward mobility for people of color, especially Black men, than the US labor market at large. There is a kernel of truth to this narrative: even given the disparities across rank and branch, the armed forces has in fact provided more opportunities for advancement and promotion than most civilian workplaces.[20] At the same time, "official military racial neutrality confronts the racism of many soldiers and the communities from which they come, as well as the racist discourses that have supported military actions since the beginning of the Republic."[21] The narrative of military color-blind opportunity for advancement obscures both the everyday practices of racism that many soldiers experience and how racial discourse has been central to the imperial expansion of the United States.

Military color-blind rhetoric grows out of a deeper history of color-blind ideology that was linked in the 1970s to the New Right's reinvention of conservative racial discourse along color-blind lines.[22] With this deeper history in mind, a military color-blind frame of abstract liberalism can operate within the broader role that military culture and institutions, war, and imperialism have played in the formation of US white supremacy. In relation, for instance, to the Vietnam War, Kathleen Belew describes the "overspills of state violence from wars" directly fueling a burgeoning white power movement within the United States.[23] In 2019, a survey conducted by Military Times and the Syracuse University Institute for Veterans and Military Families found that more than one-third of active-duty troops and more than half of minority service members reported having "personally witnessed examples of white nationalism or ideological-driven racism within the ranks in recent months," an increase from similar surveys conducted in previous years.[24] The prevalence of military claims for color blindness amid a rising tide of white supremacy in military ranks points to how color-blind racism can operate within military institutions in articulation with racial violence and white supremacy.[25] Military color-blind ideology joins with and gives meaning to different elements of racial violence, including white supremacy.[26] One way this color blindness develops meaning is through soldiers' explanations of Afghan civilization as "backward" and containing cultural elements that make foreign oversight necessary. In the sense that Stuart Hall examined articulation as a way to "think how an ideology empowers people, enabling them to begin to make some sense or intelligibility of their historical situation," we might consider soldiers' civilizational discourses about Afghanistan as a way of making sense of their historical position on the terrain of US imperialism.[27]

As US imperial wars rage on, racist explanations persist of "cultural backwardness" as justifying military intervention. Such cultural racism is continuous with historical forms of imperialism. It also informs an imperial feminism that imagines Afghan women as helpless victims who must be "saved." The imagined Afghan woman is also defined in contrast to the female soldier who is framed as a model of modernity and women's empowerment. While these relationships of race, gender, and culture mark imperial continuities, they are also a historically specific iteration of imperialism. Current military discourses of color-blind liberalism are different from the "military multiculturalism" Melani McAlister wrote about during the Gulf War (1990–1991). She argued that the US armed forces' racial diversity served as evidence of the country's status as a "world citizen" that justified military violence allegedly in the service of an imagined global humanity. "As the military would represent the diversity of the United States, the United States, as represented in its military, would contain the world."[28] Some scholars have interpreted gendered counterinsurgency as a relatively straightforward extension of the military's strategy of cynically deploying its diversity to demonstrate humanitarian motives.[29] Although this explanation is partially useful for understanding the diverse character of the first iterations of the Lioness teams and FETs, it does not account for the emphasis on color blindness that I observed to centrally inform military racial discourse.

Gendered counterinsurgency as a particular iteration of military multiculturalism also does not explain how the program's most established versions (CSTs) were marked by whiteness. Departing from the military's self-representation in the 1990s as "a microcosm of a pluralist American society," gendered counterinsurgency reconfigured meanings associated with women's military labor. CSTs were less multicultural symbols than they were vehicles for a white femininity that distinguished a post-9/11 imperial feminism.[30] Anne McClintock classically examined race, gender, and class as formed in imperial encounters "*in and through* relation to each other—if in contradictory and conflictual ways."[31] If viewed through this lens of articulated categories, CSTs reveal how whiteness, heterosexuality, and middle-class domesticity come into formation through one another in post-9/11 imperial encounters.

Counterinsurgent women in Iraq and Afghanistan position themselves by building upon colonial feminisms that have historically placed white women in a hierarchy above colonized men.[32] Yet in contrast to Victorian tropes of "anachronistic space," where women, the colonized, and working classes are imagined as outside of modernity, post-9/11 female counterinsurgents make their place at the center of history through imperial imaginations of the Afghan Other whose monolithic "culture" is considered to be the source of gendered repression.[33] At the same time as military and popular media represent CSTs through whiteness, a color-blind racism is also at work through military language that everyone is "green," masking racism as it occurs in the everyday experiences of soldiers such as Claudine. A color-blind discourse underpins the forms of cultural racism at work in soldiers' understandings of Afghanistan as a place "backward" in time. Military color-blind racism works in two directions, disavowing white supremacy as it occurs in the halls of West Point while also enabling cultural racisms injected into soldiers' understandings of Afghan civilization as anachronistic. This color-blind racism also informs the continuing significance of emotional labor as gendered counterinsurgency became more prevalent in special operations and in relation to combat. I explore this continuation of emotional labor and its relationship to sexuality in women's accounts before returning to how emotion, sexuality, and color-blind racism came together to target Afghan women for "liberation" and represent US servicewomen as models of liberal feminism.

Continuities of Emotional Labor: From "Female Engagement" to "Cultural Support"

I met most of the women I interviewed through a strong network of female West Point graduates. Claudine introduced me to Cindy, who had deployed on a CST in 2012 with a Ranger regiment. Cindy, a white woman originally from the Midwest, had recently graduated from West Point and joined the 82nd Airborne Division as a signal officer with a light infantry division. Her story represents how the CSTs continued to reflect ideas of women as newly valuable emotional experts of war. It also thickens the concept of gendered counterinsurgency with the notion of servicewomen as being both more skilled at soothing and calming civilian subjects of military intervention and, in her words, "biologically different" from male soldiers in a way that was both valuable to intelligence gathering and "distracting" to male soldiers.

Cindy's experience echoes feminist scholars of war and militarism's identification of sex as one facet of biological difference between men and women shaping military social relations. In Cynthia Enloe's words, "military men's sexualized relations with women—and other men's attempts to control those relations—have been a major thread running through international politics for at least the last two centuries."[34] In my interviews with former CST members, one of the more delicate topics involved sex between CST members and the special operations units they were attached to. Early in the program's history, CSTs were derided as "casual sex teams" within the army.[35] In Cindy's CST class, about one-third of the women who made it through selection and training deployed with direct-action units, while two-thirds deployed with village stability operations. Much of the conversation about sex between CSTs and their attached units was directed at this latter category of VSO teams, in which CSTs lived in remote areas with Special Forces units that were trying to establish internal defense forces. These were also the CSTs for which no secondary information is available and whose members my direct interactions with were more limited.[36]

The anxiety and rumors swirling about these sexual relationships reflect a dynamic related to what Enloe identifies as a sexualized thread running through international politics. Enloe thinks more broadly about ideas of femininity and masculinity serving as a "protective camouflage" that is part of how US military bases maintain themselves on foreign soil. The model of on-base housing—"the suburb with family houses, grass to mow, men employed as soldiers and civilian women as unpaid housewives"—depended on gendered notions of home and labor to, in Enloe's words, keep married soldiers happy and their wives at least "silently resigned."[37] The suburban base model is one example of how broader societal norms of femininity and masculinity enable military power, here the ability to maintain enough trappings of suburban life to keep married soldiers and their families content.

In contrast to Enloe's example of the middle-class domesticity reflected in on-base housing as bolstering US military basing abroad, sexual relationships between CSTs and Special Forces members, outside of marriage and in remote deployment locations, threatened to corrode the normative glue shoring up the occupation. The comparison serves to highlight the difference between accepted domestic norms captured in suburban models of base housing versus the intense anxiety over military personnel having sex with each other. These anxieties are reflected in Cindy's and many of her fellow servicewomen's memories of serving as CSTs, often in the form of taking preemptive action to protect themselves from any misunderstanding about their intentions or roles on deployment.

The sorts of anxieties Cindy experienced reflect long-standing military concern over mixed-gender units as compromising "unit cohesion." This concern is visible in a study undertaken by the Marine Corps in 2015 to form, test, and study mixed-gender combat units.[38] Military scrutiny is directed at not only sexuality but also biological differences between men and women. Women's presence within masculinist military institutions has long been a source of ambivalence. During times of war, women have been tapped as a source to bolster enlistment, while in postwar contractions, as Deborah Cowen writes, women become "a convenient pressure valve to manage volatility in the labour force."[39] Enloe has written of the conflicting military need to recruit women for certain types of roles while main-taining intact ideas of military masculinity. She describes instructions to military women in the 1980s to wear their hair short but not so short as to look "unfemi-nine" and reminding them that "some of the best soldiers wear lipstick."[40] Enloe discusses military studies on how pregnancy and menstruation affect military service as well as how physiological differences bear on women's upper-body strength.[41] In the context of growing anxiety over maintaining military masculine culture as women came to represent increasing numbers and participate in more permanent military roles, Enloe frames these studies as a "search for a dif-ference which can justify women's continued exclusion from the military's ideo-logical core—combat."[42] CST members' stories are a particularly salient articulation of how women at the tail end of combat exclusion experienced such justifications and developed their own understandings of biological differences between male and female soldiers. At the same time, when Cindy served on a CST there was a more complex concern over female soldiers' sexuality that was combined with the desire to exploit women's sexual difference to collect intelligence.

Women's narratives of serving on CSTs are formed through these dual ten-sions of biological difference and sexuality. Cindy was in fact drawn to the CST program because of the physical challenges of its selection, training, and deploy-ment. She had previously enjoyed the physical feats associated with her support role as a signal officer with a light infantry division, and the high level of physical fitness required to join the CST was an attractive challenge. Many CST partici-pants were proud of the high physical standards the program required, linking this point of pride to broader attitudes toward physicality and fitness within the military.[43] Physical standards were also a prominent aspect of the debate over gender-integrated combat units, echoing Enloe's "ideological sandbags" of female hormones and upper-body strength serving as barriers to women's integration.[44]

When combat exclusion was rescinded in 2013, all military branches were given the opportunity to undertake studies on how gender integration would af-fect their "force readiness," then to ask for exemptions for the integration of cer-tain units. The Marine Corps did in fact request exemption from integration of its infantry and artillery units, which was denied in 2015 when the secretary of de-fense announced the integration of all military jobs in all branches. In response to the denial of its request, the Marine Corps increased physical standards for its infantry in a deliberate attempt to exclude women.[45] It is within this broader meaning of what the military refers to as "physical standards" that Cindy and many other servicewomen saw meeting and exceeding these standards as a way to "prove themselves" as being equal to male peers. Cindy went out of her way to address the "upper-body strength" arguments that Enloe writes about, explain-ing to me that women can achieve the same level of strength as men (specifically in order to carry the very heavy load that infantry service requires); it just requires doing the same exercises as men with greater frequency and duration.

Even as she dismantled sexist "upper-body strength" arguments, Cindy disagreed with the way in which CSTs had been used in policy discussions to exemplify women's ability to serve in infantry units. She drew attention to the fact that she did not physically carry the same items (and hence weight) as the infantrymen she was attached to. Drawing attention to the difference between the CST and its infantry team, she was adamant in our conversation that CSTs could not be proof for women's fitness to serve in the infantry. To the contrary, she had a particular understanding of female biological difference and sexuality that posed problems for gender-integrated units. Cindy recalled seeing the advertisement for CSTs (figure 10) and feeling enthused by the physical and mental challenges the program posed, describing in our interview her desire to fulfill a sense of "duty," "obligation," and "being where it's hardest." She was in the third iteration of the CST program, also using the language of a "week from hell" to describe the selection. During her CST's training, her team learned that CST 2—the previous class—had experienced its first casualty. This was Ashley White, the first member of a CST to be killed in action. She died in an explosion during a night raid in Kandahar and became the subject of the popular book *Ashley's War*. Cindy had met Ashley in airborne school and, because they were both enthusiastic runners, the two had trained together and stayed in touch. When we spoke, Cindy remembered how Ashley's death cast a shadow on her team's training, serving as a reminder of their deployment's dangerous nature.

Cindy explained how her purpose on the CST was "to interact with the Afghan women and children . . . to keep them calm and to put a female face on the American military or ISAF [International Security Assistance Force]. . . . Then we were conducting physical searches, and we were talking to women and children." Describing her attachment to a direct-action unit, she recalls how "we were there to interact with women and children. To basically get information. Or if there were nefarious items that were hidden, under burkas and things of that nature." She explained how when she went out on patrols, she would downplay her role within a platoon to the Afghans she interacted with. Even though CSTs were in fact one component of a small circle consulted on whether to apprehend suspected insurgents, she would give the impression that she had no authority on the team. Cindy recalled a range of reactions to her presence during patrols, emphasizing how interpersonal conflict within households often resulted in civilians volunteering information to her. "And then you get that random scorned woman who'll pull you aside and be like 'Hey, I just married into this family. It's really sad but unfortunately I'm infertile and I can't have children, so they mistreat me. They hate me because they say I have no value, so I'm just going to tell you everything I know.'"

FEMALE SOLDIERS

BECOME A PART OF HISTORY
Join the US Army Special Operations Command
Female Engagement Team Program

The Female Engagement Team (FET) program will challenge you. You will undergo intense mental and physical training designed to prepare you for the rigors associated with conducting tactical operations with Special Forces and Ranger units in Afghanistan. You will be trained to think critically, interact with local Afghan women and children, and integrate as a member of an elite unit. Once trained, you will be assigned to the FET program for up to 1 year as either a Screener or a Cultural Support Team member.

Minimum Requirements:
- E-4 - E-8, 01 - 03, WO1 - CW3
- current minimum GT Score of 100 or better
- PT Score of 210 with at least 70 pts in each event
- meet height and weight IAW AR 600-9
- minimum Secret clearance
- must carry 35 lbs six miles in at least 1 hr and 39 mins
- pre-screened by current unit of assignment

For more information:
visit our website - http://www.soc.mil/CST/CST.html
call - 910-396-0645 (DSN 236)
910-432-6283 (DSN 239)
email - cst@soc.mil

FIGURE 10. Early cultural support team recruitment poster that uses previous terminology of female engagement teams (2011).

To get this sort of information, Cindy highlighted the argument that Edith, Courtney, and Rochelle made about the utility of women's "emotional expertise" in counterinsurgency warfare. Cindy described how "you have different tools as a woman that you can use that I don't think a man would be successful in." She gave the example of a little boy in a village who they thought "knew something." A Ranger was questioning the little boy, who was terrified of how, in her words, the Ranger "looked like a storm trooper, wearing his helmet and carrying a rifle. But for me to kneel next to the little kid and take off my helmet and maybe put my

hand on his shoulder and say 'there,' I can do that with my voice. This guy probably could not or would not. And that kid was crying, and we couldn't get anything out of him. But you can turn the tables with a completely different energy."
Cindy remembered with pride how it took her all of fifteen minutes to identify the
correct location of Taliban activity when her unit had been in the wrong location.

Cindy understood women as possessing an "innate" emotional expertise that
framed her contributions as a CST. She explained her ability to extract information from the young boy as a form of emotional labor, in particular the ability to make him feel safe. Her recollection speaks to the CSTs' continuation of
deploying emotional labor in their interactions with the occupied population as
well as internally, as in Edith's case. Interviews with Cindy's counterparts in
other CST missions also echoed servicewomen's emotional labor in relation to
the male Rangers and Green Berets they were attached to. For example, Amanda
was an army captain deployed on a CST to Uruzgan from 2011 through the beginning of 2012. After completing CST training, Amanda was attached to a
VSO. She recalled living in an adobe hut with a thatched roof, the same building as the male operators. The elements of the deployment that stood out in her
mind were her inability to shower for the full forty-seven days she was on the
mission, cooking over an open fire, and spearheading radio and education programs in the village. In a discussion about misperceptions of women in combat
at a conference on the CST program, she talked about the "misnomer that when
you put the uniform on, you're asexual. It's just not true. I'm still female. I'm always a female. That's just who I am." Using different language than the trainer
who spoke of a "third gender," Amanda understood her role through the male-
female dyad that the "third gender" ideology also maintained. She framed herself as categorically female in response to the sorts of societal perceptions that
led to the trainer's notion of a "third gender" soldier category.

In a statement reaffirming her femininity at the same time as her ability to
provide emotional counseling to the men on her team, Amanda said,

> I think there can be a calming effect to that [being female]. Where you
> have obviously gung ho men and you have gung ho women, but we're
> still women. And you're going to have things that they're going to talk
> to us about that they're not going to talk to their male counterpart. And
> that's totally fine. I don't mind being that voice of reason to talk about
> your daughter who's having this problem in high school. Or you have
> concerns about your girlfriend or your wife. Of course you can talk to
> me about that. I think that had a humanizing effect to the team. That
> you were dealing with human issues even though we were living like
> animals.

In close relation to the language of humanitarianism that FETs used to describe their role in counterinsurgency, Amanda mobilized the cognates of "human" and "humanizing" to think about her role in relation to male soldiers.

Amanda's fellow CST Elizabeth also spoke during the conference of how the men on her team "liked talking to us about personal things that maybe they couldn't talk about with their team guys because maybe it would be seen as weakness." In the interviews with these CST members compiled by the Army Women's Museum, many women referred to the role they adopted as emotional confidants for male team members. Amanda explained her role as providing emotional guidance through the trope of humanity, arguing that their emotional role allowed them to lend a "humanizing effect to the team," in contrast to the animalistic conditions in which they lived. Servicewomen's narratives reflected the official counterinsurgency discourse of "humanizing" the occupation in relation to its Afghan subjects. Amanda's rhetoric of emotion also redirected the notion of the "humanized" soldier toward the male soldiers on the team. Female soldiers' presence made the conditions of war more "human" for male soldiers who otherwise became animalistic on their own. The rhetoric of "humanizing" is closely linked to that of civilizing, here used to make the male soldier more domestic, more human, and more civilized alongside parallel discussions of civilizing Afghan society.

Amelia, who was also deployed on a VSO mission, recalled that how she was perceived affected her relationships with Afghan civilians as well as with male soldiers. She explained that having servicewomen on her deployment was an asset because

> we were not threatening, we were just there. For Afghan men, we were fascinating because we were these independent women, in just a different role than they see for most of their women there. But we were nonthreatening to them, so they could talk to us openly. And same for American soldiers. For the marines, just having us there helped kind of calm things down a little bit. And we would do things to try to give back to them. Like we baked for them frequently. That was not our role and I don't want anyone to think that we were a baking team, but we would do things like that and it really helped. Like a motherly touch or whatever. We would bake cookies and cinnamon buns. It really helped bring the team together and have more of a family feeling.

Amelia's logic resembled that of the trainer who spoke of FETs as a "third gender" who could interact in a nonthreatening way with Afghan men thanks to their placement outside of normative male and female gender roles. Particularly when CSTs were deployed on VSO missions when they were stationed for long periods at remote locations with Green Berets, the rhetoric of women as nonthreatening was as significant to their interaction with fellow male soldiers as it was to inter-actions with Afghan civilians.

Like Edith, Amelia emphasized women's "natural" ability to soothe and calm, but this time in relation to male special operators as opposed to the subjects of a home raid. As in Amelia's recollection, baking was often a way for CSTs to per-form domesticity to make themselves intelligible to the male teams. Amelia de-scribed this as creating a "motherly touch or whatever." Yet her hesitation about performing this role was clear in her caveat that she didn't want anyone to think they were the "baking team." Other FET and CST members also described with great ambivalence how they were able to ingratiate themselves with male sol-diers by baking and cooking, but it came with the risk of being perceived more as domestic caregiver than lethal soldier. What Amelia described as employing a "motherly touch" was a way to make the conditions of war more "human" for the men on her team, which represents counterinsurgency's specific valoriza-tion of female soldiers' emotional labor. This valorization occurs through main-taining binary definitions of femininity and masculinity, for instance, feminine as associated with the home and domestic labor. As it is performed by white women such as Cindy, Amelia, and Amanda, this domestic labor begins to bring into view a white femininity that became very prominent in later media repre-sentations of CSTs. The emotional labor Amelia described, along with her dis-comfort with how it seemed to confuse people about whether they were the "baking team," addresses how such activities maintained rather than disrupted dominant paradigms of masculinity and femininity.

Framing War: Modernity as Sexual Freedom

The intersection of gendered physical differences with sexual desire was inter-twined with CST members' explanations of women's "natural" ability to soothe and calm both the subjects of a home raid and the male teams they were attached to. Female counterinsurgents spoke of the "natural desire" of all young Afghan men to impress women as a valuable route to extract information. Cindy de-scribed finding adolescent Afghan men on patrols as "like striking gold. You get that young guy who has never met a young lady who is not his sister or mom ever in his entire life. And he can't stop grinning. Like, he cannot prevent him-self from grinning. My counterpart—she's very pretty. She would smile and talk to him. He would just want to impress her with all this great information. Like—'I'm an important person here.' Of course you're not. But he would try and prove his importance to try and impress by relinquishing some information."

Multiple FET and CST interview subjects told stories like this, often emphasizing how they were able to exploit sexual desire to extract information. Cindy's discussion of her sexuality was also a statement of her modernity.

In her critique of the "frames" of war—"the ways of selectively carving up experience as essential to the conduct of war"—Judith Butler examines how sexual and feminist politics have provided a certain "frame" for the war effort.[46] Butler analyzes these forces in relation to the sexual freedom of gay people, but Cindy's discussion of her sexuality as a source of power and an index of modernity reflected Butler's broader analysis of sexual and feminist politics as a "frame" to bolster the war effort. Cindy's framing of her own modernity and sexuality relied on an understanding of Afghan men as outside the modern space of sexual liberation she occupied. She imagined her modern sexuality to be so shocking and enticing to Afghan men that she could use it to gain intelligence. Cindy's framing of sexuality worked in tandem with a military feminism that saw gendered counterinsurgency as an opportunity to further women's equality within the military. This framing of feminist and sexual politics in support of war forecloses analysis of war's degradation of women's and all people's safety in Afghanistan, structural gender-based and sexual violence within the US military, racial differentiation whereby soldiers can and cannot make claims for sexual freedom, and the production of Afghan gender politics through a highly modern nexus of Cold War geopolitics and military aid.

Cindy's positive association of female sexuality departed from the military studies Enloe describes in which hormonal differences between men and women are used to disqualify women from combat roles. Cindy explained her gender as at once intriguing and disarming Afghan subjects to emphasize the value her difference from male soldiers added to the intelligence-gathering aspect of a counterinsurgency campaign. The dynamic between Afghan men and US servicewomen was a more systematized concern within official military discourse. The *Commander's Guide to Female Engagement Teams* emphasizes the importance of using military women to interact with Afghan men. The guide references a Marine Corps officer and a cultural adviser deployed to Helmand Province who say, "'Here, as elsewhere in Helmand, the presence of female marines softened the interaction with local men and children.'" The guide goes on to recount how the female marines "quoted a local man who opened his home to the FET as saying, 'Your men come to fight, but we know the women are here to help.'"[47] Unlike Cindy's emphasis of her feminine intrigue as an intelligence asset, the guide emphasizes the assumption of servicewomen as less threatening than male soldiers, thus "softening" the interaction with civilians in order to build the sorts of relationships that are important to counterinsurgency. Multiple trainers used the quote about men being "there to fight" versus women as "here to help." This way of thinking of female counterinsurgency as "softening the blow" of an otherwise violent military intervention was pervasive. The goal of collecting intelligence connects both the element of pseudosexualized attraction Cindy spoke of and the notion of servicewomen as "here to help" in official military discourse. Both of these elements are crucial to understanding how female counterinsurgency's architects and participants made sense of the teams' role in fighting war.

The idea in Cindy's narrative of her foreign, implicitly white feminine intrigue posing a certain benefit to intelligence collection reconfigures the idea, widespread in military culture, that servicewomen pose a (latently sexual) "distraction" to male soldiers and that this is a danger to "unit cohesion," particularly in the context of combat. Yet here women's sexuality is deployed against the enemy and thus is allegedly helpful to the mission, as opposed to when it is deployed against their own unit and therefore potentially harmful. While many interviewees spoke in detail about the relationships they were able to foster with Afghan civilians (men, women, children, and adolescents), of equal importance was their relationship to the male combat units they were attached to. Just as Cindy spoke of adolescent men's "natural desire" to impress women, she also raised what she understood to be a biological dynamic between men and women that made a qualitative difference in mixed-gender units as compared with all-male field units. This difference gave her pause about whether the integration of combat units under way when we spoke in 2017 was a positive development.

Several women I interviewed articulated the notion of difference and distraction in relation to bathing and bodily scent. Those on remote bases brought up, as part of an attempt to give me a better sense of the context and difficulty of their deployments, how they had access to "sun showers" once a week—a makeshift shower made of water bottles. In several interviews, women's access to hygiene and especially showers were some of their most detailed memories. Cindy described this single weekly shower as the impetus to becoming a "distraction":

> I'm married. I'm an athlete. I'm not feminine—OK. And even me—if I use Bath and Body Works body wash—like your favorite that your mom sends you in your care package. Like you use that and you're fresh out of the shower and you put on your uniform and you just walk into the day room, they [male soldiers] will all look at you and be like, "you smell like a flower." And you'll be like—ugh—like, oh, "that's that distraction thing." It's very subtle, little things. Like if someone says a joke and all the guys are there, a lot of people will look at the woman in the room to see if I thought it was funny. Because I think once you put a woman into play, there becomes some kind of dominance hierarchy. It could be very subconscious. But I think the guys can sense that if I talk to

one of them more than another or if I have an inside joke with one of them, that there is a hierarchy forming.

For Cindy, distraction was manifest through smell. Using the notion of "dominance hierarchy," or a vertical hierarchy formed in the animal kingdom in which each member of a pack is subordinate to the next, she also developed a primatological understanding of adding a female to an all-male setting as fundamentally changing the hierarchical relationship between what she conceived as a "pack."[48] As in popular understandings of animal behavior, sex was mapped onto relationship hierarchies, with inside jokes changing the map of relationships within her unit. Given how she understood her effect of changing the dynamic of the all-male unit, Cindy chose to mostly spend time by herself instead of attempting to socialize with the men. For a portion of her deployment, she had a CST counterpart who was attached to another platoon but located on the same base. After this counterpart was injured, however, she was the only woman on the entire base. She filled her time outside of missions by taking an online course, studying at her desk, and watching science fiction DVDs.

Beth, Cindy's contemporary, also recalled taking sun showers during her deployment. Beth was a Marine Corps logistics officer by training, deployed on a FET with a special operations task force in 2009–2010. She volunteered for the deployment, thrilled at the opportunity to work with special operations and to go outside the wire and interact with women and children. She spent much of the deployment conducting searches, describing her position as a woman as "an invaluable tool" in relation to collecting information. Echoing the section in the *Commander's Guide to Female Engagement Teams* on women as "softening" military presence, Beth explained her utility in terms of her observation that "women in general tend to disarm people—I mean personality wise." She also went into villages in support of a VSO when the operational detachment was trying to identify a village to embed itself in. Her role was to gather information on whether the village contained residents who might be able to aid this mission.

Although Beth's time with the operational detachments (a small group of Green Berets) was generally positive, she recalled her attachment to marines, in contrast, as a time when she had never been treated so poorly in her life. Marines spread rumors about her and fabricated inaccurate statements they attributed to her. "I had no voice. Nobody had my back." She made sense of this through the fact that the marines in particular—who were some of the first to deploy as part of the new Marine Special Operations Command—did not want CSTs attached to them. The idea of women being "a distraction" was the main reason Beth gave for this reaction, explaining how interactions between men and women will always be complicated by "some sort of bond of attraction" that, she argued, "men tend to have a harder time keeping in check." She elaborated the various patterns of desire during deployments, emphasizing the threat that other CST members' relationships to male soldiers posed to her own reputation. "To use the metaphor of bad apple/good tree, you can have a tree that bears good fruit, and one bad apple is the only thing everyone is going to talk about. You could have a bunch of great professional women, but all you need is that one who is hooking up with every guy or having an affair with someone, and that is all people will remember and talk about."

In another attempt to explain the unavoidable, physical nature of distraction, Beth again used bathing to discuss biological difference. "My first deployment, we were taking sun showers—we only got to shower once a week. I would have to tell my women, 'I know you're using like Garnier Fructis or whatever to wash your hair.' Just understand, a woman would walk by after showering, and it was like pheromone central. It's not like she's dolled up. She's not going out on a Saturday night. But she most certainly didn't smell like this sweaty nasty dude that's next to the guy, because we tend to take care of ourselves, we tend to smell better. And that is already a distraction. You can't ignore the senses." Even more overtly than in Cindy's description, for Beth the "distraction" was inescapable—a sensory matter that could not be ignored but only overcome through sheer force of will. The biological, inescapable nature of the problem became part of how she understood the dynamic between military men and women as being fixed in nature.

International militaries' recruitment of women has been framed by feminist scholars mainly in terms of a (male) labor shortage. Indeed, the period of female counterinsurgency overlapped with a period of military labor shortages leading to the broadening of criteria for recruitment, including qualified acceptance of women's labor. Within a frame of masculinity as "intimately tied to militarism," attempts to recruit women are a "political high wire act" in which those committed to a masculinized military recruit women in a way that "will not subvert the fundamentally masculinized culture of the military."[49] This reflects the gradual history of women's integration into the US military, which is punctuated with caps on women's numbers, rank, and type of military service. Enloe's theory is also a reflection of the relationship of women's integration to shortages of male recruits in some roles. This was especially apparent in the integration of the military academies in the 1970s. In contrast to other pieces of integration that had occurred before, such as specializations that were experiencing difficulty filling their ranks, the military academies never had trouble filling their slots with men. Accordingly, gender integration of service academies drew the most protest from the military services, with Congress ultimately overriding attempts to block integration.

In many ways, women's understandings of their work on CSTs reflect an attempt to walk the high wire Enloe writes of, using aspects of their gender difference to the benefit of the counterinsurgency mission without destabilizing the fundamentally masculine military culture. Beth's and Cindy's narratives indicated how an important aspect of walking this high wire was not to cross over into a sexual realm. Biological difference, on the other hand, they understood as inescapable; they would always be the subject of attention and desire following a shower or in relation to their scent. But there is also something altogether different about the type of recruitment undertaken for female counterinsurgency teams. Rather than the inability to recruit enough men, as Enloe writes has historically been the source of female recruitment, the military confronted shortages of women capable of doing the sorts of activities required on missions in Iraq and Afghanistan. Overall, the share of women among enlisted ranks rose from 2 to 14 percent, and among commissioned officers the share rose from 4 to 16 percent between the end of military conscription in 1973 and 2011, when the military was most intensively deploying female counterinsurgency teams.[50] Although this is a large relative increase, the overall increase of roughly 15 percent remained stable in gendered counterinsurgency's key post-9/11 years, pointing to how the military has had to move women internally from specializations they were formerly restricted to in order to fill counterinsurgency demands. Deployments of women in such special operative roles newly attributed value to the association of femininity—and often an implicitly white femininity—with being "softer" and "less threatening." At the same time, women's biological difference from men, especially how this was tied to a concern about sexual distraction, emerged as a concern at both official and everyday levels. All of these gendered maneuvers amounted to a particular version of femininity that was useful to special operations missions. Female recruitment has reinforced masculinity's dominance within military culture, going even a step beyond Enloe's argument that women's integration leaves masculinity's dominance untouched. Female soldiers occupy an impossible paradox in which counterinsurgency frames their sexuality as a valuable tool for intelligence collection at the same time as it is a dangerous threat to "unit cohesion."

Ambassadors for Women's Rights: Color-Blind Women Saving Brown Women from Brown Men

Intertwined with arguments that women are both the emotional experts of war and potential sexual distractions is the argument that US female soldiers can claim a form of solidarity with Afghan women by virtue of being women. Cindy made this argument in another instance she recalled of being on a raid with US

Army Rangers and Afghan National Army soldiers when someone had ruined the family's cabinets while searching them. Cindy recalled a Ranger waving his hands at her to "do something" because a group of women inside the house was loudly protesting the ruined cabinets. Cindy thought that the woman making the most noise was in fact waging forceful protest to distract them from valuable information inside the house. "I basically turned on the fellow woman 'men are so stupid' kind of attitude with her," Cindy recalled, describing how she acted very reverent toward the woman and kept apologizing for the soldiers' destruction. This caught the woman off guard, and Cindy was able to sustain conversation and distract her while her assistant questioned a different young woman who surrendered valuable information. Cindy also intentionally appeared frazzled, handing out water and apologizing for how she did not have the power to get the men to pay for or fix the cabinets.

By presenting herself as a powerless member of the invading force, Cindy was in fact able to get more information than her male counterparts could, information that was often linked to lethal targeting. She emphasized how "we're only trained in direct questions," which was different than the more formal intelligence gathering and the emotional manipulation she had improvised. In addition to echoing gendered arguments about emotion, Cindy constructed a faux solidarity with the woman whose home she had invaded, arguing that she was a more "natural ally" as a fellow woman. This explanation was much more widespread than Cindy's personal recollections, structuring meaning in popular and media accounts of gendered counterinsurgency as well as individual servicewomen's experiences.

Ronda, a CST member deployed on a VSO mission in Kandahar in 2013, used similar language about her own gender serving as a "natural" boon to creating solidarity with civilian women. She was one of the only two women living on a remote base with the Operational Detachment Alpha—the primary fighting force for Green Berets—and its infantry uplift. She recounted bringing a sense of "home" to the detachment via the care packages her family sent, from which she made a small storage area for food that she shared with the other soldiers. She described the deployment as rewarding because of the example she served of liberated empowered womanhood. "Just getting out there and letting the girls see that there's more out there than what you have here, that was very empowering. I think they really appreciated it; in full kit I look like a dude. That first instance when you take off your helmet and they see your hair and see you are female—a lot of times they have never seen a female before that didn't just take care of the garden and take care of the kids. That was very empowering." Ronda understood herself not only as a "natural" ally of Afghan women thanks to her own gender but also as an example of feminist empowerment. The "very empowering" nature of the deployment is a description in relation to the Afghan women she interacted with, for whom her independence and her role performing culturally "male" security work served as an example of liberated empowerment. It was also a description of her own experience *feeling* empowered both by serving as this sort of example and being a CST member when women were technically banned from the sorts of missions she was doing.

Similarly, Amanda spoke of how when she would go out into the village, "you see the light especially in the females' eyes when they see other females from a different country. Kind of give them perspective that there is more to the world than Afghanistan; it was really nice to see the light in their eyes of what else there is." She thought that this "light" came from the stories she shared through her interpreter of what New York City was like or what it was like to be a woman and a soldier.

In a broader reflection of what Amanda and Ronda spoke of as modeling liberated womanhood, a 2012 US Army news article about FETs quoted a team member who described the "positive responses from the Afghan population" she believed they received. "I think seeing our FET out there gives Afghan women hope that change is coming. . . . They definitely want the freedom American women enjoy."[51] Like Amanda and Ronda, the FET member framed herself as a model of liberal freedom, holding herself up as an example and a contrast to the oppressed Afghan woman. Such media coverage echoes the military's own deliberate framing of female counterinsurgency teams as vehicles for Afghan women's empowerment.

A public affairs article published on the US Army's website begins with photographs and descriptions of a FET visit to an orphanage to distribute school supplies and clothing. Humanitarian rhetoric blends with a related narrative of Afghan women as needing foreigners to amplify their voices. The article features an interview with the officer in charge of the FET who explained, "In the mission of aiding Afghanistan in getting back on its feet, governing itself, and securing itself, we want to make sure that women's needs are met as well. . . . The FET is a way to get the Afghan women's voices heard."[52] The story also features photographs of a multicultural group of Black and Latina women accompanying the white officer interviewed and photographed. The "military multiculturalism" at work in this particular story about FETs makes the liberated Western soldier into a model for Afghan women who need to be "saved." It is also markedly different from how parallel representations of CSTs foregrounded white femininity, in contrast to FETs' multiculturalism and departure from the military multiculturalism McAlister observed in the Gulf War moment of the 1990s. The officer's explanation draws together arguments about the Afghanistan War as being motivated by humanitarian values with the notion of "women's voices" as being powerful symbols of a helpless population in need of rescue.[53] A new imperial feminism combines humanitarian rhetoric with the framing of female soldiers as models for women's rights. Female counterinsurgents were often fond of pointing to the irony of how public affairs coverage of the teams framed them as vehicles for Afghan women's empowerment at the same time as they were denied equal opportunity to join combat units.

Military and popular media narratives of servicewomen as exemplars of women's rights dovetail with the notion of all service members as global ambassadors. A US Army news article, for example, describes the job of the FETs as "part soldier and part diplomat."[54] The notion of being an ambassador for women's rights was articulated through arguments about culture, historicity, and religion. Beth recalled her time in Afghanistan as "like going into a time warp. Imagine huts. And tons of women, tons of men and children, in these *huts*. And the only person who has a cell phone is the tribal leader. . . . We had to tell these women, 'the reason your children are getting sick is because you're not boiling your water.' I mean, that's insane. Look at when the Bible was written—people then even knew how to boil their water. They talk about clean and unclean, kosher, and they know what's going to rot. How did Jesus get the memo and you didn't?" Beth used biblical metaphors extensively in our conversation, referring to biblical time to describe what it was like to be in Afghanistan and wondering aloud "how do these people survive? When I do read parts of the Bible or other historical-type writings, I'm thinking these people aren't even as advanced as that. How did that happen?" Beth used a type of social evolutionism that, in one mode, places Afghans as being backward in time, framing biblical time as comparatively more advanced than the society before her. She was confounded by Afghanistan's underdevelopment, asking "how did this happen?" Her lack of understanding is not surprising given the training in "cultural sensitivity" she received prior to her deployment that included only the most superficial treatment of Afghanistan's history. It is also informed by a paternalistic racism that paints the Afghan Other as savage.

In a second mode of social evolutionism that looks forward in time, Beth emphasized how she could bring Afghans into the future. She placed herself further ahead on a temporal scale, implying that Afghans could potentially "catch up," which also draws attention away from the history of serial wars that created the conditions before her eyes. This second mode is less pejorative and more focused on "helping" Afghans into the future, yet it is still underpinned by the racist paternalism that imagines the Afghan Other as in need of Western assistance to modernize. Through tropes of evolutionism, religiosity, and modernity, Beth created an understanding of the savage Other that pervaded many of her peers' recollections of deployment to Afghanistan. As female counterinsurgents described their interactions with Afghan women, they thickened this description of savagery by emphasizing the nobility with which women in particular faced such difficult living conditions.

In her *Military Review* article, an army lieutenant colonel expands this notion of women's rights by promoting more FET training and coordination, arguing that "Westerners often think that Afghan women are powerless, not only because of cultural constraints but also because Afghan men do not support rights or opportunities for women. This generally isn't the case. In fact, women's rights activist Sima Wali states, 'the stereotype of Afghan men as women haters and oppressors is incorrect. Most Afghan men are committed to the cause of better conditions and freedom for Afghan women.'"[55] The lieutenant colonel argues for a more nuanced understanding of Afghan women's rights, noting that female counterinsurgents can be part of a broader strategy for the military to show "trust and respect to Afghan traditions and Islamic values." This trust and respect, however, is strategic and often related to intelligence gathering.

The notion of the West protecting Afghan women's rights was strikingly effective at winning public support for the US invasion of Afghanistan.[56] Such arguments rely on the one-dimensional figure of the uniformly oppressed Afghan woman who also appears in military trainings on Afghan language and culture. The *Military Review* article's argument that Afghan women are not powerless and that not all Afghan men are oppressors recognizes the cracks that often appeared in imperial feminism's essentialist understandings of women's repression. These cracks were also evident in many interviews with FET and CST participants as an element of surprise that, in the words of one FET member quoted in an article for the army's website, "there are strong people under those burkas."[57] The limited interaction US servicewomen had with Afghan women served to disprove many of the assumptions they initially arrived in Afghanistan with of local women as oppressed and without agency. Such assumptions were garnered through societal attitudes at large as well as specifically from the cultural sensitivity units that were part of military predeployment training.

The same army article begins with the story of Warrant Officer Caitlin Purinton who, when she "lifted up the thin blue cloth of the burka, . . . would not have been surprised to see despair in the eyes of the woman underneath who spends more of her life hidden behind the garment that conceals her from head to toe. Instead, she ducked under the burka and saw the vibrant smile and heard the giggle of a vivacious young woman, who, like most Afghan women, is as curious about American female Soldiers as the female Soldiers are about them."[58] After describing the team's work with a local maternity clinic, the article explains how "most of the female soldiers expected the Afghan women to be downtrodden and defeated, but were pleasantly surprised to find the shy smiles of women who epitomize survivors." Both the warrant officer and the article's author presume despair and repression as they prepare themselves to confront Afghan women. The burka figures prominently in this assumption as a symbol of repression as well as physically covering the women about whom female counterinsurgents are so curious. As Rochelle described in her journals, female counterinsurgents often expressed their surprise at the moment the burka was lifted and they saw who was underneath. A heroic, industrious survivor replaces the figure of the universally repressed woman as Rochelle describes the veil being lifted. The transformation from one trope to another occurs as a surprise in this article as well as in Rochelle's and other female counterinsurgents' experiences.

As troop levels declined in Afghanistan, the Marine Corps used FETs on security cooperation and training missions—for example, to train the women's section of foreign militaries and militarized police forces in Romania, Kuwait, and Bahrain.[59] In 2019, the Marine Corps deployed a FET to Jordan to train a group of Jordanian female soldiers in areas such as medical care, marksmanship, and martial arts.[60] A similar exchange took place in 2018 between a team of female marines and Romanian servicewomen. Such trainings prepare foreign female quick-reaction forces that can interact with women and children as an alternative to foreign male military forces. Yet these examples are also part of a much larger network of training and exchange with foreign militaries that lay groundwork for future US military deployment overseas. As one FET member deployed to Romania explained in a Marine Corps promotional video, "The purpose of this training is to build relations with our allies—to get to know other countries—so that if we ever do deploy and we have to work with them, then we have that knowledge."[61] In this sense, such trainings can be seen as working in tandem with the US military's "forward strategy" that permanently stations hundreds of thousands of troops on approximately eight hundred bases outside of the United States.[62] The circulation of knowledge and labor at work within and even beyond an expansive geography of the war on terror is part of the "permanent war footing" on which the United States has long placed itself.[63]

On the special operations side, the CST program formally ended in 2014, yet special operations documents and interviews with trainers clearly indicate attempts to repurpose gendered counterinsurgency beyond the war on terror.[64] Since reviving FETs in 2015, the Marine Corps has repurposed the concept from Afghanistan to continually staff, train, and deploy teams to provide training and exchange with foreign militaries, such as in Jordan and Romania. The repurposing of such teams is linked to the globalized rhetoric of women's rights, specifically in response to the National Action Plan on Women, Peace and Security, which commits the United States to including women in areas of conflict and security.[65] The US military saw all-female teams as a way to both include US servicewomen in these areas and train foreign women.

Cecilia deployed on one of these missions in 2016. At the time, her tenth year in the Marine Corps, she oversaw maintenance for a combat logistics regiment that was deployed with an expeditionary unit—essentially a small portion of all Marine Corps capabilities on board three Navy ships—that sails around the world in order to quickly respond to military involvements. The unit also serves a pseudodiplomatic role of making US uniformed bodies strategically visible around the world. For example, this expeditionary unit spent much of its deployment training foreign militaries, including three weeks in Bahrain and two weeks in Kuwait. In these countries, the unit provided training for the US equivalent to a SWAT team and a VIP security force in skills such as martial arts as well as searching and clearing a room, handling detainees and hostages, and providing personal security in a crowd. Both countries had all-female units that were utilized in situations such as a visiting female head of state requiring private security, a hostage situation involving women, or a woman who needed to be searched. Cecilia's expeditionary unit thus repurposed the FET technology from Afghanistan to train the female units.

Cecilia's team spent several hours a day training the women's units. I interviewed several women who participated in Marine Corps FETs outside of Iraq and Afghanistan, all of which had a similar training objective. I asked what surprised them most about the mission. Every response to this question contained some degree of surprise that the women they were training did not match their prior assumptions. Cecilia expressed how she had assumed that the women would be "subservient" and "meek" but was surprised by how "they were very aggressive females. They would have no issue taking you down, yelling at you." In fact, she spent a large part of her training focusing on more nuanced tactics in searching operations that could be more effective than sheer force. Wendy, who deployed with Cecilia on the same FET, described how she too was surprised by how much she had in common with the women they trained, laughing as she recalled how some of the Bahraini women invited them out to drink and party, which they were required to decline. She explained that "a lot of girls on the FET were expecting, I don't want to say religious but by the books, supertimid females. . . . We realized that they had more rights than we thought they would. It didn't seem they were that restricted, to me. They had a lot more freedoms than I thought they would." When such marines imported the FET technology from Afghanistan, they also brought with them the veil's association with women's repression. Wendy's mention of religion reveals how the marines carried associations of women's subservience with Islam.

Mollie was the officer in charge of Cecilia and Wendy's FET. Over coffee in the small town outside of the base where she was currently stationed, Mollie explained how she became involved in the FETs when she was the only female officer in a security cooperation unit of three hundred personnel. Her executive officer pulled her in one day and announced that the Marine Corps had been tasked with developing a response to the National Action Plan on Women, Peace, and Security. He explained that "we want you to be the command representative. Because you're a woman. And it says women." Although Mollie was annoyed at her commander's reasoning, she was more perturbed that the Department of Defense had interpreted the National Action Plan to apply only internally, in relation to its own female personnel. She explained that she was personally just as committed to empowering foreign women and proposed the FETs as a way to do this. In her brief about the National Action Plan to her unit, she argued that "the US is supposed to portray that we are a model to work for in terms of integration of females, yet we tend to bow to their customs and courtesies," alluding to the limited role her own unit allowed her to play when it participated in security cooperation missions with all-male foreign militaries. Here she framed the US military as a potential model of liberal human rights and women's rights. Mollie's only apprehension about repurposing the FETs to showcase women's empowerment was that gender segregation of US forces mirrored gendered discrimination in the country receiving foreign military training.

Mollie's own experience enduring sexism throughout her military career made her question how valid a model of universal rights the US military could be. She painted her experience overseeing the FET as overwhelmingly positive, mainly coming from the pride she felt for the women on her team, especially their adaptability. Her recollections of working closely with "twenty other strong women," as she put it, contrasted with a career of confronting sexism beginning in boot camp, where she remembers being taught to hate other women and see them as her competition. "You bash other women to fit in with the men. You become a passive person. You don't stand up when people make snide comments." Mollie's career rising through the ranks as an officer was checkered with discriminatory experiences ranging from subtle, judgmental looks to the overt example of an officer wanting to work with her after reading her biography, then, after being told "*she will be here in a few weeks*," responded, "I don't want a female to work for me." Mollie repurposed female counterinsurgency teams to showcase US military women as models of empowered womanhood for societies she understood as repressive to their own women. But women such as Cecilia and Wendy who served on her team found the assumption of universal women's repression to be inaccurate the more they interacted with foreign women.

Like Mollie, Rickie, a former Marine Corps officer who was a veteran when I met her near Quantico, also described her motivations for joining a FET as rooted in a military feminist response to the sexism she had encountered throughout her career. She had heard of the FETs and Lioness teams at officer candidate school and had read the book *Band of Sisters*, an account profiling twelve women who fought in the Iraq War.[66] Mollie said that after her FET in Afghanistan received fire on a patrol and its commanding officer decided that the team was to stay inside the wire for the rest of her deployment, "I remember looking around and thinking, it's 2009. You're saying I can't do this not because I physically can't, not because I'm not smart enough, but I can't do it by the very nature that I have two X chromosomes. Something about that makes me inherently incapable of performing a mission. And it was just so frustrating." In her regular job as an adjutant (administrator), she recalled writing combat action ribbons and navy achievement medals with valor for a female platoon commander. Then, to be told "you can't leave the wire because women aren't allowed in combat. I would be like 'but we are.' What is your definition of combat? . . . I remember being very angry and very confused about it. And frustrated that it almost downplayed the role that—not myself because I was an administrator—but that these other women are doing."

Mollie offered the comparison of her husband, still an active-duty infantryman, who the general public assumes saw combat during his deployment because of his gender and title. In contrast, throughout her career she observed the reaction to fellow female marines wearing the combat action or navy achievement medals she processed as "why did you get that? You weren't in combat. Why are you wearing that? Why do you have a combat action ribbon? That's the attitude of most marines toward female marines, especially at the lower levels. . . . It all feels very much like you're twelve years old and it's a no-girls-allowed club. Then the more successful you are, the less they tend to like it." Unlike Mollie, Rickie left the Marine Corps after her time on a FET, offering the limitations she faced upon return as playing into her decision to leave military service.

If the goal of the repurposed teams was to showcase US military women's liberation, an unanticipated outcome was a feminism directed internally toward the military, sparked by the unique experience of being on an all-female team. After a career of enduring sexism and misogyny, Mollie's leadership of the FET stood out as an empowering contrast. She constantly struggled with whether to stay in the military as her list of sexist encounters grew longer, but leading the FET made her feel more responsible for the next generation of servicewomen. It also incited her own respect for other military women, which she explained as a departure from the competition and pressure to hate fellow servicewomen in order to fit in with male marines. The FET had turned her into an outspoken advocate for military women. "During the FET, I saw such great women. It frustrates me that they have to put up with this. . . . I've had so much BS like that throughout my career. Seeing how amazing these women were in high-stress situations—I want to stay in and continue to fight for that, so junior marines don't have to put up with the same sorts of sexist misogynist comments that I did." The predominant aspect of the FET in our conversation was the internal shift it provoked within Mollie, what she described as turning her into an "unapologetic feminist" responsible for more junior servicewomen. Mollie's narrative is analytically significant beyond her own experience. She spoke about how the program began as a model of US military women's empowerment but served a more substantial purpose of giving military women who had spent their careers in a masculinist and often virtually all-male environment the opportunity to be among comparatively large numbers of other women. The experience of serving on a FET, for some such as Mollie, evoked a military feminism committed to improving conditions for women serving in the military, often in response to the discovery of shared experiences of sexism and misogyny. In Mollie's case, this awakening encouraged her to reenlist, which she explained as being motivated by her desire to improve the situation for female marines who came after her.

Any conception of how a military feminism informs women's understandings of themselves must also be placed within a broader imperial feminism that outwardly targets Afghan women for uplift at the same time as it looks inward at the US military and its female soldiers as symbols of modern feminist empowerment. Military racial discourses of color blindness stifle critical engagement with the racial inequalities and exclusions within the armed forces. White supremacy works in tandem with these color-blind discourses, fueling the rise in far right extremism and white nationalism that the military itself is scrambling to reform within its own ranks. At the same time, color-blind racism operates through the civilizational and cultural evolutionary arguments that imagine Afghanistan as being backward in time. Military feminism's celebration of women's achievements in counterinsurgency is inseparable from its gaze outward that distorts Afghan women. Through this color-blind racism, imperialism abroad is connected to gendered and racial forms of repression within military ranks.

Color-Blind Racism and the Civilizational Imperative for Intervention

Female counterinsurgents explained the sexism they encountered during military service by turning the language of repressed Afghan women into a mirror that reflects the military's own problematic gender politics. In describing the poor treatment she experienced as a FET member, Rickie claimed that the FETs were about winning hearts and minds not only "with the people in Afghanistan but [also] with the [male] teams that you're serving on day in and day out." Her comment echoes Mollie's desire for the FETs to showcase women's capabilities in the military, this time in relation to not only foreign militaries but also their male colleagues. In a harder-edged critique, three FET trainers compare US military leadership to Taliban attitudes about women. In their *Small Wars Journal* article, the authors highlight a series of assumptions about the unimportance of "engaging" local women and the unwillingness of military leadership to adequately staff and train FETs. As advocates of the FET program, they lay out the "tactical benefits" of reaching Afghan women and a series of case studies and best practices demonstrating the program's effectiveness. They conclude that "our reluctance to employ all but a few allied servicewomen in tactical counterinsurgency operations mirror-images the Taliban. . . . Who is shielding their women from Afghan society more: Pashtun men or US commanders?"[67] Challenging US commanders as potentially just as repressive as the Taliban toward women, the authors employ a racist civilizational argument that uses the category of "Pashtun men" to insult US commanders. Even as it rhetorically draws out similarities between the US military and the Taliban in an effort to ridicule the US military for its own treatment of servicewomen, the argument relies on the image of a savage enemy Other. US military commanders' greatest delegitimation comes from breaking down the binary of civilized US military versus barbaric Taliban to reveal similarities between them.

Such notions of the savage enemy Other are maintained in part through humanitarian narratives of female counterinsurgency teams providing help for people who cannot take care of themselves. This blending of humanitarian rhetoric with a liberal notion of women's rights was at work in the FET promotional video featuring Jill Biden. Clad in a pink floral dress, Biden sits in front of a piano with pictures of her own children and one of her dancing with her husband at a ball. As she explains how the teams are there to help Afghan women with "the things like all American women are concerned about," she draws a similar link to Cindy's in her story of turning on the "fellow woman" attitude toward the woman in a home raid.[68] Both statements rely on the assumption of a universal woman whose concerns—Biden names health care, education, and small business support—represent those of women globally. Jennifer Fluri has noted that all of the women featured in this promotional video are phenotypically white, which is at odds with the racial diversity of some teams performing this counterinsurgent labor.[69] As discussed at the outset of this chapter, however, racial diversity is not distributed evenly within the military among rank and service, with a marked white composition among officer ranks and special operations. Rather than an extension of "military multiculturalism," CSTs operated through a specific articulation of white femininity. The myth that everyone is "green" within the military serves on the one hand to hide these disparities in diversity among military ranks and, on the other, to enable a civilizational narrative about cultural difference between Afghanistan and the United States as a key site of intervention. As in Rochelle's journal entries about being in

Afghanistan as like going "back in time" to the Stone Age, servicewomen's narratives of doing the work of gendered counterinsurgency were framed in terms of a civilizational argument in which race is articulated through the language of cultural difference between Afghanistan and the United States.

Military arguments for color-blind multiculturalism, akin to the meritocracy framework Edith used to understand her own experiences, also hide the whiteness of the special operative renditions of gendered counterinsurgency, in particular the CSTs. One especially public representation of CSTs that harnessed this white femininity appeared in the book *Ashley's War*, a tremendously popular account that appeared on the *New York Times* best-seller list and had its rights sold to produce a Hollywood blockbuster featuring Reese Witherspoon. The book describes the CSTs as "the softer side of the hardest side of war" and emphasizes the heteronormative femininity of the CST members, particularly the central character of Ashley White.[70] In one of her many public appearances and writings conveying a celebratory message of feminism's triumph and the future of gender equality in the military, Gayle Tzemach Lemmon, the book's author, describes White as "a petite blond dynamo, who barely reached five-foot-three. And she was this wild mix of Martha Stewart and what we know as G.I. Jane. She was someone who loved to make dinner for her husband. . . . She also loved to put 50 pounds of weight on her back and run for miles, and she loved to be a soldier. She was somebody who had a bread maker in her office in Kandahar, and would make a batch of raisin bread, and then go to the gym and bust out 25 or 30 pull-ups from a dead hang."[71] Throughout the book, Lemmon emphasizes White's feminine domesticity through recollections of the meals she cooked for her husband in their modest single-family home in North Carolina and how she continued this domestic caregiving via baking bread and cookies for Rangers in the field.[72] Ashley's performance of domesticity is also spatially dependent on the place of her family home, aspects of which are transplanted to her deployment: she brings a bread maker to the field and bakes for the proxy male Rangers in her husband's absence. Such gendered forms of domestic labor are reminiscent of historical celebrations of women's contribution to war through hosting, entertaining, and secretarial work.[73] It is as if the author must remind the reader that Ashley is a woman even though she is doing military labor that was formerly restricted to men.

Through portrayals of Ashley's blond hair and fair skin combined with reference to her domesticity, Lemmon makes her into a culturally intelligible figure of white domestic femininity.[74] In *Manliness and Civilization*, historian Gail Bederman examines the making of "masculinity" in the late nineteenth- and early twentieth-century United States, a process that entailed the production of "a racially based ideology of male power."[75] Just as masculinity was for Bederman a category that had to be created through drawing together "anatomy, identity, and authority," a related project is at work in the depictions of female counterinsurgents as white middle-class domestic subjects. Ashley White is such a significant portrayal of CSTs because she draws together these elements of anatomy, identity, and authority that Bederman identified as so significant to the production of imperial masculinities in a previous period. Ashley White represents the articulation of meanings mapped onto femininity (such as domesticity) with whiteness. Bederman writes of class as providing "materials to remake manhood."[76] Here too, characteristics of being middle class such as the single family home and the white wedding are "materials" to make the white femininity through which the CSTs were represented.

Bederman describes "civilization" as always denoting attributes of race and gender. Given these attributions, "civilization" has been used to link male dominance to white supremacy.[77] In female counterinsurgents' descriptions of Afghanistan as a "backward" place, a related civilizational racial discourse is at work. Captured in the imagery of *Ashley's War*, CSTs in particular were represented through white femininity. At the same time, color-blind multicultural language silenced overt discussion of race, instead providing a civilizational and cultural explanation of female soldiers' capacity to bring Afghan women into modernity through sheer example.

In *Ashley's War* and during various author talks, Lemmon shows the image of Ashley White in her traditional wedding gown, with her groom in his army dress uniform, in a small Catholic church in rural Ohio. These different pieces of imagery together represent a white heteronormative middle-class femininity that was both an attractive representation of the teams to the general public and a set of normative gender traits that servicewomen could adopt as strategically useful in their interactions with male Special Forces teams. The book's pairing of white middle-class gender norms with validation of women's role in combat formed a culturally palatable argument for gender integration of military ground combat units. Unlike some of the public and media representations of the FETs, in the case of the CSTs, this white middle-class femininity was tied to women's participation in combat-intensive special operations missions. Always in tension with Ashley's domestic femininity in the book are her equal capabilities to her male counterparts in combat, including her ability to do as many pull-ups and to shoot with accuracy equal to that of male soldiers. Unlike media accounts featuring FETs performing humanitarian activities, the book emphasizes Ashley's role in combat missions, especially home raids. In connecting Ashley's white normative femininity to her participation in combat, the book offers a new military femininity that maintains certain gender-normative behaviors in relation to caregiving and sexuality, even as it disrupts former gendered restrictions of military combat roles.

Mollie's understanding of female counterinsurgency teams as showcasing women's capabilities to a sexist military reflected a similar argument. As she recounted the impressive skill set each woman on her FET added to the team, she paused to express dismay that the main media coverage she had seen involved the FET visiting a preschool and handing out soccer balls. She scoffed at this more humanitarian representation of the teams, which she read as at odds with her goal of allowing them to demonstrate women's equal capabilities to male soldiers.

In contrast to the intelligence role that FET members such as Beth emphasized and the combat featured in *Ashley's War*, academic literature largely focuses on the allegedly humanitarian dimensions of gendered counterinsurgency.[78] This focus mirrors and is perhaps a result of humanitarian media representations, but it also replicates the military's own attempts to manage public opinion and perceptions of civilians on the battlefield. While servicewomen's personal narratives emphasize combat and intelligence over the more pervasive humanitarian rhetoric, they also serve as a reminder that such humanitarian rhetoric cannot be discounted entirely as an attempt to distract the public from the continuation of violent military activities.[79] Instead, such humanitarian rhetoric is a significant site for the production of racialized and gendered forms of difference. Female counterinsurgents used the rhetoric of humanitarianism to craft understandings of themselves as models of women's empowerment. Color-blind racism bolstered an imperial feminism by targeting "culture" and "civilization" for intervention. Soldiers performed projects to rescue Afghan women from what they understood as an uncivilized, backward society, obscuring structural and historical reasons that created the conditions of poverty so prominent in soldiers' memories of their deployments. At the same time, the all-female and combat focus of the CSTs amplified even more this opportunity for servicewomen to display themselves as empowered members of the most valorized and historically masculinist domains of warfare.

CST members' memories combine racialized arguments about civilization, religion, and historicity to make sense of deployments that took place in the shadows before they were caught in the spotlight of a national conversation about military gender inclusion. Ashley White's media representation as a particular articulation of white domestic heterosexual femininity captures how CSTs operated through shifting meanings of race, class, gender, and sexuality within the US military. CSTs' specific conglomeration of racial, sexual, gender, and class meaning illustrates how a new imperial feminism has come to operate through gender essentialisms and color-blind racisms.

A specific iteration of liberal feminism has emerged within the military that uses women such as Ashley White to demonstrate increasing military gender equality. Within a liberal feminist paradigm, the gender equality indicated by women's inclusion in combat is considered to be a "good" thing. A more comprehensive view from the women Ashley served with, however, reveals multiple new racial and gendered forms of inequality that prefigured combat integration. Women made themselves intelligible within combat roles by performing accepted gender norms of domesticity and caregiving, further entrenching the notion of women as the emotional experts of war. Combat integration in the forms explored here effectively strengthens gender stereotypes. At the same time, military language that "we are all green" delegitimizes the racism that soldiers such as Claudine experience. Color-blind racism at once fuels imperialism abroad by couching racist arguments that Afghan people require military occupation to shepherd them into modern life in a language of "culture" and "civilization." The ties that bind these racialized and gendered practices within the military to the work of occupation abroad undermine a liberal feminist celebration of combat integration as a marker for greater gender equality. A new imperial feminism consolidates gender and racial repression among military ranks with a racial evolutionism used to imagine the subjects of occupation.

CONCLUSION

After I thought I had concluded this book, the Taliban rapidly secured military victory over the entirety of Afghanistan in August 2021, intersecting with a stunning airlift from Kabul of US and international forces and some of their allies. During the evacuation, marines quickly assembled a female engagement team to search Afghan women and children, underscoring the evolving life span of such gendered military labor. Of the thirteen US service members killed by a suicide bomber during the evacuation, two were young women—Nicole Gee, a maintenance technician, and Johanny Rosario, a supply chief—who were searching evacuees when the attack happened. Media coverage of their deaths featured a photograph posted the week before the attack: "clad in body armor with her hair pulled back in a tight bun, Marine Sgt. Nicole Gee cradled the barefoot Afghan infant in her arm as softly as she could through thick work gloves. 'I love my job,' the 23-year-old wrote in an Instagram caption."[1]

Such media representation echoes the forms of military femininity and emotional labor I have explored here. It also speaks to how gendered warfare has continued in new forms. Media and official political narratives were quick to mark the Kabul airlift as the official "end" of the Afghanistan War. Yet it is inaccurate to describe the post-9/11 wars as over. The war continues in Afghanistan in the form of devastated infrastructure and physical insecurity for Afghan people, not to mention bombs that continue to fall. It continues through injuries that women such as Edith will live with until the last veteran of these wars receives their last disability payment as we enter the twenty-second century.[2] It continues through immigration restrictions, terrorism prosecutions, surveil-

198

lance, and Islamophobia. The post-9/11 wars have morphed in form and expanded in geography to cover eighty-five countries, over 40 percent of the countries on the surface of Earth.[3] As we enter the third decade of the war on terror, a key challenge remains to grapple with the contours of US imperialism.

The post-9/11 wars have metastasized. The Kabul airlift underscores the decline of US hegemony as the Pentagon's budget continues to climb and the forever wars expand in all directions, spreading across half the globe and reaching even into Earth's atmosphere. The defeats in Iraq and Afghanistan mark a turning point, so we can read the autopsy report more clearly now. We can see the signs of decay that were there all along: in military training, in how the US wars in Vietnam become abstract "lessons learned," and in the treatment of women and minorities in the armed services.

Over the past two decades, the military has experimented with development projects and humanitarian rhetoric to fight endless wars. Although this experiment has rarely resulted in development projects that achieve their own stated aims, or soldiers embracing civilian-centric approaches to fighting war, it has transformed the institutional relationship between the development and defense sectors. New forms of defense funding have tempted development practitioners to dabble in counterinsurgency projects. Humanitarian workers now face high-stakes questions about the safety and ethical implications of their relationship to military actors, who are more present than ever in areas such as the Horn of Africa and parts of West Africa. Gendered uses of counterinsurgency have given rise to a new imperial feminism that frames female soldiers as models of liberated empowerment, in contrast to the imagined Afghan woman. This imperial feminism contains new forms of military femininity that define women's roles through gender essentialisms such as emotion, even as women are integrated into combat. It also contains color-blind and cultural forms of racism that structure soldiers' own experiences of military racism and inform the racial construction of war's targets. These forces of military humanitarianism and imperial feminism shape the lingering imprint of the post-9/11 wars.

With counterinsurgency's return, development projects and humanitarian relief were reframed as military tools to "win the hearts and minds" of local populations. The District Stability Framework (DSF) embodied this attempt to "translate" development "best practices" for military use. Here the US Agency for International Development (USAID) used private development contractors to provide new forms of predeployment training. In these civilian-directed trainings and in traditional military spaces such as war colleges, instructors actively used imperial histories of counterinsurgency to make the present. Malaya, Vietnam, the Philippines, Algeria, and Haiti all haunted post-9/11 military classrooms as examples of how the military had always been involved in development and humanitarianism. Such uses of history also erased the body counts of military occupation, rewriting imperial wars as playbooks of sanitized tactics. For example, defense intellectuals and classroom instructors skip over the murderous legacy of the Vietnam War–era Phoenix Program and teach the Civil Operations and Revolutionary Development Support Program as a successful example worthy of replication in Iraq and Afghanistan.[4]

The modern assembly of imperialism plays out through the lived experiences of the development contractors, soldiers undergoing training, and female counterinsurgents I interviewed. I chose to focus on these figures because they occupy the complex position of both directly perpetuating US imperialism abroad and falling victim to military abuses of their labor and health. This lens onto empire is wholly different than more widespread perceptions of the military as a monolithic force. Violence is carried out through PowerPoint presentations so numbing that one almost forgets that they too enable death and destruction. Lived experiences reveal an impartial and unstable process of manufacturing US imperial hegemony. While USAID could translate development best practices into military language through the DSF, its contractors were less successful in convincing soldiers to begin thinking of themselves as "armed social workers." During simulations, soldiers found that conducting a survey about village needs came into direct conflict with the aggressive stance their captain instructed them to take on patrol. Counterinsurgency elevated feminized specializations such as working with civilians. This gendering of military jobs in counterinsurgency provoked more pervasive resistance to soldiers' new roles. At times, soldiers articulated this resistance by reasserting masculinity's definition through combat. Contrary to the DSF's intention of convincing soldiers to take seriously the importance of working with civilians, its implementation backfired to further entrench traditional associations of combat with masculinity.

Some of the most fraught examples of soldiers as simultaneous victims and perpetrators of imperialism come from the experiences of women who served on all-female counterinsurgency teams. Female soldiers were placed in dangerous and underrecognized positions of vulnerability because of a lack of training and structural biases within Veterans Affairs. During the years leading up to women's integration into combat units, the military defined women as the emotional experts of war as it placed them in these dangerous positions. The dominant understanding of female counterinsurgency teams as a humanitarian guise to distract the public from military violence completely misses these teams' relationship to combat. This relationship is crucial to understanding gendered counterinsurgency because it undermines liberal feminist arguments for women's increasing equality within the military.

A closer, more critical look within these programs reveals how integration has happened through new forms of repression that strengthened gender essentialisms. A new military femininity has come to value servicewomen's differences from male soldiers in a way that is at odds with established theorizations of women's bodies as "foreign" within masculinist military institutions.[5] Yet women's emotional labor is valued through reinforcement of gender essentialisms, such as the assumption of women's "natural" ability to soothe and calm victims of violent military interventions. This warped military praise for emotional labor is strategic, always linked to intelligence collection and the threat of violence. Gender integration has happened through new forms of repression that enforce gender stereotypes at the same time as lack of training and veteran health care have unnecessarily endangered female soldiers.

A new military femininity, defined through women's emotional labor, is part of a more expansive imperial feminism through which servicewomen imagine themselves as models of empowered womanhood, in contrast to the imagined helpless, oppressed Afghan woman. Color-blind language of "culture" and "civilization" thinly veils racist imperial rhetoric of "saving brown women from brown men."[6] At the same time as this rhetoric of imperial "rescue" resembles Gayatri Spivak's critique, here it is a multiracial group of US military women using civilizational and cultural language to describe their ability to liberate Afghan women. Yet unlike the military's emphasis on multicultural diversity, which Melani McAlister found during the Gulf War (1990–1991), post-9/11 gendered counterinsurgency used color-blind language of all soldiers as "green" to demonstrate how these wars were not racially motivated. Military color-blind language of "we are all green" in practice enabled cultural and civilizational forms of racism about Afghans as being unable to take care of themselves. Soldiers employed military color-blind understandings of race when they made cultural arguments that the brand of liberal feminism they brought to Afghanistan was superior to the "culturally backward" civilization they found before them. As such, the new imperial feminism operates through race in a way that is distinct from the 1990s and earlier imperial moments.

At the same time as color-blind racisms inform military imaginations of Afghanistan, they also shape the military's understanding of itself as a color-blind institution. Turned inward, claims that "we are all green" erase the experiences of women such as Claudine as well as the actual diversity of women performing counterinsurgent labor. In contrast to the multiculturalism that the US military has strategically deployed (for instance, in the 1990s) to mark its position as a citizen of the world acting in the service of global humanity, cultural support teams were publicly represented through a white femininity.[7] Their white composition also reflected the lack of diversity within military special operations more generally and within the officer corps of various military services. Rather than a "military multiculturalism" at work in gendered counterinsurgency, a more accurate description would be a specific iteration of military color-blind racism. This color-blind argument has worked to silence overt discussion of racial imperialism in spaces of foreign military occupation. It has also worked to obscure the disconnection between US public representations of white military femininity and the actual diversity of female counterinsurgents, who are themselves often shaped through experiences of racism and white supremacy within the military.

The new imperial feminism prizes a white femininity that is continuous with US promotion of racism in the early twentieth century.[8] As embodied in Ashley White's fair skin, blond hair, and adherence to traditional gender roles in her marriage to a male soldier, this white femininity maintains certain gender-normative expectations of domestic caregiving and sexuality while also disrupting traditional military associations of combat with masculinity. The new military femininity's delicate touch departs from the "rugged masculinity" associated with late nineteenth-century US promotions of racist imperialism. These militarized understandings of race and gender are all part of the new imperial feminism. The framing of women's presence in combat units as a milestone for gender equality papers over the painful and exploitative experiences of women such as Edith and ignores female counterinsurgents' imperialist imaginations of themselves as liberating Afghan women.

Gender theorist Joan Scott analyzes how "politics construct gender and gender constructs politics."[9] Applying Scott's insight here, we can see how women's integration into military combat is narrowly couched as a "policy issue," concealing how complex social practices make policy. That is, fortified gender essentialisms, color-blind racism, and civilizational narratives of liberating Afghan women show the broad political, historical, and cultural machinations through which policy is made. We have seen how military policy shorthand of "combat integration" stands in for a process that, in practice, reinforces gender stereotypes. Women's integration into combat units has produced a particular military femininity that, while useful to special operations in its ability to wield emotion and normative feminine traits such as motherhood, has actually reinforced masculinity's dominance within military culture. Women have used some aspects of their gender difference from male soldiers to bolster counterinsurgency work at the same time as, particularly in relation to sexuality, they have walked Cynthia Enloe's "high wire act" so that they do not destabilize a dominant masculinist military culture that relies on dyadic understandings of male and female.[10] Even though female engagement team members and trainers use the language of a "third gender" to talk about gendered counterinsurgency, they are describing the maintenance of masculine-feminine binaries through a biologically female soldier who strategically blends legibly "masculine" traits such as military dress and weaponry with "feminine" traits of emotion and domesticity. Ironically, the maintenance of a male-female dyad becomes most clear in the instances when soldiers use the language of a "third gender."

Recent steps to include transgender people in military service again raise the issue of whether and how military gender inclusion still upholds gender binaries and essentialisms. In 2016, the Obama administration ended the military's longstanding ban on transgender people openly serving, only for the Trump administration to reinstate the ban in 2017. Among President Joe Biden's first executive orders in 2021 was a reversal of Donald Trump's transgender ban, returning the US military to the Obama-era policy of transgender inclusion. Military transgender inclusion raises a parallel set of questions to my argument that women's inclusion in combat indicates a new imperial feminism rather than an unequivocally positive marker of rising gender equity. A study coauthored by three former military surgeons general found that the ban on military service by transgender people harmed military recruitment, cohesion, and medical care.[11] The transgender ban also promoted discrimination and transphobia while dangerously framing trans-competent health care as a public burden rather than a human right. Yet, as with combat inclusion, transgender inclusion highlights the inseparability of winning rights on the home front from continued military violence abroad.

In her concept of "homonationalism," Jasbir Puar captures how liberal gay rights discourses and corresponding forms of inclusion and recognition rely on "the shoring up of the respectability of homosexual subjects in relation to the performative reiteration of the pathologized perverse (homo- and hetero-) sexuality of racial others, in specific, Muslim others upon whom Orientalism and neo-Orientalist projections are cast."[12] Military transgender inclusion is formed through the connections Puar traces between sexuality, race, gender, nation, class, and ethnicity that sustain permanent war. Women's inclusion in combat and the move to a more developmental, "culturally sensitive" military as captured in the DSF saw the promotion of racist and culturally essentialist visions of Afghan culture. Modern military feminism and its concomitant figure of the liberated Western woman is produced in contrast to the pathologized Afghan Other.

At the same time, gender inclusion happened through reinforcing gender essentialisms, leaving male-female binaries in place, and shoring up military masculinity. Military transgender inclusion seems to follow this pattern in that it includes only binary-identified trans people. The policy then enforces gender binaries as it excludes the many trans and genderqueer people who do not identify their gender as "female" or "male" or fit neatly in these boxes. Like counterinsurgent uses of the "third gender" language without actually dismantling a male-female binary, transgender inclusion actually maintains this same binary, including only those who are intelligible within a male-female dyad. Just as a particular brand of homosexuality has operated as a "regulatory script" for both queerness and particular racial and national norms, transgender military inclusion has already begun on the basis of "good" versus "bad" trans soldiers.

Take, for instance, Shawn Skelly, who was the first transgender veteran to receive a presidential appointment, under Barack Obama, and who Biden also appointed to his transition team. Skelly's loyal military service is part of her story as a trans hero of sorts and places her within a homonational frame unavailable to whistleblower Chelsea Manning (a former army intelligence analyst who disclosed thousands of classified reports and diplomatic cables from the wars in Iraq and Afghanistan to WikiLeaks). Manning's anti-imperial stance places her outside a national imaginary that includes and recognizes only those trans bodies that leave US empire untroubled. Will military transgender inclusion depend on this sorting of "good" versus "bad" trans soldiers as it moves ahead?[13] Will inclusion of transgender soldiers depend on racial and sexual Others being cast out of the national imaginary or racial and sexual Others abroad being pathologized and cast as potential terrorists? In the way Puar argues homonationalism has acted to normalize the post-9/11 response, will trans inclusion grease the gears of permanent war rather than, God forbid, throw a wrench in the machine?

Gendered constructions of humanitarianism and development as counterinsurgency tools that can win the hearts and minds of populations under military occupation have worked hand in glove with a new imperial feminism to promote endless wars. As I conclude this book, US global hegemony appears to be on the brink of massive decline. I introduced this work using Giovanni Arrighi's compelling framework of the post-9/11 wars marking the "terminal crisis" of US hegemony, following from the "signal crisis" apparent in the Vietnam War era. If the post-9/11 wars marked a terminal crisis of US hegemony, the coronavirus crisis has sounded a death knell. On the global stage, China airlifts medicine and medical gear after successfully containing the same virus that has turned the United States inside out, killing hundreds of thousands of (disproportionately poor, Black, and Latino) people. Yet the US military budget is certainly not poised to mirror this decline in global standing. Proposed spending on war and security for fiscal year 2023 is $1.4 trillion.[14] In the post-9/11 period framing this book, the base military budget has more than doubled.[15] At the same time, other public institutions have been decimated by budget cuts, most notably the Department of Health and Human Services.[16] The COVID-19 pandemic laid bare the weaknesses created by this budgetary imbalance. A gutted Centers for Disease Control and Prevention failed massively to roll out virus testing early on in the pandemic, crippling the country's ability to manage viral spread. One is only left to wonder if fewer people would have died had the response been coordinated by the federal pandemic response program that the Trump administration eliminated when it increased the defense budget.

Without irony, political leaders have referred to the United States and indeed the world as "at war" with the coronavirus.[17] Yet military tools repurposed to fight the COVID-19 pandemic have floundered. To give only one example, the US Navy's hospital ships deployed to New York and Los Angeles were limited in their capacity to treat COVID-19 patients because the ships were designed for combat trauma cases.[18] Military tools are built to fight wars. They cannot effectively be repurposed to suddenly secure peoples' health and well-being in the face of an emergency. Instead, the rhetoric of being "at war with COVID" shines a light on the massive imbalance between spending on war and defense and spending on public health and other tools that could actually keep people safe. This speaks to the deeply entrenched political economy of militarism and imperialism in the United States that even in this pandemic moment of stark contrast and extreme urgency, following Biden's election and even claims, however dubious, that he is ending the forever wars, the defense budget continues to grow.

Military humanitarianism and new forms of imperial feminism are part of a vast machinery of perpetual war. The USNS *Comfort*—the very hospital ship stationed in New York at the height of the city's fight against the COVID-19 pandemic—is often associated with the term "military humanitarianism." The ship was deployed to Haiti in 2010 to treat earthquake victims before traveling in 2011 to nine Caribbean and Latin American countries on a medical humanitarian mission.[19] Yet these examples are mere surface reflections of a much deeper current of military attempts to repurpose humanitarian rhetoric and practice as counterinsurgency weapons. When military public relations photographs of the *Comfort* are allowed to stand in for a more comprehensive definition of military humanitarianism, we miss this deeper current, mistakenly categorizing the entire enterprise as a mask for more sinister military motives. A deeper look inside these military public relations exercises reveals massive changes in the relationship between military institutions and the development and humanitarian sectors. In military trainings, colonial visions, seeing the world through Lawrence of Arabia's eyes, are used to imagine the soldier as parenting the occupied other in a racial evolutionary framework. Attempts to value feminized military jobs such as civil affairs backfire, leaving soldiers with even stronger associations of combat with masculinity. These military ways of seeing and new institutional relationships are significant, even if military humanitarian projects do not accomplish any of their stated aims.

Beyond even the direct costs of the post-9/11 wars' $8 trillion price tag, the indirect costs of permanent war have become painfully evident as millions of people have lost their jobs and their health insurance during the pandemic. The high "opportunity costs of war" include stronger health care, education, and social safety nets whose absence is now brutally apparent.[20] These effects will be felt for generations to come. As the US combat mission in Afghanistan technically drew down over the course of the summer of 2021, the former head of the US Army's mission commented that it would be "impossible to argue" that the war on terror had been worth it.[21] Testimonies from leaders such as Secretary of Defense Lloyd Austin leading up to the troop withdrawal indicate how "withdrawal" was conceived as more of "a step down with an option of reescalation as necessary."[22] Even within official rhetoric of "ending" the forever wars, a new enemy is lurking.

When President Biden addressed the US public in conclusion to the Kabul airlift, he described "a new world" in which "the terror threat has metastasized across the world, well beyond Afghanistan." He listed Al Shabab in Somalia, Al Qaeda affiliates in Syria and the Arabian Peninsula, and ISIS affiliates stretching from the Middle East across the African and Asian continents. Citing "over-the-horizon capabilities," or the ability to carry out drone strikes and other intelligence and surveillance operations remotely, Biden preemptively clarified, lest anyone really believe that the war on terror is over, that the US would "maintain the fight against terrorism in Afghanistan and other countries. We just don't need to fight a ground war to do it." The bodies of ten Afghan civilians (including seven children) killed in a drone strike during the Kabul evacuation are a grim preview of what we might expect as the wars are increasingly fought through such "over-the-horizon capabilities."[23]

We would also do well to reject the binary of "boots on the ground" versus "over-the-horizon" capabilities. Contrasting air war as the opposite of ground war endorses the US government's marketing of the drone as a "flying guillotine that kills only the right people."[24] The weapon that killed ten civilians in Kabul during the evacuation was called a "ninja bomb," its name evoking the stealth and precise character of drone war that is billed as a contrast to ground war.[25] The binary of air war versus boots on the ground completely misses how military training and assistance continues in the background of both of these forms of war and is often the glue securing basing rights that enable drone war. For example, when the Trump administration withdrew approximately seven hundred US troops from Somalia in late 2019, it repositioned many of them in Kenya, where they could continue to carry out drone strikes.[26] As the drawdown from Somalia completed in 2020, the US Africa Command representatives described doing the same training, advising, and assistance mission virtually and "commuting" to Somalia from Djibouti, Kenya, and the command's headquarters in Stuttgart, Germany.[27] When Biden appeared alongside Iraqi commander in chief Prime Minister Mustafa Al-Kadhimi in July 2021 touting an agreement to formally end the US combat role in

Iraq by the end of that year, officials quickly clarified that in practice the mission would continue its training, assistance, and support role, just as it had already been doing for more than a year before this announcement. A temporary combat mission became a long-term if not permanent training mission.

Such forms of training—and training as an entrenchment of permanent war—will continue if not expand in the next chapter of the post-9/11 era. I have shown military trainings to be a rich site at which the labor of empire becomes visible. It is here that what otherwise can appear to be a monolithic military is broken down into some of its constituent parts, where living, breathing people struggle with the meaning of their work and develop understandings of social difference. Training will continue to be an important site where US imperialism takes new forms as it is haunted by its own history.

History haunts the present in the halls of war colleges and other military-education settings. In these trainings, mostly composed of US troops, we have seen how military instructors can, for instance, interpret the Vietnam War through a lens of experimental science in which tactics are separated from politics and certain tactics can and should be recuperated as valuable and replicable. Given the work we have seen this selective historical memory do to promote permanent war, official US government descriptions of the Kabul airlift as a humanitarian rescue mission and even a success are especially pernicious.[28] Afghan people rarely appear at all in such descriptions. When they do, it is often women and children, whose status underscores their need for humanitarian uplift. This is another iteration of the one-dimensional, oppressed figure of the Afghan woman that informed US servicewomen's understandings of themselves as global ambassadors for women's rights. The imaginary Afghan in need of rescue that appeared in DSF trainings still circulates through the next chapter of the post-9/11 wars. The liberal feminist narratives of rescuing Afghan women and girls that underpinned the invasion of Afghanistan persist. They provoke us to bring a more critical anti-imperial lens to bear as we might imagine the high school history textbooks of the future explaining the Kabul airlift as a humanitarian rescue mission and tomorrow's military instructors picking over the Afghanistan War for tactics they argue can be separated from politics to produce abstract "lessons learned" for the next war.

Some defense practitioners claim that ongoing wars against terrorism will be fought on the home front. Counterinsurgency is central to these emergent conversations. After a conglomeration of right-wing, white supremacist, militia, and conspiracy groups overtook the US Capitol on January 6, 2021, former Central Intelligence Agency officer and director of counterterrorism Robert Grenier claimed that "we may be witnessing the dawn of a sustained wave of violent insurgency within our own country, perpetuated by our own countrymen."[29]

Grenier, whose views on counterterrorism and counterinsurgency were formed in the key turning point of the mid-2000s, went on to argue that the United States had become a "candidate for a comprehensive counterinsurgency program." The spectacle of January 6 brought to life the feeling that many living within the United States and certainly those witnessing it from outside had long been experiencing of the country being a powder keg waiting to spark. As Grenier's words remind us, understanding counterinsurgency remains crucial. It is a key piece of the puzzle of US militarism and its afterlives.

Counterinsurgency's cousin—stabilization—has become institutionalized within the military to the point of the US Marine Corps establishing its own trainers and curriculum on the topic after initially subcontracting the work. The DSF and anything smacking of nation building may be history in Afghanistan, but the broader enterprise of stability lives on. USAID continues to describe some of its development projects in Africa, Asia, Europe, and the Middle East as "countering violent extremism," including programs focusing on women and girls.[30] Official development projects continue to be conceived as weapons to fight terrorism and promote stability, perhaps even as an alternative to the large-scale deployments of ground combat troops that have become unpalatable. The history of development in colonial counterinsurgencies and of USAID as a Cold War weapon reveals the deep entanglement of development and militarism. Tracking the form this entanglement takes will remain important. In new historical and political-economic turning points, investigating the changing shape the new imperial feminism takes in the context of militarized development will provide insight into how forms of social difference established in the post-9/11 context continue to inform our present.

Counterinsurgency has always bubbled just below the surface of influence in the US military even at moments when its prominence is less obvious.[31] As Grenier reminds us, military imaginations of urban insurgency include "ungoverned spaces" of Los Angeles alongside Beirut.[32] Military writing on this topic refers to "feral cities" and "deglobalization" as some of the most pressing security threats of the twenty-first century.[33] As military theorists continue to look to cities near and far as future sites of insurgency, flows of military equipment and technologies, funding, personnel, and ideas have intensified during the post-9/11 wars.[34] Counterinsurgency surveillance technologies developed for use in Iraq and Afghanistan have flowed back into the United States through domestic policing.[35]

From its origin in the violent formation of the United States through the Indian Wars, counterinsurgency has been here all along.[36] The return of counterinsurgency rhetoric, whether referring to foreign wars or the enemy within, should raise our alarms to ask about the history this rhetoric grows from and the practices associated with it. If nothing else, this book should warn against any rosy view of militarized tactics that were neither successful in their application in the post-9/11 wars nor appropriate for replication at home. As counter-insurgency rhetoric is turned back upon the domestic sphere, the country also learned that nearly one in five of the US Capitol rioters served in the military.[37] These are glaring indicators of the violence that has circulated through foreign US imperial excursions and back again into domestic spaces. Whatever shape the post-9/11 period will take next, it remains centrally important to understand the detailed and multifaceted dimensions of the modern assembly of imperialism. Such an understanding is a first step toward remaking a less violent world.

Stepping away from the liberal feminist interpretation of women in combat as a positive gain for women's equality, it is time to return to feminist critiques of imperialism in order to imagine something new. Instead of a military feminism that uses false cultural imaginations of Afghan women requiring foreign rescue, let us build an anti-imperial feminism that learns from Cold War history to lessen support of authoritarian regimes and paramilitaries that create more violence in all people's lives. Instead of celebrating women's achievements within the military while turning a blind eye to the promotion of endless wars abroad, let us work toward more educational and economic opportunities so that the burden of military service does not disproportionately fall on those with limited economic options. Instead of warped uses of humanitarianism to win hearts and minds in a counterinsurgency, let us build less militarized, less destructive US engagement abroad that begins from knowledge of local priorities, politics, and history. Instead of being at war with women, it is time for an anti-imperial feminism and a reinvention of humanitarian theory and practice. In imagining a new world during the Algerian revolution, Frantz Fanon conceptualized a "new humanism" based on human relationships that were fundamentally different from the violent, racist colonial past.[38] Following this book's investigation of modern imperialism, a parallel imagination is in order to deconstruct the components of imperial violence in pursuit of alternatives to perpetual war.

Notes

INTRODUCTION

1. Center for Army Lessons Learned, *Commander's Guide to Female Engagement Teams: Observations, Insights, Lessons* (Washington, DC: US Army, 2011), 59.

2. The US military defines FETs through biology and sex in its use of the word "female." I use the terms "female counterinsurgency" and "female soldier" to intentionally capture military representations and understandings of sex and biology. At times I use my own terminology of "gendered counterinsurgency" (in conversation with Laleh Khalili's "gendered practices of counterinsurgency") when I am not examining a specific military reference to a team but rather using this phrase to draw attention to the relational production of social difference. For the sake of grammatical clarity I use "female soldier" throughout, although the term is certainly problematic and should further indicate the need to examine how gendered military categories are produced. Laleh Khalili, "Gendered Practices of Counterinsurgency," *Review of International Studies* 37, no. 4 (2011): 1471–91.

3. Giovanni Arrighi, *The Geometry of Imperialism* (New York: Verso, 1983), 173.

4. In defining imperialism through new forms of US financial and military power, I both draw on and depart from the large body of work (addressed later in greater detail) that, in light of the post-9/11 wars, revisited classical theories of imperialism, in particular the relationship between capitalism and imperialism. Gillian Hart returns to the concept of imperialism by way of recent work on race, the rise of the New Right, and counterinsurgency in a global conjunctural frame. She identifies three broad regional patterns of financial reconfiguration that, together, "generated massive capital inflows into the US from the 1980s that helped drive intensified militarism under Reagan." These "shifts in interconnected financial and military relations of the US to different regions of the non-Western world" comprise new forms of US imperialism from the 1980s onward. Retaining the word "imperialism" is valuable because it signals these shifts in US financial and military power. Imperialism is also redefined through the distinct features of what Giovanni Arrighi called "world-hegemony" in his argument that classical theories of imperialism have been rendered obsolete by the post–World War II Pax Americana. Gillian Hart, "Why Did It Take So Long? Trump-Bannonism in a Global Conjunctural Frame," *Geografiska Annaler, Series B: Human Geography* 102, no. 3 (2020): 239–66.

5. The Direct Combat Exclusion Rule (1994), which repealed some previous restrictions on women on combat ships and aircraft, stated that women still could not be assigned to units below the brigade level (a unit with three thousand to five thousand persons) whose primary mission was ground combat. Kristy Kamarck, *Women in Combat: Issues for Congress* (Washington, DC: Congressional Research Services, 2016), 6.

6. Through 2015, the Marine Corps sought exemption from integrating infantry units based on an internal study that found all-male infantry units to be superior to mixed-gender units in areas such as speed, weapons accuracy, and evacuations ability. The study was widely condemned for biases in methodology and analysis that favored all-male units. Although its request was denied, the Marine Corps continued to fight gender integration by elevating infantry standards and maintaining separate boot camps, sparking two federal lawsuits: *Hegar v. Panetta, C 12-06005 EMC* (California, 2013) and *Baldwin et al. v. Panetta et al., C 12-cv-00832* (District of Columbia, 2012). See also Tom Bowman,

211

"Controversial Marine Corps Study on Gender Integration Published in Full," National Public Radio, November 4, 2015; and US Marine Corps, "Marine Force Integration Plan—Summary," 2015, https://www.documentcloud.org/documents/2394531-marine-corps-force-integration-plan-summary.html.

7. Katie Rogers, "Kristen Griest on Course to Become First Female Army Officer Trained to Lead Troops into Combat," *New York Times*, April 28, 2016.

8. Scott Neuman, "First Female Soldiers Graduate from Army Ranger School," National Public Radio, August 21, 2015; and Gayle Tzemach Lemmon, *Ashley's War: The Untold Story of a Team of Women Soldiers on the Special Ops Battlefield* (New York: Harper, 2015).

9. Charles Hirschkind and Saba Mahmood, "Feminism, the Taliban, and Politics of Counter-Insurgency," *Anthropological Quarterly* 75, no. 2 (2002): 341.

10. Samantha Power, "Our War on Terror," *New York Times*, July 29, 2007.

11. Jennifer Ryan, "Samantha Power: 'Being the Only Woman in the UN Made Me a Feminist,'" *Irish Times*, November 13, 2017.

12. Episode 164 of *The Irish Times Women's Podcast*, hosted by Kathy Sheridan. For a critique of feminist human rights advocates' singular focus on sexual violence in conflict and how it obscures the politics of empire, see Karen Engle, *The Grip of Sexual Violence in Conflict: Feminist Interventions in International Law* (Stanford, CA: Stanford University Press, 2020).

13. Chandra Talpade Mohanty, "Cartographies of Struggle: Third World Women and the Politics of Feminism," in *Feminism without Borders: Decolonizing Theory, Practicing Solidarity* (Durham, NC: Duke University Press, 2003), 54. Critiques of liberal feminism's individualist subject include Norma Alarcón, "The Theoretical Subject(s) of *This Bridge Called My Back* and Anglo-American Feminism," in *Criticism in the Borderlands: Studies in Chicano Literature, Culture, and Ideology*, ed. Héctor Calderon and José David Saldívar, 28–40 (Durham, NC: Duke University Press, 1991); Gloria Anzaldúa, *Borderlands/La Frontera: The New Mestiza* (San Francisco: Aunte Lute Books, 1987); Inderpal Grewal and Caren Kaplan, eds., *Scattered Hegemonies: Postmodernity and Transnational Feminist Practices* (Minneapolis: University of Minnesota Press, 1994); and Sistren with Honor Ford-Smith, *Lionhart Gal: Life Stories of Jamaican Women* (Toronto: Sister Vision, 1987).

14. Feminist scholarship has pointed to the First World Conference on Women held in Mexico City in 1975 as a key turning point in this separation of sexual equality from broader issues of liberation. At this conference, liberal feminists from the United States and Western Europe argued, against women affiliated with the Non-Aligned Movement, that women's legal and economic status should drive the agenda of women's conferences, leaving all topics outside of sexual equality to (men in) the General Assembly. See Chiara Bonfiglioli and Kristen Ghodsee, "Vanishing Act: Global Socialist Feminism as the 'Missing Other' of Transnational Feminism," *Feminist Review* 126, no. 1 (2020): 168–72.

15. Two influential examples of this scholarship are Martha Nussbaum, *Sex and Social Justice* (New York: Oxford University Press, 1999), and Susan Moller Okin, *Justice, Gender and the Family* (New York: Basic Books, 1989). For an alternative reading of the liberal subject as possible to place in a collective form and offering a more radical future, see Zillah Eisenstein, *The Radical Future of Liberal Feminism* (New York: Longman, 1981).

16. Chandra Talpade Mohanty, "Under Western Eyes: Feminist Scholarship and Colonial Discourse," in *Feminism without Borders: Decolonizing Theory, Practicing Solidarity* (Durham, NC: Duke University Press, 2003): 17–42. For critiques of liberal feminism in relation to the post-9/11 wars, see Deepa Kumar, *Islamophobia and the Politics of Empire* (Chicago: Haymarket Books, 2012); and Jasbir Puar, *Terrorist Assemblages: Homonationalism in Queer Times* (Durham, NC: Duke University Press, 2017).

17. On hegemony as a form of power or leadership that is both "ethico-political" and economic and operates through the production of consent (which is very different from uses of the term that are synonymous with dominance), see Antonio Gramsci, *Selections from the Prison Notebooks*, ed. Quintin Hoare and Geoffrey Nowell Smith (New York: International Publishers, 1971), 161–62; David Forgacs, "Hegemony," in *The Antonio Gramsci Reader, Selected Writings, 1916–1935*, ed. David Forgacs (New York: New York University Press, 2000), 422–24; Jim Glassman, "Hegemony," in *International Encyclopedia of Human Geography*, ed. Rob Kitchin and Nigel Thrift, 80–90 (Amsterdam: Elsevier, 2009); Stuart Hall, *The Hard Road to Renewal: Thatcherism and the Crisis of the Left* (New York: Verso, 1988); Stuart Hall, Chas Critcher, Tony Jefferson, John Clarke, and Brian Roberts, *Policing the Crisis: Mugging, the State, and Law and Order* (London: Palgrave, 1978); Peter Ives, *Language and Hegemony in Gramsci* (London: Pluto, 2004); Adam David Morton, *Unravelling Gramsci: Hegemony and the Passive Revolution in Global Political Economy* (London: Pluto, 2007); and Joel Wainwright, "Was Gramsci a Marxist?," *Rethinking Marxism* 22, no. 4 (2010): 617–24.

18. I use the terms "development" and "humanitarianism," although not interchangeably. Where I, drawing on Hart, define development as a project of political-economic intervention in the third world, entangled with the development of capitalism, the word "humanitarianism" denotes interventions related to human suffering and disaster. In contrast to development and human rights discourse, Bornstein and Redfield point to how humanitarianism "emphasizes the physical (and increasingly psychological) condition of suffering people above all else," often in "exceptional states of misfortune." In military uses of the term, humanitarianism can mean the alleviation of suffering in the strategic interest of the counterinsurgency. More common still is the word "stabilization" (discussed in chapter 2), which is a category of development performed for a specific military objective by military actors. Development workers I interviewed were especially anxious to differentiate "real development" from "stabilization" in the context of widespread critique over aid's militarization. Since this distinction denies the relationship that development has historically shared with security, even when it is not performed by the military, I use the phrase "militarized development" to describe projects that contractors and some military personnel might prefer to describe as "stabilization." Erica Bornstein and Peter Redfield, eds., *Forces of Compassion: Humanitarianism between Ethics and Politics* (Santa Fe: School for Advanced Research Press, 2011), 4, 6. On defining development, see Gillian Hart, "Development Critiques in the 1990s: *Culs de Sac* and Promising Paths," *Progress in Human Geography* 25, no. 4 (2001): 649–58; and Gillian Hart, "D/developments after the Meltdown," *Antipode* 41, s1 (2009): 119–20.

19. Derek Gregory, "'The Rush to the Intimate': Counterinsurgency and the Cultural Turn," *Radical Philosophy* 150 (2008): 11.

20. David Kilcullen, "Two Schools of Classical Counterinsurgency," *Small Wars Journal* (blog), January 27, 2007, https://smallwarsjournal.com/blog/two-schools-of-classical-counterinsurgency.

21. Khalili, "Gendered Practices of Counterinsurgency," 1475.

22. In one Marine Corps class, the instructor used a slide that read "The Corps protected American citizens and business interests by intervening in the Dominican Republic (1916–1924), Haiti (1915–1934), and Nicaragua (1912–1933). In addition to providing stability and security during these Small Wars, Marines developed CA [civil affairs] doctrine 'on the fly' as they built roads and schools, taught local citizens how to become civil servants, and raised the overall standard of living of these countries."

23. Jennifer Greenburg, "'The One Who Bears the Scars Remembers': Haiti and the Historical Geography of US Militarized Development," *Journal of Historical Geography* 51 (2016): 52–63.

24. Jennifer Greenburg, "'Going Back to History': Haiti and US Military Humanitarian Knowledge Production," *Critical Military Studies* 4, no. 2 (2018): 121–39.

25. Giovanni Arrighi, Terence K. Hopkins, and Immanuel Wallerstein, *Anti-Systemic Movements* (New York: Verso, 1989).

26. The section of the *Counterinsurgency Field Manual* titled "Population Control," for instance, describes conducting a village census in order to know who resides in each household. US Army and US Marine Corps, *Counterinsurgency Field Manual* (Chicago: University of Chicago Press, 2007): 180–81. See also Oliver Belcher, "Anatomy of a Village Razing: Counterinsurgency, Violence, and Securing the Intimate in Afghanistan," *Political Geography* 62 (2018): 94–105.

27. David Kilcullen, "Twenty-Eight Articles: Fundamentals of Company-Level Counterinsurgency," *Marine Corps Gazette* 90, no. 7 (2006): 33.

28. By "Western" I mean the *idea* of "the West" as "a historical, not a geographical construct," a concept that signifies difference in relation to the notion of "Western" as "developed, industrialized, urbanized, capitalist, secular, and modern." Stuart Hall, "The West and the Rest: Discourse and Power," in *Formations of Modernity*, ed. Stuart Hall and Bram Gieben (Cambridge, UK: Polity, 1992), 277.

29. On the entanglement of the domestic and the foreign and the metaphorical weight of these terms, see Amy Kaplan, *The Anarchy of Empire in the Making of US Culture* (Cambridge, MA: Harvard University Press, 2002).

30. Cynthia Enloe, *Bananas, Beaches and Bases: Making Feminist Sense of International Politics* (Oakland: University of California Press, 2000); Cynthia Enloe, *Does Khaki Become You? The Militarisation of Women's Lives* (Boston: South End, 1983); Cynthia Enloe, *Maneuvers: The International Politics of Militarizing Women's Lives* (Oakland: University of California Press, 2000); and Catherine Lutz, *Homefront: A Military City and the American Twentieth Century* (Boston: Beacon, 2001).

31. Deborah Cowen, *Military Workfare: The Soldier and Social Citizenship in Canada* (Toronto: University of Toronto Press, 2008), 180.

32. Cynthia Enloe describes masculinity and militarism as "knitting needles; wielded together, they can knit a sturdy institutional sock. But even such a sturdy sock—the military—is not immune to holes." Enloe, *Maneuvers*, 235. See also Lutz, *Homefront*, 62.

33. Aaron Belkin, *Bring Me Men: Military Masculinity and the Benign Facade of American Empire, 1898–2001* (New York: Columbia University Press, 2012), 4. On military masculinities, see Zillah Eisenstein, *Sexual Decoys: Gender, Race and War in Imperial Democracy* (London: Zed Books, 2007); and Paul Higate, *Military Masculinities: Identity and the State* (Westport: Praeger, 2003).

34. For example, Paula Broadwell, "CST: Afghanistan," *Foreign Policy*, February 8, 2011, https://foreignpolicy.com/2011/02/08/cst-afghanistan/; and Jeanita Pisachubbe, "Female Engagement Team Brings Aid to School, Orphanage," February 15, 2011, https://www.army.mil/article/51804.

35. Elizabeth Mesok, "Affective Technologies of War: US Female Counterinsurgents and the Performance of Gendered Labor," *Radical History Review* 123 (2015): 60–86; Keally McBride and Annick T. R. Wibben, "The Gendering of Counterinsurgency in Afghanistan," *Humanity: An International Journal of Human Rights, Humanitarianism, and Development* 3, no. 2 (2012): 199–215.

36. For instance, Jennifer Terry describes reference to military women as "emblems" of the military's humanitarian rhetoric, while Khalili theorizes a "new metropolitan warrior femininity" at work in promoting contemporary US military counterinsurgency, which "deploys the language of humanitarian rescue." Elizabeth Mesok conceptualizes the Lioness teams and FETs as "affective technologies of war," or a militarized performance of affective labor that is articulated through purported racial difference between US ser-

vicewomen and their military subjects. McBride and Wibben approach the FETs as a humanitarian reframing of military occupation, emphasizing media representations of the teams as fulfilling a "civilizational" imperative of protecting women's rights, reminiscent of colonial feminism. Jennifer Terry, "Significant Injury: War, Medicine, and Empire in Claudia's Case," *Women's Studies Quarterly* 37, no. 1–2 (2009): 215; Khalili, "Gendered Practices of Counterinsurgency," 1488; Mesok, "Affective Technologies of War"; and McBride and Wibben, "The Gendering of Counterinsurgency in Afghanistan." See also Jennifer Terry, *Attachments to War: Biomedical Logics and Violence in Twenty-First-Century America* (Durham, NC: Duke University Press, 2017).

37. Jennifer Fluri, "Armored Peacocks and Proxy Bodies: Gender Geopolitics in Aid/Development Spaces of Afghanistan," *Gender, Place and Culture* 4 (2011): 535. See also Judith Butler, *Gender Trouble: Feminism and the Subversion of Identity* (New York: Routledge, 1990). On conservative gendered expectations of female soldiers in counterinsurgency, see Jennifer Fluri, "States of (in)Security: Corporeal Geographies and the Elsewhere War," *Environment and Planning D: Society and Space* 32 (2014): 795–814.

38. Arlie Russell Hochschild, *The Managed Heart: The Commercialization of Human Feeling* (Oakland: University of California Press, 1983), 7.

39. Hochschild, *The Managed Heart*, 14; Karl Marx, *Capital: A Critique of Political Economy*, Vol. 1 (New York: Penguin, 1976): 341–438, esp. 356–58; and Karl Marx, "Economic and Philosophic Manuscripts of 1844," in *The Marx-Engels Reader*, ed. Robert C. Tucker, 66–125 (New York: Norton, 1978).

40. Cowen, *Military Workfare*, 16–18.

41. The meaning of gender continues to evolve within the military, as discussed more fully in the conclusion's treatment of transgender inclusion. Inspired by Joan Wallach Scott's understanding of gender as a relational term to understand the production of masculinity and femininity, I ask how associations between emotional labor and femininity are formed through practices that are both material and meaningful. This is a different orientation than equations of gender with women, or definitions of gender along biologically deterministic and binary male-female lines. Joan Wallach Scott, *Gender and the Politics of History* (New York: Columbia University Press, 2018); and Joan Wallach Scott, "Gender: A Useful Category of Historical Analysis," *American Historical Review* 91, no. 5 (1986): 1053–75.

42. David Galula, *Pacification in Algeria, 1956–1958* (Santa Monica, CA: Rand, 2006); David Kilcullen, *The Accidental Guerrilla: Fighting Small Wars in the Midst of a Big One* (Oxford: Oxford University Press, 2009); and John A. Nagl, *Learning to Eat Soup with a Knife: Counterinsurgency Lessons from Malaya and Vietnam* (Chicago: University of Chicago Press, 2005).

43. David Kilcullen, "Countering Global Insurgency," *Small Wars Journal*, November 30, 2004, 40.

44. Laleh Khalili, *Time in the Shadows: Confinement in Counterinsurgencies* (Stanford, CA: Stanford University Press, 2013), 18.

45. Julian Go and Anne L. Foster, eds., *The American Colonial State in the Philippines: Global Perspectives* (Durham, NC: Duke University Press, 2003): 9. See also Vina Lanzona, *Amazons of the Huk Rebellion: Gender, Sex, and Revolution in the Philippines* (Madison: University of Wisconsin Press, 2009); Paul Kramer, *Blood of Government: Race, Empire, the United States and the Philippines* (Chapel Hill: University of North Carolina Press, 2006); and Vicente Rafael, *Motherless Tongues: The Insurgency of Language amid Wars of Translation* (Durham, NC: Duke University Press, 2016).

46. Kramer, *Blood of Government*, 13.

47. Gail Bederman, *Manliness and Civilization: A Cultural History of Gender and Race in the United States, 1880–1917* (Chicago: University of Chicago Press, 1995), 192–93.

48. Kaplan, *The Anarchy of Empire in the Making of US Culture*, 17.

49. Lester Langley, *The Banana Wars: United States Intervention in the Caribbean, 1898–1934* (Lanham: Rowman & Littlefield, 2002).

50. Mary Renda, *Taking Haiti: Military Occupation and the Culture of US Imperialism, 1915–1940* (Chapel Hill: University of North Carolina Press, 2001); and Brenda Gayle Plummer, *Haiti and the United States: The Psychological Moment* (Athens: University of Georgia Press, 2003).

51. Michael Sherry, *In the Shadow of War*, qtd. in Lutz, *Homefront*, 47.

52. David Vine, *Base Nation: How US Military Bases Abroad Harm America and the World* (New York: Metropolitan Books, 2015), 17–18.

53. The notion of a "positive American world order" comes from Peter Gowan's analysis of Paul Nitze, author of the policy paper "United States Objectives and Programs for National Security," better known as NSC-68, and compatriot of Dean Acheson, who wrote of his own involvement in a foreign policy school that pursued this positive aim from 1946 to 1953. Peter Gowan, "Triumphing toward International Disaster: The Impasse in American Grand Strategy," *Critical Asian Studies* 36, no. 1 (2004): 3–36. See also Vijay Prashad, *The Darker Nations: A People's History of the Third World* (New York: New Press, 2007), 39.

54. I. F. Stone, qtd. in Samuel Huntington, "Transnational Organizations in World Politics," *World Politics* 25, no. 3 (1973): 333–68.

55. Neil Smith, *American Empire: Roosevelt's Geographer and the Prelude to Globalization* (Oakland: University of California Press, 2003), 349.

56. Lutz, *Homefront*, 90. See also Joseph Masco, "'Survival Is Your Business': Engineering Ruins and Affect in Nuclear America," *Cultural Anthropology* 23, no. 2 (2008): 361–98.

57. Marilyn B. Young, *The Vietnam Wars, 1945–1990* (New York: HarperCollins, 1991), ix.

58. In 1950 Acheson, Truman's secretary of state, oversaw the production of a report to the National Security Council, NSC-68, that outlined the new US policy of containment of communism. See also Young, *The Vietnam Wars*, 25–26.

59. The phrase "prose of counterinsurgency" comes from Ranajit Guha, which Jordan Camp uses to analyze responses to the Watts and Detroit rebellions. Jordan T. Camp, *Incarcerating the Crisis: Freedom Struggles and the Rise of the Neoliberal State* (Oakland: University of California Press, 2016), 53; Ranajit Guha, "The Prose of Counter-Insurgency," in *Selected Subaltern Studies*, ed. Ranajit Guha and Gayatri Chakravorty Spivak, 45–86 (New York: Oxford University Press, 1988).

60. Mahmood Mamdani, *Good Muslim, Bad Muslim: America, the Cold War, and the Roots of Terror* (New York: Doubleday, 2004), 95.

61. Mahmood Mamdani, "Good Muslim, Bad Muslim—An African Perspective," Social Science Research Council, November 1, 2001, https://items.ssrc.org/after-september-11/good-muslim-bad-muslim-an-african-perspective/.

62. Mamdani, *Good Muslim, Bad Muslim*, 126, 132–33.

63. Derek Gregory, *The Colonial Present: Afghanistan, Palestine, Iraq* (Malden, MA: Blackwell, 2004), 36.

64. Mamdani, *Good Muslim, Bad Muslim*, 13. See also Timothy Mitchell, "McJihad: Islam in the US Global Order," *Social Text* 20, no. 4 (2002): 1–18.

65. Neil Smith, "Scales of Terror and the Resort to Geography: September 11," *Environment and Planning D: Society and Space* 19 (2001): 631 (emphasis in original).

66. Thomas Barnett, "The Pentagon's New Map," *Esquire*, March 1, 2003; and Thomas Barnett, *The Pentagon's New Map: War and Peace in the Twenty-First Century* (New York: Putnam, 2004). See also Gillian Hart, "Denaturalizing Dispossession: Critical Ethnography in an Age of Resurgent Imperialism," *Antipode* 38, no. 5 (2006): 979–80. On imagina-

tive geographies, see Gregory, *The Colonial Present*; and Derek Gregory and Allan Pred, eds., *Violent Geographies: Fear, Terror, and Political Violence* (New York: Routledge, 2007).

67. Joint Resolution to Authorize the Use of United States Armed Forces against Those Responsible for the Recent Attacks Launched against the United States, S.J. Res 23, 107th Cong. (2001).

68. Kenneth Katzman and Clayton Thomas, *Afghanistan: Post-Taliban Governance, Security, and U.S. Policy* (Washington, DC: Congressional Research Services, 2017).

69. Giovanni Arrighi, *Adam Smith in Beijing: Lineages of the Twenty-first Century* (New York: Verso, 2007), 176.

70. George Packer, *The Assassins' Gate: America in Iraq* (New York: Farrar, Straus and Giroux, 2005), 23.

71. Packer, 28.

72. Packer, 40.

73. On the reckless and inaccurately preemptive nature of the Iraq invasion, see Thomas Ricks, *Fiasco: The American Military Adventure in Iraq* (New York: Penguin, 2006). For a history of the Coalition Provisional Authority and administrators' ineptitude and nepotism, see Rajiv Chandrasekaran, *Imperial Life in the Emerald City: Inside Iraq's Green Zone* (New York: Knopf, 2006).

74. Neta Crawford, "The US Budgetary Costs of the Post-9/11 Wars," Costs of War Project, September 1, 2021, https://watson.brown.edu/costsofwar/files/cow/imce/papers/2021/Costs%20of%20War_U.S.%20Budgetary%20Costs%20of%20Post-9%2011%20Wars_9.1.21.pdf.

75. Linda Bilmes, "The Credit Card Wars: Post-9/11 War Funding Policy in Historical Perspective," Costs of War Project, November 8, 2017, https://watson.brown.edu/costsofwar/files/cow/imce/papers/2017/Linda%20J%20Bilmes%20_Credit%20Card%20Wars%20FINAL.pdf.

76. Neta Crawford and Catherine Lutz, "Human Cost of the Post-9/11 Wars: Direct War Deaths in Major War Zones, Afghanistan and Pakistan (October 2001–May 2021); Iraq (March 2003–August 2021); Syria (September 2014–August 2021); Yemen (October 2002–August 2021); and Other Post-9/11 War Zones," Costs of War Project, September 1, 2021, https://watson.brown.edu/costsofwar/files/cow/imce/papers/2021/Costs%20of%20War_Direct%20War%20Deaths_9.1.21.pdf.

77. This number includes people forcibly displaced in and from Afghanistan, Iraq, Pakistan, Yemen, Somalia, the Philippines, Libya, and Syria, focusing on the eight most violent wars the United States has launched or participated in since the global war on terror began. David Vine, Cala Coffman, Katalina Khoury, Madison Lovasz, Helen Bush, Rachael Leduc, and Jennifer Walkup, "Creating Refugees: Displacement Caused by the United States' Post–9/11 Wars," Costs of War Project, August 19, 2021, https://watson.brown.edu/costsofwar/files/cow/imce/papers/2021/Costs%20of%20War_Vine%20et%20al_Displacement%20Update%20August%202021.pdf.

78. This number does not include military contractors killed in Iraq and Afghanistan, which, though difficult to count, could double the first decade's body count. Both of these numbers include a small number of Department of Defense civilian employees. I have also added to this published data the thirteen service members killed in the Kabul evacuation. For even comparison, I list US uniformed dead *in* Iraq and Afghanistan, although the most recent numbers grow beyond seven thousand if Operation Enduring Freedom deaths in Cuba, Djibouti, Eritrea, Ethiopia, Jordan, Kenya, Kyrgyzstan, Pakistan, the Philippines, Seychelles, Sudan, Tajikistan, Turkey, Uzbekistan, and Yemen are included. Crawford and Lutz, "Human Cost of the Post-9/11 Wars"; and Catherine Lutz, "US and Coalition Casualties in Iraq and Afghanistan," Costs of War Project, February 21, 2013, https://watson.brown.edu/costsofwar/files/cow/imce/papers/2013/USandCoalition.pdf.

79. Post-9/11 veterans have much higher disability ratings than veterans from other conflicts, which is often linked to the greater frequency and length of deployments, more exposure to combat, and higher rates of survival from injuries that historically would have resulted in death. Linda Bilmes, "The Long-Term Costs of United States Care for Veterans of the Afghanistan and Iraq Wars," Costs of War Project, August 18, 2021, https://watson.brown.edu/costsofwar/files/cow/imce/papers/2021/Costs%20of%20War _Bilmes_Long-Term%20Costs%20of%20Care%20for%20Vets_Aug%202021.pdf. On injured veterans, see also Kenneth T. MacLeish, *Making War at Fort Hood* (Princeton, NJ: Princeton University Press, 2013); and Zoe Wool, *After War: The Weight of Life at Walter Reed* (Durham, NC: Duke University Press, 2015).

80. Arrighi, *Adam Smith in Beijing*, 8–9.

81. In the 1983 afterword to *The Geometry of Imperialism*, Arrighi develops the notion of a "struggle for world-hegemony," which replaces classical theories of "imperialism" that he argues the post–World War II Pax Americana has rendered obsolete. Arrighi, *The Geometry of Imperialism*, 155–73. See also Giovanni Arrighi, "Hegemony Unravelling—I," *New Left Review* 32 (2005): 23–80; and Giovanni Arrighi, "Hegemony Unravelling—II," *New Left Review* 33 (2005): 83–116.

82. Arrighi develops the concept of "world-hegemony" by engaging with Harvey's extension of classical theories of imperialism in *The New Imperialism*. On post-9/11 rediscoveries of the classical theories of imperialism Arrighi departs from, see Samir Amin, *Obsolescent Capitalism: Contemporary Politics and Global Disorder* (New York: Zed Books, 2003); David Harvey, *The New Imperialism* (New York: Oxford University Press, 2003); and Ellen Meiksins Wood, *Empire of Capital* (New York: Verso, 2003).

83. Arrighi, "Hegemony Unravelling-I," 32 (emphasis in original); Giovanni Arrighi and Beverly J. Silver, *Chaos and Governance in the Modern World System* (Minneapolis: University of Minnesota Press, 1999); and Giovanni Arrighi and Beverly Silver, "Capitalism and World (Dis)order," *Review of International Studies* 27 (2001): 257–79. On Arrighi's "move to globalize Gramsci," see Gillian Hart, "Forging Connections: Giovanni Arrighi's Conceptions of the World," paper presented at Dynamics of the Global Crisis, Antisystemic Movements and New Models of Hegemony, Museo Nacional Centro de Arte Reina Sofía, Madrid, 25–29 May 2009, 4. For a comprehensive discussion of Gramsci and geography, see Jordan T. Camp, "Gramsci and Geography," in *Oxford Bibliographies in Geography*, ed. Barney Warf (New York: Oxford University Press, 2022).

84. On legal and economic dimensions, see Shaina Potts, "Law as Geopolitics: Judicial Territory, Transnational Economic Governance, and American Power," *Annals of the Association of American Geographers* 110, no. 4 (2019): 1192–207. On the military dimension of bases, see Vine, *Base Nation*.

85. Gramsci, *Selections from the Prison Notebooks*, 184.

86. Arrighi, *Adam Smith in Beijing*, 176–77.

87. Arun Kundnani, *The Muslims Are Coming! Islamophobia, Extremism, and the Domestic War on Terror* (New York: Verso, 2015).

88. Judith Butler, *Frames of War: When Is Life Grievable?* (New York: Verso, 2009), 26.

89. Butler, 105.

90. Rosa Luxemburg, *The Accumulation of Capital* (New York: Monthly Review Press, 1951); and Raya Dunayevskaya, *Philosophy and Revolution* (New York: Delacorte, 1973). See also Anthony Brewer, *Marxist Theories of Imperialism: A Critical Survey* (New York: Routledge, 1990).

91. Luxemburg, *The Accumulation of Capital*, 464.

92. Lis Mandl, "Rosa Luxemburg and the Women's Question," In Defence of Marxism, January 15, 2009, https://www.marxist.com/rosa-luxemburg-and-the-womens-question .htm.

93. Hannah Arendt, *The Modern Challenge to Tradition: Fragmente eines Buchs* (Göttingen: Wallsteid Verlag, 2018); and Hannah Arendt, *Thinking without a Banister: Essays in Understanding, 1953–1975* (New York: Schocken Books, 2018).

94. Hannah Arendt, *The Origins of Totalitarianism* (New York: Harcourt, 1968), 150–51. Giovanni Arrighi's and David Harvey's divergent readings of Arendt inform the difference between "world-hegemony" and extensions of classical theories of imperialism. Arrighi writes, "Arendt's observation refers to accumulation of power and capital *within states*, whereas mine refers to the accumulation of power and capital in an evolving *system of states.*" Arrighi, *Adam Smith in Beijing*, 229.

95. Francisca de Haan, "Continuing Cold War Paradigms in Western Historiography of Transnational Women's Organizations: The Case of the Women's International Democratic Federation (WIDF)," *Women's History Review* 19, no. 4 (2010): 547–73; and Kristen Ghodsee, *Second World, Second Sex: Socialist Women's Activism and Global Solidarity during the Cold War* (Durham, NC: Duke University Press, 2019). On how these linkages also informed postwar Black freedom struggles in the United States in relation to global decolonization, see John Munro, *The Anticolonial Front: The African American Freedom Struggle and Global Decolonisation, 1945–1960* (Cambridge: Cambridge University Press, 2017).

96. Bonfiglioli and Ghodsee, "Vanishing Act."

97. Chandra Talpade Mohanty, Minnie Bruce Pratt, and Robin L. Riley, "Introduction: Feminism and US Wars—Mapping the Ground," In *Feminism and War: Confronting US Imperialism*, ed. Robin Riley, Chandra Talpade Mohanty, and Minnie Bruce Pratt (New York: Zed Books, 2008), 3.

98. Jennifer Fluri, "'Rallying Public Opinion' and Other Misuses of Feminism," in *Feminism and War: Confronting US Imperialism*, ed. Robin Riley, Chandra Talpade Mohanty, and Minnie Bruce Pratt, 143–57 (New York: Zed Books, 2008).

99. Gayatri Chakravorty Spivak, "Can the Subaltern Speak?" in *Marxism and the Interpretation of Culture*, ed. Lawrence Grossberg and Cary Nelson, 271–313 (Urbana: University of Illinois Press, 1988).

100. Butler, *Frames of War*, 129.

101. Angela Y. Davis, "A Vocabulary for Feminist Praxis: On War and Radical Critique," in *Feminism and War: Confronting US Imperialism*, ed. Robin Riley, Chandra Talpade Mohanty, and Minnie Bruce Pratt (New York: Zed Books, 2008), 21. See also Eisenstein, *Sexual Decoys*.

102. Gramsci, *Selections from the Prison Notebooks*, 178. On the method of conjunctural analysis see also Camp, *Incarcerating the Crisis;* Jordan T. Camp and Jennifer Greenburg, "Counterinsurgency Reexamined: Racism, Capitalism, and US Military Doctrine," *Antipode* 52, no. 2 (2020): 430–51; Hall et al., *Policing the Crisis*; Hart, "Why Did It Take So Long?"; and Hart, "D/developments after the Meltdown."

103. Closely linked to conjunctural analysis is what Gramsci called the "relations of force" composed of political, economic, and military relations that are formed through spatial and international connections. Gramsci, in historico-political analysis, "distinguish[ed] organic movements (relatively permanent) from movements which may be termed 'conjunctural' (and which appear as occasional, immediate, almost accidental)." Gramsci, *Selections from the Prison Notebooks*, 175–85. On the stakes of this distinction with respect to economism and volunteerism, see Gillian Hart, *Disabling Globalization: Places of Power in Post-Apartheid South Africa* (Oakland: University of California Press, 2002).

104. Stuart Hall, "The Problem of Ideology—Marxism without Guarantees," in *Stuart Hall: Critical Dialogues in Cultural Studies*, ed. Kuan-Hsing Chen and David Morley, 25–46 (London: Routledge, 1996). See also Gillian Hart, "Geography and Development: Critical Ethnographies," *Progress in Human Geography* 28, no. 1 (2004): 91–100; Hart, *Disabling*

Globalization, esp. 28–29; and Stuart Hall, "Gramsci's Relevance for the Study of Race and Ethnicity," *Journal of Communication Inquiry* 10, no. 5 (1986): 5–27.

105. Mark Duffield, *Global Governance and the New Wars: The Merging of Development and Security* (London: Zed Books, 2001): 15–16.

106. Mark Duffield, *Development, Security and Unending War: Governing the World of Peoples* (Cambridge, UK: Polity, 2007), 24. Duffield draws heavily on Cowen and Shenton to argue that development emerged to manage Europe's nineteenth-century surplus populations, found its way into colonial government discourses in the post–World War I era, and reemerged to define official development discourse in the post–Cold War era. Hart's "D/developments after the Meltdown," drawing on Corbridge, argues that the sort of focus Cowen and Shenton bring to the continuity of development obscures how official development policy grew out of the end of colonial empires and rising forms of US hegemony. Michael Cowen and Robert Shenton, *Doctrines of Development* (New York: Routledge, 1996); Stuart Corbridge, "Review of *Doctrines of Development,*" *Antipode* 29, no. 2 (1997): 218–20.

107. Such a contingent understanding of development draws on scholars such as Frederick Cooper, who have considered development's emergence in response to crises of colonial government, and Hart's emphasis on the "moments of crisis and redefinition" within her framework of "D/development" that distinguishes between the intertwined processes of capitalism's spatially uneven development and "Development" as projects of intervention in the third world. Frederick Cooper, "Modernizing Bureaucrats, Backward Africans, and the Development Concept," in *International Development and the Social Sciences: Essays on the History and Politics of Knowledge,* ed. Frederick Cooper and Randall Packard (Oakland: University of California Press, 1997), 64–69; and Hart, "D/developments after the Meltdown."

108. Gregory, "The Rush to the Intimate," 19.

109. Gregory, 20.

110. Laleh Khalili, "The New (and Old) Classics of Counterinsurgency," *Middle East Report* 255 (2010): 5; Laleh Khalili, "Scholar, Pope, Soldier, Spy," *Humanity: An International Journal of Human Rights, Humanitarianism, and Development* 5, no. 3 (2014): 417–34.

111. Gregory, "The Rush to the Intimate," 19.

112. On role players, see Nomi Stone, "Living the Laughscream: Human Technology and Affective Maneuvers in the Iraq War," *Cultural Anthropology* 32, no. 1 (2017): 149–74.

113. Neta Crawford and Catherine Lutz, "Human Cost of the Post-9/11 Wars."

114. Ryan Toews claims that we must understand the political economy of imperialism in relation to counterinsurgency doctrine and knowledge production rather than framing the military simply as an extension of state power. I take these insights further by examining social practices of knowledge production, including military contractors as embodying some of the political-economic forces scholarship on imperialism identifies. This approach is distinct from, for instance, Harvey's political-economic analysis of "the new imperialism." Ryan Toews, "Counterinsurgency as Global Social Warfare," in *Destroy, Build, Secure: Readings on Pacification,* ed. Tyler Wall, Parastou Saberi, and Will Jackson, 46–67 (Ottawa: Red Quill Books, 2017).

115. I refer to increasing interest in multisited approaches such as the one employed here. It is also important to distinguish analytical and empirical differences between the mixed methodological approach pursued here and recent ethnographies of military lives— such as MacLeish, *Making War at Fort Hood;* Stone, "Living the Laughscream"; and Wool, *After War*—and classic texts, such as Catherine Lutz, *Homefront.*

116. Kilcullen, "Twenty-Eight Articles."

117. Brooks R. Brewington, "Combined Action Platoons: A Strategy for Peace Enforcement" (Air University: Subject Area Strategic Issues, 1996); and Curtis L. Williamson III,

"The US Marine Corps Combined Action Program (CAP): A Proposed Alternative Strategy for the Vietnam War" (Air University: Subject Area History, 2002). The US military used this program (and reading sources such as this) as a template to establish similar teams in Afghanistan.

118. For a recent example of a West Point cadet publishing "lessons learned" for counterinsurgency based on the Marine Corps occupation of Haiti, see Nick Kramer, "Lessons from American Counterinsurgency Operations during the Occupation of Haiti," *Small Wars Journal*, June 16, 2021.

119. Khalili, *Time in the Shadows*, 54.

120. Emily Gilbert, "The Gift of War: Cash, Counterinsurgency, and 'Collateral Damage,'" *Security Dialogue* 46, no. 5 (2015): 403–21.

121. Lorraine Dowler, "The Hidden War: The 'Risk' to Female Soldiers in the US Military," in *Reconstructing Conflict: Integrating War and Post-War Geographies*, ed. Colin Flint and Scott Kirsch, 295–314 (Burlington, VT: Ashgate, 2011).

122. All personal names used in this book, except those of public officials, are pseudonyms.

123. The US government established Provincial Reconstruction Teams in Afghanistan and Iraq to combine military forces with civilian representatives from organizations such as USAID, the Department of State, the Department of Agriculture, and the Department of Justice and contractors to support provincial governments in a wide variety of programs, from police training to agricultural development to budget preparation. Provincial Reconstruction Teams were emblematic of the "whole of government" approach discussed in chapter 1 and the controversy of embedding civilian development workers with military forces.

1. DOCTRINAL TURNING POINTS IN THE NEW IMPERIAL WARS

1. On NGOs and interventions in Haiti, see Greg Beckett, *There Is No More Haiti: Between Life and Death in Port-au-Prince* (Oakland: University of California Press, 2019); Paul Farmer, *The Uses of Haiti* (Monroe, ME: Common Courage, 1994); Erica Caple James, *Democratic Insecurities: Violence, Trauma, and Intervention in Haiti* (Oakland: University of California Press, 2010); Chelsey L. Kivland, *Street Sovereigns: Young Men and the Makeshift State in Urban Haiti* (Ithaca, NY: Cornell University Press, 2020); and Mark Schuller, *Killing with Kindness: Haiti, International Aid, and NGOs* (New Brunswick, NJ: Rutgers University Press, 2012).

2. On Walter Benjamin's notion of the telescoping of the past through the present, see Walter Benjamin, *The Arcades Project* (Cambridge, MA: Harvard University Press, 1999); Susan Buck-Morss, *The Dialectics of Seeing: Walter Benjamin and the Arcades Project* (Cambridge, MA: MIT Press, 1989); Allan Pred, *The Past Is Not Dead: Facts, Fictions, and Enduring Racial Stereotypes* (Minneapolis: University of Minnesota Press, 2004).

3. Laleh Khalili, *Time in the Shadows: Confinement in Counterinsurgencies* (Stanford, CA: Stanford University Press, 2013), chap. 1.

4. Derek Gregory, "'The Rush to the Intimate': Counterinsurgency and the Cultural Turn," *Radical Philosophy* 150 (2008): 11.

5. Thomas Ricks, *Fiasco: The American Military Adventure in Iraq* (New York: Penguin, 2006).

6. Gregory, "The Rush to the Intimate," 19.

7. US Army, *Counterguerrilla Operations*, Field Manual 90-8 (Washington, DC: Department of the Army, 1986); US Marine Corps, *Small Wars Manual* (Washington, DC: US Marine Corps, 1940); and US Marine Corps, *Counterinsurgency Operations* (Washington, DC: US Marine Corps, 1980).

8. Roberto González, *American Counterinsurgency: Human Science and the Human Terrain* (Chicago: Prickly Paradigm, 2009); and David Price, "Faking Scholarship," in

The Counter-Counterinsurgency Manual: Or, Notes on Demilitarizing Anthropology, by the Network of Concerned Anthropologists (Chicago: Prickly Paradigm, 2009), 59–76.

9. The 2008 *Stability Operations Field Manual* marked the second time the army worked with a private publisher in this fashion. See promotional materials for *The US Army Stability Operations Field Manual*, www.press.umich.edu/1308805/us_army _stability_operations_field_manual.

10. Price, "Faking Scholarship," 70–71.

11. Price, 71.

12. Sarah Sewall, "Introduction to the University of Chicago Press Edition," in *The US Army and Marine Corps Counterinsurgency Field Manual*, by US Army and Marine Corps (Chicago: University of Chicago Press, 2007), xxx.

13. Sewall, xxxi.

14. US Army and US Marine Corps, *Counterinsurgency Field Manual*, 62–64.

15. US Army and US Marine Corps, 155, 170.

16. US Army and US Marine Corps, 51.

17. US Army and US Marine Corps, 54–55.

18. US Army and US Marine Corps, 67.

19. US Army and US Marine Corps, 50.

20. US Army and US Marine Corps, 73–75.

21. Steven Aftergood, "Army Updates Counterinsurgency Doctrine," Federation of American Scientists, May 21, 2014; US Army and US Marine Corps, *Counterinsurgency Field Manual*, 2; US Army and US Marine Corps, *Insurgencies and Countering Insurgencies*, Field Manual 3-24 (Washington, DC: Department of the Army, 2014), 1–2.

22. Adam Elkus, "FM 3–24, Social Science, and Security," *Small Wars Journal*, May 20, 2014, para. 1.

23. Bing West, "The 2014 Counterinsurgency Field Manual Requires Pre-Publication Review," *Small Wars Journal*, June 14, 2014, para. 16.

24. Oliver Belcher, "Anatomy of a Village Razing: Counterinsurgency, Violence, and Securing the Intimate in Afghanistan," *Political Geography* 62 (2018): 104.

25. US Military Joint Chiefs of Staff, *Counterinsurgency*, JP 3-24 (Washington, DC: Joint Staff Pentagon, 2021).

26. US Department of Defense, *Instruction: Stability Operations; Number 3000.05* (Washington, DC: US Department of Defense, 2005).

27. US Department of Defense, 3.

28. US Army, *The US Army Stability Operations Field Manual*, Field Manual 3-07 (Washington, DC: US Army, 2008); and US Army, *US Army Stability Operations Field Manual* (Ann Arbor: University of Michigan Press, 2009). For a precursor to this notion of the military centrally including humanitarian relief and other noncombat operations, see US Military Joint Chiefs of Staff, "Military Operations Other Than War," in *Joint Doctrine for Military Operations Other Than War*, JP 3-7 (Washington, DC: Joint Staff Pentagon, 1995).

29. William Caldwell, "Foreword," in *Stability Operations* (Washington, DC: US Army, 2008), para. 3.

30. US Army, *US Army Stability Operations Field Manual*, 10.

31. US Army, 31.

32. The 2009 version of DOD Directive 3000.05 again emphasizes the equal importance of stabilization to combat but this time also emphasizes a renewed conversation about a "whole of government approach." The 2010 National Security Strategy also includes the language of a "whole of government approach," specifically in reference to "improving the integration of skills and capabilities within our military and civilian institutions, so they complement each other and operate seamlessly." Where the 2002 and 2005 National Secu-

rity Strategies discuss development as an instrument of national security and the 2010 document follows this trajectory, the explicit reference to "stability" and a "whole of government approach" distinguishes the 2010 policy from its precedents. The Obama White House, *National Security Strategy* (Washington, DC: The White House, 2010), 14. See also chapter 3 of the *US Army Stability Operations Field Manual*, "Considerations to Achieve Unity of Effort."

33. US Army, *US Army Stability Operations Field Manual*, 6.

34. Paul Fishstein and Andrew Wilder, *Winning Hearts and Minds? Examining the Relationship between Aid and Security in Afghanistan* (Medford, MA: Feinstein International Center, 2012).

35. US Department of State, *Quadrennial Diplomacy and Development Review Fact Sheet* (2009).

36. US Department of State, *Quadrennial Diplomacy and Development Review: Enduring Leadership in a Dynamic World* (Washington, DC: US Department of State and USAID, 2015).

37. Laleh Khalili, "The New (and Old) Classics of Counterinsurgency," *Middle East Report* 255 (2010): 14–23. See also Catherine Lutz, "The Military Normal," in *The Counter-Counterinsurgency Field Manual: Or, Notes on Demilitarizing American Society* (Chicago: Prickly Paradigm, 2009), 23–38; and Price, "Faking Scholarship."

38. Price, "Faking Scholarship," 62.

39. Belcher, "Anatomy of a Village Razing." On counterinsurgency and pacification strategies mobilized through aid (including USAID) in Palestine and how this extends war into the most intimate aspects of life, see Lisa Bhungalia, "Managing Violence: Aid, Counterinsurgency, and the Humanitarian Present in Palestine," *Environment and Planning A* 47 (2015): 2308–23.

40. On this problematic disciplinary history, see Matthew Rech, Daniel Bos, K. Neil Jenkings, Alison Williams, and Rachel Woodward, "Geography, Military Geography, and Critical Military Studies," *Critical Military Studies* 1, no. 1 (2015): 47–60; Rachel Woodward, *Military Geographies* (Oxford, UK: Blackwell, 2004); and Joel Wainwright, *Geopiracy: Oaxaca, Militant Empiricism, and Geographical Thought* (New York: Palgrave Macmillan, 2013).

41. David Kilcullen, *The Accidental Guerrilla: Fighting Small Wars in the Midst of a Big One* (Oxford: Oxford University Press, 2009), xiii.

42. Kilcullen.

43. Kilcullen, 38.

44. US Army and US Marine Corps, *Counterinsurgency Field Manual*, 133–34.

45. Derek Gregory, "The Biopolitics of Baghdad: Counterinsurgency and the Counter-City," *Human Geography* 1, no. 1 (2008): 20. See also Khalili, "The New (and Old) Classics of Counterinsurgency."

46. Kilcullen, *The Accidental Guerrilla*, 38.

47. Doreen Massey, *Space, Place, and Gender* (Minneapolis: University of Minnesota Press, 1994), 5.

48. Massey, 5.

49. Thomas Friedman, *The World Is Flat: A Brief History of the Twenty-First Century* (New York: Picador, 2005).

50. Thomas Barnett, *The Pentagon's New Map: War and Peace in the Twenty-First Century* (New York: Penguin, 2004).

51. Kilcullen, *The Accidental Guerrilla*, 8–9.

52. Kilcullen, 13.

53. David Kilcullen, "Twenty-Eight Articles: Fundamentals of Company-Level Counterinsurgency," *Marine Corps Gazette* 90, no. 7 (2006): 33.

54. Khalili, "The New (and Old) Classics of Counterinsurgency"; Khalili, *Time in the Shadows*; and T. E. Lawrence, *Twenty-Seven Articles* (Seattle: Praetorian, 2011).

55. Jennifer Greenburg, "'Going Back to History': Haiti and US Military Humanitarian Knowledge Production," *Critical Military Studies* 4, no. 2 (2018): 121–39.

56. Kilcullen, cited in Khalili, "The New (and Old) Classics of Counterinsurgency," 17.

57. Khalili, *Time in the Shadows*, 49; and David Galula, *Counterinsurgency Warfare: Theory and Practice* (New York: Praeger, 1964), 53.

58. Khalili, "The New (and Old) Classics of Counterinsurgency," 17. See also Stathis Kalyvas, *The Logic of Violence in Civil War* (Cambridge: Cambridge University Press, 2006).

59. T. E. Lawrence, *Seven Pillars of Wisdom* (Garden City, NY: Doubleday, 1935).

60. Daniel Green, "A Soldier Reports: The Education of John Nagl," *Foreign Policy*, October 15, 2014.

61. Peter Maas, "Professor Nagl's War," *New York Times Magazine*, January 11, 2004.

62. John A. Nagl, *Learning to Eat Soup with a Knife: Counterinsurgency Lessons from Malaya and Vietnam* (Chicago: University of Chicago Press, 2005), xv.

63. Khalili, "The New (and Old) Classics of Counterinsurgency"; Anthony Short, *The Communist Insurrection in Malaya* (London: Frederick Muller, 1975).

64. Khalili, "The New (and Old) Classics of Counterinsurgency," 20.

65. Susan Carruthers, *Winning Hearts and Minds* (New York: Leicester University Press, 1995); and Paul Dixon, "'Hearts and Minds'? British Counter-Insurgency from Malaya to Iraq," *Journal of Strategic Studies* 32, no. 3 (2009): 354.

66. Dixon, "Hearts and Minds?"; and Khalili, *Time in the Shadows*, 177.

67. Carruthers, *Winning Hearts and Minds*; and Dixon, "Hearts and Minds?," 354.

68. Dixon, "Hearts and Minds?," 362.

69. John D. Kelly, "Seeing Red: Mao Fetishism, Pax Americana, and the Moral Economy of War," in *Anthropology and Global Counterinsurgency*, ed. John D. Kelly et al. (Chicago: University of Chicago Press, 2010), 70.

70. Kelly, "Seeing Red."

71. US Army and US Marine Corps, *Counterinsurgency Field Manual*, 58.

72. Robert Baden-Powell, founder of the Boy Scouts and international scouting movement, was a British army officer who had fought in Indian and African imperial wars. He founded scouting in the early twentieth century to prepare young British men, whose masculinity and preparedness he saw as threatened, for the next imperial wars. In creating this masculinist, imperialist imaginary, he was also influenced by notions of the American frontier circulating at the time. See Scott Johnston, "Courting Public Favour: The Boy Scout Movement and the Accident of Internationalism, 1907–29," *Historical Research* 88, no. 241 (2015): 508–29.

73. Stephen T. Hosmer and Sibylle O. Crane, *Counterinsurgency: A Symposium, April 16–20, 1962* (Santa Monica, CA: Rand, 1963).

74. David Galula, *Pacification in Algeria, 1956–1958* (Santa Monica, CA: Rand, 2006), 1.

75. Galula, xx.

76. Galula, xxi.

77. Galula, xxiii.

78. Galula, xxiii.

79. Galula, 105.

80. Galula, 164.

81. Greg Mortenson and David Oliver Relin, *Three Cups of Tea: One Man's Mission to Promote Peace—One School at a Time* (New York: Penguin, 2007).

82. Charles Hirschkind and Saba Mahmood, "Feminism, the Taliban, and Politics of Counter-Insurgency," *Anthropological Quarterly* 75, no. 2 (2002): 341.

83. Lila Abu-Lughod, *Do Muslim Women Need Saving?* (Cambridge, MA: Harvard University Press, 2013).

84. Galula, *Pacification in Algeria*, 246.

85. David Petraeus, "Commander of the International Security Assistance Force's Counterinsurgency Guidance," Official memorandum, Kabul, Headquarters of the International Security Assistance Force, 2010, https://smallwarsjournal.com/documents /comisafcoinguidance.pdf, 1.

86. David Petraeus, "Learning Counterinsurgency: Lessons from Soldiering in Iraq," *Military Review* 86, no. 1 (2006): 8–9.

87. Hillary Clinton, "Statement before the Senate Foreign Relations Committee," Washington, DC, January 13, 2009.

88. Joseph Nye, "Get Smart," *Foreign Affairs*, July 1, 2009.

89. Nye, "Get Smart"; and G. John Ikenberry, "Soft Power: The Means to Success in World Politics," *Foreign Affairs*, January 28, 2009.

90. Hillary Clinton, "Remarks on Development in the 21st Century," Speech, Center for Global Development, Washington, DC, January 6, 2010.

91. Clinton.

92. Jamey Essex, *Development, Security, and Aid* (Athens: University of Georgia Press, 2013); and Vijay Kumar Nagaraj, "'Beltway Bandits' and 'Poverty Barons': For-Profit International Development Contracting and the Military-Development Assemblage," *Development and Change* 46, no. 4 (2015): 585–617.

93. On the rise of this particular colonial feminism in tandem with soldier-scholars such as Petraeus and Kilcullen, see Laleh Khalili, "Gendered Practices of Counterinsurgency," *Review of International Studies* 37, no. 4 (2011): 1471–91.

94. Robert Gates, "Remarks as Delivered by Secretary of Defense Robert M. Gates," Landon Lecture, Kansas State University, Manhattan, Kansas, November 26, 2007.

95. Gates.

96. Reuben Brigety, *Humanity as a Weapon of War: Sustainable Security and the Role of the US Military* (Washington, DC: Center for American Progress, 2008), 2.

97. Brigety.

98. Brigety, 4.

99. For example, USAID, various UN organizations, Interaction (a consortium of NGOs), and the International Committee of the Red Cross developed their own institutional civil-military guidelines in this period.

100. James Ferguson, *The Anti-Politics Machine: "Development," Depoliticization, and Bureaucratic Power in Lesotho* (Minneapolis: University of Minnesota Press, 1990).

101. Office of Civilian-Military Cooperation," US Agency for International Development, updated October 15, 2020, https://www.usaid.gov/military.

102. Office of the Coordinator for Reconstruction and Stabilization," US Department of State (archive), updated January 20, 2009, https://2001-2009.state.gov/s/crs/.

103. US Army, *US Army Stability Operations Field Manual*.

104. Robin Wright, "Civilian Response Corps Gains Ground," *Washington Post*, February 15, 2008.

105. Nina Serafino, *In Brief: State Department Bureau of Conflict and Stabilization Operations (CSO)* (Washington, DC: Congressional Research Services, 2012), 2.

106. Serafino, *In Brief*, 10.

107. Nina Serafino, *Department of Defense "Section 1207" Security and Stabilization Assistance: Background and Congressional Concerns, FY2006–2010* (Washington, DC: Congressional Research Services, 2011).

108. Robert Perito, *Integrated Security Assistance: The 1207 Program* (Washington, DC: US Institute of Peace, 2008).

109. Perito.

110. Serafino, *Department of Defense "Section 1207" Security and Stabilization Assistance.*

111. Robert Grossman-Vermas and David Becker, "Metrics for the Haiti Stabilization Initiative," *PRISM* 2, no. 2 (2011): 145–58.

112. On how "stabilization" has further amplified for-profit development contracting, see Jennifer Greenburg, "Selling Stabilization: Anxious Practices of Militarized Development Contracting," *Development and Change* 48, no. 6 (2017): 1262–86.

113. Nina Serafino, *Global Security Contingency Fund: Summary and Overview* (Washington, DC: Congressional Research Services, 2014).

114. Michael Dziedzic and Michael Seidl, *Provincial Reconstruction Teams and Military Relations with International and Nongovernmental Organizations in Afghanistan* (Washington, DC: United States Institute of Peace, 2005).

115. Joe Bryan, "War without End? Military Humanitarianism and the Limits of Biopolitical Approaches to Security in Central America and the Caribbean," *Political Geography* 47 (2015): 33–42.

116. Nick Turse, *Tomorrow's Battlefield: US Proxy Wars and Secret Ops in Africa* (Chicago: Haymarket Books, 2015); and Stephanie Savell, "The 'War on Terror' Accelerates in Africa," *The American Prospect*, October 19, 2021.

117. Perito, *Integrated Security Assistance.*

118. Academy for Educational Development representative, interview, Washington, DC, July 2009.

119. Essex, *Development, Security, and Aid,* 31.

2. THE "SOCIAL WORK" OF WAR

1. *Atterbury-Muscatatuck 2016,* marketing brochure, Internet Archive, https://web .archive.org/web/20170113232002/http://www.atterburymuscatatuck.in.ng.mil/Portals /18/Users/053/53/53/Guide_rev_2016.2.pdf.

2. Oliver Belcher, "Staging the Orient," *Annals of the Association of American Geographers* 104, no. 5 (2014): 1022.

3. For example, Jake Kosek, *Understories: The Political Life of Forests in Northern New Mexico* (Durham, NC: Duke University Press, 2006), chap. 6; and Catherine Lutz, *Homefront: A Military City and the American Twentieth Century* (Boston: Beacon, 2001).

4. On the direct economic relationship between military spending and opportunity costs of job creation and other social programs, see Heidi Garrett-Peltier, "Job Opportunity Cost of War," Costs of War Project, May 24, 2017, https://watson.brown.edu/costsofwar /files/cow/imce/papers/2017/Job%20Opportunity%20Cost%20of%20War%20-%20 HGP%20-%20FINAL.pdf.

5. Zack Whitman Gill, "Rehearsing the War Away: Perpetual Warrior Training in Contemporary US Army Policy," *TDR: The Drama Review* 53, no. 3 (2009): 141. See also Stephen Graham, "War and the City," *New Left Review,* 44 (2007): 121–32; Scott Magelssen, "Rehearsing the 'Warrior Ethos': 'Theatre Immersion' and the Simulation of Theatres of War," *TDR: The Drama Review* 53, no. 1 (2009): 47–72; and Nomi Stone, "Living the Laughscream: Human Technology and Affective Maneuvers in the Iraq War," *Cultural Anthropology* 32, no. 1 (2017): 149–74.

6. The role of the town Fayetteville, North Carolina, in simulating the fictitious country "Pineland" in army trainings is among the most notable of such examples. See Lutz, *Homefront,* 102–4.

7. US Army and US Marine Corps, *Counterinsurgency Field Manual* (Chicago: University of Chicago Press, 2007), 1.

8. Laleh Khalili, "The New (and Old) Classics of Counterinsurgency," *Middle East Report* 255 (2010): 14–23; David Price, "Faking Scholarship," in *The Counter-Counterinsurgency Manual: Or, Notes on Demilitarizing Anthropology*, by The Network of Concerned Anthropologists (Chicago: Prickly Paradigm, 2009): 59–76.

9. Khalili, "The New (and Old) Classics of Counterinsurgency," 15; Sir Charles W. Gwynn, *Imperial Policing* (London: Macmillan, 1939).

10. Price, "Faking Scholarship," 70.

11. Laleh Khalili, "Gendered Practices of Counterinsurgency," *Review of International Studies* 37, no. 4 (2011): 1473.

12. US Army, *US Army Stability Operations Field Manual* (Ann Arbor: University of Michigan Press, 2009).

13. James Ferguson, *The Anti-Politics Machine: "Development," Depoliticization, and Bureaucratic Power in Lesotho* (Minneapolis: University of Minnesota Press, 1990).

14. Ferguson, *The Anti-Politics Machine*; Timothy Mitchell, *Rule of Experts: Egypt, Techno-Politics, Modernity* (Oakland: University of California Press, 2002); Timothy Mitchell, *Colonising Egypt* (Oakland, University of California Press, 1991); and Nikolas Rose, *Powers of Freedom: Reframing Political Thought* (Cambridge: Cambridge University Press, 1999).

15. Tania Li, *The Will to Improve: Governmentality, Development, and the Practice of Politics* (Durham, NC: Duke University Press, 2007), 11. Li distinguishes her attention to the "switch" from closure to openings from scholars of expert discourse emphasizing closure, including Hubert Dreyfus and Paul Rabinow, *Michel Foucault: Beyond Structuralism and Hermeneutics* (Brighton: Harvester, 1982); Mitchell, *Rule of Experts*; Ferguson, *The Anti-Politics Machine*; Rose, *Powers of Freedom*.

16. In Lesotho, Ferguson found that development institutions, "while 'failing' in their own terms, nonetheless have regular effects, which include the expansion and entrenchment of bureaucratic state power." Although I do not adopt Ferguson's emphasis on political closure in his argument that development operates as an "anti-politics machine," I am provoked by his insights to ask what regular effects failure produces. Ferguson, *The Anti-Politics Machine*, xiv.

17. David Keane, *Inside the Taliban*, Documentary (National Geographic, 2007).

18. George Lakoff, *Moral Politics: How Liberals and Conservatives Think* (Chicago: University of Chicago Press, 2002), 108.

19. Gayatri Chakravorty Spivak, "Can the Subaltern Speak?" in *Marxism and the Interpretation of Culture*, ed. Lawrence Grossberg and Cary Nelson, 271–313 (Urbana: University of Illinois Press, 1988).

20. For an example of such paternalism in the context of British colonial Africa, see Frederick Lugard, *The Dual Mandate in British Tropical Africa* (London: W. Blackwood and Sons, 1922).

21. Catherine Lutz and Jane Collins, *Reading National Geographic* (Chicago: University of Chicago Press, 1993), 18–19. See also George Stocking, *Victorian Anthropology* (New York: Simon and Schuster, 1991); and George Stocking, *Race, Culture, and Evolution: Essays in the History of Anthropology* (Chicago: University of Chicago Press, 1982).

22. Michael Latham, *Modernization as Ideology: American Social Science and "Nation Building" in the Kennedy Era* (Chapel Hill: University of North Carolina Press, 2000), 204.

23. Nick Turse, *Kill Anything That Moves: The Real American War in Vietnam* (New York: Metropolitan Books, 2013), 190.

24. Latham, *Modernization as Ideology*, 208; and Turse, *Kill Anything That Moves*, 190–91.

25. For a prominent example of this thinking, see David Kilcullen, "Countering Global Insurgency," *Small Wars Journal* 2, no. 2 (2004).

26. Deborah Cowen and Emily Gilbert, "Fear and the Familial in the US War on Terror," in *Fear: Critical Geopolitics and Everyday Life*, ed. Rachel Pain and Susan Smith, 49–58 (Burlington, VT: Ashgate, 2008).

27. Paul Collier, *Wars, Guns, and Votes: Democracy in Dangerous Places* (New York: Harper, 2009).

28. US Agency for International Development Office of Military Affairs, *District Stability Framework* (Washington, DC: USAID, 2011), 3. See also US Army, *US Army Stability Operations Field Manual*.

29. US Agency for International Development Office of Military Affairs, *District Stability Framework*, 4.

30. US Agency for International Development Office of Military Affairs, 7.

31. Mitchell, *Rule of Experts*, 93.

32. For example, Mitchell's mapmaker is "holding the feddan comb [an instrument devised to deal with shrinkage of the map paper] in one hand, trying to keep the cardboard flat and its threads taut, walking the pair of dividers with the other hand, making sure its point does not slip as he reads the measurement off the scale, cursing the heat that has shrunk his paper, and trying to prevent the whole sheet lifting into the air under the ceiling fans whirling above his head." Mitchell, *Rule of Experts*, 116.

33. Li makes this argument in relation to Mitchell, *Rule of Experts*. Li, *The Will to Improve*, 10.

34. David Kilcullen, "Twenty-Eight Articles: Fundamentals of Company-Level Counterinsurgency," *Marine Corps Gazette* 90, no. 7 (2006): 29–35.

35. US Marine Corps, *Marine Corps Planning Process* (Washington, DC: Department of the Navy Headquarters, 2001).

36. Some of the most extreme rejections came from this Marine Corps training, in which marines formerly assigned to infantry and artillery had been sent without a choice to be trained in civilian interaction. Whereas army personnel volunteered for this specialization and underwent an intensive screening process followed by seventeen weeks of training, many marines were reassigned against their will. In the army, one could advance their career through promotion within the active duty ranks of civil affairs. In contrast, in the Marine Corps, civil affairs was considered a "secondary military occupational specialization," meaning that time spent within this specialization hurt rather than helped chances for promotion within a primary specialization. Yet army civil affairs trainees still expressed critiques similar to those of marines, demonstrating the more widespread nature of these critiques beyond just those forcibly reassigned. For more details, see Jennifer Greenburg, "Selling Stabilization: Anxious Practices of Militarized Development Contracting," *Development and Change* 48, no. 6 (2017): 1262–86.

37. David Galula, *Counterinsurgency Warfare: Theory and Practice* (New York: Praeger, 1964).

38. Khalili, "Gendered Practices of Counterinsurgency."

39. Lakoff, *Moral Politics*.

40. Belcher, "Staging the Orient," 1019; and Ben Anderson, "Population and Affective Perception: Biopolitics and Anticipatory Action in US Counterinsurgency Doctrine," *Antipode* 43, no. 2 (2010): 208, qtd. in Belcher, "Staging the Orient."

41. Derek Gregory, "'The Rush to the Intimate': Counterinsurgency and the Cultural Turn," *Radical Philosophy* 150 (2008): 8–23.

42. Belcher, "Staging the Orient," 1017.

43. Magelssen, "Rehearsing the 'Warrior Ethos,'" 53.

44. David Petraeus, "Commander of the International Security Assistance Force's Counterinsurgency Guidance," official memorandum, Kabul: Headquarters of the International Security Assistance Force, 2010, *Small Wars Journal*, https://smallwarsjournal .com/documents/comisafcoinguidance.pdf.

3. COLONIAL "LESSONS LEARNED"

1. Emily Gilbert, "The Gift of War: Cash, Counterinsurgency, and 'Collateral Damage,'" *Security Dialogue* 46, no. 5 (2015): 403–21.

2. Gilbert, 403–21. See also Emily Gilbert, "Money as a Weapons System," *Critical Military Studies* 1, no. 3 (2015): 202–19.

3. Stephen T. Hosmer and Sibylle O. Crane, *Counterinsurgency: A Symposium, April 16–20, 1962* (Santa Monica, CA: Rand, 1963).

4. US Army and US Marine Corps, *Counterinsurgency Field Manual* (Chicago: University of Chicago Press, 2007); and US Army, *The US Army Stability Operations Field Manual: FM 3-07* (Washington, DC: US Army, 2008).

5. On the transition from the physical to the "human" terrain, see Derek Gregory, "'The Rush to the Intimate': Counterinsurgency and the Cultural Turn," *Radical Philosophy* 150 (2008): 8–23.

6. US Army and US Marine Corps, *Counterinsurgency Field Manual*; and David Price, "Faking Scholarship," in *The Counter-Counterinsurgency Manual: Or, Notes on Demilitarizing Anthropology*, by The Network of Concerned Anthropologists, 59–76 (Chicago: Prickly Paradigm, 2009).

7. Jon T. Hoffman, *Chesty: The Story of Lieutenant General Lewis B. Puller, USMC* (New York: Random House, 2001); and Smedley Butler, *War Is a Racket* (New York: Round Table, 1935).

8. Sir Charles W. Gwynn, *Imperial Policing* (London: Macmillan, 1939).

9. Laleh Khalili, *Time in the Shadows: Confinement in Counterinsurgencies* (Stanford, CA: Stanford University Press, 2013), 19.

10. Hoffman, *Chesty*, 37.

11. Marine Corps School, *Small Wars Operations* (Quantico, VA: Marine Barracks, 1935), section 1-5, 5.

12. David Galula, *Pacification in Algeria, 1956–1958* (Santa Monica, CA: Rand, 2006); Stathis Kalyvas, *The Logic of Violence in Civil War* (Cambridge: Cambridge University Press, 2006; and John A. Nagl, *Learning to Eat Soup with a Knife: Counterinsurgency Lessons from Malaya and Vietnam* (Chicago: University of Chicago Press, 2005).

13. US Marine Corps, *Small Wars Manual* (Washington, DC: US Marine Corps, 1940), section 1-14, 28.

14. US Marine Corps, section 1-17, 32.

15. US Marine Corps, section 1-14, 28.

16. Lt. Col. John Nagl popularized this quote during his 2007 appearance on *The Daily Show* with Jon Stewart, but it is also attributed to retired Marine Corps general and former secretary of defense James Mattis.

17. Joe Bryan and Denis Wood, *Weaponizing Maps: Indigenous Peoples and Counterinsurgency in the Americas* (New York: Guilford, 2015).

18. Bryan and Wood, chap. 3.

19. Marine Corps School, *Small Wars Operations*.

20. Marine Corps School, section 1-8, 19–22.

21. Harold Utley, "An Introduction to the Tactics and Techniques of Small Wars," *Marine Corps Gazette* 15, no. 5 (1931): 52.

22. Harold Utley, "The Tactics and Techniques of Small Wars: Part II—Intelligence," *Marine Corps Gazette* 18, no. 2 (1933): 44–48.

23. For Haitian perspectives on what this brutality meant, see Roger Gaillard, *Premier Écrasement du Cacoïsme: 1915* (Port-au-Prince: Le Natal, 1981).

24. Jennifer Greenburg, "'The One Who Bears the Scars Remembers': Haiti and the Historical Geography of US Militarized Development," *Journal of Historical Geography* 51 (2016): 52–63; and Patricia J. Lopez, "Clumsy Beginnings: From 'Modernizing Mission' to Humanitarianism in the US Occupation of Haiti (1915–34)," *Environment and Planning A* 47, no. 11 (2015): 2240–56.

25. Greenburg, "'The One Who Bears the Scars Remembers.'"

26. Frederick Cooper, "Modernizing Bureaucrats, Backward Africans, and the Development Concept," in *International Development and the Social Sciences: Essays on the History and Politics of Knowledge*, ed. Frederick Cooper and Randall Packard, 64–92 (Oakland: University of California Press, 1997).

27. Sibylle Fischer, *Modernity Disavowed: Haiti and the Cultures of Slavery in the Age of Revolution* (Durham, NC: Duke University Press, 2004); and Michel-Rolph Trouillot, *Silencing the Past: Power and the Production of History* (Boston: Beacon, 1997).

28. Laurent Dubois, *Haiti: The Aftershocks of History* (New York: Metropolitan Books, 2012), 13. See also Ada Ferrer, *Freedom's Mirror: Cuba and Haiti in the Age of Revolution* (New York: Cambridge University Press, 2014); Patrick Geggus and Norman Fiering, eds., *The World of the Haitian Revolution* (Bloomington: Indiana University Press, 2009); and C.L.R. James, *The Black Jacobins: Toussaint Louverture and the San Domingo Revolution* (New York: Vintage Books, 1989).

29. Mary Renda, *Taking Haiti: Military Occupation and the Culture of US Imperialism, 1915–1940* (Chapel Hill: University of North Carolina Press, 2001), 156.

30. Derek Gregory, *The Colonial Present: Afghanistan, Palestine, Iraq* (Malden, MA: Blackwell, 2004), 248; Joseph Conrad, *Heart of Darkness* (Portland, OR: Tin House Books, 2013); and Rudyard Kipling, "The White Man's Burden: The United States and the Philippine Islands," *McClures Magazine*, 1899.

31. Major Kelly Webster, "Lessons from a Military Humanitarian in Port-Au-Prince," *Small Wars Journal*, March 28, 2010, 1.

32. Michel-Rolph Trouillot, *Global Transformations: Anthropology and the Modern World* (New York: Palgrave Macmillan, 2003).

33. Akin to Hart's conception of Stephen Bannon as the organic intellectual of the Trumpist coalition, military organic intellectuals such as Nagl and Petraeus can be understood as creating cross-class alliances within and beyond military institutions that promote counterinsurgency. Gillian Hart, "Why Did It Take So Long? Trump-Bannonism in a Global Conjunctural Frame," *Geografiska Annaler: Series B, Human Geography* 103, no. 3 (2020): 239–66. On different categories and roles of intellectuals, including the organic intellectual who is linked to their class origin and fulfills a culturally productive role reflective of this link, see Antonio Gramsci, *Selections from the Prison Notebooks*, ed. Quintin Hoare and Geoffrey Nowell Smith, 4–23 (New York: International Publishers, 1971).

34. Khalili, *Time in the Shadows*, 178.

35. Nagl, *Learning to Eat Soup with a Knife*.

36. Khalili, *Time in the Shadows*, 179–80.

37. On the history of US proxy warfare, see Mahmood Mamdani, *Good Muslim, Bad Muslim: America, the Cold War, and the Roots of Terror* (New York: Doubleday, 2004).

38. Frantz Fanon, *Toward the African Revolution: Political Essays* (New York: Grove, 1964), 184.

39. Nick Turse, *Kill Anything That Moves: The Real American War in Vietnam* (New York: Metropolitan Books, 2013), 26.

40. Turse, 5.

41. Hosmer and Crane, *Counterinsurgency*, iii.

42. Hosmer and Crane, 15.

43. David Milne, *America's Rasputin: Walt Rostow and the Vietnam War* (New York: Hill and Wang, 2008), 7.

44. Milne, *America's Rasputin*, 6.

45. Walt Whitman Rostow, *The Stages of Economic Growth: A Non-Communist Manifesto* (Cambridge: Cambridge University Press, 1991), 101.

46. Michael E. Latham, *Modernization as Ideology: American Social Science and "Nation Building" in the Kennedy Era* (Chapel Hill: University of North Carolina Press, 2000), 183.

47. Milne, *America's Rasputin*, 60.

48. Huntington, qtd. in Latham, *Modernization as Ideology*, 151.

49. Latham, 176.

50. Nagl, *Learning to Eat Soup with a Knife*, 89.

51. Nagl, xv.

52. Nagl, 92.

53. Nagl, 98.

54. J.B.P.R., "The Emergency in Malaya: Some Reflections on the First Six Years," *The World Today* 10, no. 11 (1954): 481, cited in Nagl, *Learning to Eat Soup with a Knife*, 105.

55. US Marine Corps, "Development and Pacification," 1969, folder 26, box 34, Vietnam Collection, USMC Archives, Quantico (emphasis added).

56. US Marine Corps, "Development and Pacification," 1969, folder 26, box 34, Vietnam Collection, USMC Archives, Quantico, 130–32.

57. Foucault distinguished disciplinary modes of power from "government," or the "conduct of conduct," which arranges "things so that people, following their own self-interest, will do as they ought." See Tania Li, *The Will to Improve: Governmentality, Development, and the Practice of Politics* (Durham, NC: Duke University Press, 2007), 5; Donald Moore, *Suffering for Territory: Race, Place, and Power in Zimbabwe* (Durham, NC: Duke University Press, 2005); and Michel Foucault, "Governmentality," in *The Foucault Effect: Studies in Governmentality*, ed. Graham Burchell, Colin Gordon, and Peter Miller, 87–104 (Chicago: University of Chicago Press, 1991).

58. David Kilcullen, "Twenty-Eight Articles: Fundamentals of Company-Level Counterinsurgency," *Marine Corps Gazette* 90, no. 7 (2006): 33.

59. US Army and US Marine Corps, *Counterinsurgency Field Manual*, 296.

60. Center for Army Lessons Learned, *Commander's Guide to Female Engagement Teams: Observations, Insights, Lessons* (Washington, DC: US Army, 2011).

61. Alistair Horne, *A Savage War of Peace: Algeria 1954–1962* (New York: Penguin, 2006), 18.

62. Horne, 18.

63. Horne, 197–200. See also Henri Alleg, *The Question* (Lincoln: University of Nebraska Press, 2006); and Frantz Fanon, *The Wretched of the Earth* (New York: Grove, 2004).

64. Albert Camus, cited in Horne, *A Savage War of Peace*, 205.

65. Alf Andrew Heggoy, *Insurgency and Counterinsurgency in Algeria* (Bloomington: Indiana University Press, 1972), 237.

66. Heggoy, 90.

67. Heggoy, 176–77.

68. Heggoy, 181.

69. Marnia Lazreg, *Torture and the Twilight of Empire: From Algiers to Baghdad* (Princeton, NJ: Princeton University Press, 2008), 145.

70. Lazreg, 145.

71. Ryme Seferdjeli, "The French Army and Muslim Women during the Algerian War (1954–62)," *Hawwa: Journal of Women of the Middle East and the Islamic World* 3, no. 1 (2005): 51.

72. Lazreg, *Torture and the Twilight of Empire*, 147.

73. Lazreg, 148.

74. Frantz Fanon, "Algeria Unveiled," in *A Dying Colonialism* (New York: Grove, 1967), 44.

75. Fanon, 63, 59, 61.

76. Fanon, 38.

77. Fanon, 62 (emphasis in original).

78. Lazreg, *Torture and the Twilight of Empire*, 150.

79. Fanon, "Algeria Unveiled," 42.

80. Ato Sekyi-Otu, *Fanon's Dialectic of Experience* (Cambridge, MA: Harvard University Press, 1996).

81. Fanon, "Algeria Unveiled," 59. See also Alice Cherki, *Frantz Fanon: A Portrait* (Ithaca, NY: Cornell University Press, 2006).

82. Fanon, "Algeria Unveiled," 59.

83. Lazreg, *Torture and the Twilight of Empire*, 148.

84. Homa Hoodfar, "The Veil in Their Minds and on Our Heads: Veiling Practices and Muslim Women," in *Women, Gender, Religion: A Reader,* ed. Elizabeth Castelli, 420–46 (New York: Palgrave Macmillan, 2001).

85. Center for Army Lessons Learned, *Commander's Guide to Female Engagement Teams*, 76.

86. Center for Army Lessons Learned, 76.

87. Center for Army Lessons Learned, 3.

88. Center for Army Lessons Learned, 3.

89. The Obama White House, "Female Engagement Teams: The Changing Face of the US Marines," YouTube, 2012, https://www.youtube.com/watch?v=dN0w8uPnX3s.

90. Elizabeth Mesok, "Affective Technologies of War: US Female Counterinsurgents and the Performance of Gendered Labor," *Radical History Review* 123 (2015): 60–86.

91. Seferdjeli, "The French Army and Muslim Women," 49.

4. SOOTHING OCCUPATION

1. The animal metaphor "lioness" is striking in that it signifies hunting, which stands in contrast to the way female counterinsurgents described their work as calming civilians down. Early participants in the Marine Corps pilot program that coined the name "Lioness" theorized in interviews that its violent connotations were intended to convince commanders to sign off on the pilot by signaling the program's wartime value in the context of what one female trainer called a "toxic masculinity environment."

2. Catherine Lutz, "Emotion, Thought, and Estrangement: Emotion as a Cultural Category," *Cultural Anthropology* 1, no. 3 (1986): 288.

3. Michael Hardt and Antonio Negri, *Empire* (Cambridge, MA: Harvard University Press, 2000); and Susanne Schultz, "Dissolved Boundaries and 'Affective Labor': On the Disappearance of Reproductive Labor and Feminist Critique in Empire," trans. Frederick Peters, *Capitalism Nature Socialism* 17, no. 1 (2006): 77–82.

4. Elizabeth Mesok, "Affective Technologies of War: US Female Counterinsurgents and the Performance of Gendered Labor," *Radical History Review* 123 (2015): 61.

5. Sylvia Yanagisako, "Immaterial and Industrial Labor: On False Binaries in Hardt and Negri's Trilogy," *Focaal—Journal of Global and Historical Anthropology* 64 (2012): 20. See also Johanna Oksala, "Affective Labor and Feminist Politics," *Signs: Journal of*

Women in Culture and Society 41, no. 2 (2016): 280–303; and Schultz, "Dissolved Boundaries and 'Affective Labor.'"

6. Lutz, "Emotion, Thought, and Estrangement," 288.

7. Lutz, 300.

8. Lutz, 290.

9. Catherine Lutz, "Feminist Theories and the Science of Emotion," in *Science and Emotions after 1945: A Transatlantic Perspective,* ed. Frank Biess and Daniel M. Gross (Chicago: University of Chicago Press, 2014), 343.

10. Lila Abu-Lughod and Catherine Lutz, "Introduction: Emotion, Discourse, and the Politics of Everyday Life," in *Language and the Politics of Emotion,* ed. Catherine Lutz and Lila Abu-Lughod (Cambridge: Cambridge University Press, 1990), 15.

11. Susan Griffin, *Woman and Nature: The Roaring Inside Her* (New York: Harper and Row, 1978).

12. Nel Noddings, *Caring: A Feminine Approach to Ethics and Moral Education* (Oakland: University of California Press, 2013); and Sara Ruddick, *Maternal Thinking: Toward a Politics of Peace* (Boston: Beacon, 1989). See also Lutz, "Feminist Theories and the Science of Emotion," 248.

13. Alison Jaggar, "Love and Knowledge: Emotion in Feminist Epistemology," *Inquiry* 32, no. 2 (1989): 151–76.

14. For example, Cynthia Enloe, *Does Khaki Become You? The Militarisation of Women's Lives* (Boston: South End, 1983).

15. Lutz, "Feminist Theories and the Science of Emotion," 354.

16. David Kilcullen, "Twenty-Eight Articles: Fundamentals of Company-Level Counterinsurgency," *Marine Corps Gazette* 90, no. 7 (2006): 33.

17. Donna Alvah, *Unofficial Ambassadors: American Military Families Overseas and the Cold War* (New York: New York University Press, 2007).

18. Jaggar, "Love and Knowledge."

19. Noddings, *Caring*; and Ruddick, *Maternal Thinking.*

20. Ruddick, *Maternal Thinking.*

21. Catherine Lutz, "Engendered Emotion: Gender, Power, and the Rhetoric of Emotional Control in American Discourse," in *Language and the Politics of Emotion,* ed. Catherine Lutz and Lila Abu-Lughod, 69–91 (Cambridge: Cambridge University Press, 1990).

22. Ruddick, *Maternal Thinking,* 148.

23. Arlie Russell Hochschild, *The Managed Heart: The Commercialization of Human Feeling* (Oakland: University of California Press, 1983).

24. Riverbend, *Baghdad Burning: Girl Blog From Iraq* (New York: Feminist Press, 2005), 6.

25. Riverbend, 8.

26. Meg McLagan and Daria Sommers, *Lioness,* Documentary (Room 11 Productions, 2008).

27. Paul Sullivan, deputy secretary for communications, California Department of Veterans Affairs, personal correspondence, April 2016.

28. Aaron Glantz, *The War Comes Home: Washington's Battle against America's Veterans* (Oakland: University of California Press, 2009), 112.

29. Glantz, 114–16.

30. Department of Veterans Affairs, *VA Health Care Fact Sheet 16-4: Combat Veteran Eligibility* (2011).

31. *Hearing on Reclaiming the Process: Examining the VBA Claims Transformation Plan as a Means to Effectively Serve Our Veterans,* 112th Congress (2012), statement of Linda Halliday, assistant inspector general, Department of Veterans Affairs.

32. Servicewomen's Action Network representative, private conversation, 2017.

33. Swords to Ploughshares Institute for Veteran Policy, *Veterans and Their Families Reference Guide* (2015); and Department of Veterans Affairs Office of Inspector General, *Review of Combat Stress in Women Veterans Receiving VA Health Care and Disability Benefits* (Washington, DC: VA Office of Inspector General, 2010).

34. Swords to Ploughshares Institute for Veteran Policy, *Veterans and Their Families Reference Guide*, 5; and Department of Veterans Affairs Office of Inspector General, *Review of Combat Stress in Women Veterans Receiving VA Health Care and Disability Benefits*.

35. Swords to Ploughshares Institute for Veteran Policy, *Defining a New Age of Women Veteran Care: Findings from California Community Providers* (2016), 3.

36. Megan Katt, "Blurred Lines: Cultural Support Teams in Afghanistan," *Joint Forces Quarterly* 75 (2014): 106–13.

37. Katt, 108.

38. Jaggar, "Love and Knowledge."

39. Katt, "Blurred Lines," 107.

40. Center for Army Lessons Learned, *Commander's Guide to Female Engagement Teams: Observations, Insights, Lessons* (Washington, DC: US Army, 2011), 4.

41. Center for Army Lessons Learned, 1, 63.

42. Diana Staneszewki, "Female Engagement Teams," in *Civil Affairs Afghanistan Newsletter* (Washington, DC: US Army Center for Lessons Learned, n.d.), 36. See also Claire Russo and Shannon Spann. *Female Networking Operations: A Tactical Tool for Strategic Advantage* (McLean, VA: Orbis Operations, 2011).

43. On the category of "the population" as a biopolitical dimension of counterinsurgency that is more expansive than the notion in military doctrine of the population's "approval," see Ben Anderson, "Population and Affective Perception: Biopolitics and Anticipatory Action in US Counterinsurgency Doctrine," *Antipode* 43, no. 2 (2010): 205–36; Michael Dillon, "Governing through Contingency: The Security of Biopolitical Governance," *Political Geography* 26, no. 1 (2007): 41–47; Derek Gregory, "The Biopolitics of Baghdad: Counterinsurgency and the Counter-City," *Human Geography* 1, no. 1 (2008): 6–27; and Julian Reid, "The Biopolitics of the War on Terror: A Critique of the 'Return of Imperialism' Thesis in International Relations," *Third World Quarterly* 26, no. 2 (2005): 237–52.

44. Paula Broadwell, "CST: Afghanistan," *Foreign Policy*, February 8, 2011.

45. Derek Gregory, "'The Rush to the Intimate': Counterinsurgency and the Cultural Turn," *Radical Philosophy* 150 (2008): 8–23.

46. Jaggar, "Love and Knowledge."

47. Center for Army Lessons Learned, *Commander's Guide to Female Engagement Teams*, 4.

48. Center for Army Lessons Learned, 59.

49. Charles Stadtlander, "Soldiers Prep to Pave New Path in War," US Army, April 21, 2011, http://www.army.mil/article/55289.

50. Jessica Binsch, "Female Troops Take on New Role in Afghanistan," *Marine Corps Times*, April 8, 2010.

51. Jaggar, "Love and Knowledge."

52. Lutz, "Feminist Theories and the Science of Emotion," 350; and Jaggar, "Love and Knowledge," 164.

53. Kilcullen, "Twenty-Eight Articles," 33.

54. Human Rights Watch, "Booted: Lack of Recourse for Wrongfully Discharged US Military Rape Survivors," May 19, 2016, https://www.hrw.org/report/2016/05/19/booted/lack-recourse-wrongfully-discharged-us-military-rape-survivors.

55. Personal correspondence, 2018.

56. Lorraine Dowler, "The Hidden War: The 'Risk' to Female Soldiers in the US Military," in *Reconstructing Conflict: Integrating War and Post-War Geographies,* ed. Colin Flint and Scott Kirsch (Burlington, VT: Ashgate, 2011), 296.

57. Didier Fassin, *Humanitarian Reason: A Moral History of the Present* (Oakland: University of California Press, 2011), 1.

58. For example, Jeanita Pisachubbe, "Female Engagement Team Brings Aid to School, Orphanage," US Army, February 14, 2011, https://www.army.mil/article/51804.

59. Deborah Cowen and Emily Gilbert, "Fear and the Familial in the US War on Terror," in *Fear: Critical Geopolitics and Everyday Life,* ed. Rachel Pain and Susan Smith, 49–58 (Burlington, VT: Ashgate, 2008).

60. Center for Army Lessons Learned, *Commander's Guide to Female Engagement Teams,* 63.

61. Julia Watson, "Female Engagement Teams: The Case for More Female Civil Affairs Marines," *Marine Corps Gazette,* 2011, 3.

62. Watson, 3.

63. Gilbert Herdt, ed., *Third Sex, Third Gender–Beyond Sexual Dimorphism in Culture and History* (New York: Zone Books, 1993); Will Roscoe, *Changing Ones: Third and Fourth Genders in Native North America* (New York: St. Martin's, 1998); and Evan B. Towle and Lynn Marie Morgan, "Romancing the Transgender Native: Rethinking the Use of the 'Third Gender' Concept," *GLQ: A Journal of Lesbian and Gay Studies* 8, no. 4 (2002): 472.

64. In this sense, her argument is more like accounts of being treated like a "third gender" person while doing academic fieldwork abroad. See Jillian Schwedler, "The Third Gender: Western Female Researchers in the Middle East," *Political Science and Politics* 39, no. 3 (2006): 425–28.

65. US Agency for International Development, *The Development Response to Violent Extremism and Insurgency* (Washington, DC: USAID, 2011), 1. The 2011 USAID document captures the time during which Rochelle was deployed, but USAID's understanding of poverty as vulnerability to terrorist recruitment stretches far beyond this moment. For an example of how this understanding continued into at least the next decade, see US Agency for International Development, *Policy for Countering Violent Extremism through Development Assistance* (Washington, DC: USAID, 2020).

66. President of the United States, "National Security Strategy," 2010, 26.

67. Nadège Clitandre, "Haitian Exceptionalism in the Caribbean and the Project of Rebuilding Haiti," *Journal of Haitian Studies* 17, no. 2 (2011): 151. On the making of the Other more generally, see Edward W. Said, *Orientalism* (New York: Vintage Books, 1979).

68. Valerie Kaussen, "Do It Yourself: International Aid and the Neoliberal Ethos in the Tent Camps of Port-Au-Prince," *NACLA Report on the Americas* 44, no. 6 (2011): 5–7.

69. Jaggar, "Love and Knowledge."

70. Lutz, "Emotion, Thought, and Estrangement."

5. A NEW IMPERIAL FEMINISM

1. Kevin Maurer, "In New Elite Army Unit, Women Serve Alongside Special Forces, but First They Must Make the Cut," *Washington Post,* October 27, 2011.

2. Francis Kelly, *Vietnam Studies: US Army Special Forces 1961–1971* (Washington, DC: US Army, 1973).

3. Mark Brown, "Village Stability Operations: An Historical Perspective from Vietnam to Afghanistan," *Small Wars Journal,* March 28, 2013, 2.

4. US Special Operations Command, *Special Operations Forces Cultural Engagement Future Concept* (MacDill Air Force Base, FL: Headquarters, US Special Operations Command, 2011). The history of such "foreign internal defense" groups is gruesome. In the

post–Vietnam War era, this model of counterinsurgency was used in Latin America during the Cold War, including to train, support, and advise the Salvadorian military. Such US-trained military forces have been responsible for some of the worst massacres in modern Latin American history such as at El Mozote, where a US-trained Salvadorian battalion murdered more than seven hundred men, women, and children in December 1981. Mark Danner, *The Massacre at El Mozote* (New York: Vintage Books, 1993).

5. Gayle Tzemach Lemmon, *Ashley's War: The Untold Story of a Team of Women Soldiers on the Special Ops Battlefield* (New York: Harper, 2015).

6. Gayatri Chakravorty Spivak, "Can the Subaltern Speak?," in *Marxism and the Interpretation of Culture*, ed. Lawrence Grossberg and Cary Nelson, 271–313 (Urbana: University of Illinois Press, 1988).

7. Associated Press, "'They Didn't See the Pride': West Point Photo Puts Race and Gender in Spotlight," *The Guardian*, May 14, 2016.

8. Associated Press, "'They Didn't See the Pride.'"

9. Dana Farrington, "West Point Cadets at Center of Storm after Raising Fists in Photo," *National Public Radio*, May 9, 2016.

10. Farrington, "West Point Cadets at Center of Storm after Raising Fists in Photo."

11. On the racial inequity of tests regulating entry into the military, see Catherine Lutz, *Homefront: A Military City and the American Twentieth Century* (Boston: Beacon, 2001), 304n86.

12. Lutz, *Homefront*, 115–16.

13. Mary Tobin herself uses this example that "we're told we're all green." Associated Press, "'They Didn't See the Pride.'"

14. Eduardo Bonilla-Silva, *Racism without Racists: Color-Blind Racism and the Persistence of Racial Inequality in America* (New York: Rowman and Littlefield, 2018), 56. See also George Lipsitz, *The Possessive Investment in Whiteness: How White People Profit from Identity Politics* (Philadelphia: Temple University Press, 2018).

15. Eileen Patten and Kim Parker, *Women in the US Military: Growing Share, Distinctive Profile* (Washington, DC: Pew Research Center, 2011).

16. Tom Vanden Brook, "Pentagon's Elite Forces Lack Diversity," *USA Today*, August 6, 2015.

17. Joseph Votel, Proceedings of "A Look into SOCOM," The Aspen Institute, Aspen, CO, July 24, 2015.

18. Brook, "Pentagon's Elite Forces Lack Diversity."

19. Mike Copenhaver, "The Integration of Minorities into Special Operations: How Cultural Diversity Enhances Operations" (unpublished manuscript, US Army War College 2014).

20. Melani McAlister, *Epic Encounters: Culture, Media, and US Interests in the Middle East Since 1945* (Oakland: University of California Press, 2005), 254; Lutz, *Homefront*, 242.

21. Lutz, *Homefront,* 243.

22. The version of color blindness I examine here within the US military must be understood in relation to the longer history through which color-blind ideologies have taken shape over the past half century in the United States. The popular diffusion of color-blind discourse in the 2000s and its relation to a liberal multicultural project was prefigured by the conservative movement's reinvention of itself amid the crisis of hegemony in the 1970s. Committed to reversing the economic and legal gains of the civil rights movement, the new "color-blind conservatives" obscured the movements' more "radical reconstruction" goals and established a narrow color-blind narrative of the civil rights movement. This color-blind narrative, reworked to serve the purposes of the New Right, erased the Dr. Martin Luther King Jr. who advocated unionization and linked domestic poverty to militarism and imperialism. I am interested here in how this deeper history takes shape in the post-

9/11 turning point, becoming formalized and institutionalized in military trainings. This deeper history reveals how certain forces on the Right that shaped a now-dominant narrative of color blindness were committed to white supremacy and rule of law. In this way, it is not surprising that within conservative military institutions, military frames of color-blind liberalism should exist alongside overt forms of white supremacy. Jacquelyn Dowd Hall, "The Long Civil Rights Movement and the Political Uses of the Past," *Journal of American History* 91, no. 4 (2005): 1233–63.

23. Kathleen Belew, *Bring the War Home: The White Power Movement and Paramilitary America* (Cambridge, MA: Harvard University Press, 2018), 21.

24. Leo Shane, "Signs of White Supremacy, Extremism Up Again in Poll of Active-Duty Troops," *Military Times,* February 6, 2020.

25. A. C. Thompson, Ali Winston, and Jake Hanrahan, "Ranks of Notorious Hate Group Include Active-Duty Military," ProPublica, May 3, 2018.

26. It is in part through the history of color-blind ideology Dowd Hall maps out that certain iterations of white supremacy are able to draw upon this history of color-blind conservatism, giving meaning to present-day versions of color-blind racism through historical racial discourses within the New Right. I draw here on Stuart Hall's understanding of articulation in the combined sense of joining together and giving meaning through language. Stuart Hall, "Race, Articulation and Societies Structured in Dominance," in *Sociological Theories: Race and Colonialism,* 305–45 (Paris: UNESCO, 1980). On Hall's concept of articulation as a Gramscian theory of praxis, see Gillian Hart, *Disabling Globalization: Places of Power in Post-Apartheid South Africa* (Oakland: University of California Press, 2002), 28–30.

27. Stuart Hall, "On Postmodernism and Articulation: An Interview with Stuart Hall," in *Stuart Hall: Critical Dialogues in Cultural Studies,* ed. David Morley and Kuan-Hsing Chen (New York: Routledge, 1996), 142.

28. McAlister, *Epic Encounters,* 250.

29. Elizabeth Mesok, "Affective Technologies of War: US Female Counterinsurgents and the Performance of Gendered Labor," *Radical History Review* 123 (2015): 62.

30. McAlister, *Epic Encounters,* 257.

31. Anne McClintock, *Imperial Leather: Race, Gender, and Sexuality in the Colonial Contest* (New York: Routledge, 1995), 5 (emphasis in original).

32. On colonial hierarchies see Laleh Khalili, "Gendered Practices of Counterinsurgency," *Review of International Studies* 37, no. 4 (2011): 1471–91; and McClintock, *Imperial Leather,* 6.

33. McClintock, *Imperial Leather,* 40.

34. Cynthia Enloe, *Bananas, Beaches and Bases: Making Feminist Sense of International Politics* (Oakland: University of California Press, 2000), 161.

35. Susannah Robertson and Andrea Crossan, "'Make No Mistake, These Women Are Warriors,'" *The World,* Public Radio International, June 16, 2015.

36. For instance, *Ashley's War* as well as all media accounts are entirely focused on CST deployments with direct-action units. Many video interviews conducted by the Army Women's Museum, however, do feature women who served on VSO missions; however, these interviews did not address issues of sexuality.

37. Enloe, *Bananas, Beaches and Bases,* 149.

38. Joanna Walters, "'Flawed' Study Casts Doubt on Mixed-Gender Units in US Marine Corps," *The Guardian,* October 17, 2015.

39. Deborah Cowen, *Military Workfare: The Soldier and Social Citizenship in Canada* (Toronto: University of Toronto Press, 2008), 56.

40. Cynthia Enloe, *Does Khaki Become You? The Militarisation of Women's Lives* (Boston: South End, 1983), 119.

41. Enloe, 138–39.

42. Enloe, 138.

43. Kenneth T. MacLeish, *Making War at Fort Hood* (Princeton, NJ: Princeton University Press, 2013); and Zoe Wool, *After War: The Weight of Life at Walter Reed* (Durham, NC: Duke University Press, 2015).

44. Enloe, *Does Khaki Become You?*

45. Kate Germano, "Separate Is Not Equal in the Marine Corps," *New York Times*, March 31, 2018.

46. Judith Butler, *Frames of War: When Is Life Grievable?* (New York: Verso, 2009), 26.

47. Center for Army Lessons Learned, *Commander's Guide to Female Engagement Teams: Observations, Insights, Lessons* (Washington, DC: US Army, 2011), 5.

48. On the construction of "natural" phenomena in nature, see, for example, Jennifer Terry, "'Unnatural Acts' In Nature: The Scientific Fascination with Queer Animals," *GLQ: A Journal of Lesbian and Gay Studies* 6, no. 2 (2000): 151–93.

49. Cynthia Enloe, *Maneuvers: The International Politics of Militarizing Women's Lives* (Oakland: University of California Press, 2000), 235, 237–38.

50. Patten and Parker, *Women in the US Military*. In the decade since then, the proportion of women in the US armed forces has continued to slowly grow, reaching 16.9 percent active-duty enlisted and 18.9 percent active-duty officers in 2020. Female enlisted and commissioned officers are 28 percent more likely to separate from the military than their male counterparts. See US Department of Defense, *2020 Demographics: Profile of the Military Community* (Washington, DC: US Department of Defense, Office of the Deputy Assistant Secretary of Defense for Military Community and Family Policy, 2020); and US Government Accountability Office, *Female Active-Duty Personnel: Guidance and Plans Needed for Recruitment and Retention Efforts* (Washington, DC: Government Accountability Office, 2020).

51. Kimberly Lessmeister, "Stryker Brigade Females Strive for Spot on Female Engagement Team," Defense Video Imagery Distribution System, March 12, 2012, https://www.dvidshub.net/news/printable/86128.

52. Jeanita Pisachubbe, "Female Engagement Team Brings Aid to School, Orphanage," US Army, February 14, 2011, https://www.army.mil/article/51804.

53. Charles Hirschkind and Saba Mahmood, "Feminism, the Taliban, and Politics of Counter-Insurgency," *Anthropological Quarterly* 75, no. 2 (2002): 339–54.

54. Christopher McCullough, "Female Engagement Teams: Who They Are and Why They Do It," US Army, February 22, 2013, www.army.mil/article/88366.

55. Janet Holliday, "Female Engagement Teams: The Need to Standardize Training and Employment," *Military Review*, March–April 2012, 91.

56. Hirschkind and Mahmood, "Feminism, the Taliban, and Politics of Counter-Insurgency."

57. Whitney Hughes, "Female Engagement Team Finds Strength behind Burkas," US Army, November 8, 2010, https://www.army.mil/article/47832/female_engagement_team_finds_strength_behind_burkas.

58. Hughes.

59. Lindsey Pirek, "The 26th MEU Female Engagement Team Trains with Kuwaiti Police," US Marine Corps, March 4, 2016, https://www.marines.mil/News/News-Display/Article/686139/26th-meu-female-engagement-team-trains-with-kuwaiti-police/; and "Sisters in Arms: American and Romanian Female Marines Train Together in a Mission to 'Defend' the Black Sea Coast," *Daily Mail*, March 24, 2017.

60. Shaiyla Hakeem, "Fearless Females Unite, Empower One Another," Defense Visual Information Distribution Service, August 23, 2019, https://www.dvidshub.net/news/337023/fearless-females-unite-empower-one-another.

61. Sylvia Tapia, "Female Engagement Team—Spring Storm 2018," YouTube, March 16, 2018, https://www.youtube.com/watch?v=B50-6iI4GMM.

62. David Vine, *Base Nation: How U.S. Military Bases Abroad Harm America and the World* (New York: Metropolitan Books, 2015).

63. Vine, 13. See also Nikhil Pal Singh, *Race and America's Long War* (Oakland: University of California Press, 2017); and David Vine, *The United States of War: A Global History of America's Endless Conflicts, from Columbus to the Islamic State* (Oakland: University of California Press, 2020).

64. A Special Forces document from 2011 titled "Special Operations Forces: Cultural Engagement Future Concept" conceptualizes how the cultural support "capability" may be developed and used more globally. The document studies the uses of CSTs in Iraq and Afghanistan in order to generalize their applicability to global war.

65. The Obama White House, *The United States National Action Plan on Women, Peace, and Security* (Washington, DC: The White House, 2011).

66. Kristen Holmstedt, *Band of Sisters: American Women at War in Iraq* (Mechanicsburg, PA: Stackpole Books, 2007).

67. Matt Pottinger, Hali Jilani, and Claire Russo, "Trying to Win Afghanistan without Afghan Women," *Small Wars Journal*, February 18, 2010, 9.

68. The Obama White House, "Female Engagement Teams: The Changing Face of the US Marines." YouTube, 2012, https://www.youtube.com/watch?v=dN0w8uPnX3s.

69. Jennifer Fluri, "States of (in)Security: Corporeal Geographies and the Elsewhere War," *Environment and Planning D: Society and Space* 32, no. 5 (2014): 795–814.

70. Lemmon, *Ashley's War*, 108.

71. Gayle Tzemach Lemmon, "Meet the Women Fighting on the Front Lines of an American War," TED Talk, May 28, 2015, https://www.ted.com/talks/gayle_tzemach _lemmon_meet_the_women_fighting_on_the_front_lines_of_an_american_war.

72. Lemmon, *Ashley's War*, 134–40.

73. Lutz, *Homefront*, 59–64.

74. Gail Bederman, *Manliness and Civilization: A Cultural History of Gender and Race in the United States, 1880-1917* (Chicago: University of Chicago Press, 1995); and Mary Louise Pratt, *Imperial Eyes: Travel Writing and Transculturation* (London: Routledge, 1992).

75. Bederman, *Manliness and Civilization*, 5.

76. Bederman, 17.

77. Bederman, 23.

78. Fluri, "States of (in)Security"; Khalili, "Gendered Practices of Counterinsurgency"; and Mesok, "Affective Technologies of War."

79. Derek Gregory, "'The Rush to the Intimate': Counterinsurgency and the Cultural Turn," *Radical Philosophy* 150 (2008): 8–23; and Khalili, "Gendered Practices of Counterinsurgency."

CONCLUSION

1. Alex Horton and Travis M. Andrews, "Deaths of 2 Marines in Kabul Underscore the Evolving Roles of Women in the Military," *Washington Post*, August 28, 2021.

2. The cost of caring for post-9/11 war veterans will reach between $2.2 and $2.5 trillion by 2050. This is the largest single long-term economic cost of the post-9/11 wars, in part the result of the extraordinarily high proportion of post-9/11 veterans who qualify for lifetime disability payments. Most of this sum has not been paid, nor have adequate budgetary commitments been made to ensure that the US government makes good on its promise to these veterans. Linda Bilmes, "The Long-Term Costs of United States Care for Veterans of the Afghanistan and Iraq Wars," Costs of War Project, August 18, 2021, https://watson

.brown.edu/costsofwar/files/cow/imce/papers/2021/Costs%20of%20War_Bilmes_Long -Term%20Costs%20of%20Care%20for%20Vets_Aug%202021.pdf.

3. Stephanie Savell, "United States Counterterrorism Operations 2018–2020," Costs of War Project, February 2021, https://watson.brown.edu/costsofwar/files/cow/imce/papers /2021/US%20Counterterrorism%20Operations%202018-2020%2C%20Costs%20of%20 War.pdf.

4. David Kilcullen, "Countering Global Insurgency," *Small Wars Journal,* November 30, 2004.

5. Lorraine Dowler, "The Hidden War: The 'Risk' to Female Soldiers in the US Military," in *Reconstructing Conflict: Integrating War and Post-War Geographies,* ed. Colin Flint and Scott Kirsch, 295–314 (Burlington, VT: Ashgate, 2011).

6. Gayatri Chakravorty Spivak, "Can the Subaltern Speak?," in *Marxism and the Interpretation of Culture,* ed. Lawrence Grossberg and Cary Nelson, 271–313 (Urbana: University of Illinois Press).

7. Melani McAlister, *Epic Encounters: Culture, Media, and US Interests in the Middle East since 1945* (Oakland: University of California Press, 2005).

8. Gail Bederman, *Manliness and Civilization: A Cultural History of Gender and Race in the United States, 1880–1917* (Chicago: University of Chicago Press, 1995).

9. Joan Wallach Scott, *Gender and the Politics of History* (New York: Columbia University Press, 2018), 27.

10. Cynthia Enloe, *Maneuvers: The International Politics of Militarizing Women's Lives* (Oakland: University of California Press, 2000), 235.

11. Donald C. Arthur, Gale Pollack, Alan Steinman, Nathaniel Frank, Diane H. Mazur, and Aaron Belkin, *DoD's Transgender Ban Has Harmed Military Readiness* (San Francisco: Palm Center, 2020).

12. Jasbir Puar, *Terrorist Assemblages: Homonationalism in Queer Times* (Durham, NC: Duke University Press, 2017), 228.

13. Mia Fischer, *Terrorizing Gender: Transgender Visibility and the Surveillance Practices of the US Security State* (Lincoln: University of Nebraska Press, 2019); and C. Riley Snorton, *Black on Both Sides: A Racial History of Trans Identity* (Minneapolis: University of Minnesota Press, 2017).

14. William Hartung, "Fueling the Warfare State: America's $1.4 Trillion 'National Security' Budget Makes Us Even Less Safe," TomDispatch, July 7, 2022.

15. Neta Crawford, "The US Budgetary Costs of the Post-9/11 Wars," Costs of War Project, September 1, 2021, https://watson.brown.edu/costsofwar/files/cow/imce/papers /2021/Costs%20of%20War_U.S.%20Budgetary%20Costs%20of%20Post-9%2011%20 Wars_9.1.21.pdf.

16. Catherine Lutz and Neta Crawford, "Fighting a Virus with the Wrong Tools," The Hill, March 28, 2020.

17. In one among many examples, in a virtual summit of world leaders on March 26, 2020 the director of the World Health Organization claimed that "we are at war" with the coronavirus. In another example, Joe Biden used this phrase in the March 15, 2020 Democratic primary debate.

18. Uri Friedman, "We Can't Rely on Just the Military," *The Atlantic,* April 8, 2020; and Kathleen Hicks and Joseph Federici, "Regaining Lost Ground: Defense Support in the Coronavirus Pandemic," Center for Strategic and International Studies, March 20, 2020, https://www.csis.org/analysis/regaining-lost-ground-defense-support-coronavirus -pandemic.

19. On the important link between these medical humanitarian missions and basing agreements, see Joe Bryan, "War without End? Military Humanitarianism and the Lim-

its of Biopolitical Approaches to Security in Central America and the Caribbean," *Political Geography* 47 (2015): 33–42.

20. Heidi Garrett-Peltier, "Job Opportunity Cost of War," Costs of War Project, May 24, 2017, https://watson.brown.edu/costsofwar/files/cow/imce/papers/2017/Job%20Opportunity%20Cost%20of%20War%20-%20HGP%20-%20FINAL.pdf.

21. Bevan Hurley, "Retired Army General Stanley McChrystal Admits War on Terror Was Not Worth It," *The Independent,* August 8, 2021.

22. Spencer Ackerman, qtd. in Dan Spinelli, "We Have the War on Terror to Thank for Donald Trump," *Mother Jones,* August 10, 2021.

23. Eric Schmitt, "Military Analysis Raises Questions about Deadly Drone Strike in Kabul," *New York Times,* September 5, 2021.

24. Spencer Ackerman, "Victims of a Drone Strike, Momentarily Visible," Forever Wars Substack, August 30, 2021, https://foreverwars.substack.com/p/victims-of-a-drone-strike-momentarily.

25. In a ReThink Media–curated media roundup of post-9/11 war coverage, Emily Blout reflects on the nickname of the "ninja bomb," a new weapon that deploys six blades instead of explosives in an effort to reduce civilian deaths, as serving to "sanitize and glorify the deadly weapon." Emily Blout, "ReThink Roundup," August 28–31, 2021, https://mailchi.mp/rethinkmedia.org/drone-roundup-how-to-survive-americas-kill-list-us-admits-to-killing-another-78-civilians-in-raqqa-2501769?e=51152cb385.

26. Helene Cooper, "Trump Orders All American Troops Out of Somalia," *New York Times,* December 4, 2020.

27. Meghann Myers, "US Troops Now 'Commuting to Work' to Help Somalia Fight al-Shabab," *Military Times,* April 21, 2021.

28. Among many press and official US government descriptions of the Kabul airlift, Biden called the evacuation an "extraordinary success." Joe Biden, "Remarks by President Biden on the Drawdown of US Forces in Afghanistan," The White House, July 8, 2021.

29. Robert Grenier, "How to Defeat America's Homegrown Insurgency," *New York Times,* January 27, 2021.

30. US Agency for International Development, *Policy for Countering Violent Extremism through Development Assistance* (Washington, DC: USAID, 2020).

31. Following US defeat in Vietnam in the 1970s, counterinsurgency was rearticulated as "low-intensity conflict" in the 1980s and in relation to the Cold War in Central America. In the 1980s and 1990s, the US military became preoccupied with "military operations in the urban terrain," which saw the future of warfare as located in the "broken cities of the world." Ralph Peters, "Our Soldiers, Their Cities," *Parameters* 26 (1996): 43–50, qtd. in Mike Davis, *Planet of Slums* (London: Verso, 2006). See also Jordan T. Camp and Jennifer Greenburg, "Counterinsurgency Reexamined: Racism, Capitalism, and US Military Doctrine," *Antipode* 52, no. 2 (2020), 442; Mike Davis, "The Pentagon as Global Slumlord," TomDispatch, April 19, 2004; Stephen Graham, *Cities under Siege: The New Military Urbanism* (New York: Verso, 2010); Laleh Khalili, "Pacifying Urban Insurrections," *Historical Materialism* 25, no. 2 (2017): 115–30; and William Leogrande, "Central America: Counterinsurgency Revisited," *NACLA Report on the Americas* 21, no. 1 (1987): 3–5.

32. Robert Killebrew, qtd. in Khalili, "Pacifying Urban Insurrections," 116.

33. David Kilcullen, *Out of the Mountains: The Coming Age of the Urban Guerrilla* (London: C. Hurst, 2013); and Richard Norton, cited in Khalili, "Pacifying Urban Insurrections."

34. Jessica Katzenstein, "The Wars Are Here: How the United States' Post-9/11 Wars Helped Militarize US Police," Costs of War Project, September 16, 2020, https://watson

.brown.edu/costsofwar/files/cow/imce/papers/2020/Police%20Militarization
_Costs%20of%20War_Sept%2016%202020.pdf.

35. Jordan T. Camp and Christina Heatherton, "Total Policing and the Global Surveillance Empire Today: An Interview with Arun Kundnani," and "Broken Windows, Surveillance, and the New Urban Counterinsurgency: An Interview with Hamid Khan," in *Policing the Planet: Why the Policing Crisis Led to Black Lives Matter,* ed. Jordan T. Camp and Christina Heatherton, 83–93, 151–155 (New York: Verso, 2016).

36. Roxanne Dunbar-Ortiz, *An Indigenous Peoples' History of the United States* (Boston: Beacon, 2014).

37. Tom Dreisbach and Meg Anderson, "Nearly One in Five Defendants in Capitol Riot Cases Served in the Military," National Public Radio, January 21, 2021.

38. Importantly, Fanon rejects a liberal European humanism, whose racism undermined its principles. At the same time, he retains the goal of a "more human and fundamentally different future from the dehumanized and violent experience of colonial rule." Such an antiracist, anticolonial humanism provides a helpful starting point for considering a future beyond perpetual war. Nigel Gibson, *Fanon: The Postcolonial Imagination* (Cambridge, UK: Polity, 2003), 181.

Selected Bibliography

PRIMARY SOURCES

Government Documents, Speeches, and White Papers

Biden, Joe. "Remarks by President Biden on the Drawdown of US Forces in Afghanistan." The White House, July 8, 2021.

Brigety, Reuben. *Humanity as a Weapon of War: Sustainable Security and the Role of the US Military.* Washington, DC: Center for American Progress, 2008.

Clinton, Hillary. "Remarks on Development in the 21st Century." Speech, Center for Global Development, Washington, DC, January 6, 2010.

———. "Statement before the Senate Foreign Relations Committee." Washington, DC, January 13, 2009.

Department of Veterans Affairs Office of Inspector General. *Review of Combat Stress in Women Veterans Receiving VA Health Care and Disability Benefits.* Washington, DC: VA Office of Inspector General, 2010.

Dziedzic, Michael, and Michael Seidl, *Provincial Reconstruction Teams and Military Relations with International and Nongovernmental Organizations in Afghanistan.* Washington, DC: United States Institute of Peace, 2005.

Fishstein, Paul, and Andrew Wilder. *Winning Hearts and Minds? Examining the Relationship between Aid and Security in Afghanistan.* Medford, MA: Feinstein International Center, 2012.

Gates, Robert. "Remarks as Delivered by Secretary of Defense Robert M. Gates." Landon Lecture, Kansas State University, Manhattan, Kansas, November 26, 2007.

Hicks, Kathleen, and Joseph Federici, "Regaining Lost Ground: Defense Support in the Coronavirus Pandemic." Center for Strategic and International Studies, March 20, 2020. https://www.csis.org/analysis/regaining-lost-ground-defense-support-corona virus-pandemic.

Kamarck, Kristy. *Women in Combat: Issues for Congress.* Washington, DC: Congressional Research Services, 2016.

Katzman, Kenneth, and Clayton Thomas. *Afghanistan: Post-Taliban Governance, Security, and U.S. Policy.* Washington, DC: Congressional Research Services, 2017.

The Obama White House. *National Security Strategy.* Washington, DC: The White House, 2010.

———. *The United States National Action Plan on Women, Peace, and Security.* Washington, DC: The White House, 2011.

Patten, Eileen, and Kim Parker. *Women in the US Military: Growing Share, Distinctive Profile.* Washington, DC: Pew Research Center, 2011.

Perito, Robert. *Integrated Security Assistance: The 1207 Program.* Washington, DC: US Institute of Peace, 2008.

Serafino, Nina. *Department of Defense "Section 1207" Security and Stabilization Assistance: Background and Congressional Concerns, FY2006–2010.* Washington, DC: Congressional Research Services, 2011.

———. *Global Security Contingency Fund: Summary and Overview.* Washington, DC: Congressional Research Services, 2014.

———. *In Brief: State Department Bureau of Conflict and Stabilization Operations (CSO)*. Washington, DC: Congressional Research Services, 2012.

US Agency for International Development Office of Military Affairs. *The Development Response to Violent Extremism and Insurgency*. Washington, DC: USAID, 2011.

———. *District Stability Framework*. Washington, DC: USAID, 2011.

———. *Policy for Countering Violent Extremism through Development Assistance*. Washington, DC: USAID, 2020.

US Department of State. *Quadrennial Diplomacy and Development Review: Enduring Leadership in a Dynamic World*. Washington, DC: US Department of State and USAID, 2015.

US Government Accountability Office. *Female Active-Duty Personnel: Guidance and Plans Needed for Recruitment and Retention Efforts*. Washington, DC: Government Accountability Office, 2020.

Military Doctrine, Publications, and Other Military Primary Sources

Binsch, Jessica. "Female Troops Take on New Role in Afghanistan." *Marine Corps Times*, April 8, 2010.

Brewington, Brooks R. "Combined Action Platoons: A Strategy for Peace Enforcement." Air University: Subject Area Strategic Issues, 1996.

Brown, Mark. "Village Stability Operations: An Historical Perspective from Vietnam to Afghanistan." *Small Wars Journal*, March 28, 2013.

Caldwell, William. "Foreword." In *Stability Operations*. Washington, DC: Headquarters, Department of the Army, 2008.

Center for Army Lessons Learned. *Commander's Guide to Female Engagement Teams: Observations, Insights, Lessons*. Washington, DC: US Army, 2011.

Copenhaver, Mike. "The Integration of Minorities into Special Operations: How Cultural Diversity Enhances Operations." Unpublished manuscript, US Army War College, 2014.

Elkus, Adam. "FM 3–24, Social Science, and Security." *Small Wars Journal*, May 20, 2014.

Hakeem, Shaiyla. "Fearless Females Unite, Empower One Another." Defense Visual Information Distribution Service, August 23, 2019. https://www.dvidshub.net/news/337023/fearless-females-unite-empower-one-another.

Holliday, Janet. "Female Engagement Teams: The Need to Standardize Training and Employment." *Military Review*, March–April 2012.

Hughes, Whitney. "Female Engagement Team Finds Strength behind Burkas." US Army, November 8, 2010. https://www.army.mil/article/47832/female_engagement_team_finds_strength_behind_burkas.

Katt, Megan. "Blurred Lines: Cultural Support Teams in Afghanistan." *Joint Forces Quarterly* 75 (2014): 106–13.

Kelly, Francis. *Vietnam Studies: US Army Special Forces 1961–1971*. Washington, DC: US Army, 1973.

Kramer, Nick. "Lessons from American Counterinsurgency Operations during the Occupation of Haiti." *Small Wars Journal*, June 16, 2021.

Lessmeister, Kimberly. "Stryker Brigade Females Strive for Spot on Female Engagement Team." Defense Video Imagery Distribution System, March 12, 2012. https://www.dvidshub.net/news/printable/86128.

Marine Corps School. *Small Wars Operations*. Quantico, VA: Marine Barracks, 1935.

McCullough, Christopher. "Female Engagement Teams: Who They Are and Why They Do It." US Army, February 22, 2013. www.army.mil/article/88366.

Myers, Meghann. "US Troops Now 'Commuting to Work' to Help Somalia Fight al-Shabab." *Military Times*, April 21, 2021.

Petraeus, David. "Commander of the International Security Assistance Force's Counter-insurgency Guidance." Official memorandum, Kabul: Headquarters of the International Security Assistance Force, 2010. https://smallwarsjournal.com/documents /comisafcoinguidance.pdf.

——. "Learning Counterinsurgency: Lessons from Soldiering in Iraq." *Military Review* 86, no. 1 (2006): 2–12.

Peters, Ralph. "Our Soldiers, Their Cities." *Parameters* 26 (1996): 43–50.

Pirek, Lindsey. "The 26th MEU Female Engagement Team Trains with Kuwaiti Police." US Marine Corps, March 4, 2016. https://www.marines.mil/News/News-Display /Article/686139/26th-meu-female-engagement-team-trains-with-kuwaiti-police/.

Pisachubbe, Jeanita. "Female Engagement Team Brings Aid to School, Orphanage." US Army, February 14, 2011. https://www.army.mil/article/51804.

Pottinger, Matt, Hali Jilani, and Claire Russo. "Trying to Win Afghanistan without Afghan Women." *Small Wars Journal*, February 18, 2010.

Russo, Claire, and Shannon Spann. *Female Networking Operations: A Tactical Tool for Strategic Advantage*. McLean, VA: Orbis Operations, 2011.

Sewall, Sarah. "Introduction to the University of Chicago Press Edition." In US Army and Marine Corps, *The US Army and Marine Corps Counterinsurgency Field Manual*, xxi–xliii. Chicago: University of Chicago Press, 2007.

Shane, Leo. "Signs of White Supremacy, Extremism Up Again in Poll of Active-Duty Troops." *Military Times*, February 6, 2020.

Stadtlander, Charles. "Soldiers Prep to Pave New Path in War." US Army, April 21, 2011. http://www.army.mil/article/55289.

Staneszewki, Diana. "Female Engagement Teams," in *Civil Affairs Afghanistan Newsletter*. Washington, DC: US Army Center for Lessons Learned, n.d.

US Army. *Counterguerrilla Operations*. Field Manual 90-8. Washington, DC: Department of the Army, 1986.

——. *US Army Stability Operations Field Manual*. Ann Arbor: University of Michigan, 2009.

——. *The US Army Stability Operations Field Manual: Field Manual 3-07*. Washington, DC: US Army, 2008.

US Army and US Marine Corps. *Counterinsurgency Field Manual*. Chicago: University of Chicago Press, 2007.

——. *Insurgencies and Countering Insurgencies*. Field Manual 3-24. Washington, DC: Department of the Army, 2014.

US Department of Defense. *Instruction: Stability Operations; Number 3000.05*. Washington, DC: US Department of Defense, 2005.

——. *2020 Demographics: Profile of the Military Community*. US Department of Defense: Office of the Deputy Assistant Secretary of Defense for Military Community and Family Policy, 2020.

US Marine Corps. *Counterinsurgency Operations*. Washington, DC: US Marine Corps, 1980.

——. "Marine Force Integration Plan—Summary." 2015. https://www.documentcloud .org/documents/2394531-marine-corps-force-integration-plan-summary.html.

——. *Marine Corps Planning Process*. Washington, DC: Department of the Navy Headquarters, 2001.

——. *Small Wars Manual*. Washington, DC: US Marine Corps, 1940.

US Military Joint Chiefs of Staff. *Counterinsurgency*. JP 3-24. Washington, DC: Joint Staff Pentagon, 2021.

——. *Joint Doctrine for Military Operations Other Than War*. JP 3-7. Washington, DC: Joint Staff Pentagon, 1995.

US Special Operations Command. *Special Operations Forces Cultural Engagement Future Concept*. MacDill Air Force Base, FL: Headquarters, US Special Operations Command, 2011.

Utley, Harold. "An Introduction to the Tactics and Techniques of Small Wars." *Marine Corps Gazette* 15, no. 5 (1931): 50–53.

———. "The Tactics and Techniques of Small Wars: Part II—Intelligence." *Marine Corps Gazette* 18, no. 2 (1933): 44–48.

Vietnam Collection. US Marine Corps Archives, Quantico, VA.

Votel, Tom. Proceedings of "A Look into SOCOM." The Aspen Institute, Aspen, CO, July 24, 2015.

Watson, Julia. "Female Engagement Teams: The Case for More Female Civil Affairs Marines." *Marine Corps Gazette*, 2011.

Webster, Kelly. "Lessons from a Military Humanitarian in Port-Au-Prince." *Small Wars Journal*, March 28, 2010.

West, Bing. "The 2014 Counterinsurgency Field Manual Requires Pre-Publication Review." *Small Wars Journal*, June 14, 2014.

Williamson, Curtis L., III. "The US Marine Corps Combined Action Program (CAP): A Proposed Alternative Strategy for the Vietnam War." Air University: Subject Area History, 2002.

SECONDARY SOURCES

Abu-Lughod, Lila. *Do Muslim Women Need Saving?* Cambridge, MA: Harvard University Press, 2013.

Abu-Lughod, Lila, and Catherine Lutz. "Introduction: Emotion, Discourse, and the Politics of Everyday Life." In *Language and the Politics of Emotion*, ed. Catherine Lutz and Lila Abu-Lughod, 1–23. Cambridge: Cambridge University Press, 1990.

Alarcón, Norma. "The Theoretical Subject(s) of *This Bridge Called My Back* and Anglo-American Feminism." In *Criticism in the Borderlands: Studies in Chicano Literature, Culture, and Ideology*, ed. Héctor Calderon and José David Saldívar, 28–40. Durham, NC: Duke University Press, 1991.

Alleg, Henri. *The Question*. Lincoln: University of Nebraska Press, 2006.

Alvah, Donna. *Unofficial Ambassadors: American Military Families Overseas and the Cold War*. New York: New York University Press, 2007.

Amin, Samir. *Obsolescent Capitalism: Contemporary Politics and Global Disorder*. New York: Zed Books, 2003.

Anderson, Ben. "Population and Affective Perception: Biopolitics and Anticipatory Action in US Counterinsurgency Doctrine." *Antipode* 43, no. 2 (2010): 205–36.

Anzaldúa, Gloria. *Borderlands/La Frontera: The New Mestiza*. San Francisco: Aunte Lute Books, 1987.

Arendt, Hannah. *The Modern Challenge to Tradition: Fragmente eines Buchs*, ed. Barbara Hahn and James McFarland, with Ingo Kieslich and Ingebord Nordmann. Göttingen: Wallsteid Verlag, 2018.

———. *The Origins of Totalitarianism*. New York: Harcourt, 1968.

———. *Thinking without a Banister: Essays in Understanding, 1953–1975*, ed. Jerome Kohn. New York: Schocken Books, 2018.

Arrighi, Giovanni. *Adam Smith in Beijing: Lineages of the Twenty-First Century*. New York: Verso, 2007.

———. *The Geometry of Imperialism*. New York: Verso, 1983.

———. "Hegemony Unravelling—I." *New Left Review* 32 (2005): 23–80

———. "Hegemony Unravelling—II." *New Left Review* 33 (2005): 83–116.

Arrighi, Giovanni, Terence K. Hopkins, and Immanuel Wallerstein. *Anti-Systemic Movements*. New York: Verso, 1989.

Arrighi, Giovanni, and Beverly J. Silver. "Capitalism and World (Dis)order." *Review of International Studies* 27 (2001): 257–79.

——. *Chaos and Governance in the Modern World System*. Minneapolis: University of Minnesota Press, 1999.

Arthur, Donald C., Gale Pollack, Alan Steinman, Nathaniel Frank, Diane H. Mazur, and Aaron Belkin. *DoD's Transgender Ban Has Harmed Military Readiness*. San Francisco: Palm Center, 2020.

Barnett, Thomas. *The Pentagon's New Map: War and Peace in the Twenty-First Century*. New York: Penguin, 2004.

Beckett, Greg. *There Is No More Haiti: Between Life and Death in Port-au-Prince*. Oakland: University of California Press, 2019.

Bederman, Gail. *Manliness and Civilization: A Cultural History of Gender and Race in the United States, 1880–1917*. Chicago: University of Chicago Press, 1995.

Belcher, Oliver. "Anatomy of a Village Razing: Counterinsurgency, Violence, and Securing the Intimate in Afghanistan." *Political Geography* 62 (2018): 94–105.

——. "Staging the Orient." *Annals of the Association of American Geographers* 104, no. 5 (2014): 1012–29.

Belew, Kathleen. *Bring the War Home: The White Power Movement and Paramilitary America*. Cambridge, MA: Harvard University Press, 2018.

Belkin, Aaron. *Bring Me Men: Military Masculinity and the Benign Facade of American Empire, 1898–2001*. New York: Columbia University Press, 2012.

Benjamin, Walter. *The Arcades Project*. Cambridge, MA: Harvard University Press, 1999.

Bhungalia, Lisa. "Managing Violence: Aid, Counterinsurgency, and the Humanitarian Present in Palestine." *Environment and Planning A* 47 (2015): 2308–23.

Bilmes, Linda. "The Credit Card Wars: Post-9/11 War Funding Policy in Historical Perspective." Costs of War Project, November 8, 2017. https://watson.brown.edu/cost sofwar/files/cow/imce/papers/2017/Linda%20J%20Bilmes%20_Credit%20Card%20 Wars%20FINAL.pdf.

——. "The Long-Term Costs of United States Care for Veterans of the Afghanistan and Iraq Wars." Costs of War Project, August 18, 2021. https://watson.brown.edu/costsofwar /files/cow/imce/papers/2021/Costs%20of%20War_Bilmes_Long-Term%20Costs %20of%20Care%20for%20Vets_Aug%202021.pdf.

Bonfiglioli, Chiara, and Kristen Ghodsee. "Vanishing Act: Global Socialist Feminism as the 'Missing Other' of Transnational Feminism." *Feminist Review* 126, no. 1 (2020): 168–72.

Bonilla-Silva, Eduardo. *Racism without Racists: Color-Blind Racism and the Persistence of Racial Inequality in America*. New York: Rowman and Littlefield, 2018.

Bornstein, Erica, and Peter Redfield, eds. *Forces of Compassion: Humanitarianism between Ethics and Politics*. Santa Fe, NM: School for Advanced Research Press, 2011.

Broadwell, Paula. "CST: Afghanistan." *Foreign Policy*, February 8, 2011.

Brewer, Anthony. *Marxist Theories of Imperialism: A Critical Survey*. New York: Routledge, 1990.

Bryan, Joe. "War without End? Military Humanitarianism and the Limits of Biopolitical Approaches to Security in Central America and the Caribbean." *Political Geography* 47 (2015): 33–42.

Bryan, Joe, and Denis Wood. *Weaponizing Maps: Indigenous Peoples and Counterinsurgency in the Americas*. New York: Guilford, 2015.

Buck-Morss, Susan. *The Dialectics of Seeing: Walter Benjamin and the Arcades Project*. Cambridge, MA: MIT Press, 1989.

Butler, Judith. *Frames of War: When Is Life Grievable?* New York: Verso, 2009.

———. *Gender Trouble: Feminism and the Subversion of Identity.* New York: Routledge, 1990.

Butler, Smedley. *War Is a Racket.* New York: Round Table, 1935.

Camp, Jordan T. "Gramsci and Geography." In *Oxford Bibliographies in Geography,* ed. Barney Warf. New York: Oxford University Press, 2022.

———. *Incarcerating the Crisis: Freedom Struggles and the Rise of the Neoliberal State.* Oakland: University of California Press, 2016.

Camp, Jordan T., and Jennifer Greenburg, "Counterinsurgency Reexamined: Racism, Capitalism, and US Military Doctrine." *Antipode* 52, no. 2 (2020): 430–51.

Camp, Jordan T., and Christina Heatherton, eds. *Policing the Planet: Why the Policing Crisis Led to Black Lives Matter.* New York: Verso, 2016.

Carruthers, Susan. *Winning Hearts and Minds.* New York: Leicester University Press, 1995.

Chandrasekaran, Rajiv. *Imperial Life in the Emerald City: Inside Iraq's Green Zone.* New York: Knopf, 2006.

Cherki, Alice. *Frantz Fanon: A Portrait.* Ithaca, NY: Cornell University Press, 2006.

Clitandre, Nadège. "Haitian Exceptionalism in the Caribbean and the Project of Rebuilding Haiti." *Journal of Haitian Studies* 17, no. 2 (2011): 146–53.

Collier, Paul. *Wars, Guns, and Votes: Democracy in Dangerous Places.* New York: Harper, 2009.

Conrad, Joseph. *Heart of Darkness.* Portland, OR: Tin House Books, 2013.

Cooper, Frederick. "Modernizing Bureaucrats, Backward Africans, and the Development Concept." In *International Development and the Social Sciences: Essays on the History and Politics of Knowledge,* ed. Frederick Cooper and Randall Packard, 64–92. Oakland: University of California Press, 1997.

Corbridge, Stuart, "Review of *Doctrines of Development.*" *Antipode* 29, no. 2 (1997): 218–20.

Cowen, Deborah. *Military Workfare: The Soldier and Social Citizenship in Canada.* Toronto: University of Toronto Press, 2008.

Cowen, Deborah, and Emily Gilbert. "Fear and the Familial in the US War on Terror." In *Fear: Critical Geopolitics and Everyday Life,* ed. Rachel Pain and Susan Smith, 49–58. Burlington, VT: Ashgate, 2008.

Cowen, Michael, and Robert Shenton. *Doctrines of Development.* New York: Routledge, 1996.

Crawford, Neta. "The US Budgetary Costs of the Post-9/11 Wars." Costs of War Project, September 1, 2021. https://watson.brown.edu/costsofwar/files/cow/imce/papers /2021/Costs%20of%20War_U.S.%20Budgetary%20Costs%20of%20Post-9%20 11%20Wars_9.1.21.pdf.

Crawford, Neta, and Catherine Lutz. "Human Cost of the Post-9/11 Wars: Direct War Deaths in Major War Zones, Afghanistan and Pakistan (October 2001–May 2021); Iraq (March 2003–August 2021); Syria (September 2014–August 2021); Yemen (October 2002–August 2021); and Other Post-9/11 War Zones." Costs of War Project, September 1, 2021. https://watson.brown.edu/costsofwar/files/cow/imce/papers /2021/Costs%20of%20War_Direct%20War%20Deaths_9.1.21.pdf.

Danner, Mark. *The Massacre at El Mozote.* New York: Vintage Books, 1993.

Davis, Angela Y. "A Vocabulary for Feminist Praxis: On War and Radical Critique." In *Feminism and War: Confronting US Imperialism,* ed. Robin Riley, Chandra Talpade Mohanty, and Minnie Bruce Pratt, 19–26. New York: Zed Books, 2008.

Davis, Mike. *Planet of Slums.* London: Verso, 2006.

de Haan, Francisca. "Continuing Cold War Paradigms in Western Historiography of Transnational Women's Organizations: The Case of the Women's International Democratic Federation (WIDF)." *Women's History Review* 19, no. 4 (2010): 547–73.

Dillon, Michael. "Governing through Contingency: The Security of Biopolitical Governance." *Political Geography* 26, no. 1 (2007): 41–47.

Dixon, Paul. "'Hearts and Minds'? British Counter-Insurgency from Malaya to Iraq." *Journal of Strategic Studies* 32, no. 3 (2009): 353–82.

Dowd Hall, Jacquelyn. "The Long Civil Rights Movement and the Political Uses of the Past." *Journal of American History* 91, no. 4 (2005): 1233–63.

Dowler, Lorraine. "The Hidden War: The 'Risk' to Female Soldiers in the US Military." In *Reconstructing Conflict: Integrating War and Post-War Geographies*, ed. Colin Flint and Scott Kirsch, 295–314. Burlington, VT: Ashgate, 2011.

Dreyfus, Hubert, and Paul Rabinow. *Michel Foucault: Beyond Structuralism and Hermeneutics*. Brighton, UK: Harvester, 1982.

Dubois, Laurent. *Haiti: The Aftershocks of History*. New York: Metropolitan Books, 2012.

Duffield, Mark. *Development, Security and Unending War: Governing the World of Peoples*. Cambridge, UK: Polity, 2007.

——. *Global Governance and the New Wars: The Merging of Development and Security*. London: Zed Books, 2001.

Dunayevskaya, Raya. *Philosophy and Revolution*. New York: Delacorte, 1973.

Dunbar-Ortiz, Roxanne. *An Indigenous Peoples' History of the United States*. Boston: Beacon, 2014.

Eisenstein, Zillah. *The Radical Future of Liberal Feminism*. New York: Longman, 1981.

——. *Sexual Decoys: Gender, Race and War in Imperial Democracy*. London: Zed Books, 2007.

Engle, Karen. *The Grip of Sexual Violence in Conflict: Feminist Interventions in International Law*. Stanford, CA: Stanford University Press, 2020.

Enloe, Cynthia. *Bananas, Beaches and Bases: Making Feminist Sense of International Politics*. Oakland: University of California Press, 2000.

——. *Does Khaki Become You? The Militarisation of Women's Lives*. Boston: South End, 1983.

——. *Maneuvers: The International Politics of Militarizing Women's Lives*. Oakland: University of California Press, 2000.

Essex, Jamey. *Development, Security, and Aid*. Athens: University of Georgia Press, 2013.

Fanon, Frantz. "Algeria Unveiled." In *A Dying Colonialism*, 35–67. New York: Grove, 1967.

——. *Toward the African Revolution: Political Essays*. New York: Grove, 1964.

——. *The Wretched of the Earth*. New York: Grove, 2004.

Farmer, Paul. *The Uses of Haiti*. Monroe, ME: Common Courage, 1994.

Fassin, Didier. *Humanitarian Reason: A Moral History of the Present*. Oakland: University of California Press, 2011.

Ferguson, James. *The Anti-Politics Machine: "Development," Depoliticization, and Bureaucratic Power in Lesotho*. Minneapolis: University of Minnesota Press, 1990.

Ferrer, Ada. *Freedom's Mirror: Cuba and Haiti in the Age of Revolution*. New York: Cambridge University Press, 2014.

Fischer, Mia. *Terrorizing Gender: Transgender Visibility and the Surveillance Practices of the US Security State*. Lincoln: University of Nebraska Press, 2019.

Fischer, Sibylle. *Modernity Disavowed: Haiti and the Cultures of Slavery in the Age of Revolution*. Durham, NC: Duke University Press, 2004.

Fluri, Jennifer. "Armored Peacocks and Proxy Bodies: Gender Geopolitics in Aid/Development Spaces of Afghanistan." *Gender, Place & Culture* 4 (2011): 519–36.

——. "'Rallying Public Opinion' and Other Misuses of Feminism." In *Feminism and War: Confronting US Imperialism*, ed. Robin Riley, Chandra Talpade Mohanty, and Minnie Bruce Pratt, 143–57. New York: Zed Books, 2008.

——. "States of (in)Security: Corporeal Geographies and the Elsewhere War." *Environment and Planning D: Society and Space* 32 (2014): 795–814.

Forgacs, David. "Hegemony." In *The Antonio Gramsci Reader, Selected Writings, 1916–1935*, ed. David Forgacs, 422–24. New York: New York University Press, 2000.

Foucault, Michel. "Governmentality." In *The Foucault Effect: Studies in Government Rationality*, ed. Graham Burchell, Colin Gordon, and Peter Miller, 87–104. Chicago: University of Chicago Press, 1991.

Friedman, Thomas. *The World Is Flat: A Brief History of the Twenty-First Century*. New York: Picador, 2005.

Gaillard, Roger. *Premier Écrasement du Cacoïsme: 1915*. Port-au-Prince: Le Natal, 1981.

Galula, David. *Counterinsurgency Warfare: Theory and Practice*. New York: Praeger, 1964.

——. *Pacification in Algeria, 1956–1958*. Santa Monica, CA: Rand, 2006.

Garrett-Peltier, Heidi. "Job Opportunity Cost of War." Costs of War Project, May 24, 2017. https://watson.brown.edu/costsofwar/files/cow/imce/papers/2017/Job%20 Opportunity%20Cost%20of%20War%20-%20HGP%20-%20FINAL.pdf.

Geggus, Patrick, and Norman Fiering, eds. *The World of the Haitian Revolution*. Bloomington: Indiana University Press, 2009.

Ghodsee, Kristen. *Second World, Second Sex: Socialist Women's Activism and Global Solidarity during the Cold War*. Durham, NC: Duke University Press, 2019.

Gibson, Nigel. *Fanon: The Postcolonial Imagination*. Cambridge, UK: Polity, 2003.

Gilbert, Emily. "The Gift of War: Cash, Counterinsurgency, and 'Collateral Damage.'" *Security Dialogue* 46, no. 5 (2015): 403–21.

——. "Money as a Weapons System." *Critical Military Studies* 1, no. 3 (2015): 202–19.

Gill, Zack Whitman. "Rehearsing the War Away: Perpetual Warrior Training in Contemporary US Army Policy." *TDR: The Drama Review* 53, no. 3 (2009): 139–55.

Glantz, Aaron. *The War Comes Home: Washington's Battle against America's Veterans*. Oakland: University of California Press, 2009.

Glassman, Jim. "Hegemony." In *International Encyclopedia of Human Geography*, ed. Rob Kitchin and Nigel Thrift, 80–90. Amsterdam: Elsevier, 2009.

Go, Julian, and Anne L. Foster, eds. *The American Colonial State in the Philippines: Global Perspectives*. Durham, NC: Duke University Press, 2003.

González, Roberto. *American Counterinsurgency: Human Science and the Human Terrain*. Chicago: Prickly Paradigm, 2009.

Gowan, Peter. "Triumphing toward International Disaster: The Impasse in American Grand Strategy." *Critical Asian Studies* 36, no. 1 (2004): 3–36.

Graham, Stephen. *Cities under Siege: The New Military Urbanism*. New York: Verso, 2010.

——. "War and the City." *New Left Review* 44 (2007): 121–32.

Gramsci, Antonio. *Selections from the Prison Notebooks*, ed. Quintin Hoare and Geoffrey Nowell Smith. New York: International Publishers, 1971.

Green, Daniel. "A Soldier Reports: The Education of John Nagl." *Foreign Policy*, October 15, 2014.

Greenburg, Jennifer. "'Going Back to History': Haiti and US Military Humanitarian Knowledge Production." *Critical Military Studies* 4, no. 2 (2018): 121–39.

——. "'The One Who Bears the Scars Remembers': Haiti and the Historical Geography of US Militarized Development." *Journal of Historical Geography* 51 (2016): 52–63.

——. "Selling Stabilization: Anxious Practices of Militarized Development Contracting." *Development and Change* 48, no. 6 (2017): 1262–86.

Gregory, Derek. "The Biopolitics of Baghdad: Counterinsurgency and the Counter-City." *Human Geography* 1, no. 1 (2008): 6–27.

——. *The Colonial Present: Afghanistan. Palestine. Iraq.* Malden, MA: Blackwell, 2004.
——. "'The Rush to the Intimate': Counterinsurgency and the Cultural Turn." *Radical Philosophy* 150 (2008): 8–23.
Gregory, Derek, and Allan Pred, eds. *Violent Geographies: Fear, Terror, and Political Violence.* New York: Routledge, 2007.
Grewal, Inderpal, and Caren Kaplan, eds. *Scattered Hegemonies: Postmodernity and Transnational Feminist Practices.* Minneapolis: University of Minnesota Press, 1994.
Griffin, Susan. *Woman and Nature: The Roaring Inside Her.* New York: Harper and Row, 1978.
Grossman-Vermas, Robert, and David Becker. "Metrics for the Haiti Stabilization Initiative." *PRISM* 2, no. 2 (2011): 145–58.
Guha, Ranajit. "The Prose of Counter-Insurgency." In *Selected Subaltern Studies,* ed. Ranajit Guha and Gayatri Chakravorty Spivak, 45–86. New York: Oxford University Press, 1988.
Gwynn, Sir Charles W. *Imperial Policing.* London: Macmillan, 1939.
Hall, Stuart. "Gramsci's Relevance for the Study of Race and Ethnicity." *Journal of Communication Inquiry* 10, no. 5 (1986): 5–27.
——. *The Hard Road to Renewal: Thatcherism and the Crisis of the Left.* New York: Verso, 1988.
——. "On Postmodernism and Articulation: An Interview with Stuart Hall." In *Stuart Hall: Critical Dialogues in Cultural Studies,* ed. David Morley and Kuan-Hsing Chen, 131–50. New York: Routledge, 1996.
——. "The Problem of Ideology—Marxism without Guarantees." In *Stuart Hall: Critical Dialogues in Cultural Studies,* ed. Kuan-Hsing Chen and David Morley, 25–46. London: Routledge, 1996.
——. "Race, Articulation and Societies Structured in Dominance." In *Sociological Theories: Race and Colonialism* (Paris: UNESCO, 1980): 305–45.
——. "The West and the Rest: Discourse and Power." In *Formations of Modernity,* ed. Stuart Hall and Bram Gieben, 276–331. Cambridge, UK: Polity, 1992.
Hall, Stuart, Chas Critcher, Tony Jefferson, John Clarke, and Brian Roberts. *Policing the Crisis: Mugging, the State, and Law and Order.* London: Palgrave, 1978.
Hardt, Michael, and Antonio Negri. *Empire.* Cambridge, MA: Harvard University Press, 2000.
Hart, Gillian. "Denaturalizing Dispossession: Critical Ethnography in an Age of Resurgent Imperialism." *Antipode* 38, no. 5 (2006): 977–1004.
——. "D/developments after the Meltdown." *Antipode* 41, no. s1 (2009): 117–41.
——. "Development Critiques in the 1990s: *Culs de Sac* and Promising Paths." *Progress in Human Geography* 25, no. 4 (2001): 649–58.
——. *Disabling Globalization: Places of Power in Post-Apartheid South Africa.* Oakland: University of California Press, 2002.
——. "Forging Connections: Giovanni Arrighi's Conceptions of the World." Paper presented at Dynamics of the Global Crisis, Antisystemic Movements and New Models of Hegemony. Museo Nacional Centro de Arte Reina Sofía, Madrid, May 25–29, 2009.
——. "Geography and Development: Critical Ethnographies." *Progress in Human Geography* 28, no. 1 (2004): 91–100.
——. "Why Did It Take So Long? Trump-Bannonism in a Global Conjunctural Frame." *Geografiska Annaler: Series B, Human Geography* 103, no. 3 (2020): 239–66.
Harvey, David. *The New Imperialism.* New York: Oxford University Press, 2003.
Heggoy, Alf Andrew. *Insurgency and Counterinsurgency in Algeria.* Bloomington: Indiana University Press, 1972.

Herdt, Gilbert, ed. *Third Sex, Third Gender—Beyond Sexual Dimorphism in Culture and History*. New York: Zone Books, 1993.

Higate, Paul. *Military Masculinities: Identity and the State*. Westport, CT: Praeger, 2003.

Hirschkind, Charles, and Saba Mahmood. "Feminism, the Taliban, and Politics of Counter-Insurgency." *Anthropological Quarterly* 75, no. 2 (2002): 339–54.

Hochschild, Arlie Russell. *The Managed Heart: The Commercialization of Human Feeling*. Oakland: University of California Press, 1983.

Hoffman, Jon T. *Chesty: The Story of Lieutenant General Lewis B. Puller, USMC*. New York: Random House, 2001.

Holmstedt, Kristen. *Band of Sisters: American Women at War in Iraq*. Mechanicsburg, PA: Stackpole Books, 2007.

Hoodfar, Homa. "The Veil in Their Minds and on Our Heads: Veiling Practices and Muslim Women." In *Women, Gender, Religion: A Reader*, ed. Elizabeth Castelli, 420–46. New York: Palgrave Macmillan.

Horne, Alistair. *A Savage War of Peace: Algeria 1954–1962*. New York: Penguin, 2006.

Hosmer, Stephen T., and Sibylle O. Crane. *Counterinsurgency: A Symposium, April 16–20, 1962*. Santa Monica, CA: Rand, 1963.

Human Rights Watch. "Booted: Lack of Recourse for Wrongfully Discharged US Military Rape Survivors." May 19, 2016, https://www.hrw.org/report/2016/05/19/booted/lack-recourse-wrongfully-discharged-us-military-rape-survivors.

Huntington, Samuel. "Transnational Organizations in World Politics." *World Politics* 25, no. 3 (1973): 333–68.

Ikenberry, G. John. "Soft Power: The Means to Success in World Politics." *Foreign Affairs*, January 28, 2009.

Ives, Peter. *Language and Hegemony in Gramsci*. London: Pluto, 2004.

J.B.P.R. "The Emergency in Malaya: Some Reflections on the First Six Years." *The World Today* 10, no. 11 (1954): 477–87.

Jaggar, Alison. "Love and Knowledge: Emotion in Feminist Epistemology." *Inquiry* 32, no. 2 (1989): 151–76.

James, C.L.R. *The Black Jacobins: Toussaint Louverture and the San Domingo Revolution*. New York: Vintage Books, 1989.

James, Erica Caple. *Democratic Insecurities: Violence, Trauma, and Intervention in Haiti*. Oakland: University of California Press, 2010.

Johnston, Scott. "Courting Public Favour: The Boy Scout Movement and the Accident of Internationalism, 1907–29." *Historical Research* 88, no. 241 (2015): 508–29.

Kalyvas, Stathis. *The Logic of Violence in Civil War*. Cambridge: Cambridge University Press, 2006.

Kaplan, Amy. *The Anarchy of Empire in the Making of US Culture*. Cambridge, MA: Harvard University Press, 2002.

Katzenstein, Jessica. "The Wars Are Here: How the United States' Post-9/11 Wars Helped Militarize US Police." Costs of War Project, September 16, 2020. https://watson.brown.edu/costsofwar/files/cow/imce/papers/2020/Police%20Militarization_Costs%20of%20War_Sept%2016%202020.pdf.

Kaussen, Valerie. "Do It Yourself: International Aid and the Neoliberal Ethos in the Tent Camps of Port-Au-Prince." *NACLA Report on the Americas* 44, no. 6 (2011): 5–7.

Keane, David. *Inside the Taliban*. Documentary, National Geographic, 2007.

Kelly, John D. "Seeing Red: Mao Fetishism, Pax Americana, and the Moral Economy of War." In *Anthropology and Global Counterinsurgency*, ed. John D. Kelly, Beatrice Jauregui, Sean T. Mitchell, and Jeremy Walton, 67–84. Chicago: University of Chicago Press, 2010.

Khalili, Laleh. "Gendered Practices of Counterinsurgency." *Review of International Studies* 37, no. 4 (2011): 1471–91.

——. "The New (and Old) Classics of Counterinsurgency." *Middle East Report* 255 (2010): 14–23.

——. "Pacifying Urban Insurrections." *Historical Materialism* 25, no. 2 (2017): 115–30.

——. "Scholar, Pope, Soldier, Spy." *Humanity: An International Journal of Human Rights, Humanitarianism, and Development* 5, no. 3 (2014): 417–34.

——. *Time in the Shadows: Confinement in Counterinsurgencies.* Stanford, CA: Stanford University Press, 2013.

Kilcullen, David. *The Accidental Guerrilla: Fighting Small Wars in the Midst of a Big One.* Oxford: Oxford University Press, 2009.

——. "Countering Global Insurgency." *Small Wars Journal,* November 30, 2004.

——. *Out of the Mountains: The Coming Age of the Urban Guerrilla.* London: C. Hurst, 2013.

——. "Twenty-Eight Articles: Fundamentals of Company-Level Counterinsurgency." *Marine Corps Gazette* 90, no. 7 (2006): 29–35.

——. "Two Schools of Classical Counterinsurgency." *Small Wars Journal* (blog), January 27, 2007. https://smallwarsjournal.com/blog/two-schools-of-classical-counter insurgency.

Kipling, Rudyard. "The White Man's Burden: The United States and the Philippine Islands." *McClures Magazine,* 1899.

Kivland, Chelsey L. *Street Sovereigns: Young Men and the Makeshift State in Urban Haiti.* Ithaca, NY: Cornell University Press, 2020.

Kosek, Jake. *Understories: The Political Life of Forests in Northern New Mexico.* Durham, NC: Duke University Press, 2006.

Kramer, Paul. *Blood of Government: Race, Empire, the United States and the Philippines.* Chapel Hill: University of North Carolina Press, 2006.

Kumar, Deepa. *Islamophobia and the Politics of Empire.* Chicago: Haymarket Books, 2012.

Kundnani, Arun. *The Muslims are Coming! Islamophobia, Extremism, and the Domestic War on Terror.* New York: Verso, 2015.

Lakoff, George. *Moral Politics: How Liberals and Conservatives Think.* Chicago: University of Chicago Press, 2002.

Langley, Lester. *The Banana Wars: United States Intervention in the Caribbean, 1898–1934.* Lanham, MD: Rowman and Littlefield, 2002.

Lanzona, Vina. *Amazons of the Huk Rebellion: Gender, Sex, and Revolution in the Philippines.* Madison: University of Wisconsin Press, 2009.

Latham, Michael E. *Modernization as Ideology: American Social Science and "Nation Building" in the Kennedy Era.* Chapel Hill: University of North Carolina Press, 2000.

Lawrence, T. E. *Seven Pillars of Wisdom.* Garden City, NY: Doubleday, 1935.

——. *Twenty-Seven Articles.* Seattle: Praetorian, 2011.

Lazreg, Marnia. *Torture and the Twilight of Empire: From Algiers to Baghdad.* Princeton, NJ: Princeton University Press, 2008.

Lemmon, Gayle Tzemach. *Ashley's War: The Untold Story of a Team of Women Soldiers on the Special Ops Battlefield.* New York: Harper, 2015.

——. "Meet the Women Fighting on the Front Lines of an American War." TED Talk, May 28, 2015. https://www.ted.com/talks/gayle_tzemach_lemmon_meet_the _women_fighting_on_the_front_lines_of_an_american_war.

Leogrande, William. "Central America: Counterinsurgency Revisited." *NACLA Report on the Americas* 21, no. 1 (1987): 3–5.

Li, Tania. *The Will to Improve: Governmentality, Development, and the Practice of Politics*. Durham, NC: Duke University Press, 2007.

Lipsitz, George. *The Possessive Investment in Whiteness: How White People Profit from Identity Politics*. Philadelphia: Temple University Press, 2018.

Lopez, Patricia J. "Clumsy Beginnings: From 'Modernizing Mission' to Humanitarianism in the US Occupation of Haiti (1915–34)." *Environment and Planning A* 47, no. 11 (2015): 2240–56.

Lugard, Frederick. *The Dual Mandate in British Tropical Africa*. London: W. Blackwood and Sons, 1922.

Lutz, Catherine. "Emotion, Thought, and Estrangement: Emotion as a Cultural Category." *Cultural Anthropology* 1, no. 3 (1986): 287–309.

——. "Engendered Emotion: Gender, Power, and the Rhetoric of Emotional Control in American Discourse." In *Language and the Politics of Emotion*, ed. Catherine Lutz and Lila Abu-Lughod, 69–91. Cambridge: Cambridge University Press, 1990.

——. "Feminist Theories and the Science of Emotion." In *Science and Emotions after 1945: A Transatlantic Perspective*, ed. Frank Biess and Daniel M. Gross, 342–64. Chicago: University of Chicago Press, 2014.

——. *Homefront: A Military City and the American Twentieth Century*. Boston: Beacon, 2001.

——. "The Military Normal." In *The Counter-Counterinsurgency Field Manual: Or, Notes on Demilitarizing American Society*, 23–38. Chicago: Prickly Paradigm, 2009.

——. "US and Coalition Casualties in Iraq and Afghanistan." Costs of War Project, February 21, 2013. https://watson.brown.edu/costsofwar/files/cow/imce/papers/2013/USandCoalition.pdf.

Lutz, Catherine, and Jane Collins. *Reading National Geographic*. Chicago: University of Chicago Press, 1993.

Luxemburg, Rosa. *The Accumulation of Capital*. New York: Monthly Review Press, 1951.

MacLeish, Kenneth T. *Making War at Fort Hood: Life and Uncertainty in a Military Community*. Princeton, NJ: Princeton University Press, 2013.

Magelssen, Scott. "Rehearsing the 'Warrior Ethos': 'Theatre Immersion' and the Simulation of Theatres of War." *TDR: The Drama Review* 53, no. 1 (2009): 47–72.

Mamdani, Mahmood. *Good Muslim, Bad Muslim: America, the Cold War, and the Roots of Terror*. New York: Doubleday, 2004.

——. "Good Muslim, Bad Muslim—An African Perspective." Social Science Research Council, November 1, 2001. https://items.ssrc.org/after-september-11/good-muslim-bad-muslim-an-african-perspective/.

Mandl, Lis. "Rosa Luxemburg and the Women's Question." In Defence of Marxism, January 15, 2009. https://www.marxist.com/rosa-luxemburg-and-the-womens-question.htm.

Marx, Karl. *Capital: A Critique of Political Economy*, Vol. 1. New York: Penguin, 1976.

——. "Economic and Philosophic Manuscripts of 1844." In *The Marx-Engels Reader*, ed. Robert C. Tucker, 66–125. New York: Norton, 1978.

Masco, Joseph. "'Survival Is Your Business': Engineering Ruins and Affect in Nuclear America." *Cultural Anthropology* 23, no. 2 (2008): 361–98.

Massey, Doreen. *Space, Place, and Gender*. Minneapolis: University of Minnesota Press, 1994.

McAlister, Melani. *Epic Encounters: Culture, Media, and US Interests in the Middle East since 1945*. Oakland: University of California Press, 2005.

McBride, Keally, and Annick T. R. Wibben. "The Gendering of Counterinsurgency in Afghanistan." *Humanity: An International Journal of Human Rights, Humanitarianism, and Development* 3, no. 2 (2012): 199–215.

McClintock, Anne. *Imperial Leather: Race, Gender, and Sexuality in the Colonial Contest*. New York: Routledge, 1995.

McLagan, Meg, and Daria Sommers. *Lioness*. Documentary, Room 11 Productions, 2008.

Mesok, Elizabeth. "Affective Technologies of War: US Female Counterinsurgents and the Performance of Gendered Labor." *Radical History Review* 123 (2015): 60–86.

Milne, David. *America's Rasputin: Walt Rostow and the Vietnam War*. New York: Hill and Wang, 2008.

Mitchell, Timothy. *Colonising Egypt*. Oakland: University of California Press, 1991.

——. "McJihad: Islam in the US Global Order." *Social Text* 20, no. 4 (2002): 1–18.

——. *Rule of Experts: Egypt, Techno-Politics, Modernity*. Oakland: University of California Press, 2002.

Mohanty, Chandra Talpade. "Cartographies of Struggle: Third World Women and the Politics of Feminism." In *Feminism without Borders: Decolonizing Theory, Practicing Solidarity*, 43–84. Durham, NC: Duke University Press, 2003.

——. "Under Western Eyes: Feminist Scholarship and Colonial Discourse." In *Feminism without Borders: Decolonizing Theory, Practicing Solidarity*, 17–42. Durham, NC: Duke University Press, 2003.

Mohanty, Chandra Talpade, Minnie Bruce Pratt, and Robin L. Riley. "Introduction: Feminism and US Wars—Mapping the Ground." In *Feminism and War: Confronting US Imperialism*, ed. Robin Riley, Chandra Talpade Mohanty, and Minnie Bruce Pratt, 1–18. New York: Zed Books, 2008.

Moore, Donald. *Suffering for Territory: Race, Place, and Power in Zimbabwe*. Durham, NC: Duke University Press, 2005.

Morton, Adam David. *Unravelling Gramsci: Hegemony and the Passive Revolution in Global Political Economy*. London: Pluto, 2007.

Mortenson, Greg, and David Oliver Relin. *Three Cups of Tea: One Man's Mission to Promote Peace—One School at a Time*. New York: Penguin, 2007.

Munro, John. *The Anticolonial Front: The African American Freedom Struggle and Global Decolonisation, 1945–1960*. Cambridge: Cambridge University Press, 2017.

Nagaraj, Vijay Kumar. "'Beltway Bandits' and 'Poverty Barons': For-Profit International Development Contracting and the Military-Development Assemblage." *Development and Change* 46, no. 4 (2015): 585–617.

Nagl, John A. *Learning to Eat Soup with a Knife: Counterinsurgency Lessons from Malaya and Vietnam*. Chicago: University of Chicago Press, 2005.

Noddings, Nel. *Caring: A Feminine Approach to Ethics & Moral Education*. Oakland: University of California Press, 2013.

Nussbaum, Martha. *Sex and Social Justice*. New York: Oxford University Press, 1999.

Nye, Joseph. "Get Smart." *Foreign Affairs*, July 1, 2009.

Okin, Susan Moller. *Justice, Gender and the Family*. New York: Basic Books, 1989.

Oksala, Johanna. "Affective Labor and Feminist Politics." *Signs: Journal of Women in Culture and Society* 41, no. 2 (2016): 280–303.

Packer, George. *The Assassins' Gate: America in Iraq*. New York: Farrar, Straus and Giroux, 2005.

Plummer, Brenda Gayle. *Haiti and the United States: The Psychological Moment*. Athens: University of Georgia Press, 2003.

Potts, Shaina. "Law as Geopolitics: Judicial Territory, Transnational Economic Governance, and American Power." *Annals of the Association of American Geographers* 110, no. 4 (2019): 1192–207.

Prashad, Vijay. *The Darker Nations: A People's History of the Third World*. New York: New Press, 2007.

Pratt, Mary Louise. *Imperial Eyes: Travel Writing and Transculturation*. London: Routledge, 1992.

Pred, Allan. *The Past Is Not Dead: Facts, Fictions, and Enduring Racial Stereotypes*. Minneapolis: University of Minnesota Press, 2004.

Price, David. "Faking Scholarship." In *The Counter-Counterinsurgency Manual: Or, Notes on Demilitarizing Anthropology*, ed. The Network of Concerned Anthropologists, 59–76. Chicago: Prickly Paradigm, 2009.

Puar, Jasbir. *Terrorist Assemblages: Homonationalism in Queer Times*. Durham, NC: Duke University Press, 2017.

Rafael, Vicente. *Motherless Tongues: The Insurgency of Language amid Wars of Translation*. Durham, NC: Duke University Press, 2016.

Rech, Matthew, Daniel Bos, K. Neil Jenkings, Alison Williams, and Rachel Woodward. "Geography, Military Geography, and Critical Military Studies." *Critical Military Studies* 1, no. (2015): 47–60.

Reid, Julian. "The Biopolitics of the War on Terror: A Critique of the 'Return of Imperialism' Thesis in International Relations." *Third World Quarterly* 26, no. 2 (2005): 237–52.

Renda, Mary. *Taking Haiti: Military Occupation and the Culture of U.S. Imperialism, 1915–1940*. Chapel Hill: University of North Carolina Press, 2001.

Ricks, Thomas. *Fiasco: The American Military Adventure in Iraq*. New York: Penguin, 2006.

Riverbend. *Baghdad Burning: Girl Blog From Iraq*. New York: Feminist Press, 2005.

Roscoe, Will. *Changing Ones: Third and Fourth Genders in Native North America*. New York: St. Martin's, 1998.

Rose, Nikolas. *Powers of Freedom: Reframing Political Thought*. Cambridge: Cambridge University Press, 1999.

Rostow, Walt. *The Stages of Economic Growth: A Non-Communist Manifesto*. Cambridge: Cambridge University Press, 1991.

Ruddick, Sara. *Maternal Thinking: Toward a Politics of Peace*. Boston: Beacon, 1989.

Said, Edward W. *Orientalism*. New York: Vintage Books, 1979.

Savell, Stephanie. "United States Counterterrorism Operations 2018–2020." Costs of War Project, February 2021. https://watson.brown.edu/costsofwar/files/cow/imce/papers/2021/US%20Counterterrorism%20Operations%202018-2020%2C%20Costs%20of%20War.pdf.

Schuller, Mark. *Killing with Kindness: Haiti, International Aid, and NGOs*. New Brunswick, NJ: Rutgers University Press, 2012.

Schultz, Susanne. "Dissolved Boundaries and 'Affective Labor': On the Disappearance of Reproductive Labor and Feminist Critique in Empire." Translated by Frederick Peters. *Capitalism Nature Socialism* 17, no. 1 (2006): 77–82.

Schwedler, Jillian. "The Third Gender: Western Female Researchers in the Middle East." *Political Science and Politics* 39, no. 3 (2006): 425–28.

Scott, Joan Wallach. "Gender: A Useful Category of Historical Analysis." *The American Historical Review* 91, no. 5 (1986): 1053–75.

——. *Gender and the Politics of History*. New York: Columbia University Press, 2018.

Seferdjeli, Ryme. "The French Army and Muslim Women during the Algerian War (1954–62)." *Hawwa: Journal of Women of the Middle East and the Islamic World* 3, no. 1 (2005): 40–79.

Sekyi-Otu, Ato. *Fanon's Dialectic of Experience*. Cambridge, MA: Harvard University Press, 1996.

Short, Anthony. *The Communist Insurrection in Malaya*. London: Frederick Muller, 1975.

Singh, Nikhil Pal. *Race and America's Long War*. Oakland: University of California Press, 2017.

Sistren with Honor Ford-Smith. *Lionhart Gal: Life Stories of Jamaican Women.* Toronto: Sister Vision, 1987.

Smith, Neil. *American Empire: Roosevelt's Geographer and the Prelude to Globalization.* Oakland: University of California Press, 2003.

——. "Scales of Terror and the Resort to Geography: September 11." *Environment and Planning D: Society and Space* 19 (2001): 631–37.

Snorton, C. Riley. *Black on Both Sides: A Racial History of Trans Identity.* Minneapolis: University of Minnesota Press, 2017.

Spivak, Gayatri Chakravorty. "Can the Subaltern Speak?" In *Marxism and the Interpretation of Culture,* ed. Lawrence Grossberg and Cary Nelson, 271–313. Urbana: University of Illinois Press, 1988.

Stocking, George. *Race, Culture, and Evolution: Essays in the History of Anthropology.* Chicago: University of Chicago Press, 1982.

——. *Victorian Anthropology.* New York: Simon and Schuster, 1991.

Stone, Nomi. "Living the Laughscream: Human Technology and Affective Maneuvers in the Iraq War." *Cultural Anthropology* 32, no. 1 (2017): 149–74.

Swords to Ploughshares. *Defining a New Age of Women Veteran Care: Findings From California Community Providers.* San Francisco: Swords to Ploughshares, 2016.

Terry, Jennifer. *Attachments to War: Biomedical Logics and Violence in Twenty-First-Century America.* Durham, NC: Duke University Press, 2017.

——. "Significant Injury: War, Medicine, and Empire in Claudia's Case." *Women's Studies Quarterly* 37, no. 1–2 (2009): 200–25.

——. "'Unnatural Acts' in Nature: The Scientific Fascination with Queer Animals." *GLQ: A Journal of Lesbian and Gay Studies* 6, no. 2 (2000): 151–93.

Toews, Ryan. "Counterinsurgency as Global Social Warfare." In *Destroy, Build, Secure: Readings on Pacification,* ed. Tyler Wall, Parastou Saberi, and Will Jackson, 47–67. Ottawa: Red Quill Books, 2017.

Towle, Evan B., and Lynn Marie Morgan. "Romancing the Transgender Native: Rethinking the Use of the 'Third Gender' Concept." *GLQ: A Journal of Lesbian and Gay Studies* 8, no. 4 (2002): 469–97.

Trouillot, Michel-Rolph. *Global Transformations: Anthropology and the Modern World.* New York: Palgrave Macmillan, 2003.

——. *Silencing the Past: Power and the Production of History.* Boston: Beacon, 1997.

Turse, Nick. *Kill Anything That Moves: The Real American War in Vietnam.* New York: Metropolitan Books, 2013.

——. *Tomorrow's Battlefield: U.S. Proxy Wars and Secret Ops in Africa.* Chicago: Haymarket Books, 2015.

Vine, David. *Base Nation: How US Military Bases Abroad Harm America and the World.* New York: Metropolitan Books, 2015.

——. *The United States of War: A Global History of America's Endless Conflicts, from Columbus to the Islamic State.* Oakland: University of California Press, 2020.

Vine, David, Cala Coffman, Katalina Khoury, Madison Lovasz, Helen Bush, Rachael Leduc, and Jennifer Walkup. "Creating Refugees: Displacement Caused by the United States' Post-9/11 Wars." Costs of War Project, August 19, 2021. https://watson.brown.edu/costsofwar/files/cow/imce/papers/2021/Costs%20of%20War_Vine%20et%20al_Displacement%20Update%20August%202021.pdf.

Wainwright, Joel. *Geopiracy: Oaxaca, Militant Empiricism, and Geographical Thought.* New York: Palgrave Macmillan, 2013.

——. "Was Gramsci a Marxist?" *Rethinking Marxism* 22, no. 4 (2010): 617–24.

Wood, Ellen Meiksins. *Empire of Capital.* New York: Verso, 2003.

Woodward, Rachel. *Military Geographies.* Oxford, UK: Blackwell, 2004.

Wool, Zoe. *After War: The Weight of Life at Walter Reed*. Durham, NC: Duke University Press, 2015.

Yanagisako, Sylvia. "Immaterial and Industrial Labor: On False Binaries in Hardt and Negri's Trilogy." *Focaal—Journal of Global and Historical Anthropology* 64 (2012): 16–23.

Young, Marilyn B. *The Vietnam Wars, 1945–1990*. New York: HarperCollins, 1991.

Index

female engagement teams (FETs) (*continued*)
intelligence collection, 7, 18, 20, 143,
145–49; media representation of, 145, 154,
156, 195–96; multiculturalism of, 16, 185;
purpose and program, 1–3, 19, 24–25, 94,
142–43, 193; recruitment, *175*, 182–83;
repurposed for training foreign militaries,
188–90; sexism and misogyny and, 190–92;
training and documentation for, 121, 139,
143–46, 200. See also *Commander's Guide
to Female Engagement Teams* (2011); cultural support teams (CSTs); Lioness teams
femininity: DSF contractors and, 89, 92, 100;
emotional labor and, 132–34, 136, 143, 146,
149, 150, 162, 215n41; humanitarianism
and, 88–89, 176–77, 214n36; military
masculinity and, 7–8, 63, 99, 134, 172–73,
178, 182–83, 202; new military, 2, 6, 8–10,
195, 199, 201, 202; white, 16, 170, 178, 180,
183, 185, 193–95, 201–2
feminism. See liberal feminism; military
feminism; new imperial feminism
Ferguson, James, 64, 227n16
First World Conference on Women (1975),
212n14
Fluri, Jennifer, 9, 193
food-denial operations, 47, 114, 118, 119
foreign disaster relief, 113
foreign internal defense groups, 164, 172,
235n4
foreign policy, 14, 50–55, 85, 216n53
Foucault, Michel, 231n57
French colonialism, 111, 118; Algeria and, 26,
46–48, 121–28; Haiti and, 112; Indochina
and, 115, 122
Friedman, Thomas, 42–43

Galula, David, 39–40, 43–46, 85, 116;
Pacification in Algeria, 1956-1958, 46–49
Gates, Robert, 51–52, 54
Gee, Nicole, 198
gender construct politics, 202. See also "third
gender" concept
gendered counterinsurgency, 8, 26, 94, 127,
179, 199, 200; color-blindness and, 194, 201,
202; combat invisibility and, 10, 141; definition and usage, 5, 211n2; emotional labor
and, 131–32, 136, 161, 162, 171; humanitarian dimension of, 9, 196; institutionalization of, 144, 164; military masculinity and,
170, 183
gender inclusion, 8, 134, 196, 201, 203–4, 215n41
Glantz, Aaron, 139–40

globalization, 13, 42–43
Global Security Contingency Fund, 55
Gowan, Peter, 216n53
Gramsci, Antonio, 15–16, 19, 218n83, 219n103
"green," soldiers as, 135, 165, 167–68, 171, 193,
197, 201
Green Berets, 3, 164, 168, 176, 177, 181, 184
Gregory, Derek, 20, 31, 41, 93, 94, 113
Grenier, Robert, 207–8
Griest, Kristen, 3
grievances, 73, 75, 81
Griffin, Susan, 133
Gulf War, 170, 185, 201

Haiti: Cité Soleil stabilization initiative,
29–30, 55; earthquake (2010), 23, 43, 104,
105, 112, 205; independence and racializa-
tion, 112–13; US intervention and small
wars doctrine, 6, 12, 26, 106, 108, 110–12,
213n22
Hall, Stuart, 169–70, 237n26
Hardt, Michael, 132
Hart, Gillian, 211n4, 213n18, 220nn106-7,
230n33
Harvey, David, 218n82, 219n51, 220n114
headscarves. See veils
health care, 92–93, 203; coronavirus and,
204–5, 206; medical support or outreach,
145, 146, 153, 161; Muslim women's access
to, 120, 123, 127; for veterans, 10, 130,
140–41, 201, 239n2
hegemony: US, 4, 12, 15, 134, 199–200, 204,
220n106, 236n22; world, 2, 15, 211n4,
218nn81–82, 219n51
Helmand province, 37–38, 39, 179
hierarchies, 92, 133; colonial, 30, 34, 50, 67,
170; dominance, 180–81
Hirschkind, Charles, 48
Hochschild, Arlie, 9, 132, 136, 161
home raids, 7, 27, 94, 130, 164; emotional labor
and, 2, 21, 131, 133, 135–38, 174–76; intelligence gathering and, 146–47, 150; invasion
of privacy and, 155; soldiers' recollections
of, 154, 155; solidarity tactics and, 183–84;
violence and casualties, 162, 174
homonationalism, 203, 204
Horne, Alistair, 122, 123
households, targeting, 6–7, 214n26
humanism, 209, 242n38
humanitarianism: development and, 2, 3,
4–6, 20–21, 52, 199–200, 213n18; of female
counterinsurgency teams, 8–9, 26–27, 131,
145–46, 153–54, 196, 214n36; femininity